QUICK & EASY cooking

Dear Laura & Matt.,

CONGRATULATIONS

QUICK & EASY
cooking

MORE THAN 400 RECIPES

&

Best Wishes for Happy
cooking and eating for ever
and ever,

from
The Dhillons
7 Sept. 2014,

**Reader's
Digest**

CONTENTS

GREAT FOOD IN MINUTES

Creative cooking is not only for those who have hours to spend in the kitchen. The recipes collected here can be prepared and cooked in 30 minutes, with an emphasis on fresh, healthy ingredients and a little help from a well-stocked pantry.

THE NUTRITIONAL BALANCE

Fast food can also be healthy food — all of these recipes are designed to offer a good nutritional balance as well as minimum cooking.

Fast-cooked food not only gives you more time to spend on other things, it carries a health bonus, as the most valuable nutritional components of food are best conserved by reducing the amount of time they are exposed to heat.

Also, when good-quality ingredients are cooked for the minimum amount of time, they retain all their fresh, intense flavours.

STEPS TO SUCCESS

HEAT The first important ingredient is heat: before you even wash your hands, turn on the oven or the grill (broiler) or chargrill pan to preheat, or put a kettle or saucepan of water on to boil.

Domestic ovens vary a great deal in how long they take to come to the required temperature. In general, about 10–15 minutes have been allowed for preheating the oven. An electric fan oven usually does not need to be preheated. But if you know that your oven is slow to heat up, preset it to the required temperature as long in advance as you need to, before you start to assemble the ingredients.

Grills must be properly preheated before use. For fast, even cooking, it is best to have the grill on high in order to avoid any cool patches, and to keep an eye on the food. If any tender items such as fish seem in danger of burning, drop the grill rack a few centimetres (an inch) away from the heat source, or take the food off the rack and sit it on the base of the grill tray.

For best results — and quicker cooking — charcoal barbecues should be lit well in advance so that you are cooking on coals, not flames. Light a gas barbecue at least 5 minutes before cooking to allow the hotplate or grill to heat thoroughly.

ORGANISATION The next secret of successful fast cooking is organisation. Make sure you have all the ingredients you need at hand — a dish can easily be ruined if you have to spend time hunting for the sesame oil, for example, while the contents of the wok are seconds away from burning.

Before you begin to prepare a recipe, read it through to familiarise yourself with the method, so you won't have to waste time stopping to read each step. Then assemble the ingredients, dishes and tools so that everything you need is within easy reach. This is especially important when the recipe demands items that you don't use every day.

Clear an adequate working space with plenty of elbow room. Remove utensils from your working area after use — clutter will slow you down.

Healthy eating Use fresh ingredients and oils that are high in monounsaturated fatty acids for the best nutritional value and use fresh herbs and natural seasonings to enhance their flavours.

MICROWAVE SHORTCUTS

These quick tips for making the most of a microwave oven are based on a 650 watt oven.

SOFTEN BUTTER from the refrigerator by warming on High 20 seconds.

WARM LEMONS for a few seconds on High and they will yield more juice.

MAKE CRISPY BACON by placing 3–4 slices on a microwave rack over folded paper towel; cook on High 2 minutes, then turn and cook 1–2 minutes.

MAKE FAT-FREE PAPPADUMS by cooking one at a time on High 40–60 seconds.

MELT CHOCOLATE by breaking small pieces into a bowl and leaving it uncovered. It's best to melt all chocolate on Medium or Low and to stir and check every 10 seconds or so during the cooking time, as chocolate will hold its shape even when melted. Keep checking, and expect to stir the last few bits of chocolate in. To melt chocolate for a quick decoration, place it in one corner of a microwave roasting bag and melt it in the microwave oven. Then snip off the corner tip of the bag and drizzle a pattern over a dessert or cake.

TOAST NUTS such as cashew nuts; 30 g (1 oz) nuts, cooked on High 5 minutes, will turn a golden, toasted colour.

TIME-SAVING TECHNIQUES

Use these handy shortcuts when preparing or cooking. You'll save time
in the kitchen and have dinner on the table in minutes.

SCISSOR-SNIP HERBS AND VEGETABLES

It's much quicker to scissor-snip fresh herbs than to chop them on a board
with a knife. Snip the herbs with sharp kitchen scissors straight into the pan
or bowl, or over a finished dish as a garnish. Hold the bunch firmly and snip
from the top, including the tender stems of coriander (cilantro), chives, mint
and parsley. Fresh basil is best roughly torn, as the leaves blacken when cut.

Kitchen scissors are also useful for snipping spring onions (scallions),
trimming tough stalks off leafy vegetables, or topping and tailing snow peas
(mangetout) and green beans.

PREPARING BACON AND HAM

A sharp pair of kitchen scissors is great for chopping and trimming bacon,
ham and salami. It's a quick way to trim bacon of excess fat before cooking,
or for snipping it into small pieces. Cooked bacon can also be scissor-cut to
size, holding each rasher in a pair of tongs if it's hot.

CRUSHING GARLIC

The chef's way to crush garlic is very fast. Lay the unpeeled clove on its side
on a chopping board and crush it by pressing on it with the flat of a large
knife blade. Remove the skin, then finely chop the garlic with a pinch of salt.
Or leave the garlic partly crushed and add it to the food as it cooks.

SMALL PIECES

The smaller the piece of food, the more quickly it will cook. Cut potatoes into
smaller chunks if you are boiling them for mashing. Also, cut vegetables into
small pieces if you are adding them to soups or for quick roasting.

Bite-sized chunks of tender meats, such as boneless, skinless chicken breast
or boned shoulder or leg of lamb, are great for skewers or stir-fries.

MASH IN NO TIME

The quickest way to mash potatoes is to use a hand-held stick blender, with
a little warm milk, cream or crème fraîche, some freshly ground black pepper
and a knob of butter. To keep mashed potato light and fluffy before serving,
cover with a clean tea towel (dish towel) — this absorbs the steam rather than
allowing it to condense and fall back into the pan. Or serve potatoes roughly
crushed with butter and parsley, using a large fork to break down any large
chunks. Don't use a food processor, as it makes mashed potato gluey.

COOK EXTRA QUANTITIES

Soups, stews and casseroles freeze well, so if a recipe is suitable for freezing, simply double up the ingredients, then freeze half for an easy meal that just needs reheating another day. (Remove it from the freezer and thaw overnight in the refrigerator.) Left-over cooked pasta is great for salads or a pasta bake; any left-over rice can be stir-fried the next day; and cooked potatoes or vegetables can be used for a tasty hash.

SKINNING CHICKEN

If you have bought chicken breasts with the skin on and you want to remove it fast, grip the skin while holding the chicken with paper towel, then pull firmly. Sometimes pulling the skin off a drumstick can be made easier if you use a sharp knife to cut the skin around the bird's 'ankle' first.

THINNING OR FLATTENING MEAT

Steaks and fillets of meat for grilling (broiling) or frying cook faster and more evenly if they are uniformly flat, with no thick areas. Place the meat between two layers of plastic wrap or baking (parchment) paper and pound gently with a meat mallet or rolling pin to a regular thickness. (Schnitzels or escalopes are already flattened out so that they cook quickly, and are excellent for a fast meal.) Homemade burgers, too, should be fairly flat — aim for about 10 cm (4 inches) in diameter and 2 cm (¾ inch) thick — so that they cook all the way through without burning on the outside.

NO-FUSS DUSTING

To dust pieces of meat or fish with flour before cooking, put 2–3 tablespoons of plain (all-purpose) flour, with seasoning and dried herbs if you like, into a plastic bag or a bowl with a lid. Drop in the pieces of meat or fish, a few at a time, cover the bowl or hold the bag shut at the top, and give it a good shake until the pieces are evenly coated.

NO-MESS CRUMBS

To make crumbs or broken pieces from biscuits or chocolate, put them in a sturdy plastic bag and bash against a benchtop, or crush with a rolling pin.

CUTTING EDGE

Keep your knives and scissors sharp — it makes much faster work of cutting and chopping, and it's safer too; you are more likely to have an accident using a blunt knife than a sharp one.

VEGETABLE PREPARATION SHORTCUTS

Here's how to make short work of some of the more fiddly tasks in vegetable preparation.

CHOPPING ONIONS Leave the root end intact when peeling the onion, then cut the onion in half lengthwise. Put each half cut side down, and make fine vertical cuts through to the root end, stopping just short of it. Cut across these slices so that the onion falls into dice.

QUICK-TRIM VEGETABLES When trimming or slicing vegetables of a similar shape, such as green beans or spring onions (scallions), line them up on a board, then trim or slice across the whole row.

SKINNING TOMATOES AND FRENCH SHALLOTS (ESCHALOTS) Put in a heatproof bowl and pour over boiling water. Leave 1 minute, drain, cover with cold water, then peel with a knife.

QUICKEST COOKING METHODS

Here are six of the fastest ways to cook. They are not only quick but because these methods help retain as many nutrients as possible, they're healthy too!

GRILLING

Grilling (broiling) is a quick method of cooking that suits tender cuts of meat and fish, and shellfish. Make sure the grill (broiler) is preheated before cooking begins. The heat can then be adjusted with the temperature dial or by raising or lowering the grill tray if it can't be adjusted by a temperature dial. Meats such as sausages and bacon contain sufficient fat for grilling, but leaner cuts such as boneless, skinless chicken breast will need a light brushing of oil or basting liquid. Use a grill rack so that fat drips down into the tray.

Grilling is excellent for tomatoes, mushrooms, capsicums (bell peppers), and eggplant (aubergine) and zucchini (courgette) slices brushed with a little oil. It is a great way to brown the top of a dish, such as a breadcrumb gratin.

STIR-FRYING

Lean cuts of meat and poultry are perfect for stir-frying, as are firm-textured fish and shellfish, vegetables, rice and noodles. Use an oil that can withstand a high cooking temperature, such as peanut oil. Don't use olive oil – it will burn, and only use sesame oil to sprinkle over at the end of cooking, not at the outset. Have all your ingredients prepared before you start cooking. Marinate meat and poultry first for 30 minutes or so, to help to tenderise and add extra flavour. Use a wok or large deep frying pan and get it very hot before adding the oil, to ensure an even heat. Add 1–2 tablespoons oil and swirl it around; when it is hot enough, it will sizzle. When you add the food, start with the ingredients that take the longest to cook, such as carrots, and add the tender ones, such as bean sprouts, last. Keep the ingredients moving.

STEAMING

Food is steamed by setting it above simmering water or stock. The natural flavour, colour, shape and texture, as well as water-soluble vitamins and minerals, are retained in the food. This moist method of cooking is ideal for delicate foods such as fish, chicken and vegetables, including new potatoes.

There are several ways of steaming, but the chief points to remember are that the pan containing the water must not be allowed to boil dry and the water must not go off the boil. Sliced onions, chopped celery or fennel, lemon slices, fresh herb sprigs or warm spices can be added to the boiling water so that their flavours waft upwards and seep into the foods as they cook. Never sprinkle salt over vegetables, as it will draw out the moisture and nutrients.

CHARGRILLING

Chargrilling uses a ridged cast-iron pan on a high heat on the stovetop to quickly sear food on the outside. It's fast and healthy, as it uses less oil than frying, and gives attractive markings to the food. It is ideal for thin cuts of meat, as well as for seafood and thick slices of zucchini, eggplant and other summer vegetables. You can even chargrill haloumi cheese.

Choose a ridged grill pan with deep ridges and grooves so that the food doesn't sit in the fat or juices that drip from it while cooking. Always make sure that the pan is really hot before using, otherwise the food will stick to the surface. To test, splash a few drops of water on the heated surface — they should splutter and disappear instantly.

Brush the food (not the pan) lightly with oil. If it has been marinated, drain off the excess before placing it in the pan. Cook on one side, then turn over using tongs. Don't turn too soon, or it will stick — as the food chars, it will come away from the grill pan naturally. If you have time, allow meat to rest, covered on a warmed plate, 3–5 minutes before serving; this gives the muscle fibres time to 'relax' so the juices are distributed evenly throughout the meat.

EN PAPILLOTE

Parcels of sweet and savoury foods can be wrapped in squares of foil or baking (parchment) paper, then cooked in a microwave, oven or steamer. This method seals in all the flavour and nutrients. It is a good way to cook fish or lean cuts of meat that might otherwise dry out in the heat of the oven or disintegrate under the grill. It also prevents the odour of fish from permeating the house while it cooks. Herbs, spices and shredded vegetables such as onion and carrots can be enclosed in the parcel to flavour the food while it cooks. Serving individual portions still wrapped in their parcels is a simple and fun way to present the food.

MICROWAVING

A microwave oven allows you to prepare food in much less time than a conventional oven. It's also brilliant for quickly thawing food and reheating leftovers, as well as softening butter, melting chocolate and heating liquids. Packs of baby spinach leaves and frozen peas can be cooked in their packs (pierce the bags first with a sharp knife) to save on washing up.

Cooking times vary depending on the power level and quantity of food in the microwave, so it's best to follow the manufacturer's instructions. Always slightly undercook food, then stir (if appropriate) and allow to rest for a few minutes. Return to the microwave if it needs a little longer. Keep the dish covered to help the food cook more quickly and to stop it drying out or splashing the inside of the oven.

TIME-SAVING EQUIPMENT

Speed up your preparation and cooking with the right equipment. Here's a guide
to the most suitable tools for fast cooking, and how to put them to the best use.

POTS AND PANS

Use pots and pans that are the right size for the ingredients. It is a waste to
boil up a large saucepan of water for a few vegetables. There are exceptions.
Always use a large saucepan for pasta: it will cook quicker with plenty of
water to swim in. Use a large frying pan with plenty of space when browning
meat. It is also important not to overcrowd a wok when stir-frying, so choose
a large wok that gives you plenty of room. It can double as a large saucepan
and be used for steaming as well as stir-frying, so buy one with a lid.

A frying pan with a single heatproof handle allows you to shake the pan
vigorously when frying over a high heat. A two-handled iron frying pan or
shallow flameproof casserole dish that can be used on the stovetop and also
fit under the grill or go into the oven is another time-saver.

A pasta pan with a separate strainer basket, which you just lift out, makes
draining pasta easy. Bamboo steamers are stackable, so you can steam several
layers of food at once. Metal steamers are also available in various sizes.

Not all pots and pans are equal when it comes to heat conduction. Heat
makes food stick to the surface of a pan; to avoid this, nonstick surfaces are
designed to be relatively poor heat conductors. Copper pans lined with tin, or
copper-based stainless steel pans and saucepans, are ideal heat conductors for
fast cooking. Cast-iron saucepans with a strong enamel coating also conduct
heat well, though they are heavy to use. Stainless steel saucepans are much
lighter, virtually indestructible, and they perform very well.

ELECTRICAL EQUIPMENT

You can purée a soup or sauce in a blender, or a liquidiser, in a fraction of
the time it takes to push it through a sieve by hand, and it is much smoother.

The chopping, grating and shredding blades of a food processor can
prepare large amounts of raw food in seconds. They are especially useful for
chopping a succession of ingredients, such as when making a vegetable soup.
They make soft white breadcrumbs or dried brown breadcrumbs in seconds.

A hand-held stick blender purées soup faster than a food processor or
blender as you can use it in the saucepan. The result is not quite as smooth,
but many cooks prefer the slightly thicker texture. Hand-held blenders are
useful for taking the lumps out of sauces, or mashing pumpkin or potato.

If you use a lot of spices, invest in an extra coffee grinder for grinding them
into powder in seconds. It will also make small amounts of breadcrumbs.
And an electric hand mixer takes only seconds to whip cream or meringue.

GADGETS AND TOOLS

BRUSHES Invest in a small stiff brush for cleaning the vegetables, and don't use it for anything else. Natural fibre or plastic bristles are both equally efficient, but natural bristles must be left to dry out completely after each use. A pastry brush is

the quickest way to baste food under the grill (broiler) with oil or a marinade — choose natural bristles, as plastic bristles will melt if they touch a hot surface. A pastry brush is also useful for cleaning out the tiny holes in a hand grater.

CHERRY-STONER Using a single cherry-stoner is quicker than removing cherry stones by hand; it can also remove olive pits.

CHOPPING BOARD Choose a large chopping board that sits firmly on the workbench. It will make chopping easier, and nothing will fall over the edges.

GRATER A stainless-steel grater makes fast work of small items. If you need only one or two carrots grated, it is quicker to do it by hand than in a food processor. Making pastry can also be quicker if you grate hard butter into the flour before rubbing it in.

JAR OPENER A tool with large rings at the end that will grip firmly stuck jar and bottle tops and open them easily saves time and temper.

KNIFE SHARPENER Blunt knives slow you down. Use a knife sharpener and take a few seconds to hone the blades of knives and kitchen scissors to a fine, razor-sharp edge every time you use them. It will make short work of cutting and slicing.

LEMON SQUEEZER A cone-shaped hand-held squeezer will let you squeeze citrus juice straight into the salad bowl or saucepan.

POTATO MASHER A hand-held potato masher is very useful, because food processors and blenders can turn potatoes (and potato-based soups, too) into a gluey mass. It is also quicker to clean.

SALAD SPINNER A simple plastic spinner is the most effective way to dry salad leaves. Put washed leaves into the basket and rotate it to spin the water out.

STRAINER Wire mesh strainers strain off all liquid better than a colander.

VEGETABLE PEELER A swivel-headed potato peeler will make a smooth job of peeling other vegetables, or cutting vegetables such as zucchini (courgettes) into ribbon shapes. It will remove strings from celery and shave chocolate and strips of parmesan. Learn to use it in smooth long strokes away from yourself.

ZESTER A zester makes swift work of removing zest from citrus fruit. Holes at the end of the blade shave off thin strips of zest without lifting the bitter white pith beneath.

CHAPTER 1

Soups

CARROT, ORANGE AND FETTA SOUP

TIME **30 MINUTES** SERVES **4**

INGREDIENTS

1 tablespoon olive oil

1 onion, finely chopped

4 carrots, finely chopped

1 clove garlic, crushed

2$\frac{1}{2}$ cups (625 ml) vegetable stock

juice of 1 small orange

2 tablespoons chopped fresh tarragon,
    plus leaves to garnish

salt and freshly ground black pepper

100 g (3$\frac{1}{2}$ oz) fetta, crumbled

METHOD

1 Heat oil in a large saucepan and fry onion, carrots and garlic over medium heat about 5 minutes, or until softened but not browned.

2 Add stock, orange juice and half the chopped tarragon and bring to a boil. Reduce heat, cover and simmer gently 6–8 minutes, or until tender. If you have time, allow soup to cool for a few minutes before puréeing.

3 Reserve about a quarter of the vegetables and process the remainder of the soup in a food processor or blender until almost smooth (it's best to leave some texture and not process to a completely smooth purée). Season to taste with salt and pepper.

4 Return purée to pan with reserved cooked vegetables and heat until boiling. Ladle into bowls and add some crumbled fetta to each one. Sprinkle with remaining chopped tarragon and whole leaves.

NUTRIENTS PER SERVING

677 kJ, 162 kcal, 6 g protein, 11 g fat (4.5 g saturated), 10 g carbohydrate

VARIATION

PARSNIP, LEMON AND THYME SOUP You can make the soup with 4 parsnips instead of carrots, and fry them with onion and garlic in step 1. Replace orange juice with juice of $\frac{1}{2}$ lemon, and tarragon with chopped fresh thyme. Cook up to the end of step 2, then tip into a food processor or blender and process until smooth. Season, return to pan and swirl in 100 ml (3$\frac{1}{2}$ fl oz) light sour cream. Omit fetta. Sprinkle with chopped fresh thyme.

COOK'S TIP

This soup freezes well. Prepare it to the end of step 3, add reserved cooked vegetables and then cool quickly. Pour into freezer-proof container and freeze for up to 1 month. Serve with toast spread with tapenade or other topping.

TOMATO AND RED LENTIL SOUP

TIME **30 MINUTES** SERVES **4**

INGREDIENTS

2½ cups (625 ml) chicken or
    vegetable stock
2 tablespoons olive oil
3 French shallots (eschalots), chopped
2–3 cloves garlic, chopped
1 red chilli, seeds removed, chopped
⅔ cup (160 g) red lentils, rinsed and
    drained
410 g (15 oz) can chopped tomatoes
1 tablespoon shredded fresh basil,
    plus leaves to garnish
100 g (3½ oz) soft cream cheese
    (optional)
salt and freshly ground black pepper

METHOD

1 Heat stock in a medium saucepan.
2 Heat oil in a large saucepan. Add French shallots, garlic and chilli and fry
   gently 5 minutes, until soft.
3 Add lentils to pan with heated stock and tomatoes. Bring to a boil, cover
   and simmer 10 minutes. Add half the shredded basil and simmer about
   5 minutes.
4 Beat soft cream cheese, if using, in a small bowl until softened. Stir
   in remaining shredded basil.
5 Process the soup in a food processor or blender to a purée. Season to taste
   with salt and pepper. Ladle into bowls with spoonfuls of cream cheese
   mixture and garnish with basil leaves.

NUTRIENTS PER SERVING

1260 kJ, 301 kcal, 10 g protein, 20 g fat (8 g saturated fat), 20 g carbohydrate

PEA AND ASPARAGUS SOUP
TIME **30 MINUTES** SERVES **4**

METHOD

1 Heat stock in a large saucepan. Add spring onions and frozen peas and bring to a boil.

2 Add asparagus stems and a pinch of salt to the pan. Reduce heat, cover and simmer 10–15 minutes, or until asparagus is tender.

3 Meanwhile, add bacon to a frying pan and fry until crisp and golden. Transfer to a plate and set aside.

4 If there is not enough bacon fat in the pan for frying, add 1–2 tablespoons vegetable oil and heat. Fry diced bread 2–3 minutes over high heat, turning the croutons frequently, until golden. Drain on paper towels.

5 When the peas and asparagus are done, process the soup to a purée in a food processor or blender.

6 Return purée to pan and heat until boiling. Add all but 12 of the reserved asparagus tips to the soup and simmer about 5 minutes, or until tender.

7 Pour soup into four warmed serving bowls. Swirl 2 teaspoons crème fraîche or sour cream into each and sprinkle with reserved bacon pieces, croutons and remaining asparagus tips. Top with some freshly ground black pepper.

INGREDIENTS

2¹/₂ cups (625 ml) chicken or vegetable stock

8–9 spring onions (scallions), roughly chopped

3¹/₃ cups (500 g) frozen peas

150 g (5 oz) small asparagus spears, tips removed and set aside, stems roughly chopped

salt

3 slices rindless bacon (bacon strips), diced

1–2 tablespoons vegetable oil, if needed

2 slices day-old white bread, diced

2 tablespoons crème fraîche or sour cream

freshly ground black pepper

NUTRIENTS PER SERVING
1381 kJ, 330 kcal, 13 g protein, 21 g fat (9 g saturated fat), 24 g carbohydrate

GREEN GAZPACHO WITH SMOKED SALMON

TIME **30 MINUTES** SERVES **4**

INGREDIENTS

1 large green capsicum (bell pepper),
    seeds removed, chopped
1 Lebanese or other small cucumber,
    seeds removed, chopped
1 small onion, chopped
1 ripe avocado, stoned and peeled
1 clove garlic, chopped
4 tablespoons roughly chopped fresh
    flat-leaf (Italian) parsley
2½ cups (625 ml) vegetable stock
3 tablespoons white balsamic vinegar
    or white wine vinegar
3 tablespoons extra virgin olive oil
salt and freshly ground black pepper
250 g (8 oz) smoked salmon,
    cut into strips

METHOD

1 Place capsicum, cucumber, onion, avocado, garlic, parsley, stock, vinegar and oil in a food processor or blender. Season with salt and black pepper, then process until lightly textured.
2 Chill, covered, in the refrigerator until needed. Ladle into serving bowls and top with strips of salmon.

NUTRIENTS PER SERVING

1354 kJ, 323 kcal, 16 g protein, 27 g fat (5 g saturated fat), 5 g carbohydrate

VARIATION

RED-HOT GAZPACHO Place 1 slice white bread in a food processor or blender with 1 chopped red capsicum (bell pepper), 1 chopped red onion, a 410 g can (15 oz) tomatoes with onion and garlic, 1 small cucumber, peeled, seeds removed, chopped, 1 red chilli, finely chopped (remove seeds for a milder taste), 1 cup (250 ml) vegetable stock, 3 tablespoons each olive oil and red wine vinegar and 2 tablespoons chopped fresh mint. Season with salt and freshly ground black pepper. Process until smooth. Ladle into bowls and add a few ice cubes to each one. Top with torn fresh basil and ready-made garlic croutons. Divide a 180 g (6 oz) can tuna, drained and flaked, or 200 g (7 oz) fresh tuna, grilled and thinly sliced, among the bowls.

CHICKEN, THYME AND MUSHROOM SOUP
TIME **25 MINUTES** SERVES **4**

METHOD

1 Heat oil in a large saucepan and fry chicken 5 minutes, or until golden brown all over. Remove from pan with a slotted spoon and set aside. Add onion, garlic and celery to pan and cook 5 minutes.

2 Add mushrooms, thyme, sherry and worcestershire sauce. Season lightly and cook 2–3 minutes, stirring occasionally. If you have time, allow soup to cool a little before puréeing.

3 Tip mixture into a food processor or blender, add half the stock and process until smooth. Return mixture to pan with reserved chicken and remaining stock. Bring to a boil, then reduce heat and simmer 3 minutes. Stir in 2 tablespoons light sour cream or crème fraîche and heat through. Adjust seasoning to taste.

4 Ladle into bowls and serve topped with a swirl of the remaining light sour cream or crème fraîche and a sprinkling of fresh thyme, if using.

NUTRIENTS PER SERVING
1041 kJ, 249 kcal, 17 g protein, 16 g fat (5 g saturated fat), 7 g carbohydrate

INGREDIENTS

2 tablespoons olive oil

200 g (7 oz) boneless, skinless chicken breast, finely diced

1 red onion, chopped

1 clove garlic, finely chopped

2 celery stalks, chopped

250 g (8 oz) button mushrooms, roughly chopped

1 tablespoon chopped fresh thyme or 1 teaspoon dried thyme, plus extra fresh thyme, to garnish (optional)

1 tablespoon dry sherry

1 tablespoon worcestershire sauce

3 cups (750 ml) chicken stock

4 tablespoons light sour cream or crème fraîche

salt and freshly ground black pepper

PRAWN, SPRING ONION AND EGG RIBBON SOUP
TIME **20 MINUTES** SERVES **4**

INGREDIENTS

4 cups (1 litre) fish or chicken stock

1 lemongrass stem, white part only, crushed

2.5 cm (1 inch) piece fresh ginger, peeled and thinly sliced

4 large spring onions (scallions), sliced

$^1/_2$ cup (100 g) jasmine rice (Thai fragrant rice) or long-grain rice or basmati rice

salt and freshly ground black pepper

2 tablespoons rice vinegar or white wine vinegar

175 g (6 oz) cooked peeled prawns (shrimp)

3 cups (200 g) bean sprouts, trimmed

3 eggs, lightly beaten

4 teaspoons chilli oil, or to taste

METHOD

1 Put stock, lemongrass, ginger and spring onions in a large saucepan and bring to a boil.

2 Stir in rice and return to a boil. Reduce heat, cover and simmer gently 8 minutes.

3 Season, add vinegar, prawns and bean sprouts. Return to a boil, reduce heat and simmer 1 minute.

4 Pour eggs into simmering soup in a steady, continuous drizzle. They should set into ribbons within a few seconds. Immediately remove pan from heat and ladle soup into bowls. Drizzle each serving with chilli oil to taste.

NUTRIENTS PER SERVING

1207 kJ, 288 kcal, 16 g protein, 9 g fat (2 g saturated fat), 34 g carbohydrate

VARIATION

For a vegetarian soup, use vegetable stock and replace prawns with cubes of smoked or plain tofu.

COOK'S TIP

Both crushed lemongrass and crushed ginger are available in jars and are useful when you're short on time. A generous teaspoon of each will give a good flavour to the soup.

SPICY PRAWN AND CHILLI SOUP

TIME **25 MINUTES** SERVES **4**

INGREDIENTS

5 cups (1.25 litres) chicken stock

2 lemongrass stems, finely sliced

2.5 cm (1 inch) piece fresh ginger,
    peeled and julienned

4 small red chillies, seeds removed,
    finely sliced

juice of 4 limes

3 tablespoons fish sauce

2 kaffir lime (makrut) leaves, shredded,
    plus 4 kaffir lime (makrut) leaves,
    to garnish

500 g (1 lb) raw prawns (uncooked
    shrimp), peeled and deveined

2 tablespoons chopped fresh coriander
    (cilantro) leaves

METHOD

1 Heat stock in a large saucepan.

2 Add lemongrass, ginger, chillies,
   lime juice and fish sauce to the
   simmering stock. Continue to
   simmer over medium–low heat,
   1–2 minutes.

3 Add shredded lime leaves and
   prawns and simmer a further
   10 minutes. Add coriander and
   stir through.

4 Pour soup into a warmed serving
   bowl, garnish with remaining lime
   leaves and serve immediately.

NUTRIENTS PER SERVING

536 kJ, 128 kcal, 18 g protein, 1 g fat
(<1 g saturated fat), 1 g carbohydrate

VARIATION

Instead of prawns, use strips of boneless, skinless chicken breast.

COOK'S TIP

Known as *nam pla* in Thailand and *nuoc nam* in Vietnam, fish sauce is
available from Asian food stores and larger supermarkets.

CARAMELISED ONION, BEEF AND BEER SOUP

TIME 30 MINUTES SERVES 4

METHOD

1 Heat butter and two-thirds of the oil in a large, heavy-based saucepan or flameproof casserole dish. Stir in onions and sugar. Cover pan and cook 10 minutes over medium heat, stirring occasionally. Remove lid and increase heat slightly. Cook a further 5 minutes, stirring frequently, or until onions are softened and golden brown.

2 While onions are caramelising, heat a heavy-based frying pan until very hot. Brush steak slices with remaining oil and season lightly. Fry 3 minutes each side, turning once, or until golden brown but still pink inside. Remove from heat and cover with foil to keep warm. Set aside.

3 Add garlic, beer and bay leaf to onions. Bring to a boil, then reduce heat to a simmer. Cook, uncovered, 5 minutes. Add stock and adjust seasoning. Cook until boiling, then remove from heat.

4 Slice reserved steak into thin, ribbon-like strips, adding any juices from the meat to the soup. Discard bay leaf. Ladle soup into wide bowls and place a few meat strips in the centre of each serving. Sprinkle with parsley.

INGREDIENTS

30 g (1 oz) butter
2 tablespoons olive oil
500 g (1 lb) onions, thinly sliced
2 teaspoons caster (superfine) sugar
300 g (10 oz) fillet steak, thickly sliced
salt and freshly ground black pepper
1 clove garlic, crushed
1 cup (250 ml) dark beer, such as
   Guinness
1 bay leaf
3 cups (750 ml) beef stock
2 tablespoons chopped fresh flat-leaf
   (Italian) parsley, to garnish

NUTRIENTS PER SERVING

1427 kJ, 341 kcal, 22 g protein, 19 g fat (7 g saturated fat), 14 g carbohydrate

VARIATION

Instead of beer, use extra stock with 2 tablespoons worcestershire sauce or soy sauce. Use fresh thyme instead of bay leaf.

COOK'S TIP

Make the basic onion soup up to 2 days in advance. Cool quickly, cover and store in the refrigerator. Cook steak at time of serving. If you have some leftover roast beef or lamb, use it instead of the steak. Slice the meat into thin ribbons and add to the soup during the last few minutes of cooking to heat through.

CHUNKY FISH SOUP

TIME **30 MINUTES** SERVES **4**

INGREDIENTS

2¹/₂ cups (625 ml) fish stock
2 tablespoons vegetable oil
1 onion, finely chopped
1 bulb fennel, finely chopped, fronds
 reserved to garnish
²/₃ cup (150 ml) dry white wine
 or vermouth
410 g (15 oz) can chopped tomatoes
1 bay leaf
1 teaspoon sugar

salt and freshly ground black pepper
500 g (1 lb) firm fish fillets or cutlets,
 skin and bones removed, cut into
 chunks
2 tablespoons chopped fresh flat-leaf
 (Italian) parsley, plus leaves to garnish
1 tablespoon cornflour (cornstarch)
2 tablespoons milk
2 tablespoons thick (heavy/double) cream

METHOD

1 Heat stock in a medium saucepan.
2 Heat oil in a large, heavy-based saucepan. Cook onion and fennel over medium heat 5 minutes, or until softened.
3 Pour off any surplus oil from pan. Add stock, wine, tomatoes, bay leaf and sugar and season with salt and pepper. Bring to a boil, reduce heat, cover and simmer 10 minutes.
4 Add fish and chopped parsley. Cover and simmer gently 5 minutes.
5 Blend cornflour and milk in a bowl. When fish is cooked, remove bay leaf, stir cornflour into the soup and simmer until thickened slightly.
6 Stir in cream and heat gently 1–2 minutes. Serve the soup garnished with the reserved fennel fronds and parsley.

NUTRIENTS PER SERVING

1389 kJ, 332 kcal, 22 g protein, 19 g fat (8 g saturated fat), 12 g carbohydrate

VARIATION

You can use any firm-fleshed fish, such as snapper, orange roughy, hake, cod, salmon or shark, to make this dish. Alternatively, you can use equal quantities of peeled and deveined prawns (shrimp) and shucked scallops.

SMOKED FISH, BEAN AND LEEK SOUP

TIME **30 MINUTES** SERVES **4**

INGREDIENTS

2¹/₂ cups (625 ml) fish, chicken
 or vegetable stock
2 tablespoons extra virgin olive oil
1 onion, finely chopped
2 leeks, trimmed and sliced
2 x 400 g (14 oz) cans butterbeans
 (lima beans), with their liquid
500 g (1 lb) smoked fish, such as haddock
 or cod, skin removed, diced
freshly ground black pepper
2 tablespoons chopped fresh flat-leaf
 (Italian) parsley, to garnish

METHOD

1 Heat stock in a medium saucepan.
2 Heat oil in large saucepan. Add onion and leeks and cook gently 5 minutes, stirring occasionally. Add stock and bring to a boil, reduce heat, cover and simmer 5 minutes.
3 Add butterbeans and their liquid to the pan and mash roughly. Return to a boil, reduce heat, cover and let simmer.
4 Add smoked fish and simmer until heated through and opaque.
5 Season with pepper (the smoked fish should make the soup salty enough). Ladle into bowls and sprinkle over parsley.

NUTRIENTS PER SERVING

1594 kJ, 381 kcal, 38 g protein, 10 g fat (1 g saturated fat), 34 g carbohydrate

VARIATION

For a richer flavour, serve with a spoonful of cream swirled into each bowl.

Right Smoked fish, bean and leek soup (top); Chunky fish soup (bottom)

3 Add watercress, with stalks, to onion and potatoes. Cook over medium heat, stirring, 2 minutes, or until watercress has wilted. Add stock and season lightly. Cook a further few minutes if the potato is not yet tender. If you have time, allow soup to cool a little before puréeing.

4 Process soup in a food processor or blender until smooth. Return to the pan.

5 Add milk and bring soup just to a boil. Ladle into bowls and sprinkle with cashews and gruyère.

NUTRIENTS PER SERVING
1424 kJ, 340 kcal, 14 g protein, 21 g fat (6 g saturated fat), 24 g carbohydrate

VARIATION

CHUNKY MUSSEL AND ROCKET SOUP Heat a 500 g (1 lb) vacuum pack of mussels 5 minutes, or according to packet instructions. Omit the watercress, cashews and gruyère from the basic recipe. Cook onion and potatoes as for step 1 and add stock. Cool a little, then purée soup. Add milk and bring to a boil. Add mussels and their juices and simmer 5 minutes. Season, then stir in 3 tablespoons thick (heavy/double) cream and 75 g (2½ oz) rocket (arugula), roughly chopped.

COOK'S TIP
This is a good recipe for using up leftover mashed potato. Add it at the end of step 3 instead of using raw potatoes. Reduce cooking time for the onion in step 1 to 5 minutes.

WATERCRESS AND ONION CREAM SOUP WITH CASHEWS

TIME 25 MINUTES SERVES 4

INGREDIENTS

1 tablespoon olive oil
1 large onion, chopped
400 g (14 oz) potatoes, chopped
⅔ cup (100 g) raw cashew nuts
100 g (3½ oz) watercress

2 cups (500 ml) vegetable stock
salt and freshly ground black pepper
½ cup (125 ml) skim or low-fat milk
½ cup (60 g) coarsely grated gruyère

METHOD

1 Heat oil in a large saucepan. Add onion and potatoes. Cover and cook over medium heat, stirring occasionally, 10 minutes or until softened.

2 Meanwhile, toast cashews in a dry pan over medium–high heat, tossing regularly, until golden brown. Remove from heat and chop roughly.

SEAFOOD NOODLE BOWL

TIME **20 MINUTES** SERVES **4**

INGREDIENTS

3 cups (750 ml) fish or chicken stock

4 spring onions (scallions), chopped

2.5 cm (1 inch) piece fresh ginger, grated

1 lemongrass stem, white part only,
   finely sliced (optional)

2 teaspoons soy sauce

225 g (8 oz) thick firm white fish fillets,
   such as blue-eye cod or hake, skin
   removed, cut into chunks

125 g (4 oz) scallops, without roe,
   thickly sliced

175 g (6 oz) cooked, peeled prawns
   (shrimp)

200 g (7 oz) bok choy, thinly sliced

300 g (10 oz) wok-ready udon (rice)
   noodles

METHOD

1 Put stock, spring onions, ginger,
   lemongrass and soy sauce in
   a large saucepan and bring to
   a boil.

2 Add fish and return to a boil. Add
   scallops, reduce heat and simmer
   gently 1 minute.

3 Stir in prawns, bok choy and
   noodles and cook until heated
   through and noodles are cooked.
   Serve immediately.

NUTRIENTS PER SERVING

977 kJ, 233 kcal, 23 g protein, 2 g fat
(0 g saturated fat), 29 g carbohydrate

VARIATION

Instead of prawns and scallops,
use cooked and shelled pipis or
clams and mussels.

GARDEN VEGETABLE BROTH WITH PARMA HAM

TIME **30 MINUTES** SERVES **4**

INGREDIENTS

2 x 410 g (15 oz) cans beef consommé
1 onion, finely chopped
1 celery stalk, finely chopped
1 small bulb fennel, finely chopped
1 small kohlrabi or turnip, finely chopped
1 potato, finely chopped
1 bay leaf
75 g (2¹/₂ oz) lean parma ham,
    torn into strips
4 savoy cabbage leaves, cored
    and finely shredded
salt and freshly ground black pepper

METHOD

1 Bring consommé and ¹/₂ cup (125 ml) water to a boil in a large
   saucepan. Add onion, celery, fennel, kohlrabi or turnip, and potato.
   Return to a boil.
2 Add bay leaf, then reduce heat, cover and simmer 10 minutes, or until
   vegetables are almost tender.
3 Add parma ham and shredded cabbage. Return to a boil, cover, reduce
   heat and simmer a further 5 minutes, or until cabbage is tender. Season
   with salt and pepper, if needed. Discard bay leaf before serving.

NUTRIENTS PER SERVING

765 kJ, 183 kcal, 23 g protein, 4 g fat (2 g saturated fat), 16 g carbohydrate

VARIATION

For a vegetarian soup, use 4 cups (1 litre) vegetable stock, omit ham and
instead add a 400 g (14 oz) can French-style green (puy) lentils or cannellini
beans, drained and rinsed, in step 3.

COOK'S TIP

Make double the quantity of the basic vegetable soup, preparing it up to
the end of step 2. Freeze half and use within 3 months, or refrigerate for
use within a couple of days.

COOL CUCUMBER SOUP
TIME 15 MINUTES SERVES 4

METHOD

1 Chill four soup bowls in the refrigerator.
2 Place cucumber and mint in a large bowl. Stir in yogurt, cream and vinegar. Season well with salt and pepper and stir again.
3 Divide soup among the four chilled soup bowls. Add one or two ice cubes to each, if you like, to chill the mixture quickly. Garnish with sprigs of mint and serve immediately.

NUTRIENTS PER SERVING

984 kJ, 235 kcal, 10 g protein, 19 g fat (11 g saturated fat), 6.5 g carbohydrate

VARIATION

You can use sour cream instead of cream if you prefer a sharper taste, and use tarragon vinegar instead of white wine vinegar for a herbier overtone.

INGREDIENTS

1 large cucumber, trimmed and grated
4 tablespoons chopped fresh mint
2 cups (500 g) natural (plain) yogurt
150 ml (5 fl oz) cream
1 tablespoon white wine vinegar
salt and freshly ground black pepper
ice cubes (optional)
4 sprigs fresh mint, to garnish

PEA AND HAM SOUP
TIME **20 MINUTES** SERVES **4**

INGREDIENTS

2 tablespoons olive oil

1 large onion, chopped

2 2/3 cups (400 g) frozen peas

3 cups (750 ml) beef, ham or
   chicken stock

salt and freshly ground black pepper

200 g (7 oz) thickly sliced ham,
   fat removed, diced

100 ml (3 1/2 fl oz) light sour cream

1/2 teaspoon freshly grated nutmeg

METHOD

1 Heat oil in a large saucepan. Add
   onion and cook over low heat
   about 5 minutes, or until softened.
2 Stir in peas and stock and bring
   to a boil. Reduce heat, cover and
   simmer 5 minutes. Season lightly.
   If you have time, allow soup to
   cool a little before puréeing.
3 Process soup in a food processor
   or blender to a fairly rough purée.
   Return to the pan and add ham.
   Cook until just below boiling,
   then remove from heat.
4 Add sour cream and stir gently
   until almost melted. Ladle soup
   into bowls and sprinkle each with
   a little nutmeg.

NUTRIENTS PER SERVING

1313 kJ, 314 kcal, 19 g protein, 21 g fat
(8 g saturated fat), 14 g carbohydrate

VARIATION

For a vegetarian soup, replace meat
stock with vegetable stock. Use 200 g
(7 oz) diced tofu instead of ham.

SWEET POTATO AND BEAN SOUP
TIME **30 MINUTES** SERVES **4**

INGREDIENTS

30 g (1 oz) butter

2 leeks, white part only, thinly sliced

400 g (14 oz) orange sweet potatoes (kumara), thinly sliced

1/2 teaspoon ground cumin

4 cups (1 litre) vegetable stock

4 tablespoons sour cream

2 tablespoons chopped fresh coriander (cilantro) leaves

200 g (7 oz) can butterbeans (lima beans), drained and rinsed

salt and freshly ground black pepper

juice of 1/2 lemon

METHOD

1 Melt butter in a large saucepan. Add leeks and sweet potatoes, then
   cook over low heat 3 minutes, stirring occasionally, until they begin
   to soften. Add cumin and cook a further 2 minutes.
2 Add stock and bring to a boil. Reduce heat, cover and cook gently
   12 minutes, or until vegetables are tender.
3 While soup is simmering, combine sour cream and coriander in a bowl.
   Set aside for the garnish.
4 Remove pan from heat and add butterbeans to the soup. Purée in a
   blender or food processor until smooth. Return soup to the pan and
   bring to a boil, then reduce heat and simmer gently until hot.
   Season and add lemon juice.
5 Ladle soup into bowls and swirl a large spoonful of coriander cream
   through each serving.

NUTRIENTS PER SERVING

913 kJ, 218 kcal, 5 g protein, 12 g fat (7 g saturated fat), 23 g carbohydrate

VARIATION

Omit beans. After puréeing the soup, stir in a 175 g (6 oz) can crabmeat,
drained, and 2 tablespoons dry sherry.

COOK'S TIP

Make the basic soup to the end of step 3, then cool and store in the
refrigerator for up to 2 days. When ready to use, gently reheat and
complete recipe.

Left Pea and ham soup

GAZPACHO

INGREDIENTS

1 thick slice day-old white bread,
   crusts removed

4 tablespoons extra virgin olive oil

3 tablespoons red wine vinegar

salt

1 tablespoon paprika

2 x 410 g (15 oz) cans chopped tomatoes

1 red onion

4 large cloves garlic

1 large cucumber, peeled

1 red capsicum (bell pepper), quartered
   lengthwise, seeds removed

1 yellow capsicum (bell pepper), quartered
   lengthwise, seeds removed

1 green capsicum (bell pepper), quartered
   lengthwise, seeds removed

1 fresh or dried red chilli, or 1 fresh
   green chilli, halved, seeds removed

6 fresh basil and/or mint leaves, torn into
   small pieces

freshly ground black pepper

1¼ cups (310 ml) iced water

12 ice cubes (optional)

CROUTONS

1 tablespoon olive oil

1 clove garlic

3 thick slices white bread, crusts removed,
   cut into small cubes

METHOD

1 Process bread in a food processor or blender to make crumbs.
2 Put oil in a large serving bowl and whisk in vinegar and salt to make a creamy emulsion. Add paprika and breadcrumbs and stir until thoroughly combined.
3 Stir tomatoes into the mixture, then set aside.
4 Roughly chop onion and garlic in a food processor, then add to the tomato mixture. One by one, roughly chop cucumber, capsicums and chilli in a food processor, then add to the mixture.
5 Add basil and/or mint. Stir well, taste and season generously with salt and pepper. The flavour should be sharp and refreshing, with plenty of bite.
6 Stir in enough iced water to give the mixture a soup-like consistency, but do not make it too thin: the texture should be quite dense. Leave to chill, or stir in the ice cubes and serve immediately.
7 To make croutons, heat oil in a frying pan and add garlic. Fry bread cubes over medium heat, turning often, until browned. Serve with the soup.

NUTRIENTS PER SERVING
1013 kJ, 242 kcal, 6 g protein, 16 g fat (3 g saturated fat), 21 g carbohydrate

VARIATION
Put some vodka in the freezer before making the gazpacho, then add 1–2 tablespoons to each bowl just before serving.

COOK'S TIP
Using a food processor makes fast work of chopping the vegetables. You can chop them by hand, but it will take much longer.

FRENCH VEGETABLE SOUP
TIME **30 MINUTES** SERVES **4**

INGREDIENTS

30 g (1 oz) butter

2 cloves garlic, chopped

2 French shallots (eschalots), chopped

3 x 410 g (15 oz) cans chopped tomatoes

1³⁄₄ cups (435 ml) chicken or
   vegetable stock

1 teaspoon dried basil

salt and freshly ground black pepper

200 g (7 oz) small new potatoes,
   quartered

12 baby carrots, halved, or 4 small carrots,
   cut into chunks

6 large radishes, diced

12 asparagus tips

100 g (3¹⁄₂ oz) sugarsnap peas or snow
   peas (mangetout), trimmed and halved

2 cups (500 ml) cream

8 fresh basil leaves, roughly torn

parmesan or mature cheddar, grated
   (optional)

METHOD

1 Put a kettle of water on to boil. Heat butter very slowly in a large
saucepan. Add garlic and French shallots and fry gently 3 minutes,
stirring occasionally.

2 Add tomatoes, stock, dried basil, and some salt and pepper. Bring to a
boil, cover and simmer 15 minutes.

3 Put potatoes in a second saucepan and cover well with boiling water from
the kettle. Return to a boil, then reduce heat and boil gently 5 minutes.

4 Add carrots, radishes, asparagus and sugarsnap peas or snow peas to the
saucepan with potatoes. Cook 10–12 minutes, or until they are just tender.

5 Drain vegetables and add to the tomato stock. Stir in cream and heat
through gently.

6 Add fresh basil and season with salt and pepper. Ladle into bowls and
sprinkle each with parmesan or mature cheddar if desired.

NUTRIENTS PER SERVING

938 kJ, 224 kcal, 8 g protein, 12 g fat (7 g saturated fat), 22 g carbohydrate

VARIATION

Add some shredded cooked chicken or turkey to make a delicious poultry
and vegetable stew.

HEARTY CHICKEN SOUP
WITH HORSERADISH DUMPLINGS
TIME **30 MINUTES** SERVES **4**

METHOD

1 Heat oil in a large saucepan. Add onion, celery and carrots and fry 2 minutes, stirring.
2 Add chicken and cook, stirring occasionally, 3–4 minutes, or until the chicken is lightly coloured.
3 Combine flour, vegetable shortening, chives or parsley and horseradish in a bowl. Season with salt and black pepper and add just enough cold water to form a fairly dry dough. Shape into 16 pieces.
4 Add stock and peas to pan. Bring mixture to a boil, then add dumplings. Cover pan, reduce heat to a gentle simmer and cook 12 minutes, or until dumplings rise to the top and are firm. Ladle into bowls and garnish with remaining chives or parsley.

NUTRIENTS PER SERVING

2105 kJ, 503 kcal, 25 g protein, 32 g fat (10 g saturated fat), 30 g carbohydrate

VARIATION

COCK-A-LEEKIE SOUP This traditional Scottish soup featuring chicken and leeks dates from the 16th century. Omit onion, celery, carrots and peas from the basic recipe, and also omit the dumplings. Heat oil in a saucepan and add diced chicken, as in step 2. Add 2 thinly sliced leeks, white part only, and 2 slices rindless bacon (bacon strips), chopped. Add stock and bring to a boil. Stir in 1/3 cup (65 g) long-grain rice and 12 pitted prunes. Season, then reduce heat and simmer 12–15 minutes, or until rice is tender. Add a squeeze of lemon juice and sprinkle with chopped fresh parsley.

INGREDIENTS

2 tablespoons vegetable oil
1 onion, finely chopped
2 celery stalks, finely chopped
2 carrots, finely chopped
375 g (3/4 lb) boneless, skinless chicken thighs, diced
1 cup (150 g) self-raising flour
60 g (2 oz) solid vegetable shortening, grated
1 tablespoon snipped fresh chives or chopped fresh parsley, plus extra, to garnish
1 tablespoon grated horseradish, from a jar
salt and freshly ground black pepper
2 cups (500 ml) chicken stock
1 cup (150 g) frozen peas

ROASTED TOMATO, CAPSICUM
AND CHORIZO SOUP
TIME 30 MINUTES SERVES 4

INGREDIENTS

1 red onion, unpeeled, quartered

2 red capsicums (bell peppers), halved
   lengthwise, seeds removed

4 roma (plum) tomatoes, halved lengthwise

2 cloves garlic, unpeeled

2 cups (500 ml) chicken stock

salt and freshly ground black pepper

400 g (14 oz) can red kidney beans,
   drained and rinsed

100 g (3$^{1}/_{2}$ oz) chorizo, diced

2 teaspoons balsamic vinegar

4 tablespoons torn fresh basil

METHOD

1 Preheat grill (broiler) to high. Place onion, capsicums and tomatoes on
   a large baking tray, cut sides down, with garlic cloves.
2 Grill vegetables about 8 minutes, or until skins start to blacken. Allow
   to cool slightly, then peel skins from onion, capsicums and tomatoes.
   Squeeze garlic flesh from its skin.
3 Chop half the vegetables into chunks and set aside. Put remaining
   vegetables in a food processor or blender with garlic flesh and stock.
   Process until smooth, then pour into a saucepan. Add reserved chopped
   vegetables and season lightly.
4 Bring soup to a boil, stirring occasionally. Add beans, chorizo and vinegar,
   cover pan and simmer gently 2–3 minutes. Toss basil into soup just before
   serving (it will darken if added too soon).

NUTRIENTS PER SERVING
817 kJ, 195 kcal, 14 g protein, 6 g fat (2 g saturated fat), 22 g carbohydrate

VARIATION
ROASTED CHERRY TOMATO SOUP Replace roma tomatoes in basic
recipe with 350 g (12 oz) red cherry tomatoes. Grill with 1 halved, unpeeled
red onion, 1 halved, seeded red capsicum (bell pepper) and 2 cloves garlic
until skins split, as for basic recipe. Purée whole unpeeled cherry tomatoes
with stock and garlic flesh in a food processor or blender. Put in a saucepan.
Peel and chop onion and capsicum and add to pan. Omit beans and vinegar.
Add chorizo or instead add a 180 g (6 oz) can tuna, drained and flaked.
Add 2 tablespoons pesto. Simmer gently 2–3 minutes, then add fresh basil.
Ladle into bowls and sprinkle each with 100 g (3$^{1}/_{2}$ oz) crumbled fetta and
4 tablespoons pine nuts.

COOK'S TIP
You can make this soup up to 2 days in advance. Prepare to the end of step 3,
then cool, cover and store in the refrigerator. To serve, complete step 4.

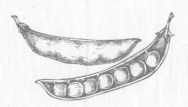

MINTED ASPARAGUS AND PEA SOUP

TIME **30 MINUTES** SERVES **4**

INGREDIENTS

200 g (7 oz) asparagus spears

1 tablespoon olive oil

2 French shallots (eschalots), chopped

175 g (6 oz) potatoes, chopped

1 cup (150 g) frozen peas

2¹/₂ cups (625 ml) vegetable stock

1 sprig fresh mint

salt and freshly ground black pepper

4 tablespoons Greek-style yogurt

¹/₄ cup (40 g) ready-toasted pine nuts, to garnish

METHOD

1 Snap off any woody ends from asparagus spears at the point where they break easily. Cut off tender tips and reserve. Roughly chop remainder.

2 Heat oil in a large, heavy-based saucepan and add French shallots, chopped asparagus and potatoes. Cover and cook over medium heat, stirring occasionally, 6–8 minutes, or until tender.

3 Set aside a handful of peas and add remainder to pan with stock and mint. Cook a further few minutes until potato is tender. If you have time, allow soup to cool a little before puréeing.

4 Process the soup in a food processor or blender to a smooth purée. Return to pan and season with salt and black pepper.

5 Blanch asparagus tips and reserved peas in a pan of boiling water 2 minutes. Drain.

6 Bring soup to a boil, then stir in blanched asparagus tips and peas. Ladle into bowls. Swirl 1 tablespoon yogurt through each and scatter pine nuts over the top.

NUTRIENTS PER SERVING

898 kJ, 214 kcal, 7 g protein, 14 g fat (3 g saturated fat), 15 g carbohydrate

COOK'S TIP

If ready-toasted pine nuts are not available, use raw. Place in a small, dry pan and toast over medium–high heat 1 minute, tossing or stirring frequently, until light golden brown.

Left Minted asparagus and pea soup

MISO NOODLE SOUP WITH TOFU

TIME **20 MINUTES** SERVES **4**

INGREDIENTS

4 cups (1 litre) boiling water

4 x 18 g (²/₃ oz) sachets miso soup powder

2 cups (180 g) sliced button mushrooms

6 spring onions (scallions), sliced

125 g (4 oz) dried rice stick noodles

90 g (3 oz) watercress, with stalks, roughly chopped

175 g (6 oz) tofu, cut into small cubes

salt

METHOD

1 Bring water to a boil in a large saucepan. Dissolve miso powder in boiling water.

2 Add mushrooms and spring onions to the pan, cover and simmer 2–3 minutes to soften vegetables. Stir in noodles and simmer gently 4 minutes.

3 Stir in watercress and tofu, then return to a boil. Season with salt, if necessary, and serve.

NUTRIENTS PER SERVING

797 kJ, 190 kcal, 9 g protein, 3 g fat (0 g saturated fat), 29 g carbohydrate

VARIATION

For a super-speedy soup, buy a 400 g (14 oz) packet ready-sliced stir-fry vegetables and add them to hot miso soup in step 2, instead of mushrooms and spring onions. Simmer until vegetables are almost tender, then add noodles and cook 4 minutes. Finally, add tofu. Omit watercress.

AROMATIC PARSNIP SOUP

TIME **30 MINUTES** SERVES **4**

INGREDIENTS

3$\frac{1}{2}$ cups (875 ml) vegetable stock

1 tablespoon vegetable oil

1 onion, chopped

1 clove garlic, chopped

2 teaspoons ground coriander

1 teaspoon ground cumin

1 teaspoon turmeric

1 large tart green apple, peeled, cored
   and cut into chunks

600 g (1 lb 5 oz) parsnips, cut into chunks

salt

1$\frac{1}{4}$ cups (310 ml) milk

4 tablespoons natural (plain) yogurt

2 tablespoons fresh coriander (cilantro)
   leaves, to garnish

METHOD

1 Warm stock in a large saucepan over low heat.
2 Heat oil in a large, heavy-based saucepan. Cook onion over medium heat 5 minutes, until softened.
3 Add garlic, coriander, cumin and turmeric and cook 1 minute.
4 Pour warmed stock into the pan and add apple, parsnips and salt to taste. Bring to a boil, then reduce heat, cover and simmer 15 minutes.
5 Remove pan from heat and stir in milk. Process soup in a food processor or blender until it forms a smooth purée. Return soup to pan and heat gently until boiling.
6 Ladle into bowls. Swirl 1 tablespoon yogurt through each and garnish with coriander leaves.

NUTRIENTS PER SERVING

966 kJ, 213 kcal, 9 g protein, 10 g fat (2 g saturated fat), 30 g carbohydrate

COOK'S TIP

If you are using a food processor or blender that will not take boiling liquids, cooling the soup by adding cold milk means that you can purée it immediately.

SPICED BEETROOT AND APPLE SOUP

TIME **30 MINUTES** SERVES **4**

INGREDIENTS

1 tablespoon olive oil

15 g ($^1/_2$ oz) butter

250 g (8 oz) raw beetroot (beets),
    peeled and roughly chopped

2 sweet apples, peeled, cored and
    cut into chunks

1 large red onion, chopped

1 tablespoon mild curry powder

2 cups (500 ml) vegetable stock

salt and freshly ground black pepper

4 tablespoons light sour cream or
    crème fraîche

2 hard-boiled (hard-cooked) eggs,
    peeled and roughly chopped

METHOD

1 Heat oil and butter in a large
   saucepan. Stir in beetroot, apples
   and onion. Cover and cook over
   medium heat 10 minutes, shaking
   pan occasionally to prevent any
   sticking. Stir in curry powder and
   cook gently a further 5 minutes.

2 Add half the stock. Purée in a
   food processor or blender until
   smooth.

3 Return soup to the pan and stir in
   the remaining stock. Season and
   heat gently until boiling. Ladle
   into bowls, swirl 1 tablespoon
   sour cream or crème fraîche into
   each and scatter with pieces of
   hard-boiled egg.

NUTRIENTS PER SERVING

1145 kJ, 273 kcal, 6 g protein, 19 g fat
(9 g saturated fat), 21 g carbohydrate

VARIATION

Instead of curry powder, you could
use 2 teaspoons grated horseradish
from a jar or 1 teaspoon dried red
chilli flakes or wasabi (Japanese
horseradish) paste.

SPICY LENTIL SOUP
TIME **30 MINUTES** SERVES **4**

METHOD
1 Heat oil in a large saucepan. Fry onion, garlic, celery and carrot over medium heat, stirring occasionally, about 5 minutes.
2 Stir in curry paste and cook 1 minute, then add lentils, tomatoes and stock. Season and bring to just below boiling.
3 Reduce heat and simmer gently about 15 minutes, or until lentils and vegetables are tender. Stir in coconut cream. Ladle into bowls. Add a drizzle of yogurt and a little fresh coriander to each.

NUTRIENTS PER SERVING
1083 kJ, 259 kcal, 9 g protein, 17 g fat (5 g saturated fat), 18 g carbohydrate

VARIATION
For a Moroccan flavour, replace curry paste with 2 teaspoons harissa paste. This is a fiery North African paste made from dried chillies, garlic, cumin, caraway seeds and tomato paste. Serve the soup with pita bread.

INGREDIENTS
2 tablespoons vegetable oil

1 onion, chopped

1 clove garlic, crushed

1 celery stalk, chopped

1 carrot, chopped

1 tablespoon medium madras curry paste

$1/3$ cup (90 g) red lentils

3 roma (plum) tomatoes, fresh or canned, chopped

2 cups (500 ml) vegetable stock

salt and freshly ground black pepper

4 tablespoons coconut cream

4 tablespoons low-fat natural (plain) yogurt

2 tablespoons fresh coriander (cilantro) leaves, to garnish

SPICY CARROT SOUP
TIME 30 MINUTES SERVES 4

INGREDIENTS

4 cups (1 litre) vegetable stock or water

1 potato, cut into small chunks

1 onion, cut into small chunks

500 g (1 lb) carrots, cut into small chunks

2 large cloves garlic, quartered

salt

2 tablespoons olive oil

1 green chilli, seeds removed, finely
    chopped

5 cm (2 inch) piece fresh ginger, peeled
    and finely chopped

1 teaspoon garam masala, Chinese
    five-spice or mixed spice

juice of 1 lemon or lime

1 teaspoon sesame oil

freshly ground black pepper

2 tablespoons chopped fresh coriander
    (cilantro) leaves, to garnish

METHOD

1 Put stock or water in a large saucepan and bring to a boil.

2 Stir in potato, onion, carrots, garlic and salt to taste. Bring back to a boil,
   reduce heat, partially cover and simmer 15–20 minutes.

3 Meanwhile, heat oil in a small pan. Fry chilli and ginger about 1 minute,
   but do not let them burn. Stir in garam masala, Chinese five-spice or mixed
   spice, and lemon or lime juice. Cook 1 minute.

4 Add sesame oil and stir over low–medium heat until the mixture thickens.
   Remove from heat and set aside.

5 When vegetables are tender, stir in the ginger mixture. Process soup in a
   food processor or blender to a purée.

6 Return purée to the pan. Season with black pepper and reheat gently.
   Ladle into bowls and garnish with coriander.

NUTRIENTS PER SERVING

707 kJ, 169 kcal, 3 g protein, 11 g fat (1 g saturated fat), 19 g carbohydrate

ZUCCHINI AND WATERCRESS SOUP

TIME **30 MINUTES** SERVES **4**

INGREDIENTS

30 g (1 oz) unsalted butter

2 onions, finely chopped

3 cups (750 ml) chicken or
vegetable stock

1 kg (2 lb) firm zucchini (courgettes),
thinly sliced

1 large bunch (300 g/10 oz) watercress,
coarse stems discarded, chopped,
plus 4 sprigs reserved, to garnish

salt and freshly ground black pepper

juice of 1 lemon

METHOD

1 Heat butter in a large saucepan
and fry onions over low heat
5 minutes, until translucent. Add
stock, cover and bring to a boil.

2 Add zucchini. Bring back to a
boil, reduce the heat, cover and
simmer 15 minutes.

3 When zucchini is tender, stir in
watercress. Remove pan from the
heat and leave to stand, covered,
5 minutes.

4 Process soup in a food processor
or blender to a purée.

5 Return purée to the pan. Add salt,
pepper and lemon juice to taste,
then reheat gently. Ladle into
bowls and garnish with reserved
sprigs of watercress.

NUTRIENTS PER SERVING

498 kJ, 119 kcal, 6 g protein, 6 g fat
(4 g saturated fat), 9 g carbohydrate

MINESTRONE

TIME **30 MINUTES** SERVES **4**

METHOD

1 Put a kettle of water on to boil.
2 Heat oil in a large saucepan and fry leek 1 minute. Add garlic and fry a further 1 minute.
3 Add celery and zucchini to the pan, stir and cook 3 minutes.
4 Add parsley, cannellini beans, tomatoes, bay leaf, white wine, pasta, lemon rind and 2 cups (500 ml) boiling water. Cover, bring back to a boil, then reduce heat and simmer 7 minutes.
5 Add cabbage and half the parmesan to the soup. Season with salt and pepper, then simmer 5 minutes.
6 Remove bay leaf. Pour the minestrone into four bowls and sprinkle remaining parmesan over each. Serve with crusty bread and, if liked, pass around a small separate bowl of pesto.

NUTRIENTS PER SERVING

2030 kJ, 485 kcal, 21 g protein, 15 g fat (3 g saturated fat), 65 g carbohydrate

COOK'S TIP

Instead of adding the parmesan at the end, you can add a small piece of parmesan rind to the soup along with the other ingredients in step 3 to give a cheesy flavour throughout. Remove rind just before serving.

INGREDIENTS

2 tablespoons olive oil
1 small leek, halved and sliced
1 clove garlic, crushed
2 celery stalks, finely sliced
2 zucchini (courgettes), halved lengthwise, sliced
1 sprig fresh parsley
400 g (14 oz) can cannellini beans, rinsed and drained
410 g (15 oz) can chopped tomatoes
1 bay leaf
$2/3$ cup (150 ml) dry white wine
2 tablespoons soup-pasta shapes
strip of zest of 1 lemon
125 g (4 oz) savoy or other green cabbage, finely shredded
$1/3$ cup (35 g) grated parmesan
salt and freshly ground black pepper
loaf of crusty bread, to serve
4 tablespoons pesto (optional), to serve

SPEEDY TWO-FISH HOTPOT
TIME **30 MINUTES** SERVES **4**

INGREDIENTS

1 tablespoon olive oil

1 small leek, white part only, thinly sliced

75 g (2¹⁄₂ oz) mild pancetta or rindless
   bacon (bacon strips), diced

1³⁄₄ cups (435 ml) fish stock

410 g (15 oz) can chopped tomatoes

¹⁄₄ teaspoon chilli powder

1 teaspoon fennel seeds

200 g (7 oz) small new potatoes, halved

salt and freshly ground black pepper

200 g (7 oz) firm thick white fish fillets,
   such as blue-eye cod, hake or cod, skin
   removed, cut into bite-sized pieces

175 g (6 oz) smoked fish, such as cod
   or haddock, preferably undyed, skin
   removed, cut into bite-sized pieces

METHOD

1 Heat oil in a large saucepan. Add leeks and pancetta or bacon and cook over medium heat, stirring occasionally, 3–4 minutes.

2 Add stock, tomatoes, chilli powder and fennel seeds. Bring to a boil. Add potatoes and season with salt and black pepper to taste. Cover, heat to just below boiling and cook 5 minutes.

3 Stir in white fish and smoked fish. Bring to a boil, then reduce heat. Cover and simmer very gently 6 minutes, or until fish flakes easily and potatoes are tender. Ladle into wide bowls to serve.

NUTRIENTS PER SERVING

1028 kJ, 246 kcal, 28 g protein, 9 g fat (2 g saturated fat), 12 g carbohydrate

VARIATION

LOUISIANA SEAFOOD CHOWDER Fry 1 chopped onion, 1 chopped celery stalk and 1 chopped green capsicum (bell pepper) in 1 tablespoon vegetable oil 5 minutes. Add 410 g (15 oz) can chopped tomatoes with torn fresh basil, 1 crushed clove garlic, 1³⁄₄ cups (435 ml) fish stock and 1 teaspoon hot chilli (pepper) sauce. Bring to a boil. Stir in ¹⁄₂ cup (100 g) long-grain rice. Reduce heat, cover and simmer 10 minutes. Add 350 g (12 oz) fresh or frozen mixed seafood (such as cubed firm white fish and small peeled prawns (shrimp)) and 100 g (3¹⁄₂ oz) frozen or drained canned corn. Season. Bring to a boil, then simmer 5 minutes, or until rice is tender and fish flakes easily.

COOK'S TIP

There are two kinds of smoked fish: hot-smoked and cold-smoked. In hot-smoking, the fish is given an initial blast of hot air and then slowly cured in the smoke from a hot woodchip or sawdust fire. This cooks it too, so it is bought ready to eat. In cold-smoking, the fish is often salted or brined before being cured over the smoke from a wood-burning fire. Some cold-smoked fish are eaten raw, while others need to be cooked further. Smoking, whether hot or cold, does not destroy the nutrients in the fish.

THREE BEAN SOUP
TIME **30 MINUTES** SERVES **4**

METHOD

1 Warm stock in a large saucepan over low heat.
2 Heat oil in a large saucepan. Add onion and cook over medium heat 5 minutes, until softened. Add garlic and cook 1 minute.
3 Add green beans and broad beans. Raise the heat and cook 3–4 minutes. Add stock and boil 5 minutes, then lower the heat and simmer 10 minutes.
4 Remove pan from heat and stir in butterbeans with their liquid.
5 Process half the soup in a food processor or blender to a purée, then return to the pan. Season with salt and black pepper and reheat. Ladle into bowls. Scatter chives and chive flowers over each.

NUTRIENTS PER SERVING

1058 kJ, 253 kcal, 13 g protein, 10 g fat (1 g saturated fat), 29 g carbohydrate

VARIATION

Chopped fresh coriander (cilantro) leaves, mint or parsley can be used as a garnish instead of chives.

INGREDIENTS

4 cups (1 litre) vegetable stock
2 tablespoons olive oil
1 onion, chopped
1 large clove garlic, crushed
250 g (8 oz) green beans, topped and tailed, cut into bite-sized pieces
2¹/₂ cups (350 g) frozen broad (fava) beans
400 g (14 oz) can butterbeans (lima beans), with their liquid
salt and freshly ground black pepper
4 tablespoons snipped fresh chives and chive flowers, to garnish

CAPSICUM AND ORANGE SOUP

TIME **30 MINUTES** SERVES 4

INGREDIENTS

2 tablespoons olive oil

1 kg (2 lb) red capsicums (bell peppers), seeds removed, roughly sliced

salt

zest of 1 orange

¾ cup (180 ml) orange juice

2 cups (500 ml) vegetable or chicken stock

METHOD

1 Heat oil in a large saucepan. Add capsicums, salt to taste and all but a few strips of orange zest to the pan.

2 Cover and cook over high heat until steam starts to escape from under the lid. Lower heat and simmer 15–18 minutes, or until capsicums are softened, shaking pan occasionally and allowing them to cook in their own juice. If you have time, allow to cool a little before puréeing.

3 Process capsicums in a food processor or blender to a smooth purée. Add orange juice and vegetable or chicken stock and process again.

4 Return soup to the pan and reheat gently. Ladle into bowls and garnish with reserved orange zest.

NUTRIENTS PER SERVING

649 kJ, 155 kcal, 2 g protein, 8 g fat (1 g saturated fat), 18 g carbohydrate

COOK'S TIP

It does not matter if some capsicums caramelise during cooking in step 2. This just adds to the richness of the soup's flavour.

Left Thai coconut soup (top); Capsicum and orange soup (bottom)

THAI COCONUT SOUP

TIME **20 MINUTES** SERVES 4

INGREDIENTS

2 cups (500 ml) chicken or vegetable stock

1 tablespoon vegetable oil

3 cloves garlic, finely chopped

2 lemongrass stems, white part only, finely chopped

6 spring onions (scallions), including green part, finely chopped

1 small red chilli, seeds removed, finely chopped

1 teaspoon red curry paste

1½ cups (375 ml) coconut milk

4 pieces dried galangal

2 teaspoons soft brown sugar

1 tablespoon lime juice

1 tablespoon fish sauce

4 kaffir lime (makrut) leaves, plus extra, to garnish

300 g (10 oz) drained canned straw mushrooms

4 tablespoons shredded coconut, lightly toasted, to garnish

1 small red chilli, finely sliced, to garnish

2 tablespoons fresh coriander (cilantro) leaves, to garnish

METHOD

1 Warm stock in a small saucepan over low heat.

2 Heat oil in a large, heavy-based saucepan. Add garlic, lemongrass, spring onions, chilli and curry paste. Cook over medium–high heat, stirring, 1–2 minutes.

3 Stir in stock, coconut milk, galangal and brown sugar. Bring to a boil, reduce heat and simmer gently 5 minutes.

4 Add lime juice, fish sauce, kaffir lime leaves and straw mushrooms to the pan. Simmer a further 2–3 minutes.

5 When the soup is ready, remove the galangal. Ladle soup into bowls and garnish with lime leaves, shredded coconut, chilli and coriander.

NUTRIENTS PER SERVING

775 kJ, 181 kcal, 5 g protein, 16 g fat (10 g saturated fat), 4 g carbohydrate

VARIATION

If you have time, you could soak about 30 g (1 oz) cloud ear fungus in warm water at least 30 minutes and use instead of the straw mushrooms.

COOK'S TIP

Galangal is sometimes available fresh, but is usually sold powdered, as slices in brine or as dried slices, in Asian food stores. The dried slices are used here, as they are the best for simmering in soups and curries.

CHILLI CRABMEAT SOUP
TIME 25 MINUTES SERVES 4

INGREDIENTS

3 cups (750 ml) fish stock

350 g (12 oz) crabmeat, brown meat
and white meat separated

6 French shallots (eschalots), roughly
chopped

1 clove garlic, chopped

75 g (2$^1/_2$ oz) basmati rice

1$^1/_2$ teaspoons dried red chilli flakes

2 teaspoons fish sauce

200 ml (7 fl oz) coconut milk

juice of 1 lime

salt and freshly ground black pepper

3 tablespoons roughly chopped fresh
coriander (cilantro) leaves, to garnish

2 spring onions (scallions), finely sliced
on the diagonal, to garnish

METHOD

1 Warm stock in a large saucepan over low heat.
2 Process brown crabmeat, French shallots, garlic and fish in a food
   processor or blender until smooth.
3 Tip mixture into the saucepan, add rice and chilli flakes. Bring to a
   boil,then reduce heat. Cover and simmer, stirring occasionally, about
   10 minutes, or until rice is just tender.
4 Stir in fish sauce, coconut milk and lime juice. Add white crabmeat and
   heat through gently. Season lightly. Ladle into bowls and sprinkle with
   coriander and spring onions.

NUTRIENTS PER SERVING

1136 kJ, 271 kcal, 20 g protein, 12 g fat (10 g saturated fat), 19 g carbohydrate

COOK'S TIP

Crabs have both delicate white meat and stronger flavoured brown meat.
Brown meat is often mixed with other ingredients or with some of the white
meat to lighten its flavour. You can buy prepared crabmeat from a fish shop
or supermarket. Store in the refrigerator and use within a day of purchase.

CRAB AND SESAME SOUP
TIME 15 MINUTES SERVES 4

INGREDIENTS

4 cups (1 litre) chicken stock

sea salt and freshly ground black pepper

2 tablespoons cornflour (cornstarch)

4 spring onions (scallions), white part only, finely sliced

125 g (4 oz) cooked crabmeat

1 teaspoon sesame oil

1 teaspoon chilli paste

1 teaspoon light soy sauce

2 tablespoons fresh coriander (cilantro) leaves

METHOD

1 Put stock in a large saucepan, season with sea salt and black pepper and bring to a simmer.

2 Blend cornflour with 3 tablespoons cold water in a small bowl to make a smooth paste. When stock is simmering, whisk in the paste until the soup is clear and thickened.

3 Add spring onions, crabmeat, sesame oil, chilli paste and soy sauce. Stir gently over medium heat 2–3 minutes, until crab is just heated through.

4 Ladle the soup into four bowls and scatter some coriander over each.

NUTRIENTS PER SERVING

273 kJ, 65 kcal, 7 g protein, 1 g fat (<1 g saturated fat), 6 g carbohydrate

CHICKEN NOODLE SOUP
TIME **15 MINUTES** SERVES **4**

METHOD

1 Bring stock and cayenne pepper to a boil in a large saucepan.
2 When stock reaches boiling point, add mushrooms, lower the heat and simmer 2 minutes. Add rice vermicelli and simmer 3 minutes, until just barely cooked. Add lettuce, then raise the heat and bring the soup to a rolling boil.
3 Remove from the heat and slowly add egg, stirring gently. It will cook very quickly to form threads. Stir in coriander and serve immediately.

NUTRIENTS PER SERVING
335 kJ, 80 kcal, 6 g protein, 2 g fat (1 g saturated fat), 8 g carbohydrate

VARIATION
Oyster mushrooms can be used instead of shiitake, and watercress can be substituted for the lettuce.

INGREDIENTS

5 cups (1.25 litres) chicken stock

$1/4$ teaspoon cayenne pepper

100 g ($3^1/_2$ oz) shiitake mushrooms, thinly sliced

40 g ($1^1/_2$ oz) rice vermicelli, lightly crushed

75 g ($2^1/_2$ oz) cos (romaine) lettuce inner leaves, finely shredded

1 large egg, lightly beaten

2 tablespoons fresh coriander (cilantro) leaves

CAULIFLOWER AND BLUE CHEESE SOUP

TIME **25 MINUTES** SERVES **4**

INGREDIENTS

1 small cauliflower, divided into small
   florets
2 small leeks, white part only, diced
1 small potato, chopped

4 cups (1 litre) vegetable stock
salt and freshly ground black pepper
125 g (4 oz) gorgonzola cheese,
   chopped

METHOD

1 Put cauliflower, leeks, potato and stock in a large saucepan. Season and
bring to a boil. Reduce heat, cover and simmer gently 15 minutes, or
until vegetables are tender. If you have time, allow soup to cool a little
before puréeing.
2 Transfer half the soup to a food processor or blender and purée until
smooth. Alternatively, use a hand-held blender straight in the pan to
process soup lightly, leaving a chunky appearance.
3 Return soup to the pan and heat gently until boiling, then remove from
heat. Add cheese, stir lightly and serve.

NUTRIENTS PER SERVING

737 kJ, 176 kcal, 10 g protein, 10 g fat (6 g saturated fat), 11 g carbohydrate

VARIATION

Instead of gorgonzola, try roquefort or dolcelatte or another soft blue-vein
cheese. Substitute broccoli or broccolini for the cauliflower.

SMOKED FISH AND CANNELLINI BEAN SOUP

TIME **25 MINUTES** SERVES **4**

INGREDIENTS

1 tablespoon olive oil
1 onion, chopped
1 celery stalk, chopped
2 small zucchini (courgettes), chopped
2½ cups (625 ml) fish or chicken stock
175 g (6 oz) smoked fish fillet, such as
   haddock or cod, skin removed, diced
salt and freshly ground black pepper
2 x 400 g (14 oz) cans cannellini beans,
   drained and rinsed
1 tablespoon chopped fresh dill
2 tablespoons thick (heavy/double) cream
   (optional)

METHOD

1 Heat oil in a large saucepan and
fry onion, celery and zucchini
5 minutes, or until softened but
not browned.
2 Add stock and bring to a boil.
Add fish and season lightly. Cover
and simmer gently 5 minutes, or
until fish flakes easily.
3 Add beans, dill and cream, if
using. Stir, then heat until almost
boiling. Ladle into bowls.

NUTRIENTS PER SERVING

1204 kJ, 288 kcal, 24 g protein, 10 g fat
(3 g saturated fat), 24 g carbohydrate

VARIATION

Instead of fish, use 150 g (5 oz)
cooked, peeled prawns (shrimp).
Add 250 g (8 oz) frozen or drained
canned corn kernels.

Right Smoked fish and cannellini bean soup

CHAPTER 2

Starters, Snacks & Light Meals

SMOKED SALMON PANCAKES

TIME **25 MINUTES** SERVES **6**

INGREDIENTS

1¼ cups (310 ml) low-fat milk

¾ cup (185 g) crème fraîche or
  sour cream

1 teaspoon lemon juice

2 eggs

4 spring onions (scallions),
  roughly chopped

2 large sprigs fresh dill

1²⁄₃ cups (250 g) self-raising flour

125 g (4 oz) smoked salmon trimmings,
  cut into thin strips

freshly ground black pepper

light olive oil, for frying

1 jar black lumpfish roe (about 50 g/
  1¾ oz) (optional)

fresh dill sprigs or snipped fresh chives,
  to garnish

METHOD

1   Put milk, 2 tablespoons crème fraîche or sour cream and lemon juice in a bowl. Whisk with a fork, then pour half the mixture into a blender. Add eggs and spring onions and blend 1 minute. Add dill and flour, and blend a further 1 minute, or until batter is fairly smooth, with tiny pieces of spring onion and dill. Add remaining milk mixture and blend again. Stir in 50 g (1¾ oz) smoked salmon and season with black pepper.

2   Preheat oven to 150°C (300°F/Gas 2). Heat a heavy non-stick frying pan until medium–hot, then add a little oil and swirl it around to coat the pan. Spoon in 2 tablespoons batter to make a pancake about 9 cm (3½ inches) in diameter. Make two or three more (depending on how many you can fit in the pan), spacing slightly apart. Cook 1 minute, or until small bubbles appear all over the surface and the tops are dry. Using a palette knife, turn pancakes over and cook on the other side about 1 minute. Take out of pan and keep warm in the oven on a baking tray (sheet) while you cook the remaining batter — there will be enough to make 18 pancakes.

3   Put 1 heaped teaspoon of remaining crème fraîche or sour cream in the middle of each pancake, then top with slivers of the remaining smoked salmon and garnish with lumpfish roe, if using, and dill or chives. Arrange on plates or a large warmed platter and serve.

NUTRIENTS PER SERVING

1461 kJ, 349 kcal, 15 g protein, 17 g fat (11 g saturated fat), 33 g carbohydrate

VARIATION

Instead of smoked salmon, use skinned and flaked smoked mackerel fillets and add a little grated horseradish from a jar to the crème fraîche or sour cream for the topping. Garnish with watercress.

HUMMUS AND CAPSICUM SLICES
TIME 10 MINUTES SERVES 4

INGREDIENTS

4 slices ciabatta, cut on the diagonal
4 tablespoons olive oil
1 clove garlic, halved
1/2 cup (110 g) hummus
2 roasted red capsicums (bell peppers),
   from a jar, thinly sliced

METHOD

1 Brush ciabatta slices with olive oil
   on both sides and rub the surfaces
   with garlic. Lightly toast on a hot
   chargrill pan until just golden,
   turning once.
2 Spread hummus over the toasts.
   Arrange red capsicum slices on
   top of the toasts.

NUTRIENTS PER SERVING
681 kJ, 163 kcal, 6 g protein, 8 g fat
(1 g saturated fat), 18 g carbohydrate

TAPENADE TOASTS
TIME 10 MINUTES SERVES 4

INGREDIENTS

8 slices baguette, cut on the diagonal
3 tablespoons black olive tapenade, from a jar

METHOD

1 Preheat grill (broiler) or chargrill pan to hot. Lightly toast baguette
   slices under the grill or on the chargrill pan, turning once.
2 Spread with black olive tapenade and serve.

NUTRIENTS PER SERVING
1008 kJ, 241 kcal, 6 g protein, 7 g fat (1 g saturated fat), 38 g carbohydrate

CHEDDAR CHUTNEY PITAS
TIME 10 MINUTES SERVES 4

INGREDIENTS

4 pitas
4 heaped tablespoons sweet chutney, such as onion and tomato
1 cup (125 g) grated mature cheddar

METHOD

1 Preheat grill (broiler) to medium. Warm pitas under the grill 1 minute
   on each side (this makes the pitas easier to open — take care not to
   toast them). Cut a slit along one edge of each pita to make a pocket.
2 Spread inside each with 1 heaped tablespoon sweet chutney. Divide
   grated cheddar among pitas, tucking it well inside the pocket. Toast
   under a hot grill, turning once, until cheese is hot and bubbling.

NUTRIENTS PER SERVING
1523 kJ, 364 kcal, 16 g protein, 14 g fat (8 g saturated fat), 43 g carbohydrate

Left Hummus and capsicum slices

RICOTTA AND PESTO BITES
TIME 10 MINUTES SERVES 4

INGREDIENTS

2 tablespoons sun-dried tomato pesto
2/3 cup (160 g) ricotta
4 slices pumpernickel
8 fresh basil leaves, torn

METHOD

1 Lightly stir pesto into ricotta to
   give a marbled effect. Spoon
   rough heaps of the mixture onto
   pumpernickel.
2 Cut each slice into four triangles
   and sprinkle with basil.

NUTRIENTS PER SERVING
793 kJ, 189 kcal, 8 g protein, 7 g fat
(3 g saturated fat), 24 g carbohydrate

GRILLED OYSTERS
TIME **30 MINUTES** SERVES 4

INGREDIENTS
60 g (2 oz) butter, softened

2 cloves garlic, crushed

3 tablespoons toasted brown breadcrumbs

1 small bunch (20 g/²⁄₃ oz) fresh parsley,
   leaves finely chopped

salt and freshly ground black pepper

coarse salt

12 oysters, such as Pacific oysters,
   on the half shell

METHOD
1 Preheat grill (broiler) to high. Mash butter in a small bowl. Mix in garlic
   and breadcrumbs.
2 Add parsley to the butter with a little salt and plenty of pepper.
3 Remove rack from grill pan and half fill pan with coarse salt. Place oysters
   firmly in the salt so they do not wobble, and top with some of the seasoned
   breadcrumb mixture.
4 Grill 1–2 minutes, or until the topping bubbles and is lightly browned.
   Serve immediately.

NUTRIENTS PER SERVING
590 kJ, 141 kcal, 4 g protein, 11 g fat (7 g saturated fat), 7 g carbohydrate

COOK'S TIP
Toasted brown breadcrumbs will keep in an airtight container in the
refrigerator for up to a month. Dry thick slices of white bread in an oven
at 150°C (300°F/Gas 2) 1 hour, or until crisp and lightly toasted. Process
in a food processor or blender to make breadcrumbs.

PRAWNS WITH CHILLI AND MANGOES
TIME **30 MINUTES** SERVES **4**

METHOD

1 Mix spring onions, ginger, garlic and chilli in a bowl and set aside. Mix tomato paste, soy sauce, sherry and sesame oil in a separate bowl. Set aside.

2 Peel mangoes, then remove the flesh from the stones and slice thinly. Arrange lettuce leaves on individual serving plates. Set aside.

3 Heat peanut oil in a wok or large frying pan. Add spring onion mixture and stir-fry 1 minute. Add prawns and continue stir-frying until just beginning to turn pink. Add mango slices and stir-fry until prawns turn completely pink and mango is heated through.

4 Add soy sauce mixture and bring to a boil. Season to taste with black pepper, then spoon over lettuce leaves and serve.

NUTRIENTS PER SERVING
912 kJ, 218 kcal, 13 g protein, 9 g fat (1 g saturated fat), 21 g carbohydrate

INGREDIENTS

3 spring onions (scallions), sliced diagonally

2.5 cm (1 inch) piece fresh ginger, grated

1 clove garlic, crushed

1 small red chilli, halved lengthwise, seeds removed, sliced

3 teaspoons tomato paste (concentrated purée)

1 tablespoon soy sauce

2 tablespoons medium sherry

$1/2$ teaspoon sesame oil

2 mangoes (about 400 g/14 oz each)

4–8 red oakleaf or frisée lettuce leaves

2 tablespoons peanut (groundnut) oil

20 peeled raw king prawns (uncooked large shrimp) (about 250 g/8 oz), deveined

freshly ground black pepper

GOAT'S CHEESE AND ROCKET SALAD

TIME **20 MINUTES** SERVES **4**

INGREDIENTS

1 tablespoon vegetable oil

3 slices rindless bacon (bacon strips),
   diced

2 small round soft goat's cheeses
   (about 100 g/3½ oz each),
   halved crosswise

100 g (3½ oz) rocket (arugula)
   or watercress, trimmed

DRESSING

1 clove garlic, crushed

1 teaspoon wholegrain mustard

3 teaspoons white wine vinegar

2 tablespoons extra virgin olive oil

salt and freshly ground black pepper

METHOD

1 Preheat oven to 240°C (460°F/Gas 8). Heat oil and fry bacon until crisp,
   then drain on paper towel.

2 To make dressing, whisk together garlic, mustard, vinegar and olive oil in
   a small bowl. Season with salt and pepper.

3 Line a baking tray with baking paper (or a baking sheet with parchment
   paper). Place goat's cheese rounds on the paper. Bake 5 minutes, or until
   cheese begins to melt and turns a toasty brown on top.

4 Meanwhile, put rocket or watercress in a mixing bowl with bacon. Pour
   over dressing and toss lightly, then arrange on individual plates.

5 Remove cheese from oven, place one round in the centre of each salad and
   serve immediately.

NUTRIENTS PER SERVING

1520 kJ, 363 kcal, 17 g protein, 32 g fat (11 g saturated fat), 2 g carbohydrate

VARIATION

For a vegetarian version, use lightly toasted pine nuts or almonds instead
of the bacon.

STUFFED MUSHROOMS WITH COUSCOUS
TIME **30 MINUTES** SERVES **4**

METHOD

1 Put couscous in a heatproof bowl and mix in stock, 1 tablespoon olive oil and $^{1}/_{2}$ teaspoon salt. Set aside so liquid can be absorbed.

2 Preheat grill (broiler) to medium–hot and line grill pan with foil. Brush gill side of mushrooms with 1 tablespoon olive oil and season. Grill, gill side up, 6 minutes, then turn over, brush with 2 teaspoons olive oil and cook a further 5 minutes, or until softened and golden.

3 Meanwhile, put walnuts on a piece of foil and grill 2 minutes, or until golden (take care not to burn them). Put in a bowl with goat's cheese and 1 tablespoon tarragon and mix together. Remove mushrooms from grill rack.

4 Divide goat's cheese mixture among mushrooms. Put filled mushrooms under the grill. Grill a further 3 minutes, or until filling begins to colour.

5 Whisk together walnut oil and red wine vinegar in a bowl, then stir in remaining tarragon. Taste couscous and adjust seasoning if necessary. Add chives to couscous and use a fork to mix them evenly through the grains. Divide couscous among serving plates, top with mushrooms and drizzle with the tarragon dressing.

INGREDIENTS

200 g (7 oz) couscous

400 ml (14 fl oz) hot beef or chicken stock

$2^{1}/_{2}$ tablespoons olive oil

salt

4 large mushrooms (about 400 g/ 14 oz), stalks removed

75 g ($2^{1}/_{2}$ oz) walnut pieces, broken if large

150 g (5 oz) medium-fat mild goat's cheese

2 tablespoons chopped fresh tarragon

2 tablespoons walnut oil

1 teaspoon red wine vinegar

freshly ground black pepper

2 tablespoons snipped fresh chives

NUTRIENTS PER SERVING
2452 kJ, 586 kcal, 18 g protein, 40 g fat (8 g saturated fat), 39 g carbohydrate

SEARED SQUID WITH BUTTER AND MINT

TIME **30 MINUTES** SERVES **4**

INGREDIENTS

500 g (1 lb) squid tubes

3 cos (romaine) lettuces, outer leaves
   discarded, finely shredded

4 tablespoons butter

2 cloves garlic, crushed

2 French shallots (eschalots),
   finely chopped

grated zest and juice of 1 lime,
   plus 1 lime, sliced, to garnish

2 tablespoons vegetable oil

salt and freshly ground black pepper

2 tablespoons finely chopped fresh mint,
   to garnish

crusty bread, to serve

METHOD

1 Halve squid lengthwise. If the flat triangles are more than 10 cm (4 inches) long, cut in half again. Score the inner surfaces to make a diamond pattern with a sharp knife, then set aside.

2 Put lettuce in a large serving bowl.

3 Warm butter in a saucepan. Add garlic and French shallots and cook very gently about 1 minute. Stir in lime zest and juice and pour the mixture over the lettuce.

4 Heat oil in a large frying pan until very hot and fry squid in batches, 2–3 minutes each batch, until the pieces have become opaque and tightened into curls.

5 Transfer squid to the serving bowl with all the juices and residue from the pan. Season with salt and pepper and toss gently into the lettuce.

6 Serve on individual plates, scatter over mint and garnish with reserved slices of lime. Accompany with slices of crusty bread.

NUTRIENTS PER SERVING

2326 kJ, 556 kcal, 28 g protein, 28 g fat (13 g saturated fat), 47 g carbohydrate

SMOKED TROUT AND WATERCRESS OPEN SANDWICH

TIME **25 MINUTES** SERVES **4**

INGREDIENTS

12 quail's eggs

50 g (1³⁄₄ oz) watercress, thick stems
   discarded, roughly chopped, plus
   4 sprigs reserved, to garnish

4 tablespoons mayonnaise

1 tablespoon lemon juice

8 thick slices rye bread

3 skinless smoked trout fillets
   (about 75 g/2¹⁄₂ oz each), flaked

freshly ground black pepper

METHOD

1 Simmer eggs in boiling water
1¹⁄₂–2 minutes, depending on
whether you prefer them slightly
soft or medium boiled. Plunge
into cold water and leave to cool.

2 Mix together chopped watercress,
mayonnaise and lemon juice in
a bowl.

3 Spread watercress mixture evenly
over each slice of rye bread, then
top with flakes of smoked trout.

4 Carefully peel shells off quail's
eggs, cut each in half and arrange
three halves on top of each open
sandwich. Grind over pepper and
garnish with watercress sprigs.

NUTRIENTS PER SERVING

1601 kJ, 382 kcal, 29 g protein, 17 g fat
(3 g saturated fat), 24 g carbohydrate

VARIATION

Instead of 12 quail's eggs, use
6 hen's eggs. Prepare as in step 1,
simmering 3–4 minutes, depending
on whether you prefer them slightly
soft or medium boiled. In step 4,
cut each egg in quarters.

PESTO AND GOAT'S CHEESE CROÛTES

TIME **15 MINUTES** SERVES **4**

INGREDIENTS

6–8 small tomatoes, thinly sliced

12 sun-dried tomatoes in oil, drained
and sliced

2 tablespoons extra virgin olive oil

3 teaspoons balsamic vinegar

salt and freshly ground black pepper

1 baguette, thickly cut on the diagonal
into 12 slices

4–5 tablespoons sun-dried tomato pesto or
2 tablespoons wholegrain mustard

200 g (7 oz) goat's cheese

METHOD

1 Preheat grill (broiler) to high.
Arrange tomato slices on four
plates and scatter over sun-dried
tomatoes.
2 Drizzle oil and vinegar over the
tomatoes and season with salt
and pepper.
3 To make croûtes, spread baguette
slices with sun-dried tomato pesto
or mustard, top with a spoonful
of goat's cheese and season with
a little pepper.
4 Put croûtes under the hot grill
1–2 minutes, or until cheese has
melted slightly.
5 Place three croûtes on each plate
with the tomato salad and serve.

NUTRIENTS PER SERVING

2373 kJ, 567 kcal, 17 g protein, 44 g fat
(11 g saturated fat), 27 g carbohydrate

COOK'S TIP

The croûtes can be assembled ahead
of time, kept in the refrigerator and
grilled just before serving.

MEDITERRANEAN TARTS

TIME **30 MINUTES** SERVES **4**

INGREDIENTS

375 g (13 oz) ready-rolled puff
pastry, thawed if frozen

4 tablespoons pesto

2 large tomatoes, thinly sliced

1 cup (250 g) ricotta

8 pitted black olives, halved

$1/2$ cup (50 g) grated parmesan

freshly ground black pepper

fresh basil leaves, to garnish

METHOD

1 Preheat oven to 220°C (400°F/Gas 6). If time allows, leave pastry, still
wrapped, at room temperature 20 minutes (this makes it easier to unroll
without cracking, but isn't essential).
2 Carefully unroll pastry, then cut into four even-sized rectangles, each
about 18 x 10 cm (7 x 4 inches). Place on a baking tray (sheet) and
prick all over with a fork. Bake 12 minutes, turning baking tray if
pastry bases are cooking or browning unevenly.
3 Spread each with 1 tablespoon pesto, then divide tomato slices evenly
among them. Dot ricotta over in small blobs, then scatter with olives.
Sprinkle with parmesan and grind over pepper.
4 Return tarts to oven and bake 5–10 minutes, or until pastry bases are
well browned and crisp and topping is slightly melted and coloured.
Serve garnished with basil.

NUTRIENTS PER SERVING

2451 kJ, 585 kcal, 19 g protein, 40 g fat (20 g saturated fat), 37 g carbohydrate

VARIATION

Brush young asparagus with olive oil and bake (while the pastry bases
are cooking, on the shelf below) 12 minutes. Spread pesto over each base.
Top with asparagus and scatter with shaved parmesan. Bake 2 minutes.

Right Mediterranean tarts

POTATO PANCAKES WITH SMOKED SALMON

TIME **30 MINUTES** SERVES **4**

METHOD

1 Put potatoes and onion in a sieve. Press with a spoon or the base of a saucer to squeeze out as much starchy liquid as possible.

2 Transfer potato mixture to a bowl. Add egg, flour, salt and pepper to taste and mix together well.

3 Pour oil into a frying pan to a depth of about 1 cm ($^1/_2$ inch) and heat until it shows a haze.

4 Put 1 tablespoon of mixture into the oil, flattening to a small pancake about 5 cm (2 inches) in diameter. Cook four to six at a time. Fry about 1 minute, or until golden on the bottom, then turn and cook other side until crisp and golden but still soft in the centre.

5 Remove pancakes from the pan, drain on paper towel and keep warm in the oven. Repeat steps 4 and 5 until you have made 12 pancakes.

6 Serve each pancake topped with a spoonful of sour cream and a few strips of salmon. Garnish with a little dill, onion slices and capers, as desired.

NUTRIENTS PER SERVING

1431 kJ, 342 kcal, 20 g protein, 18 g fat (6 g saturated fat), 28 g carbohydrate

COOK'S TIP

Smoked salmon trimmings save time as they do not need to be chopped. They taste as good as slices of smoked salmon and are considerably cheaper.

INGREDIENTS

500 g (1 lb) baking (floury) potatoes, such as pontiacs or king edwards, peeled and grated

1 medium onion, finely chopped

1 large egg

2 tablespoons wholemeal (whole-wheat) flour

salt and freshly ground black pepper

vegetable oil, for frying

$^2/_3$ cup (160 g) thick sour cream

200 g (7 oz) smoked salmon, cut into small strips

fresh dill sprigs, to garnish

red onion slices, quartered, to garnish

capers, rinsed and squeezed dry, to garnish (optional)

VEGETABLE BRUSCHETTA
TIME **30 MINUTES** SERVES **4**

INGREDIENTS

1 red and 1 yellow capsicum (bell pepper),
    seeds removed, each cut lengthwise
    into 8 pieces

2 small zucchini (courgettes),
    diagonally sliced

1 bulb fennel, thinly sliced lengthwise

1 red onion, sliced

4 tablespoons olive oil

4 thick slices ciabatta or baguette,
    cut on the diagonal

2 cloves garlic, halved

1 small tomato, halved

salt and freshly ground black pepper

6 fresh basil leaves, torn

METHOD

1 Preheat grill (broiler) to high.

2 Cover grill rack with a single layer of capsicums, zucchini, fennel and onion, with capsicums skin side down. Brush with some oil and grill, on one side only, until lightly browned but still slightly firm. If necessary, cook vegetables in batches and keep the first batch warm in the oven.

3 Toast ciabatta or baguette slices on both sides.

4 Rub the top of each slice of toast with garlic and tomato, then pile vegetables on top. Trickle over remaining oil and season with salt and pepper. Scatter basil over the top and serve while still warm.

NUTRIENTS PER SERVING

1238 kJ, 296 kcal, 11 g protein, 16 g fat (2 g saturated fat), 26 g carbohydrate

COOK'S TIP

You could brush the vegetables with oil and cook on a hot chargrill pan or plate until lightly browned but slightly firm, turning once.

BRUSCHETTA WITH ROASTED ARTICHOKE

TIME **25 MINUTES** SERVES **4**

INGREDIENTS

1 ciabatta (about 250 g/8 oz), cut on
the diagonal into 12 slices

1 red capsicum (bell pepper), seeds
removed, thinly sliced

2 tablespoons oil from jar of artichokes

12 slices salami (about 75 g/2$^1/_2$ oz)

4 tablespoons tapenade, from a jar

1 jar chargrilled or roasted artichokes
in olive oil (about 300 g/10 oz),
drained and sliced

METHOD

1   Preheat grill (broiler) to medium–
high and line grill pan with foil.
Put ciabatta on grill rack and grill
about 1 minute on each side, or
until golden. Set aside.

2   Toss capsicum in oil. Put in a
single layer on one side of grill
pan and grill 3 minutes. Put
salami slices on the other side of
grill pan and grill 2–3 minutes, or
until capsicums are lightly singed
and salami slices start to crisp.

3   Spread tapenade thinly over
toasts. Place a few capsicum and
artichoke slices on each piece,
then top with crisp salami. Return
to grill 1 minute to heat through.
Serve at once.

NUTRIENTS PER SERVING
1833 kJ, 438 kcal, 10 g protein, 30 g fat
(6 g saturated fat), 32 g carbohydrate

VARIATION

**PEAR AND GORGONZOLA
BRUSCHETTA** Rub toasted bread
at end of step 1 with 2 cut cloves
garlic. Drizzle with 2 tablespoons
walnut oil. Fry 2 cored and sliced
ripe pears in 1 tablespoon unsalted butter until tender and beginning to
brown. Put on the toasts. Add 150 g (5 oz) diced gorgonzola cheese. Grill
2 minutes, or until bubbling.

COOK'S TIP

You could brush the ciabatta slices and capsicum slices with oil and cook
them and the salami slices on a hot chargrill pan or plate until cooked,
turning as necessary.

SALMON PÂTÉ

TIME **30 MINUTES** SERVES **4**

INGREDIENTS

1 small bunch (20 g/²/₃ oz) fresh chives,
   snipped
1 small bunch (20 g/²/₃ oz) fresh dill,
   leaves chopped
1 small bunch (20 g/²/₃ oz) fresh parsley,
   leaves chopped
425 g (15 oz) can salmon, drained,
   bones and skin discarded
150 g (5 oz) cream cheese
juice of 1 lemon
1 teaspoon Tabasco sauce
salt and freshly ground black pepper
brown bread, toast fingers, Melba toast
   or water biscuits, to serve

METHOD

1　Mix chives, dill and parsley in a
   bowl and put aside.
2　Put salmon and cream cheese in
   a separate bowl and combine
   thoroughly.
3　Add lemon juice a little at a time,
   until sharp enough to suit your
   taste. Stir in Tabasco sauce and
   reserved herbs. Blend to a smooth
   purée with a hand blender. If you
   prefer a slightly coarser texture,
   blend with a wooden spoon or
   potato masher.
4　Season with salt, pepper and more
   lemon juice. Spoon pâté into a
   serving bowl or into individual
   ramekin moulds and chill about
   15 minutes.
5　Serve pâté with bread, toast or
   water biscuits as desired.

NUTRIENTS PER SERVING
1515 kJ, 362 kcal, 22 g protein, 24 g fat
(12 g saturated fat), 16 g carbohydrate

AVOCADO AND WATERCRESS CREAM

TIME **20 MINUTES** SERVES **4**

INGREDIENTS

1 bunch (250 g/8 oz) watercress,
   stems discarded
3 tablespoons fresh parsley
3 tablespoons fresh basil
4 spring onions (scallions),
   green part only
1 clove garlic, crushed

grated zest and juice of 1 lemon
2 large avocados
salt and freshly ground black pepper
2–4 tablespoons olive oil
1 tablespoon green peppercorns in brine,
   rinsed and drained, to garnish
Melba toast, to serve

METHOD

1　Put watercress, parsley, basil, spring onions, garlic, lemon zest, lemon
   juice and avocado flesh in a blender or food processor. Season with salt
   and pepper, and add enough oil to make a smooth, thick purée. Process
   until smooth, adding more oil if necessary.
2　Spoon purée into a bowl, sprinkle with green peppercorns and serve
   immediately, accompanied by Melba toast.

NUTRIENTS PER SERVING
845 kJ, 202 kcal, 3 g protein, 20 g fat (4 g saturated fat), 2 g carbohydrate

WARM CHEESE AND TOMATO DIP

TIME **25 MINUTES** SERVES **4**

INGREDIENTS

2 teaspoons olive oil

1 large onion, chopped

corn chips, soft tortillas or pitas, to serve

100 ml (3½ fl oz) thick (heavy/double)
   cream

200 g (7 oz) cheddar cheese, grated

5 tomatoes, peeled, seeds removed,
   finely chopped

2 jalapeño chillies, halved, seeds removed,
   finely chopped

salt and freshly ground black pepper

Tabasco sauce

1 red chilli, to garnish

2 lime wedges, to garnish

METHOD

1 Preheat oven to 180°C (350°F/
   Gas 4).

2 Heat oil in a small saucepan and
   gently fry onion over low heat
   10–15 minutes, until softened.

3 Put corn chips, tortillas or pitas
   in the oven to heat.

4 Add cream to onion and increase
   heat. Just before cream reaches
   simmering point, add cheese and
   stir until it melts.

5 Add tomatoes and chillies and
   heat through, stirring gently.
   Season with salt, pepper and
   Tabasco sauce.

6 Pour dip into a heated serving
   bowl, garnish with red chilli and
   lime wedges and serve with corn
   chips, tortillas or pita breads.

NUTRIENTS PER SERVING

2814 kJ, 672 kcal, 17 g protein, 53 g fat
(22 g saturated fat), 31 g carbohydrate

Right Avocado and watercress cream (top left);
Warm cheese and tomato dip (middle); Salmon
pâté (bottom)

SEAFOOD CAKES

TIME **30 MINUTES** SERVES **4**

INGREDIENTS

2 slices day-old bread (about 125 g/4 oz)

100 ml (3½ fl oz) milk

200 g (7 oz) crabmeat, flaked

200 g (7 oz) peeled cooked prawns
  (shrimp), chopped

2 large eggs, separated

2 teaspoons dijon mustard

1 tablespoon worcestershire sauce

½ cup (55 g) almond meal
  (ground almonds)

1 large pinch cayenne pepper

1 tablespoon mayonnaise

1 tablespoon chopped fresh parsley

⅓ cup (50 g) plain (all-purpose) flour

1½ cups (50 g) dry packaged
  breadcrumbs

vegetable oil, for frying

METHOD

1 Soak bread in milk in a bowl 5 minutes.

2 Put crabmeat, prawns, egg yolks, mustard, worcestershire sauce, almond meal, cayenne pepper, mayonnaise and parsley in a large bowl.

3 Squeeze bread dry. Add to bowl and stir until mixture is soft but not sloppy — add some breadcrumbs if it is too moist.

4 Put flour on one plate and breadcrumbs on another plate. Whisk reserved eggwhites with 1 tablespoon water. Divide crab mixture into eight portions and shape into patties. Dip each patty into flour, shake off the excess, then dip into eggwhites. Finally, coat with breadcrumbs.

5 Heat 1 cm (½ inch) oil in a large frying pan over medium–high heat. Fry seafood cakes 2–3 minutes on each side, until crisp and golden, then drain on paper towel.

NUTRIENTS PER SERVING

2490 kJ, 595 kcal, 38 g protein, 26 g fat (4 g saturated fat), 56 g carbohydrate

COOK'S TIP

Serve seafood cakes with lemon wedges, tartare or seafood sauce, lettuce and tomatoes, or a spicy salsa. To make a heartier meal, use the seafood cakes and salad to fill hamburger buns.

HOT CORN CAKES WITH SALAD
TIME **30 MINUTES** SERVES **4**

METHOD

1 If using canned corn, drain and set aside, then mix milk, salt, pepper and Tabasco sauce in a bowl. If using frozen corn, put in a saucepan with milk, salt, pepper and Tabasco sauce and shake over a low heat 1 minute. Turn off heat and leave to thaw.

2 To make the sour cream dressing, mix spring onions, dill and sour cream together and season to taste.

3 Put lettuce leaves, avocado and capsicum in a salad bowl. Mix olive oil and vinegar together, season and toss gently through the salad.

4 Put flour in a bowl, make a well in the centre and break in eggs. Add reserved seasoned milk, or strain in milk from defrosted corn. Beat until mixture is smooth, then stir in corn.

5 Heat 1 tablespoon vegetable oil in a frying pan. Drop six scant tablespoons of batter into the pan. Fry gently 4–5 minutes until golden underneath and set at the edges. Turn and fry a further 1–2 minutes. Drain on paper towel and keep warm while cooking the remaining corn cakes.

6 Divide salad among four plates. Arrange corn cakes on plates and garnish with dill. Put dressing in a bowl and serve separately.

NUTRIENTS PER SERVING
2792 kJ, 667 kcal, 13 g protein, 52 g fat (13 g saturated fat), 40 g carbohydrate

INGREDIENTS

200 g (7 oz) canned or frozen corn

$^1\!/_3$ cup (80 ml) milk

salt and freshly ground black pepper

few drops Tabasco sauce

1 iceberg lettuce

2 avocados, sliced

1 yellow capsicum (bell pepper), seeds removed, sliced

3 tablespoons olive oil

3 teaspoons white wine vinegar

$^3\!/_4$ cup (110 g) self-raising flour

2 large eggs

2 tablespoons vegetable oil

1 sprig fresh dill, to garnish

SOUR CREAM DRESSING

3 spring onions (scallions), finely sliced

4 sprigs fresh dill, chopped

$^2\!/_3$ cup (150 g) sour cream

salt and freshly ground black pepper

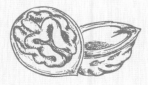

MUSHROOM AND WALNUT TURNOVERS

TIME **30 MINUTES** SERVES 6

INGREDIENTS

375 g (13 oz) ready-rolled puff
  pastry, thawed if frozen
1¼ cups (150 g) chopped walnuts
15 g (½ oz) butter
2 tablespoons thick (heavy/double)
  cream
150 g (5 oz) baby button mushrooms,
  chopped

150 g (5 oz) Swiss brown or porcini
  mushrooms, sliced
1 clove garlic, crushed
½ teaspoon mixed dried herbs
salt and freshly ground black pepper
1 egg yolk, lightly beaten with
  1 teaspoon water
1 tablespoon sesame seeds

METHOD

1 Preheat oven to 220°C (425°F/Gas 7). If time allows, leave pastry, still wrapped, at room temperature 20 minutes (this makes it easier to unroll without cracking, but isn't essential). Put walnuts on a large freezer-proof plate and put in the freezer to chill.

2 Melt butter in a non-stick frying pan. Add 1 tablespoon cream, button and Swiss mushrooms, garlic and dried herbs and cook over medium–high heat 6–7 minutes, or until mushrooms are tender and all juices have evaporated. Tip mushrooms onto the chilled plate with walnuts. Drizzle with remaining cream and season. Stir to mix with walnuts, then spread out in a single layer to cool quickly.

3 Carefully unroll pastry, then cut into six squares. Lightly brush edges with a little beaten egg yolk. Spoon mushroom and walnut filling onto one side of a diagonal centre line, then fold over to make a triangular turnover. Press edges together firmly to seal, then mark a pattern on the top with a fork. Brush all over with beaten egg yolk, sprinkle with sesame seeds and make a slit in the top to allow steam to escape.

4 Transfer turnovers to a non-stick baking tray (sheet) or a baking tray lined with baking (parchment) paper and bake 15 minutes, or until risen and lightly browned.

NUTRIENTS PER SERVING

1976 kJ, 472 kcal, 10 g protein, 38 g fat (12 g saturated fat), 24 g carbohydrate

Left Mushroom and walnut turnovers

CHEESY BEANY MUFFINS

TIME **25 MINUTES** SERVES 4

INGREDIENTS

4 wholemeal (whole-wheat) or white
  English muffins, halved crosswise
15 g (½ oz) margarine or butter, softened
400 g (14 oz) can baked beans
8 slices cheddar (about 250 g/8 oz)
12 red cherry tomatoes or baby roma
  (plum) tomatoes, halved
4 slices rindless bacon (bacon strips),
  thinly sliced
freshly ground black pepper

METHOD

1 Preheat grill (broiler) and line grill pan with foil. Put muffin halves on grill rack, cut side down, and toast base about 1 minute. Turn and thinly spread cut sides with margarine or butter (this helps to prevent the beans from soaking into the muffins). Grill, cut side up, about 1½ minutes, or until lightly browned.

2 Tip beans into a sieve over the sink and drain off some of the tomato sauce. Gently heat beans in a small saucepan until steaming hot. Divide beans among toasted muffins, then top each with a slice of cheese (make sure surfaces of muffins are completely covered with beans or cheese because any exposed parts will burn).

3 Put three halved cherry tomatoes, cut side up, on top of each, then scatter with bacon strips. Season with a little pepper. Return to grill and cook 3–5 minutes, or until bacon is cooked and cheese is melted and bubbling.

NUTRIENTS PER SERVING

2204 kJ, 526 kcal, 35 g protein, 28 g fat (16 g saturated fat), 34 g carbohydrate

LEEK AND CHEDDAR CHEESE TART

TIME **30 MINUTES** SERVES **4**

INGREDIENTS

7–8 slim leeks (about 1 kg/2 lb)

salt

250 g (8 oz) puff pastry, thawed if frozen

1 tablespoon dijon mustard

1 egg, lightly beaten

1/2 cup (60 g) grated cheddar

METHOD

1 Preheat oven to 230°C (450°/Gas 8). Put a kettle of water on to boil.

2 Trim leeks to a length of about 18 cm (7 inches) and rinse well. Arrange in a single layer in a wide saucepan or frying pan, pour over the boiling water, add a pinch of salt, return to a boil, reduce heat and simmer, covered, 6–8 minutes.

3 Meanwhile, roll out puff pastry on a lightly floured surface to a 25 cm (10 inch) square, then carefully transfer to a baking tray (sheet).

4 Cut a 1 cm (1/2 inch) strip of pastry from each side of the pastry square. Dampen edge of square with water and trim pastry strips to fit flat on top of it. Press lightly into place.

5 Drain leeks and cool under cold running water. Drain again, wrap in a tea towel (dish towel) and press gently to remove any remaining moisture.

6 Arrange leeks inside pastry case and brush with mustard. Brush beaten egg over pastry border. Sprinkle cheddar evenly over leeks.

7 Position tart on the top shelf of the oven and bake 15 minutes, or until pastry is risen and golden and cheese melted and bubbling.

8 Remove tart from oven, cut into quarters and serve hot or warm.

NUTRIENTS PER SERVING

1683 kJ, 402 kcal, 11 g protein, 26 g fat (3 g saturated fat), 31 g carbohydrate

COOK'S TIP

When you shop for this recipe, buy the well-trimmed leeks that are now available in many supermarkets. This will cut down on preparation time.

EGGPLANT PÂTÉ

TIME **30 MINUTES** SERVES **4**

INGREDIENTS

2 tablespoons olive oil

1 onion, finely chopped

1 large firm eggplant (aubergine), diced

10 sun-dried tomatoes in oil,
   drained and chopped

6 small gherkins (pickles), drained
   and chopped

3 cloves garlic, crushed

1 teaspoon chopped fresh thyme

2 tablespoons chopped fresh parsley

1 teaspoon wholegrain mustard

1 teaspoon balsamic vinegar

2 teaspoons capers, rinsed and
   squeezed dry

12 slices baguette, cut on the diagonal

salt and freshly ground black pepper

METHOD

1 Heat oil in a frying pan and fry onion 5 minutes, or until soft.

2 Add eggplant and cook gently over medium heat, stirring occasionally, 8–10 minutes, or until soft.

3 Add sun-dried tomatoes, gherkins, garlic, thyme, all but 1 teaspoon parsley, mustard, vinegar and capers. Simmer 5 minutes, stirring frequently.

4 Meanwhile, lightly toast baguette slices under a hot grill (broiler) or on a hot chargrill pan, turning once.

5 Season eggplant mixture with salt and pepper. Process in a food processor or blender or mash to a paste by hand.

6 Spoon pâté onto individual plates, sprinkle with reserved parsley and serve with the toasted slices of baguette.

NUTRIENTS PER SERVING

1577 kJ, 377 kcal, 10 g protein, 14 g fat
(1 g saturated fat), 55 g carbohydrate

PROSCIUTTO WITH PEAR AND PARMESAN
TIME **12 MINUTES** SERVES **4**

INGREDIENTS
juice of 1 lime or lemon

4 small pears, quartered and cored, each quarter cut lengthwise into 3–4 slices

freshly ground black pepper

100 g (3¹/₂ oz) mixed salad leaves

12 thin slices prosciutto or parma ham (about 200 g/7oz)

salt

100 g (3¹/₂ oz) parmesan, shaved

2–3 tablespoons extra virgin olive oil

METHOD
1 Put lime or lemon juice in a large bowl. Add pear slices, season lightly with pepper and toss with the juice gently.
2 Pile salad leaves loosely on four plates. Arrange marinated pear slices on top, then weave slices of prosciutto or parma ham around the pears. Season with salt.
3 Scatter over a few parmesan shavings, drizzle with oil and serve at once.

NUTRIENTS PER SERVING
1695 kJ, 409 kcal, 20 g protein, 31 g fat (11 g saturated fat), 11 g carbohydrate

COOK'S TIP
When you are shaving thin slices of parmesan, you will need to buy a larger piece of cheese than you actually use to give you a good grip. Use a potato peeler to shave the wafer-thin slices of parmesan.

GOAT'S CHEESE SOUFFLÉS
TIME **30 MINUTES** SERVES **4**

INGREDIENTS
¹/₃ cup (35 g) hazelnut, almond or walnut meal (ground hazelnuts, almonds or walnuts)

30 g (1 oz) butter, softened

1¹/₂ tablespoons plain (all-purpose) flour

4 tablespoons milk

salt and freshly ground black pepper

100 g (3¹/₂ oz) firm goat's cheese, finely diced

1 large egg yolk

3 large eggwhites

METHOD
1 Preheat oven to 190°C (375°F/Gas 5). Put a kettle of water on to boil. Spread out nut meal in a dry frying pan and toast gently over low heat, stirring, until golden brown.
2 Use half the butter to grease the insides of four 200 ml (7 fl oz) ramekin moulds. Divide nut meal equally among the moulds and shake to evenly coat the sides and bottoms with the meal.
3 Melt remaining butter in a saucepan, stir in flour and cook, stirring, about 30 seconds. Remove from heat and gradually stir in milk. Bring sauce to a boil, stirring, until it thickens. Add salt and pepper to taste.
4 Add just over half the goat's cheese to the sauce and stir well. When just melted, remove from heat and stir in egg yolk.
5 Whisk eggwhites until stiff. Using a large metal spoon, fold a third of eggwhites into cheese sauce to lighten it, then carefully fold in remaining eggwhites.
6 Divide remaining goat's cheese among the four ramekin moulds and spoon soufflé mixture on top. Stand moulds in a large roasting pan (baking dish) and pour in boiling water to come halfway up their sides. Bake in the top half of the oven 10 minutes, or until soufflés have risen and are lightly set and golden brown. Serve hot, straight from the oven.

NUTRIENTS PER SERVING
1193 kJ, 285 kcal, 13 g protein, 24 g fat (10 g saturated fat), 5 g carbohydrate

Right Prosciutto with pear and parmesan (top); Goat's cheese soufflés (bottom)

SPINACH AND PARMESAN SOUFFLÉS

TIME 30 MINUTES SERVES 4

INGREDIENTS

softened butter, for greasing
500 g (1 lb) baby spinach leaves
1 slice white bread (about 40 g/
   1½ oz), crusts removed
⅔ cup (150 g) crème fraîche or
   sour cream

5 eggs, separated
½ cup (50 g) grated parmesan or
   Italian-style hard cheese
salt and freshly ground black pepper
freshly grated nutmeg, to taste

METHOD

1 Preheat oven to 220°C (425°F/Gas 7). Lightly grease inside four 1 cup (250 ml) ovenproof dishes or ramekin moulds with butter. Tip spinach into a dry frying pan with only the moisture left on the leaves and stir over low heat about 2 minutes, or until wilted. Drain.

2 Tear bread into small pieces and process in a food processor or blender to make fine crumbs. Squeeze as much water as possible out of spinach, then add to crumbs with half the crème fraîche or sour cream. Process to a coarse purée. Add remaining crème fraîche or sour cream and process a few more seconds until just combined.

3 Add egg yolks and 3 tablespoons parmesan or Italian-style hard cheese to food processor. Season and add plenty of nutmeg, then process again to make a smooth purée.

4 Whisk eggwhites in a large bowl until stiff. Tip spinach mixture on eggwhites and carefully fold together with a large metal spoon. Sprinkle half the remaining parmesan or Italian-style hard cheese inside prepared ovenproof dishes or moulds and set on a baking tray (sheet). Spoon soufflé mixture into dishes. Sprinkle with remaining cheese and bake 15 minutes, or until puffed and golden brown. Serve at once.

NUTRIENTS PER SERVING

1472 kJ, 352 kcal, 17 g protein, 29 g fat (18 g saturated fat), 8 g carbohydrate

VARIATION

BOLOGNESE SOUFFLÉS Spoon 1–2 tablespoons warmed leftover bolognese sauce into the base of each dish. Top with the soufflé mix used in the basic recipe at step 4, and bake.

Left Spinach and parmesan soufflés

EGG AND LENTIL CURRY

TIME 25 MINUTES SERVES 4

INGREDIENTS

6 eggs
2 tablespoons olive oil
1 onion, finely chopped
4 cloves garlic, crushed
5 cm (2 inch) piece fresh ginger,
   grated
2 large tomatoes, roughly chopped
1 tablespoon garam masala
¼ teaspoon dried red chilli flakes,
   or to taste
2 x 400 g (14 oz) cans French-style green
   (puy) lentils, drained
4 tablespoons vegetable stock or water
salt and freshly ground black pepper

METHOD

1 Cook eggs in a saucepan of boiling water 10 minutes. Drain, put in a bowl of cold water to cool, and set aside.

2 Meanwhile, heat oil in a heavy-based saucepan and add onion. Cover and cook over a low heat 4 minutes, or until softened but not browned. Stir in garlic and ginger and cook 1 minute, then stir in tomatoes, garam masala and chilli flakes. Cover and cook gently 5 minutes.

3 Stir in lentils and stock or water and cook gently 5 minutes.

4 Meanwhile, peel and halve eggs. Season lentils with salt and pepper. Spoon into a serving bowl and arrange eggs on top.

NUTRIENTS PER SERVING

1203 kJ, 287 kcal, 17 g protein, 18 g fat (4 g saturated fat), 16 g carbohydrate

VARIATION

Instead of tomatoes, use 250 g (8 oz) sliced mushrooms or 250 g (8 oz) baby spinach leaves.

HONEY-BAKED HAM AND APPLE CROISSANTS

TIME **20 MINUTES** SERVES **4**

INGREDIENTS

4 large croissants

1 tablespoon mayonnaise

4 tablespoons crème fraîche or sour cream

1 large carrot, grated

1 sweet apple, quartered, cored and chopped

2 spring onions (scallions), finely chopped

30 g (1 oz) radishes, sliced

$^1\!/_2$ cup (50 g) pecans

salt and freshly ground black pepper

4 large slices honey-baked ham, trimmed of fat and cut in half

METHOD

1 Using a serrated knife, cut croissants open crosswise, keeping the halves still attached along one side like a hinge.

2 Mix mayonnaise and crème fraîche or sour cream together in a bowl. Add carrot, apple, spring onions, radishes and pecans. Season with salt and pepper and mix well.

3 Spoon mixture onto bottom half of each croissant, then top with ham. Close croissants and serve.

NUTRIENTS PER SERVING

2458 kJ, 587 kcal, 13 g protein, 42 g fat (17 g saturated fat), 42 g carbohydrate

COOK'S TIP

You can make the filling mixture up to 4 hours in advance and keep it covered in the fridge until you are ready to fill the croissants.

ONION TARTLETS WITH SALAD

TIME **30 MINUTES** SERVES **4**

INGREDIENTS

250 g (8 oz) puff pastry, thawed if frozen

1 egg, lightly beaten

2 small red onions, thinly sliced

4 large French shallots (eschalots), quartered

12 sprigs fresh thyme

4 tablespoons olive oil

salt and freshly ground black pepper

SALAD

100 g (3$^1\!/_2$ oz) baby spinach leaves

100 g (3$^1\!/_2$ oz) watercress, trimmed

$^1\!/_4$ cup (30 g) walnut pieces

40 g (1$^1\!/_2$ oz) stilton cheese, rind discarded

2 tablespoons thick (heavy/double) cream

3 teaspoons walnut oil

1 teaspoon sherry vinegar

METHOD

1 Preheat oven to 220°C (425°F/Gas 7).

2 Lightly flour a work surface, then cut pastry in half and roll out each piece to a rectangle about 30 x 15 cm (12 x 6 inches). Cut two large rounds from each rectangle, using a saucer as a guide, and place the pastry rounds on a large baking tray (sheet).

3 Brush beaten egg over pastry, but don't let it trickle over the edges.

4 Pile a quarter of onions and French shallots in the centre of each round, leaving a border of about 2 cm ($^3\!/_4$ inch) all around. Place 3 sprigs thyme on top of each pile.

5 Brush onion and shallot mixture lightly with oil and season to taste with salt and pepper. Put pastries in the oven and bake 20 minutes, or until they are puffed up and golden brown.

6 Meanwhile, prepare the salad. Put baby spinach, watercress and walnuts in a serving bowl.

7 Put stilton cheese and cream in a small bowl and mash together thoroughly. Beat in walnut oil and sherry vinegar until smooth. Season to taste with a good grinding of black pepper (the stilton should be salty enough, so no further salt will be necessary). Pour dressing over the salad and toss gently.

8 When pastries are cooked, serve on individual plates, with the bowl of salad on the side.

NUTRIENTS PER SERVING:

2390 kJ, 571 kcal, 11 g protein, 47 g fat (10 g saturated fat), 28 g carbohydrate

VARIATION

If you prefer a milder, sweeter blue cheese flavour, you could replace the stilton with either a blue brie, some dolcelatte or a blue castello or other creamy blue cheese.

Right Onion tartlets with salad

PITA PIZZAS

TIME **30 MINUTES** SERVES **2**

INGREDIENTS

vegetable oil, for greasing

2 wholemeal (whole-wheat) pitas

2 tablespoons tomato sauce (ketchup)

$\frac{1}{2}$ teaspoon Tabasco sauce

50 g (1$\frac{3}{4}$ oz) mozzarella, grated

50 g (1$\frac{3}{4}$ oz) mature cheddar, grated

50 g (1$\frac{3}{4}$ oz) taleggio, fontina, chaumes, gruyère or emmenthal cheese, diced or thinly sliced

1 red onion, cut into thin wedges

2 tomatoes, sliced

$\frac{1}{2}$ large red or green capsicum (bell pepper), seeds removed, finely chopped

1 clove garlic, crushed

1 tablespoon olive oil

4 black olives

1 tablespoon torn fresh basil

1 tablespoon fresh marjoram

$\frac{1}{4}$ cup (25 g) grated parmesan

METHOD

1 Preheat oven to 190°C (375°F/Gas 5). Lightly grease a baking tray (sheet) with vegetable oil.

2 Split pitas in half so there are four bases. Mix tomato sauce and Tabasco sauce in a bowl. Spread over each pita half and arrange on the baking tray.

3 Mix mozzarella and cheddar together and sprinkle over pitas.

4 Lay or scatter taleggio, fontina, chaumes, gruyère or emmenthal cheese over the grated cheese.

5 Arrange onion and tomatoes over the cheese, then scatter with capsicum.

6 Mix garlic and olive oil together and drizzle over the pizzas. Place an olive in the centre of each and bake on top shelf of oven 10 minutes.

7 Mix basil, marjoram and parmesan together in a bowl.

8 Remove pizzas from oven, sprinkle with herb and parmesan mixture, and serve hot.

NUTRIENTS PER SERVING:

2671 kJ, 638 kcal, 27 g protein, 37 g fat (13 g saturated fat), 53 g carbohydrate

VARIATION

Instead of wholemeal pitas, you can use white pitas, which have a crunchier texture when baked.

HASTY PIZZA
TIME **30 MINUTES** SERVES **4**

METHOD

1 Heat 1 tablespoon oil in a frying pan over medium heat. Fry onion gently about 3–4 minutes, until soft.

2 Put onions, tomatoes, garlic, dried basil, mixed dried herbs, salt and pepper to taste, and sugar in a bowl. Mix together and set aside.

3 Preheat grill (broiler) to high. Heat remaining oil in the frying pan, then add capsicums and stir-fry 5 minutes.

4 Meanwhile, slice round top off bread and cut remaining loaf across into four 1 cm (¹/₂ inch) thick slices. Grill on one side.

5 Turn bread over. Spread tomato mixture evenly over untoasted side of each slice. Arrange capsicums and artichokes on top, sprinkle with cheddar or mozzarella and dot with olives.

6 Grill 4–5 minutes, or until the cheese is melted and golden. Garnish with basil and serve immediately.

NUTRIENTS PER SERVING:
4315 kJ, 1031 kcal, 34 g protein, 56 g fat (15 g saturated fat), 104 g carbohydrate

VARIATION
Sliced mushrooms or avocados could be used instead of artichoke hearts. Meat eaters could add ham, salami, prawns (shrimp) or anchovy fillets.

INGREDIENTS

2 tablespoons olive oil

1 onion, chopped

410 g (15 oz) can chopped tomatoes, drained

1 clove garlic, crushed

1 teaspoon dried basil

1 teaspoon mixed dried herbs

salt and freshly ground black pepper

¹/₂ teaspoon sugar

1 green and 1 red capsicum (bell pepper), seeds removed, finely sliced into rings

1 small wholemeal (whole-wheat) or round cob loaf

400 g (14 oz) can artichoke hearts, drained and halved

200 g (7 oz) cheddar, grated, or mozzarella, diced, or a mixture of both

16 black olives

2 tablespoons fresh basil, to garnish

GREEK-STYLE PIZZA
TIME **20 MINUTES** SERVES **4**

INGREDIENTS

2 tablespoons oil from jar of
   sun-dried tomatoes
1 teaspoon balsamic vinegar
1 small red onion, thinly sliced
1 large thin crisp ready-made pizza
   base (about 250 g/8 oz), or
   2 x 150 g (5 oz) ready-made
   pizza bases

3 tablespoons sun-dried tomato paste
   (concentrated purée)
8 red cherry tomatoes, halved
1/3 cup (50 g) sun-dried tomatoes
   in oil, thinly sliced
12 pitted black or green olives
1 cup (150 g) crumbled fetta
freshly ground black pepper

METHOD

1 Preheat oven to 220°C (425°F/Gas 7). Whisk 1 tablespoon oil and the
vinegar in a bowl, add onion rings and toss to coat. Leave to marinate
for a few minutes to mellow the flavour.

2 Spread pizza base with tomato paste. Arrange reserved onion and
cherry tomatoes on top, then scatter with sun-dried tomatoes, olives
and fetta. Drizzle remaining oil over the pizza.

3 Put pizza directly on top shelf of oven, putting a baking tray (sheet) on
the shelf below to catch any drips. Bake 10 minutes, or until the base is
crisp and the topping is lightly browned. Season with pepper, cut into
wedges and serve.

NUTRIENTS PER SERVING

1818 kJ, 434 kcal, 15 g protein, 22 g fat (8 g saturated fat), 44 g carbohydrate

COOK'S TIP

To make your own pizza base, put 1³/4 cups (220 g) self-raising flour,
1/2 teaspoon baking powder and 1/4 teaspoon salt in a bowl. Stir, then
make a well in the centre and pour in 2/3 cup (150 ml) low-fat milk
and 1 tablespoon olive oil. Mix to a soft dough and roll out. Top
as for basic recipe and bake 12–15 minutes.

Left Greek-style pizza

BRAZILIAN CAPSICUMS
TIME **30 MINUTES** SERVES **4**

INGREDIENTS

4 red or yellow capsicums (bell peppers),
   halved lengthwise, seeds removed
salt and freshly ground black pepper
2 teaspoons olive oil
1 clove garlic, crushed
1 red chilli, halved lengthwise, seeds
   removed, finely chopped
1/2 teaspoon dried oregano
2 tablespoons sun-dried tomato paste
   (concentrated purée)
200 g (7 oz) medium-grain white rice
400 ml (14 fl oz) hot vegetable stock
400 g (14 oz) can pinto beans, rinsed
   and drained
50 g (1³/4 oz) mature cheddar, grated
1/3 cup (50 g) Brazil nuts, roughly chopped

METHOD

1 Preheat oven to 220°C (425°F/
Gas 7). Season inside capsicums
and place, cut side down, on a
lightly greased baking tray (sheet).
Cook in oven 12 minutes.

2 Meanwhile, heat oil in a large
saucepan and gently fry garlic and
chilli 30 seconds. Stir in oregano,
tomato paste, rice and stock and
bring to a boil. Reduce heat, cover
pan and cook 10 minutes, or until
rice is barely tender and most of
the stock has been absorbed (no
more than 2 tablespoons liquid
should be left). Stir in pinto beans
and season with salt and pepper.

3 Remove capsicums from oven and
spoon in rice filling to completely
fill. Combine cheese and Brazil
nuts, then scatter over the top.

4 Bake capsicums, uncovered,
10 minutes, or until tender and
the top is golden brown and crisp.

NUTRIENTS PER SERVING

1932 kJ, 461 kcal, 16 g protein, 16 g fat
(5 g saturated fat), 63 g carbohydrate

MOROCCAN WRAPS
TIME **25 MINUTES** SERVES **4**

INGREDIENTS

½ small cucumber, finely diced

3 ripe tomatoes, finely diced

2 spring onions (scallions), sliced

¼ teaspoon salt

2 tablespoons roughly chopped fresh mint

400 g (14 oz) can chickpeas, rinsed
    and drained

½ teaspoon ground cumin

1 clove garlic, crushed

2 tablespoons extra virgin olive oil

1 tablespoon lemon juice

1 tablespoon tahini

freshly ground black pepper

4 large soft flour tortillas

METHOD

1 Put cucumber, tomatoes and spring onions in a sieve, sprinkle with salt
   and leave to drain 5 minutes. Transfer to a bowl and mix in mint.

2 Tip chickpeas into a bowl. Mash roughly with a fork, then add cumin,
   garlic, oil, lemon juice and tahini. Mash again until fairly smooth. Season
   with pepper.

3 Spread tortillas with the chickpea mixture, leaving a 2.5 cm (1 inch) border.
   Spoon cucumber and tomato mixture down the centre of each tortilla, then
   roll up tightly to enclose.

NUTRIENTS PER SERVING

1056 kJ, 252 kcal, 8 g protein, 15 g fat (2 g saturated fat), 22 g carbohydrate

COOK'S TIP

Tortillas are more pliable for folding if warmed. The simplest way is to heat
one at a time on a plate in the microwave on High 15 seconds, or microwave
a stack of 4 tortillas together 1 minute. Alternatively, preheat the oven to 180°C
(350°F/Gas 4). Wrap tortilla stack in foil and warm 10 minutes, or according
to the packet instructions.

CALIFORNIAN WRAPS
TIME 10 MINUTES SERVES 4

INGREDIENTS
150 g (5 oz) natural (plain) yogurt
1 tablespoon chopped fresh dill
freshly ground black pepper
4 large soft flour tortillas
200 g (7 oz) firm goat's cheese,
    thinly sliced
1/4 cos (romaine) lettuce, finely shredded
50 g (1 3/4 oz) rocket (arugula) leaves
1 tablespoon sunflower seeds or toasted
    mixed seeds

METHOD
1 Put yogurt, dill and some pepper
  in a small bowl and mix well.
2 Spread about 2 tablespoons yogurt
  and dill mixture over each tortilla.
  Arrange goat's cheese down the
  centre of each tortilla. Top with
  lettuce and rocket, then scatter
  with sunflower seeds or toasted
  mixed seeds.
3 Fold in the sides of each wrap to
  meet the filling, then roll up. Cut
  in half diagonally to serve.

NUTRIENTS PER SERVING
1072 kJ, 256 kcal, 13 g protein, 13 g fat
(7 g saturated fat), 21 g carbohydrate

GRILLED TOFU AND CAPSICUM WRAPS
TIME 25 MINUTES SERVES 4

INGREDIENTS
350 g (12 oz) firm tofu pieces
3 tablespoons sun-dried tomato pesto
1 yellow and 1 green capsicum (bell
    pepper), seeds removed, diced
4 large soft flour tortillas
250 g (8 oz) tzatziki

METHOD
1 Preheat grill (broiler) to medium–high. Put tofu and sun-dried tomato
  pesto in a bowl and toss to coat.
2 Thread tofu and capsicums onto skewers. Cook under medium–hot grill
  8–10 minutes, turning several times, until capsicums are slightly charred
  and tender. Remove pieces from skewers.
3 Warm tortillas, then spread tzatziki over them, leaving a 2.5 cm
  (1 inch) border. Divide tofu and capsicum filling among the tortillas,
  spooning it onto one half of each. Fold other half over filling, then
  carefully fold again into a fan shape.

NUTRIENTS PER SERVING
1340 kJ, 320 kcal, 19 g protein, 17 g fat (4 g saturated fat), 22 g carbohydrate

COOK'S TIP
The skewers make it easier to turn the pieces of tofu and capsicum when
cooking under the grill, but they are not essential. You could brush the
tofu and capsicums with a little oil and cook on a hot chargrill pan or
plate until capsicums are done, turning several times.

TUNA AND CHEESE MELT FLAT BREADS
TIME 15 MINUTES SERVES 4

INGREDIENTS
2 x 180 g (6 oz) cans tuna, drained
3 tablespoons mayonnaise
1 tablespoon lemon juice
2 teaspoons tomato paste
    (concentrated purée)
1 small red onion, finely sliced
1 tablespoon French dressing
2 large flat breads or focaccias
6 large slices emmenthal or gruyère

METHOD
1 Put tuna, mayonnaise, lemon juice and tomato paste in a bowl and
  mash together.
2 Put onion and French dressing in a small bowl and marinate for a few
  minutes to mellow the flavour.
3 Warm flat breads or focaccias under a medium–hot grill (broiler)
  1 minute. Spread tuna mixture over the tops. Scatter with marinated
  onion, then divide emmenthal or gruyère slices between them. Cook
  under a medium–hot grill 3 minutes, or until cheese is lightly browned
  and bubbling. Cut each flat bread or focaccia into four wedges and
  serve two per person.

NUTRIENTS PER SERVING
1880 kJ, 449 kcal, 37 g protein, 19 g fat (7 g saturated fat), 32 g carbohydrate

PROVENÇALE PIPERADE

TIME **30 MINUTES** SERVES **4**

INGREDIENTS

2 tablespoons olive oil

2 red and 2 yellow capsicums (bell
    peppers), seeds removed, sliced

1 onion, thinly sliced

2 cloves garlic, crushed

$1/2$ teaspoon dried red chilli flakes,
    or to taste

$1/3$ cup (50 g) semi-dried (sun-blushed)
    tomatoes, roughly chopped

salt and freshly ground black pepper

8 eggs

1 small bunch (20 g/$2/3$ oz) fresh basil,
    leaves roughly torn

METHOD

1 Heat oil in a large non-stick frying
  pan. Add capsicums, onion, garlic
  and chilli flakes and cook over
  medium heat 10 minutes, stirring
  frequently, until softened but not
  browned.

2 Add semi-dried tomatoes. Season
  with salt and pepper, then cook
  over medium heat 7–8 minutes,
  stirring frequently, until mixture is
  very soft and thick, and most of
  the liquid has evaporated.

3 Break eggs into a bowl and add
  basil. Beat lightly with a fork.
  Pour eggs into pan and stir over
  low heat about 2 minutes, or until
  mixture thickens and looks like
  soft scrambled eggs. Serve hot.

NUTRIENTS PER SERVING

1195 kJ, 285 kcal, 16 g protein, 20 g fat
(4 g saturated fat), 10 g carbohydrate

CHILLI BEEF TORTILLAS

TIME **30 MINUTES** SERVES **4**

INGREDIENTS

12 thin minute steaks (about 350 g/
    12 oz in total)

1 teaspoon paprika

1 teaspoon ground cumin

salt and freshly ground black pepper

3 tablespoons vegetable oil

1 red onion, thinly sliced

1 yellow capsicum (bell pepper),
    seeds removed, sliced

2 chillies, preferably 1 red and
    1 green, seeds removed,
    thinly sliced

4 x 20 cm (8 inch) soft flour tortillas

1 ripe avocado, thinly sliced

METHOD

1 Lightly dust steaks with paprika and cumin and season lightly. Heat
  1 tablespoon oil in a large non-stick frying pan with a lid. Add beef (in
  batches, adding a little more oil each time) and cook over medium–high
  heat, turning once, until browned and cooked to your liking (about
  30 seconds each side for rare, 45 seconds for medium, and 1 minute
  for well done). Remove from pan and put on a board to 'rest'.

2 Add remaining oil to the pan. Add onion and cook, stirring, 2 minutes,
  or until beginning to soften. Add capsicum and chillies and cook
  3 minutes, or until vegetables are tender. Lightly season.

3 Meanwhile, cut beef into 1 cm ($1/2$ inch) strips and scatter over the
  vegetables in the pan (the steam will reheat the beef). Remove from
  heat and cover with lid to keep filling warm.

4 In another pan, heat tortillas one at a time about 30 seconds on each
  side, or heat them all together in a microwave. Spoon beef mixture
  down centre of each tortilla and add avocado slices. Roll up and serve.

NUTRIENTS PER SERVING

2005 kJ, 479 kcal, 23 g protein, 34 g fat (6 g saturated fat), 20 g carbohydrate

COUNTRY FRITTATA

TIME 30 MINUTES SERVES 4

INGREDIENTS

2 tablespoons olive oil

3 leeks, white part only, sliced

$^1/_2$ butternut pumpkin (squash) (about 500 g/1 lb), peeled and diced

2 tablespoons pine nuts

8 eggs

$^1/_2$ cup (125 ml) cream

3 tablespoons grated parmesan

2 fresh sage leaves, chopped, or 1 small bunch (20 g/$^2/_3$ oz) fresh chives, snipped

salt and freshly ground black pepper

METHOD

1 Heat oil in a large heavy-based non-stick frying pan (25–30 cm/ 10–12 inches in diameter) that can be used under the grill (broiler). Add leeks and pumpkin and cook, stirring frequently, over medium heat 10 minutes, or until just soft. Stir in pine nuts.

2 Meanwhile, break eggs into a large bowl. Add cream, parmesan and sage or chives. Season and mix well with a fork.

3 When vegetables are cooked, stir them into eggs, then tip mixture back into the pan. Reduce heat and cook gently 4–5 minutes, or until almost set. Meanwhile, preheat grill to high.

4 Slide pan under the grill and cook the frittata 2–3 minutes, or until puffed and golden brown. Serve hot or warm, cut into wedges.

NUTRIENTS PER SERVING

1890 kJ, 451 kcal, 19 g protein, 35 g fat (11 g saturated fat), 19 g carbohydrate

VARIATION

Try different combinations of vegetables instead of the butternut pumpkin and leek filling. Here is one idea: use $^1/_3$ cup (50 g) thickly sliced semi-dried (sun-blushed) tomatoes and 3 thinly sliced capsicums (bell peppers). Cook vegetables 5 minutes in step 1, and add 2 crushed cloves garlic to the egg, cream and parmesan mixture.

CORN KEDGEREE

TIME **25 MINUTES** SERVES **4**

INGREDIENTS

1 cup (200 g) basmati rice
$^{1}/_{2}$ teaspoon turmeric
600 ml (21 fl oz) boiling water
1 cup (150 g) frozen corn
1 cup (150 g) frozen peas
400 g (14 oz) skinless smoked fish fillets, such as haddock or cod, preferably undyed, cut into chunks
40 g (1$^{1}/_{2}$ oz) butter, cut into small pieces
4 hard-boiled (hard-cooked) eggs, peeled and coarsely chopped
1 green chilli, seeds removed, sliced
1 cup (30 g) fresh coriander (cilantro) leaves, coarsely chopped
grated zest of 1 lemon
1 lemon, cut into wedges, to garnish

METHOD

1 Put rice in a large saucepan and stir in turmeric and boiling water. Bring to a boil, stir once, reduce heat to low and cover. Simmer 5 minutes.
2 Sprinkle corn and peas over rice. Add fish, spreading out chunks evenly. Bring back to a boil but do not stir. When water is again bubbling steadily, reduce heat, cover pan tightly and leave to cook 10 minutes. The chunks of fish should be opaque, firm and succulent, and the liquid should have been absorbed.
3 Dot butter over fish, then use a fork to mix everything together lightly. Divide among four warm bowls. Sprinkle with chopped egg, chilli, coriander and lemon zest. Garnish with lemon wedges.

NUTRIENTS PER SERVING

2045 kJ, 488 kcal, 36 g protein, 16 g fat (7 g saturated fat), 49 g carbohydrate

NUTTY SPINACH AND MUSHROOM FRITTATA

TIME **25 MINUTES** SERVES **4**

INGREDIENTS

2 tablespoons olive oil
1 small onion, finely chopped
350 g (12 oz) small button mushrooms, quartered
250 g (8 oz) baby spinach leaves
$^{2}/_{3}$ cup (100 g) roasted cashew nuts
5 eggs
2 tablespoons chopped fresh parsley
salt and freshly ground black pepper
100 g (3$^{1}/_{2}$ oz) grated cheddar or parmesan

METHOD

1 Heat oil in a large frying pan. Fry onion over medium heat, stirring occasionally, 3–4 minutes, until softened but not browned.
2 Add mushrooms and fry, stirring frequently, a further 3–4 minutes.
3 Add spinach and cook over medium–high heat, stirring frequently, 3–4 minutes, until leaves have wilted and excess liquid has evaporated. Stir in cashew nuts and reduce heat to low.
4 Break eggs into a bowl. Add 2 tablespoons cold water and the parsley and season with salt and pepper, then beat together.
5 Pour egg mixture over spinach mixture and cook 5 minutes, until egg is set and golden. Preheat grill (broiler) to high.
6 Sprinkle cheese over the top. Place under the grill and grill 2–3 minutes, until frittata is set and the top is golden. Alternatively, place frittata on a baking tray (sheet) and cook under the grill. Serve hot or cold.

NUTRIENTS PER SERVING

1737 kJ, 415 kcal, 22 g protein, 34 g fat (10 g saturated fat), 6 g carbohydrate

Right Nutty spinach and mushroom frittata

BAKED EGGS WITH CRAB

TIME **30 MINUTES** SERVES **2**

INGREDIENTS
butter, for greasing
175 g (6 oz) can crabmeat, drained
2 teaspoons brandy
4 large eggs
salt and freshly ground black pepper
4 tablespoons cream
cayenne pepper
4 slices bread
1–2 tablespoons butter
2 sprigs fresh chervil, to garnish

METHOD
1 Preheat oven to 190°C (375°F/
   Gas 5). Lightly grease two small
   gratin or other ovenproof dishes.
   Divide crab between dishes and
   sprinkle with brandy.
2 Break two eggs carefully into each
   dish. Season with salt and pepper,
   then spoon cream over the top.
   Dust lightly with cayenne pepper.
3 Put gratin dishes on a baking tray
   (sheet) and bake 20–25 minutes,
   until the whites of the eggs are set
   but the yolks are still soft.
4 Meanwhile, toast bread, spread
   with butter and cut diagonally.
5 Garnish eggs with chervil and
   serve with the toast.

NUTRIENTS PER SERVING
1126 kJ, 269 kcal, 19 g protein, 13 g fat
(5 g saturated fat), 25 g carbohydrate

Left Indian scrambled eggs (top right);
Baked eggs with crab (middle); Speedy
eggs florentine (bottom)

SPEEDY EGGS FLORENTINE

TIME **15 MINUTES** SERVES **2**

INGREDIENTS

1/2 cup (125 g) mayonnaise

1/2 cup (125 ml) thick (heavy/double) cream

1 teaspoon horseradish cream, from a jar

2 tablespoons each chopped fresh basil, parsley and thyme

1 tablespoon snipped chives

1/2 bunch English spinach (about 175 g/ 6 oz), stems discarded

2 English muffins, halved crosswise

4 large eggs

2 teaspoons vinegar

freshly ground black pepper

METHOD

1 Put a kettle of water on to boil and preheat grill (broiler) to high.

2 Combine mayonnaise, cream, horseradish, basil, parsley, thyme and chives in a small saucepan. Heat gently until just hot. Remove from heat and keep warm.

3 Blanch spinach in boiling water 2–3 minutes, then squeeze out the excess moisture.

4 Meanwhile, toast muffins on both sides under the grill. Turn off the heat, divide spinach between each muffin half and leave under the warm grill.

5 Bring some water and the vinegar to a simmer in a shallow frying pan. Poach eggs 2–3 minutes, or until the whites are set. Carefully remove the eggs with a slotted spoon and drain on paper towel.

6 Put two muffin halves on each plate and place eggs on top of the spinach. Spoon over warm sauce and add a grinding of pepper.

NUTRIENTS PER SERVING

3297 kJ, 787 kcal, 23 g protein, 58 g fat (27 g saturated fat), 45 g carbohydrate

INDIAN SCRAMBLED EGGS

TIME **25 MINUTES** SERVES **2**

INGREDIENTS

oil, for deep-frying

1 large onion, halved lengthwise, 1/2 finely sliced, 1/2 finely chopped

2 tablespoons butter

2.5 cm (1 inch) piece fresh ginger, grated

1–2 green chillies, halved, seeds removed, finely sliced

6 large eggs

1 teaspoon ground turmeric

salt and freshly ground black pepper

2 tablespoons chopped fresh coriander (cilantro) leaves, plus 2 sprigs, to garnish

pappadums or warmed naan, to serve

METHOD

1 Heat 5 cm (2 inches) oil in a small saucepan. Deep-fry onion slices over low–medium heat until crisp and brown. Drain on paper towel.

2 Melt butter in another small saucepan. Fry chopped onion gently over low heat, stirring frequently, 6–7 minutes, or until softened.

3 Add ginger and chillies and cook a further 1 minute, then remove from heat.

4 Break eggs into a bowl, then add turmeric, salt and pepper and beat lightly. Stir into the onion mixture and cook over low heat, stirring, until thick but not dry.

5 Stir in chopped coriander, sprinkle with reserved fried onions and garnish with coriander sprigs, then serve with pappadums or naan.

NUTRIENTS PER SERVING

3358 kJ, 802 kcal, 29 g protein, 60 g fat (22 g saturated fat), 15 g carbohydrate

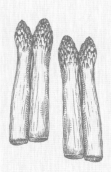

EGGS BENEDICT

TIME **25 MINUTES** SERVES **4**

INGREDIENTS

125 g (4 oz) asparagus tips
100 g (3½ oz) butter
5 eggs
1 tablespoon lemon juice
salt and freshly ground black pepper
2 tablespoons crème fraîche or sour cream
4 white or wholemeal (whole-wheat)
    English muffins, halved crosswise
8 thin slices ham or parma ham
    (about 200 g/7 oz)
2 teaspoons vinegar

METHOD

1 Drop asparagus tips into a small saucepan of boiling water and cook 2 minutes, or until just tender. Alternatively, steam 2 minutes. Drain, then cover and keep warm.

2 Fill a heavy-based frying pan with boiling water to a depth of 2.5 cm (1 inch). Bring water back to a boil, then reduce heat to a simmer.

3 Melt butter in a small saucepan until hot. Break 1 egg into a food processor or blender. Add lemon juice and seasoning. Process until just combined. While motor is running, pour hot butter through the hole in the feed tube or lid in a thin, steady stream to make a thick sauce. Briefly work in the crème fraîche or sour cream. Cover sauce to keep it warm until needed.

4 Preheat grill (broiler) to high and toast muffins under the grill. Put a muffin half on each serving plate and top with a slice of ham. Arrange asparagus on one half of each muffin and keep warm.

5 Break one of remaining eggs into a teacup. Add vinegar to the frying pan of simmering water. Carefully pour egg towards the side of the pan. Repeat with other eggs, so that they are evenly spaced. With two spoons, quickly gather whites up around each yolk. Cover pan with a lid or foil and cook 4–5 minutes, or until white is set but yolk is still soft.

6 Lift eggs out of water with a slotted spoon and set on the ham-topped muffin halves. Spoon warm sauce over asparagus and eggs, and serve.

NUTRIENTS PER SERVING

2141 kJ, 511 kcal, 25 g protein, 35 g fat (20 g saturated fat), 24 g carbohydrate

COOK'S TIP

When preparing asparagus, gently bend the spears until they snap, then discard the bases, which can be woody. To store, stand asparagus upright in a glass containing a little water and refrigerate.

SALMON AND ARTICHOKE OMELETTE

TIME 20 MINUTES SERVES 4

INGREDIENTS

8 eggs

salt and freshly ground black pepper

1 tablespoon chopped fresh dill

3 tablespoons sour cream

20 g (²/₃ oz) butter

125 g (4 oz) smoked salmon slices,
   cut into thin strips

400 g (14 oz) can or jar baby artichokes,
   rinsed, drained and sliced into quarters

METHOD

1 Break eggs into a large bowl and add 3 tablespoons water and salt and pepper to taste. Beat together thoroughly with a fork until well combined but not foamy.

2 Stir dill into sour cream and set aside. Preheat grill (broiler) to high.

3 Heat butter in a large heavy-based non-stick frying pan that can go under the grill (wrap a wooden handle with foil). As soon as the butter starts to look foamy, pour in beaten egg. Cook over high heat about 30 seconds, or until egg starts to set underneath. Using the back of a fork, gently stir the mixture so that liquid egg runs under the set mixture. Cook 30 seconds without stirring so that the omelette starts to turn brown underneath.

4 When the omelette looks almost set but is still quite moist on top, quickly top with smoked salmon strips and scatter over artichokes. Remove pan from heat and slide under the grill to cook 1 minute, or until lightly browned on top.

5 Remove pan from grill. Spoon sour cream mixture onto the omelette; it will melt to make a light sauce. Cut into wedges and serve.

NUTRIENTS PER SERVING

1120 kJ, 268 kcal, 22 g protein, 20g fat (9 g saturated fat), 2 g carbohydrate

VARIATION

VEGETARIAN OMELETTE Instead of the basic toppings, put 1 tablespoon oil in a frying pan and cook 2 thinly sliced small zucchini (courgettes) and 1 thinly sliced small red onion 3–4 minutes, to soften. Spoon over the plain omelette in step 4 and top with 125 g (4 oz) sliced or crumbled goat's cheese. Continue as for step 4. Omit sour cream and dill mixture in step 5.

EGG POTS WITH HAM AND CHEESE

TIME **25 MINUTES** SERVES **4**

INGREDIENTS

unsalted butter, for greasing

125 g (4 oz) thickly sliced ham,
  fat removed, diced

5 tablespoons thick (heavy/double) cream

4 eggs

salt and freshly ground black pepper

30 g (1 oz) finely grated mature cheddar

METHOD

1 Preheat oven to 180°C (350°C/ Gas 4). Grease four ramekin moulds well with butter.

2 Divide ham among ramekins, then spoon 1 teaspoon cream into each. Break an egg into each. Top each egg with 1 tablespoon cream, then season with salt and pepper. Sprinkle cheese over tops.

3 Put ramekin moulds in a small roasting pan (baking dish) and pour in enough hot water to come halfway up the sides of ramekins. Transfer pan to oven and bake 10–15 minutes, depending on how well you like your eggs cooked. Serve hot.

NUTRIENTS PER SERVING

1007 kJ, 241 kcal, 14 g protein, 20 g fat (11 g saturated fat), 1 g carbohydrate

VARIATION

Instead of ham, use a mixture of steamed baby spinach leaves, 30 g (1 oz) mascarpone and freshly grated nutmeg. Top with parmesan instead of cheddar.

TUNISIAN RATATOUILLE WITH EGGS

TIME **30 MINUTES** SERVES **4**

INGREDIENTS

2 tablespoons olive oil

2 onions, thinly sliced

3 green capsicums (bell peppers),
  seeds removed, sliced

3 zucchini (courgettes), thinly sliced

3 cloves garlic, crushed

1 teaspoon mild paprika

1 teaspoon ground cumin

1 good pinch cayenne pepper,
  or to taste

salt and freshly ground black pepper

410 g (15 oz) can chopped tomatoes

8 eggs

METHOD

1 Heat oil in a very large, deep frying pan that can be used under the grill (broiler). (Cover a wooden handle with foil.) Add onions and cook gently 5 minutes. Stir in capsicums, zucchini and garlic. Cover and cook over medium heat 5 minutes, stirring frequently, until just tender and beginning to colour.

2 Stir in paprika, cumin and cayenne pepper, and season to taste. Stir in tomatoes. Cover and cook gently 5 minutes.

3 Preheat grill to high. Make eight small hollows in the tomato mixture and crack an egg into each. Cook gently over low heat 2 minutes. Slide frying pan under grill and cook 2–3 minutes, or until eggs are just set. Serve immediately.

NUTRIENTS PER SERVING

1204 kJ, 288 kcal, 16 g protein, 20 g fat (5 g saturated fat), 12 g carbohydrate

VARIATION

When you add the tomatoes in step 2, also stir in 200 g (7 oz) can butterbeans (lima beans), drained and rinsed, or cooked new potatoes.

COOK'S TIP

If it is more convenient, make the ratatouille in a flameproof and ovenproof dish and do the final cooking with the eggs in the oven at 190°C (375°F/Gas 5) for about 10 minutes.

Right Tunisian ratatouille with eggs

TOMATOES WITH A SPINACH STUFFING
TIME **30 MINUTES** SERVES **2**

INGREDIENTS

1 tablespoon olive oil

250 g (8 oz) English spinach,
   stems discarded

4 large tomatoes (about 250 g/8 oz each)

125 g (4 oz) ready-toasted pine nuts

1 clove garlic, crushed

1¼ cups (125 g) grated parmesan

salt and freshly ground black pepper

METHOD

1 Preheat oven to 220°C (425°F/ Gas 7). Lightly grease a baking tray (sheet) with a little oil.

2 Heat remaining oil in a saucepan and add spinach, cover and cook 2 minutes. Uncover, stir, and cook a further 1 minute. Drain off the liquid, transfer spinach to a bowl and set aside.

3 Slice tops off tomatoes and set aside. Scoop out centre flesh of tomatoes and discard.

4 Add pine nuts, garlic and grated parmesan to the spinach, season with salt and pepper, and mix.

5 Spoon spinach mixture into the tomatoes, pressing it in firmly and piling it up. Balance tomato tops on the stuffing. Bake on top shelf of oven 12–15 minutes.

NUTRIENTS PER SERVING

4011 kJ, 958 kcal, 40 g protein, 81 g fat (18 g saturated fat), 19 g carbohydrate

COOK'S TIP

Pine nuts have a wonderful flavour, which is enhanced by toasting. If ready-toasted pine nuts are not available, use raw pine nuts. Place them in a small dry frying pan over medium–high heat and toast, stirring and turning constantly, until light golden brown.

ASPARAGUS PIPERADE
TIME **30 MINUTES** SERVES **4**

INGREDIENTS

3 tablespoons olive oil

3 cloves garlic, crushed

1 large onion, sliced

1 green chilli, seeds removed, diced

1 large red and 1 large green
   capsicum (bell pepper), seeds
   removed, sliced lengthwise

salt and freshly ground black pepper

500 g (1 lb) asparagus, woody ends
   discarded, cut into bite-sized
   pieces

410 g (15 oz) can chopped tomatoes,
   drained

8 slices crusty bread

4 large eggs, lightly beaten

4 sprigs fresh chervil, to garnish

METHOD

1 Heat 2 tablespoons oil in a large frying pan. Add garlic, onion, chilli, capsicums and salt and pepper to taste. Stir-fry 1 minute, then cover and cook over high heat 3–4 minutes, shaking pan occasionally.

2 Add asparagus, cover and cook 7–8 minutes, stirring occasionally.

3 Stir in tomatoes, increase the heat and bring to simmering point. Cook, uncovered, 2 minutes.

4 Meanwhile, brush one side of each slice of bread with a little remaining oil. Toast on a hot chargrill pan until golden, or preheat a grill (broiler) to hot and toast under the grill.

5 Add eggs to asparagus and tomato mixture and cook over medium heat, stirring, until eggs are just set.

6 Serve piperade on individual plates with toast, and garnish with chervil.

NUTRIENTS PER SERVING

2730 kJ, 652 kcal, 20 g protein, 43 g fat (20 g saturated fat), 50 g carbohydrate

Left Tomatoes with a spinach stuffing (top); Asparagus piperade (bottom)

CHAPTER 3

Salads

GREEK SALAD
TIME **15 MINUTES** SERVES **4**

INGREDIENTS

20 red cherry tomatoes, halved
1 cucumber, halved lengthwise and
    thickly sliced
375 g (13 oz) fetta, diced
3 tablespoons extra virgin olive oil
1 tablespoon lemon juice
12 black olives
freshly ground black pepper

METHOD

1 Put cherry tomatoes, cucumber
   and fetta in a serving bowl.
2 Sprinkle in oil and lemon juice.
   Add black olives and pepper to
   taste (the cheese is salty already).
   Toss well and serve.

NUTRIENTS PER SERVING
1528 kJ, 365 kcal, 16 g protein, 31 g fat
(15 g saturated fat), 5 g carbohydrate

GREEK SALAD WITH TAHINI DRESSING
TIME **20 MINUTES** SERVES **4**

INGREDIENTS

200 g (7 oz) fetta, drained
1 small cos (romaine) lettuce,
    torn into bite-sized pieces
1/2 cucumber, halved lengthwise
    and sliced
2 large roma (plum) or other well-
    flavoured ripe tomatoes (about
    350 g/12 oz in total), sliced
1 small red onion, halved and sliced

20 pitted kalamata olives or other
    pitted black olives
4 tablespoons extra virgin olive oil
1 tablespoon tahini
1 tablespoon lemon juice
freshly ground black pepper
4 large sprigs fresh flat-leaf (Italian)
    parsley

METHOD

1 Soak fetta in a small bowl of cold water for a few minutes while
   preparing the rest of the salad (this will remove excess saltiness from
   the cheese).
2 Divide lettuce among four individual serving plates, then top with
   cucumber, tomato and onion slices. Scatter with olives.
3 Whisk oil, tahini, lemon juice and a little pepper in a bowl, or shake
   together in a screw-top jar. Scissor-snip parsley into the dressing.
4 Drain fetta and crumble into small pieces. Scatter about two-thirds over
   the individual salads. Drizzle dressing over salads, then scatter with
   remaining fetta. Serve at room temperature.

NUTRIENTS PER SERVING
1736 kJ, 415 kcal, 13 g protein, 37 g fat (11 g saturated fat), 8 g carbohydrate

COOK'S TIP

In Greece, wild purslane, which has a mild taste and crunchy texture,
is often used instead of cos lettuce. Rocket (arugula) leaves, although more
peppery in flavour, make another good substitute.

Right Greek salad with tahini dressing

WITLOF, PEAR AND ROQUEFORT SALAD
TIME 15 MINUTES SERVES 4

INGREDIENTS

6 whole fresh walnuts or 12 shelled
    walnut halves
3 witlof (Belgian endive)
2 dessert pears, such as Comice or
    Williams, quartered and cored, each
    quarter cut lengthwise into 3 slices
100 g (3¹/₂ oz) roquefort cheese,
    crumbled
4 tablespoons fresh chervil or
    2 tablespoons fresh tarragon,
    to garnish (optional)

DRESSING

3 teaspoons white wine vinegar
salt
1¹/₂ tablespoons extra virgin olive oil
2 tablespoons walnut oil

METHOD

1 If using fresh walnuts, crack the shells and remove the kernels. Roughly
   chop the kernels or the shelled walnut halves and set aside.
2 Arrange witlof leaves on individual plates. Arrange pear slices decoratively
   over the witlof.
3 Scatter cheese and walnuts over the pears.
4 To make the dressing, put vinegar in a bowl, add salt, olive oil and walnut
   oil and whisk, then pour a little over each salad. Scatter with chervil or
   tarragon, if using.

NUTRIENTS PER SERVING

1281 kJ, 306 kcal, 6 g protein, 28 g fat (7 g saturated fat), 9 g carbohydrate

SALAD NIÇOISE

TIME **25 MINUTES** SERVES **4**

METHOD

1 Put eggs in a small saucepan and cover with water. Bring to a boil, then reduce heat and simmer 4 minutes. Remove from heat, cover and leave to stand.

2 To make the croutons, heat oil in a frying pan. Add garlic and fry over medium heat. Add bread cubes and fry until crisp and golden, stirring frequently, then drain on paper towel and set aside to cool.

3 To make the dressing, put sugar, vinegar and salt to taste in a large salad bowl. Add garlic, mustard and oil and whisk to a thick emulsion.

4 Put tuna, onion, anchovies and their oil, capers and olives in the bowl with the dressing. Toss gently.

5 Separate lettuce leaves and slice the heart into small pieces. Add to the salad bowl and scatter over cherry tomatoes.

6 Shell eggs and cut into quarters lengthwise. Toss the salad, making sure every leaf is coated with dressing, then add the egg quarters. Serve the croutons in a separate dish.

NUTRIENTS PER SERVING

2239 kJ, 535 kcal, 33 g protein, 38 g fat (6 g saturated fat), 17 g carbohydrate

VARIATION

You can also add artichoke hearts, sliced red capsicum (bell pepper) or cooled steamed green beans to the salad when you add the tomatoes.

INGREDIENTS

4 eggs

425 g (15 oz) can tuna, drained and flaked

1 red onion, thinly sliced

45 g (1 1/2 oz) can anchovy fillets

50 g (1 3/4 oz) capers, rinsed and squeezed dry

1 cup (125 g) pitted black olives

3 baby cos (romaine) lettuces

200 g (7 oz) red cherry tomatoes, halved

CROUTONS

2 tablespoons olive oil

1 clove garlic, crushed

2 thick slices wholemeal (whole-wheat) bread, crusts removed, cut into cubes

DRESSING

1/2 teaspoon caster (superfine) sugar

3 teaspoons white wine vinegar

salt

1 clove garlic, crushed

1–2 teaspoons dijon mustard

2 tablespoons extra virgin olive oil

TUNA WITH MOROCCAN SPICES AND BEAN SALAD

TIME **25 MINUTES** SERVES **4**

INGREDIENTS

4 tuna steaks (about 100 g/
  3¹/₂ oz each)

4 teaspoons ras el hanout

300 g (10 oz) green beans

2 tablespoons honey

grated zest and juice of 2 lemons

4 tomatoes, halved and sliced

400 g (14 oz) can cannellini beans,
  rinsed and drained

2 tablespoons olive oil

1 small onion, halved and sliced

2 large red capsicums (bell peppers),
  seeds removed, sliced

2 large cloves garlic, sliced

METHOD

1 Put tuna steaks on a plate and sprinkle ras el hanout over both sides to coat the fish. Set aside.

2 Put green beans in a small saucepan with just enough boiling water to cover and bring to a boil. Boil 2 minutes. Drain, rinse under cold water, drain again and put in a heatproof bowl. Add honey, lemon zest and juice and mix well. Add tomatoes and cannellini beans.

3 Heat 1 tablespoon oil in a frying pan. Add onion, capsicums and garlic and cook, stirring, over high heat 1 minute, or until very lightly cooked. Add to salad and mix well.

4 Return frying pan to heat and add remaining oil. Add tuna, scraping any spice mix from the plate onto the fish. Cook tuna over high heat 2 minutes. Turn and cook a further 2–3 minutes, pressing lightly with a spatula. The fish should be just cooked through.

5 Divide salad among four plates. Slice tuna into strips and lay them on the salad. Scrape any juices and spices from the pan and pour over tuna. Serve at once.

NUTRIENTS PER SERVING

1638 kJ, 391 kcal, 34 g protein, 16 g fat (4 g saturated fat), 28 g carbohydrate

COOK'S TIP

You will find ras el hanout among the standard spice mixes or specialty ranges in the supermarket. Traditionally, it was a blend of the best spices the seller had to offer, hence its name, which comes from the Arabic for 'head of the shop'. To make ras el hanout, use a mixture of 4 teaspoons ground coriander, ¹/₂ teaspoon ground cinnamon, ¹/₄ teaspoon ground mace or freshly grated nutmeg and 1 large pinch chilli powder. Or use a fiery African spice mix instead, such as harissa paste.

Left Tuna with moroccan spices and bean salad

PASTA NIÇOISE SALAD

TIME **20 MINUTES** SERVES **4**

INGREDIENTS

250 g (8 oz) pasta shapes, such
  as conchiglie

100 g (3¹/₂ oz) green beans

2 tablespoons extra virgin olive oil

¹/₂ tablespoon white wine vinegar

1 pinch sugar or ¹/₂ teaspoon honey

¹/₂ teaspoon dijon or wholegrain mustard

salt and freshly ground black pepper

180 g (6 oz) can tuna, drained and flaked

3 tablespoons chopped pitted black olives

1 large carrot, grated

1 hard-boiled (hard-cooked) egg, peeled
  and quartered, to garnish

METHOD

1 Cook pasta in a large saucepan of boiling water, following packet instructions.

2 Meanwhile, cook beans in a saucepan of lightly salted boiling water, 4 minutes. Drain, rinse under cold water and drain again.

3 Whisk together oil, vinegar, sugar or honey, mustard, and salt and pepper to taste in a bowl to make a dressing.

4 When pasta is al dente, drain well and transfer to a large serving bowl. Toss while hot with the dressing.

5 Add tuna, olives, carrot and beans to the pasta and toss gently, then garnish with egg.

NUTRIENTS PER SERVING

1602 kJ, 383 kcal, 18 g protein, 14 g fat (2 g saturated fat), 46 g carbohydrate

ITALIAN TOMATO AND BREAD SALAD

TIME **30 MINUTES** SERVES **4**

INGREDIENTS

¾ small loaf of country-style bread,
   1–2 days old, cut or torn into
   bite-sized chunks
1 yellow capsicum (bell pepper), seeds
   removed, cut into chunks
5 tablespoons extra virgin olive oil
2 tablespoons red wine vinegar
½ teaspoon caster (superfine) sugar
freshly ground black pepper
1 small red onion, halved and thinly sliced
500 g (1 lb) juicy ripe roma (plum)
   tomatoes, roughly chopped
2 tablespoons capers, rinsed and
   squeezed dry
1 small bunch (20 g/⅔ oz) fresh basil,
   leaves roughly torn
20 baby bocconcini (fresh baby mozzarella
   balls) (about 225 g/8 oz in total),
   drained

METHOD

1 Preheat oven to 190°C (375°F/Gas 5). Spread bread out over two-thirds of
   a large roasting pan (baking dish). Toss capsicum in 1 tablespoon oil and
   put in a single layer on remaining third of dish. Roast in oven 20 minutes,
   or until golden. Remove and leave to cool a few minutes.

2 Meanwhile, put remaining oil in a large serving bowl and whisk in vinegar,
   sugar and a little pepper. Add onion and toss well to coat in the dressing,
   then add tomatoes and capers, and mix together.

3 Add bread and yellow capsicums to the bowl. Scatter with torn basil, then
   mix well. Cover and chill until ready to serve. Arrange bocconcini over the
   salad before serving.

NUTRIENTS PER SERVING

2727 kJ, 651 kcal, 24 g protein, 39 g fat (12 g saturated fat), 51 g carbohydrate

COOK'S TIP

If you can't find bocconcini, buy two 125 g (4 oz) packs fresh mozzarella and
cut into pieces. Buy reduced-fat mozzarella, if you prefer.

WILD RICE AND FENNEL SALAD

TIME **30 MINUTES** SERVES **4**

INGREDIENTS

185 g (6$\frac{1}{2}$ oz) easy-cook wild rice
    and long-grain rice mixture
salt
250 g (8 oz) cucumber, finely diced
250 g (8 oz) fennel, trimmed and
    thinly sliced
6 spring onions (scallions), thinly sliced
125 g (4 oz) seedless red grapes, halved
$\frac{1}{2}$ cup (70 g) skinned hazelnuts, chopped
$\frac{1}{4}$ cup (30 g) raisins
grated zest of 1 orange
4–6 sprigs tarragon, to garnish

DRESSING

2 tablespoons orange juice
2 tablespoons finely chopped chervil
1 tablespoon finely chopped tarragon
2 tablespoons finely chopped parsley
4 tablespoons hazelnut or walnut oil
3 teaspoons white wine vinegar
salt and freshly ground black pepper

METHOD

1 Bring 1$\frac{3}{4}$ cups (435 ml) water to
a boil, add rice and a little salt,
cover and simmer 18–20 minutes,
or until the rice is cooked and all
the water absorbed. Alternatively,
follow packet instructions.

2 Meanwhile, put cucumber, fennel,
spring onions, grapes, hazelnuts,
raisins and orange zest in a bowl.

3 To make the dressing, put orange
juice, chervil, tarragon, parsley,
oil and vinegar in a separate bowl.
Whisk together; season to taste.

4 Drain cooked rice, rinse briefly
under cold running water, then
drain well again. Mix carefully
into salad and pour over dressing.
Just before serving, garnish with
sprigs of tarragon.

NUTRIENTS PER SERVING
1921 kJ, 459 kcal, 7 g protein, 26 g fat (2 g saturated fat), 50 g carbohydrate

COOK'S TIP
This salad can be made in advance and left to stand at room temperature
for 30 minutes before serving.

CHICKEN AND SUGARSNAP PEA NOODLE SALAD

TIME **25 MINUTES** SERVES **4**

INGREDIENTS

200 g (7 oz) sugarsnap peas
200 g (7 oz) dried medium egg noodles
1 tablespoon tahini
2 tablespoons vegetable oil
2 tablespoons lemon juice
1 tablespoon soy sauce
1 teaspoon sesame oil
1 clove garlic, crushed
2 teaspoons grated fresh ginger
250 g (8 oz) cold cooked boneless,
    skinless chicken breast, cut into
    thin strips

METHOD

1 Put sugarsnap peas in a saucepan
   of boiling water. Cook 4 minutes.
   Drain, rinse under cold water to
   halt the cooking process, and
   drain again.
2 Meanwhile, cook egg noodles,
   following packet instructions.
3 Whisk together tahini, oil, lemon
   juice, soy sauce, sesame oil, garlic
   and ginger in a small bowl to
   make a dressing.
4 Drain cooked noodles, transfer
   to a large serving bowl and toss
   while hot with the dressing. Cool
   15 minutes, then add chicken and
   sugarsnap peas and toss through.

NUTRIENTS PER SERVING

830 kJ, 198 kcal, 26 g protein, 19 g fat
(3 g saturated fat), 40 g carbohydrate

ITALIAN SUMMER SALAD

TIME **20 MINUTES** SERVES **4**

INGREDIENTS

250 g (8 oz) penne
2 tablespoons extra virgin olive oil
1 tablespoon lemon juice
1 clove garlic, crushed
1 small bunch (20 g/^{2}/$_3$ oz) fresh
    basil, leaves finely chopped
salt and freshly ground black pepper
200 g (7 oz) red and yellow cherry
    tomatoes, halved
200 g (7 oz) roasted red capsicums
    (bell peppers), finely sliced
150 g (5 oz) fresh mozzarella, diced

METHOD

1 Cook pasta in a large saucepan of salted boiling water, following
   packet instructions.
2 Meanwhile, whisk together oil, lemon juice, garlic and basil in a bowl
   to make a dressing.
3 Drain cooked pasta, transfer to a large serving bowl and toss while hot
   with dressing. Season to taste. Add cherry tomatoes, roasted capsicums
   and mozzarella and toss together until well combined.

NUTRIENTS PER SERVING

1922 kJ, 459 kcal, 18 g protein, 22 g fat (7 g saturated fat), 47 g carbohydrate

---

PASTA AND SALAMI SALAD

TIME **20 MINUTES** SERVES **4**

INGREDIENTS

250 g (8 oz) fusilli
2 tablespoons extra virgin olive oil
^{1}/$_2$ tablespoon white wine vinegar
1 pinch sugar or ^{1}/$_2$ teaspoon honey
^{1}/$_2$ teaspoon mustard
salt and freshly ground black pepper
1 green, 1 red and 1 yellow capsicum
    (bell pepper), thinly sliced
1 small red onion, thinly sliced
100 g (3^1/$_2$ oz) Italian salami slices,
    cut into thin strips
100 g (3^1/$_2$ oz) rocket (arugula)

METHOD

1 Cook pasta in a large saucepan of salted boiling water, following
   packet instructions.
2 Meanwhile, whisk together oil, vinegar, sugar or honey, mustard, and
   salt and pepper to taste in a bowl to make a dressing.
3 Drain cooked pasta, transfer to a large serving bowl and toss while hot
   with dressing. Add capsicums, onion, salami and rocket and toss.

NUTRIENTS PER SERVING

1754 kJ, 419 kcal, 14 g protein, 20 g fat (4 g saturated fat), 46 g carbohydrate

Right Italian summer salad

MELON, AVOCADO AND PRAWN SALAD
TIME 20 MINUTES SERVES 6

INGREDIENTS

1 rockmelon (cantaloupe)

2 avocados

50 g (1³/₄ oz) mixed salad leaves

350 g (12 oz) peeled cooked prawns
    (shrimp)

2 tablespoons fresh coriander (cilantro)
    leaves, to garnish

DRESSING

1 small French shallot (eschalot), chopped

¹/₂ cup (125 g) crème fraîche
    or sour cream

2 tablespoons extra virgin olive oil

1 tablespoon cider vinegar

1 pinch sugar

salt and freshly ground black pepper

METHOD

1 To make the dressing, put French shallot, crème fraîche or sour cream, oil, vinegar and sugar in a small bowl. Stir well, season to taste with salt and pepper and set aside.

2 Cut rockmelon into quarters and discard seeds. Remove skin and cut the flesh lengthwise into narrow slices.

3 Halve and stone avocados, then peel and cut the flesh lengthwise into slices the same thickness as the melon.

4 Divide mixed salad leaves among six plates. Arrange slices of melon and avocado among them. Scatter prawns on top and, using a spoon, drizzle over the dressing. Garnish with coriander leaves and serve.

NUTRIENTS PER SERVING
1439 kJ, 344 kcal, 16 g protein, 28 g fat (9 g saturated fat), 7 g carbohydrate

CREAMY MIXED BEAN SALAD
TIME **25 MINUTES** SERVES **4**

METHOD

1 Cook green beans in a saucepan of lightly salted boiling water 5–6 minutes, or until just tender. Drain, rinse under cold water and drain again.

2 Rinse kidney and cannellini beans and lentils. Drain and spread on a tea towel (dish towel) to dry.

3 To make the dressing, put yogurt, lemon juice and mustard to taste in a large bowl and stir well. Add torn basil, season to taste with salt and pepper and stir again.

4 Arrange lettuce leaves on a serving dish. Add green beans, kidney and cannellini beans, lentils, artichokes, mushrooms and spring onions to the bowl with the dressing and toss through. Spoon over lettuce leaves and garnish with basil.

NUTRIENTS PER SERVING

2503 kJ, 598 kcal, 32 g protein, 24 g fat (5 g saturated fat), 64 g carbohydrate

VARIATION

Diced cheese, strips of cooked ham, chicken or turkey or some small peeled prawns (shrimp) can be added to this creamy salad.

INGREDIENTS

250 g (8 oz) green beans, topped and tailed

400 g (14 oz) can red kidney beans

400 g (14 oz) can cannellini beans

400 g (14 oz) can lentils

1 soft lettuce, such as butterhead

300 g (10 oz) artichoke hearts in oil, drained and quartered

150 g (5 oz) button mushrooms, sliced

5 spring onions (scallions), thinly sliced

2 sprigs fresh basil, to garnish

DRESSING

1 cup (250 g) natural (plain) yogurt

juice of $1/2$ lemon

1–2 teaspoons dijon mustard

4 tablespoons torn fresh basil

salt and freshly ground black pepper

GRILLED CHICKEN AND VEGETABLE SALAD WITH MINT BUTTER DRESSING

TIME **30 MINUTES** SERVES **4**

METHOD

1 Put burghul in a large bowl, pour over stock and stir well. Cover with a saucepan lid or baking tray (sheet) and leave to soak 20–25 minutes, or until tender and most of the stock has been absorbed.

2 Meanwhile, preheat grill (broiler) to medium–hot and line grill pan with foil. Arrange eggplant, zucchini and capsicum slices on grill rack and brush with 1 tablespoon oil. Grill 15–20 minutes, or until tender and beginning to char, turning halfway through and brushing other side with 1 tablespoon oil. Check vegetables regularly and remove them as they are cooked.

3 Drain burghul. Whisk remaining oil and 1 teaspoon vinegar in the bowl, then add chicken, black-eyed peas and parsley, and return burghul to the bowl. Cut eggplant slices into halves, or quarters if large, and add to the bowl with zucchini and capsicum slices. Mix everything together well. Season to taste with salt and pepper.

4 Heat butter and remaining vinegar in a small saucepan. Stir in chopped mint to make a dressing. Spoon burghul salad onto individual plates and drizzle with mint butter dressing. Garnish with mint leaves.

NUTRIENTS PER SERVING

2347 kJ, 561 kcal, 27 g protein, 26 g fat (7 g saturated fat), 58 g carbohydrate

VARIATION

For a spicy dressing, stir a finely chopped, seeded red chilli into melted butter in step 4, or whisk in ¼ teaspoon chilli paste from a jar.

COOK'S TIP

The salad can be prepared to the end of step 3 up to 12 hours in advance and kept covered in the refrigerator. If possible, remove the salad from the fridge about an hour before you need it, then drizzle over the mint butter dressing just before serving.

INGREDIENTS

200 g (7 oz) burghul (bulgur)

600 ml (21 fl oz) hot vegetable stock

1 eggplant (aubergine), thickly sliced

2 zucchini (courgettes), thickly sliced

1 large yellow capsicum (bell pepper), seeds removed, thickly sliced

3 tablespoons olive oil

3 teaspoons red wine vinegar

200 g (7 oz) bought barbecued chicken pieces (quartered if breast), skin removed

400 g (14 oz) can black-eyed peas, rinsed and drained

2 tablespoons chopped fresh flat-leaf (Italian) parsley

salt and freshly ground black pepper

30 g (1 oz) butter

2 tablespoons chopped fresh mint, plus extra leaves, to garnish

THAI BEEF SALAD

TIME **30 MINUTES** SERVES **4**

INGREDIENTS

350 g (12 oz) crisp lettuce leaves,
  shredded

175 g (6 oz) cucumber, diced

2 carrots, coarsely grated

125 g (4 oz) bean sprouts, trimmed

2 teaspoons vegetable oil

1 clove garlic, crushed

1 teaspoon finely sliced lemongrass stem
  (white part only)

500 g (1 lb) lean steak, thinly sliced

2 tablespoons lime juice

1 small bunch (20 g/^{2}/$_3$ oz) fresh
  coriander (cilantro), leaves finely
  chopped

1 small bunch (20 g/^{2}/$_3$ oz) fresh basil,
  leaves finely chopped

2 tablespoons olive oil

1 tablespoon sweet chilli sauce

METHOD

1 Arrange lettuce, cucumber, carrots and bean sprouts on a large serving
   dish or individual plates.
2 Heat vegetable oil in a large frying pan and gently cook garlic and
   lemongrass about 30 seconds, until just golden brown.
3 Add beef and fry over high heat 1–2 minutes, stirring continuously to keep
   the slices separate. Remove meat from the pan and place on top of the
   salad vegetables.
4 Add lime juice, coriander, basil, olive oil and chilli sauce to the pan. Cook,
   stirring, 1 minute, then pour the dressing over the beef and salad and serve.

NUTRIENTS PER SERVING

1152 kJ, 275 kcal, 29 g protein, 16 g fat (4 g saturated fat), 7 g carbohydrate

THAI NOODLE SALAD
TIME **30 MINUTES** SERVES **4**

METHOD

1 Put snow peas in a saucepan of boiling water, bring back to a boil, then reduce heat and simmer 3 minutes. Remove from heat.
2 Add capsicum and vermicelli to the saucepan of hot water and snow peas and leave to stand 2 minutes. Transfer to a colander, rinse and drain.
3 To make the dressing, put lemongrass, chillies, ginger, coriander, lime juice, vegetable oil, sesame oil and soy sauce in a food processor or blender. Blend just long enough to make a thick, chunky dressing. Alternatively, chop or grind the ingredients with a pestle and mortar.
4 Put spring onions, prawns and vermicelli mixture in a serving bowl. Pour over the dressing and toss well. Serve with a bowl of prawn crackers.

NUTRIENTS PER SERVING

2737 kJ, 654 kcal, 21 g protein, 31 g fat (4 g saturated fat), 71 g carbohydrate

COOK'S TIP

The salad can be made in advance and stored for an hour or two in the refrigerator.

INGREDIENTS

200 g (7 oz) snow peas (mangetout), topped and tailed
1 yellow capsicum (bell pepper), seeds removed, thinly sliced
200 g (7 oz) dried rice vermicelli
8 spring onions (scallions), sliced diagonally
250 g (8 oz) peeled cooked prawns (shrimp)
prawn crackers, to serve

DRESSING

2 stems lemongrass, sliced
2 red chillies, seeds removed, sliced
7.5 cm (3 inch) piece fresh ginger, peeled and sliced
3 tablespoons chopped fresh coriander (cilantro) leaves
juice of 2 limes
3 tablespoons vegetable oil
1 tablespoon sesame oil
2 tablespoons soy sauce

CHEF'S SALAD

TIME **20 MINUTES** SERVES **4**

INGREDIENTS

45 g (1$^1/_2$ oz) can anchovy fillets,
   drained and roughly chopped
1 clove garlic, roughly chopped
$^1/_2$ teaspoon dijon mustard
4 tablespoons extra virgin olive oil
1 tablespoon lemon juice
2 tablespoons thick (heavy/double) cream
1 cos (romaine) lettuce, torn into
   bite-sized pieces
4 tomatoes, cut into wedges
1 ripe avocado, diced
$^1/_4$ cucumber, diced
100 g (3$^1/_2$ oz) gouda cheese, diced
100 g (3$^1/_2$ oz) roast ham, diced
freshly ground black pepper

METHOD

1 Put anchovy fillets, garlic, mustard, oil and lemon juice in a food processor or blender. Blend together until dressing is smooth, then add cream and blend again for just a few seconds.
2 Put lettuce, tomatoes, avocado, cucumber, cheese and ham in a large bowl and gently mix together. Alternatively, arrange the ingredients on four individual plates.
3 Lightly drizzle anchovy dressing over the salad, season with pepper and serve at once.

NUTRIENTS PER SERVING

1991 kJ, 476 kcal, 17 g protein, 42 g fat (12 g saturated fat), 9 g carbohydrate

VARIATION

VEGETARIAN SALAD Instead of ham, add 2 hard-boiled (hard-cooked) eggs, cut into wedges. For the dressing, whisk together 1 teaspoon dijon mustard, 1 pinch caster (superfine) sugar, 1 tablespoon white wine vinegar, 4 tablespoons extra virgin olive oil and 2 tablespoons crème fraîche or light sour cream.

SMOKED TROUT WITH PEAR AND ROCKET

TIME **15 MINUTES** SERVES **4**

INGREDIENTS

1 small head rosso or treviso radicchio

50 g (1³/₄ oz) rocket (arugula)

salt and freshly ground black pepper

2 teaspoons lemon juice

2 tablespoons extra virgin olive oil

4 smoked trout fillets, skin removed,
    sliced across into strips

2 dessert pears, such as Comice or
    Williams, halved and cored, thinly sliced

walnut or brown bread, thinly sliced,
    to serve

SAUCE

2 tablespoons crème fraîche or sour cream

2 teaspoons horseradish cream, from a jar

METHOD

1 Tear radicchio into a bowl, add rocket and season to taste with salt and pepper.

2 Put lemon juice and oil in a small bowl and whisk together. Pour over salad leaves, add trout and pears and toss gently. Divide among four plates.

3 To make the sauce, mix together crème fraîche or sour cream and horseradish cream, stirring to give a pouring consistency. Spoon over trout and salad and serve with slices of bread.

NUTRIENTS PER SERVING

2293 kJ, 548 kcal, 39 g protein, 30 g fat
(9 g saturated fat), 31 g carbohydrate

Left Smoked trout with pear and rocket

LEBANESE BURGHUL AND FETTA SALAD

TIME **15 MINUTES** SERVES **4**

INGREDIENTS

200 g (7 oz) burghul (bulgur)

600 ml (21 fl oz) boiling water

salt and freshly ground black pepper

125 g (4 oz) green beans, halved

2 tablespoons olive oil

juice of 1 lemon

1 teaspoon ground cinnamon

1 teaspoon ground cumin

1 teaspoon ground coriander

¹/₂ cup (25 g) snipped fresh chives

3 tablespoons chopped fresh mint

3 tablespoons chopped fresh
    coriander (cilantro) leaves

12 pitted black olives, sliced

3 tablespoons sliced marinated or
    roasted capsicums (bell peppers),
    from a jar

1 large ripe tomato, chopped,
    or 250 g (8 oz) red cherry
    tomatoes, halved

150 g (5 oz) fetta, crumbled

METHOD

1 Tip burghul into a large heatproof bowl and add boiling water. Stir in 1 teaspoon salt and leave to stand 15–20 minutes, or until liquid is absorbed, then use a fork to fluff up the grains.

2 While burghul is soaking, blanch green beans in a small saucepan of boiling water 1–2 minutes, or in a covered bowl with 1 tablespoon water in the microwave on High 3 minutes. Drain, rinse under cold running water and drain again.

3 Mix together oil, lemon juice, ground cinnamon, cumin and coriander, and a little salt and pepper. Stir into the burghul.

4 Mix green beans into the burghul with chives, mint, fresh coriander, olives, capsicums and chopped tomato or cherry tomatoes. Add fetta, then use a fork to gently combine all ingredients.

NUTRIENTS PER SERVING

1639 kJ, 391 kcal, 14 g protein, 22 g fat (7 g saturated fat), 35 g carbohydrate

VARIATION

WARM CHICKEN AND ALMOND SALAD Instead of olives, capsicums, tomato and fetta, use 1 coarsely grated carrot and ¹/₄ Lebanese or other small cucumber, chopped. While the burghul is soaking in step 1, heat 1 tablespoon olive oil in a wok or frying pan and stir-fry 400 g (14 oz) boneless, skinless chicken breast, cut into strips, with 1 crushed clove garlic and 1 teaspoon grated fresh ginger 7–8 minutes, or until just cooked through. Season, remove from heat and mix in 3 tablespoons Greek-style yogurt and 3 tablespoons toasted flaked almonds. Serve the salad topped with the chicken and garnished with more flaked almonds.

WARM EGG AND POTATO SALAD WITH SPICY PEANUT SAUCE

TIME **25 MINUTES** SERVES **4**

INGREDIENTS

750 g (1 1/2 lb) small new potatoes

2 large carrots, cut into matchsticks

125 g (4 oz) green beans, cut into
   small lengths

1 small cauliflower, divided into
   small florets

6 eggs, at room temperature

1 tablespoon vegetable oil

1 clove garlic, crushed

2.5 cm (1 inch) piece fresh ginger,
   grated

1/4 teaspoon dried red chilli flakes

1 tablespoon lime juice

1 teaspoon light muscovado sugar or
   soft brown sugar

4 tablespoons crunchy peanut butter

1 tablespoon olive oil

1 teaspoon red wine vinegar

METHOD

1 Put potatoes in a large saucepan of boiling water and place a steamer basket on top. Cook potatoes 10–12 minutes, or until just tender. Put carrots, beans and cauliflower in the steamer basket and cook the last 8 minutes of cooking time.

2 While vegetables are cooking, add eggs to a pan of boiling water and cook 8 minutes. Remove eggs and put in a bowl of cold water to cool.

3 While vegetables and eggs are cooking, heat vegetable oil in a small saucepan and cook garlic, ginger and chilli flakes 1 minute. Add lime juice, sugar, peanut butter and 1/2 cup (125 ml) cooking water from the potatoes. Heat until steaming, stirring to mix everything together.

4 Drain potatoes and return to the pan. Add steamed vegetables. Drizzle olive oil and vinegar over all the vegetables and gently toss to coat lightly. Cover pan to keep vegetables warm. Peel eggs and cut into quarters lengthwise.

5 Tip vegetables into a warmed serving dish and arrange eggs on top. Drizzle over hot peanut sauce and serve at once.

NUTRIENTS PER SERVING

2105 kJ, 503 kcal, 22 g protein, 30 g fat (6 g saturated fat), 35 g carbohydrate

VARIATION

CHINESE VEGETABLES WITH PEANUT SAUCE Instead of potatoes and fresh vegetables, stir-fry 500 g (1 lb) frozen mixed stir-fry vegetables, following the packet instructions. Drizzle over the peanut sauce and scatter 2 tablespoons bought crunchy spicy seeds on top. Serve with rice.

WARM BUTTERBEAN AND CHARRED VEGETABLE SALAD

TIME **20 MINUTES** SERVES **4**

INGREDIENTS

2 tablespoons olive oil

1 red and 1 yellow capsicum (bell pepper), seeds removed, roughly chopped

1 onion, sliced

2 zucchini (courgettes), thinly sliced

400 g (14 oz) can butterbeans (lima beans), rinsed and drained

400 g (14 oz) can brown lentils, rinsed and drained

2 tablespoons torn fresh basil

2 tomatoes, roughly chopped

2 tablespoons sliced sun-dried tomatoes in oil

1 tablespoon balsamic vinegar

salt and freshly ground black pepper

12 large black olives, to garnish

METHOD

1 Heat oil in a large frying pan and brown capsicums, onion and zucchini over high heat, stirring occasionally.

2 Add butterbeans and lentils, and stir gently, then add basil, fresh tomatoes, sun-dried tomatoes and vinegar.

3 Season with salt and pepper, then heat through, stirring well. Turn into a warm dish, garnish with olives and serve immediately.

NUTRIENTS PER SERVING

1716 kJ, 410 kcal, 21 g protein, 13 g fat (1 g saturated fat), 52 g carbohydrate

VARIATION

Balsamic vinegar has the best flavour, but you can use a good white wine or cider vinegar instead.

COOK'S TIP

Some crusty wholemeal (whole-wheat) rolls, warmed in the oven while the salad is heating through, are all you need for a nourishing meal.

SUMMER COUSCOUS SALAD

TIME **25 MINUTES** SERVES **4**

INGREDIENTS

200 g (7 oz) couscous

400 ml (14 fl oz) boiling water or stock

salt and freshly ground black pepper

2 green or red capsicums (bell peppers),
    seeds removed, quartered lengthwise

1 zucchini (courgette), quartered
    lengthwise

1 cup (155 g) frozen broad (fava) beans
    or ⅔ cup (100 g) frozen peas

4 tablespoons vinaigrette

1–2 tablespoons lemon juice, to taste

1 cinnamon stick, bruised

4 tablespoons toasted flaked almonds,
    plus extra, to serve

400 g (14 oz) cooked boneless, skinless
    chicken breast, chopped

¼ cup (15 g) chopped fresh parsley
    or coriander (cilantro) leaves

mixed salad leaves, to serve

METHOD

1 Preheat grill (broiler) to high.
   Mix couscous with boiling water
   or stock and 1 teaspoon salt,
   then leave to soak.

2 Meanwhile, grill capsicums and
   zucchini 15 minutes, or until
   browned and just tender, turning
   frequently. Cut into small pieces.

3 Meanwhile, cook broad beans or
   peas in saucepan of boiling water
   3 minutes, then drain and rinse
   under cold running water. Pat dry.

4 Use a fork to separate and fluff up
   couscous grains. Add vinaigrette,
   lemon juice, cinnamon, almonds,
   grilled vegetables, broad beans
   and chicken. Season, add parsley
   or coriander, and stir to combine.
   Serve with salad leaves.

NUTRIENTS PER SERVING

2461 kJ, 588 kcal, 41 g protein, 27 g fat
(4 g saturated fat), 42 g carbohydrate

SUMMER TABOULEH
TIME **30 MINUTES** SERVES **4**

INGREDIENTS

250 g (8 oz) burghul (bulgur)

200 g (7 oz) small green beans, topped and tailed, cut into small pieces

1⅓ cups (200 g) frozen peas

salt

5 large spring onions (scallions), thinly sliced

2 tomatoes, diced

grated zest and juice of 1 lemon

4 tablespoons chopped fresh parsley

4 tablespoons chopped fresh mint

4 tablespoons snipped fresh chives or chopped fresh dill

2 baby cos (romaine) lettuces, to serve

DRESSING

2 tablespoons extra virgin olive oil

3 teaspoons red wine vinegar

1 teaspoon honey

3 teaspoons dijon mustard

salt and freshly ground black pepper

METHOD

1 Put burghul in a large saucepan with 700 ml (24 fl oz) cold water. Bring to a boil, reduce heat and simmer 8–10 minutes, just until burghul has absorbed all water. Remove from heat and set aside.

2 Meanwhile, put beans and peas in a saucepan of boiling salted water and cook 1–2 minutes, then rinse under cold running water, drain and leave to cool a little.

3 Put burghul in a mixing bowl. Add spring onions, tomatoes, lemon zest and juice and fluff up mixture with a fork.

4 Add beans, peas, parsley, mint, chives or dill to the salad.

5 To make the dressing, whisk all the ingredients together in a bowl. Pour over the tabouleh and mix well. Serve with lettuce leaves.

NUTRIENTS PER SERVING

1599 kJ, 382 kcal, 12 g protein, 11 g fat (1.5 g saturated fat), 60 g carbohydrate

COOK'S TIP

In the Middle East this salad is eaten by rolling a spoonful of the tabouleh inside a lettuce leaf and picking it up with the fingers.

CAJUN POTATO SALAD

TIME **30 MINUTES** SERVES **4**

INGREDIENTS

500 g (1 lb) boiling (waxy) potatoes, peeled

salt

1 small green capsicum (bell pepper), halved lengthwise, seeds removed, thinly sliced

2 celery stalks, finely sliced, plus leaves reserved, to garnish

1 small red onion, halved lengthwise and sliced into thin wedges

freshly ground black pepper

DRESSING

²/₃ cup (160 g) mayonnaise

2 teaspoons dijon mustard

Tabasco sauce, to taste

METHOD

1 Put potatoes in a saucepan of salted boiling water. Simmer 15–20 minutes, or until potatoes are tender.

2 Put capsicum, celery and onion in a salad bowl.

3 To make the dressing, mix mayonnaise and mustard in a small bowl and add Tabasco to taste.

4 Drain potatoes, cool under cold running water, drain again and add to the salad. Add the dressing and pepper and mix well. Garnish the salad with celery leaves.

NUTRIENTS PER SERVING

1448 kJ, 346 kcal, 3 g protein, 29 g fat (4 g saturated fat), 19 g carbohydrate

VARIATION

Add chopped hard-boiled (hard-cooked) eggs to the salad to turn it into a complete meal.

HOT POTATO SALAD
TIME **30 MINUTES** SERVES 4

METHOD

1 Preheat grill (broiler) to high. Put potatoes in a saucepan of salted boiling water and simmer 15–20 minutes, or until potatoes are tender.

2 Meanwhile, grill sausages about 10 minutes, or following packet instructions, turning often, until cooked through and browned.

3 Heat vegetable oil in a small saucepan. Add French shallot and garlic and fry 3 minutes, until soft and just turning brown.

4 Add parsley, chives, mustard and flour and cook, stirring constantly, 1 minute.

5 Remove pan from heat and add lemon juice, vinegar, olive oil and sugar. Return pan to heat and bring mixture slowly to a boil, stirring constantly, until it is smooth and thick. Add salt and pepper to taste, then remove pan from heat.

6 Drain potatoes and put in a serving dish. Slice sausages and mix with potatoes, then pour over the hot dressing. Crumble cheese over the top and serve.

NUTRIENTS PER SERVING
2917 kJ, 697 kcal, 25 g protein, 48 g fat (17 g saturated fat), 43 g carbohydrate

VARIATION
Garlic chives add a stronger, much more garlicky flavour to the salad, but if they are difficult to find you can use ordinary chives instead.

INGREDIENTS

650 g (1 lb 7 oz) small new potatoes

salt and freshly ground black pepper

500 g (1 lb) spicy vegetarian sausages

2 tablespoons vegetable oil

1 French shallot (eschalot), chopped

1 large clove garlic, chopped

1 small bunch (20 g/²/₃ oz) fresh parsley, leaves chopped

1 small bunch (20 g/²/₃ oz) fresh garlic chives, chopped

1 teaspoon dijon mustard

3 teaspoons plain (all-purpose) flour

1 tablespoon lemon juice

2 tablespoons white wine vinegar

4 tablespoons olive oil

3 teaspoons caster (superfine) sugar

100 g (3¹/₂ oz) cheddar or cheshire cheese

CHINESE SALAD WITH MINI RICE AND SESAME PATTIES

TIME **30 MINUTES** SERVES **4**

INGREDIENTS

75 g (2^1/$_2$ oz) long-grain rice
200 ml (7 fl oz) vegetable stock
^{1}/$_2$ teaspoon grated orange zest
juice of 1 orange
100 ml (3^1/$_2$ fl oz) peanut
   (groundnut) or vegetable oil
1 teaspoon soy sauce
salt and freshly ground black pepper
^{1}/$_4$ red cabbage (about 250 g/8 oz),
   finely shredded

1 cup (125 g) walnut pieces, broken
   into smaller pieces if large
3 tablespoons sesame seeds
1 egg, lightly beaten
^{1}/$_2$ Chinese cabbage (about 300 g/
   10 oz), shredded
100 g (3^1/$_2$ oz) young, tender bok
   choy leaves, halved lengthwise
   if large

METHOD

1 Put rice and stock in a saucepan and bring to a boil. Stir, cover and simmer gently 10 minutes, or until rice is tender and has absorbed all the stock. Reduce heat to low and leave rice uncovered 1 minute, stirring occasionally, to dry it a little. Tip rice into a bowl, spread out and leave to cool.

2 Meanwhile, put orange zest, juice, half the oil and the soy sauce in a large bowl. Season with salt and pepper and whisk together. Add red cabbage and toss together well, then leave to marinate to soften the cabbage a little, while you finish preparations.

3 Put walnut pieces in a large, dry non-stick frying pan. Toast over medium heat about 3 minutes, turning frequently until golden. Tip onto a plate and set aside.

4 Add sesame seeds and beaten egg to cooked rice. Stir together and season with salt and pepper. Heat remaining oil in the frying pan and drop in small teaspoonfuls of egg and rice mixture to make little pancakes, about 2.5 cm (1 inch) in diameter (you may need to do this in two batches, depending on the size of the pan). Cook over medium–high heat 2 minutes, or until lightly browned, then turn over and cook the other side 1^1/$_2$–2 minutes.

5 Add Chinese cabbage, bok choy and reserved walnuts to marinated red cabbage and toss to coat in the dressing. Divide salad among individual plates, top with rice and sesame pancakes, and serve.

NUTRIENTS PER SERVING

1695 kJ, 405 kcal, 13 g protein, 29 g fat (3 g saturated fat), 24 g carbohydrate

Left Chinese salad with mini rice and sesame patties

TROPICAL SALAD WITH LIME DRESSING

TIME **20 MINUTES** SERVES **4**

INGREDIENTS

1 bunch (250 g/8 oz) watercress,
   thick stems discarded
2 ripe but firm avocados, sliced crosswise
2 ripe but firm papaya, halved, seeds
   removed, sliced lengthwise

DRESSING

grated zest and juice of 1 lime
salt and freshly ground black pepper
^{1}/$_4$ teaspoon sugar
3 tablespoons extra virgin olive oil
3 tablespoons vegetable oil

METHOD

1 To make the dressing, put lime zest, 2 tablespoons lime juice, salt, pepper and sugar in a mixing bowl. Whisk in the oils. Taste and add more lime juice if necessary, then set aside.

2 Arrange watercress, avocados and papaya on individual serving plates. Pour dressing over and serve immediately.

NUTRIENTS PER SERVING

1976 kJ, 472 kcal, 4 g protein, 42 g fat (7 g saturated fat), 20 g carbohydrate

VARIATION

Mangoes can be substituted for the papaya and the watercress replaced with baby spinach leaves.

COOK'S TIP

When choosing an avocado, pick one that feels heavy for its size. An avocado is ripe when it yields to light pressure; it can then be kept for 3 to 4 days in the refrigerator. Unripe avocados will ripen in 1 to 2 days if kept in a warm room.

SNOW PEA AND PICKLED GINGER SALAD

TIME **15 MINUTES** SERVES **4**

INGREDIENTS

350 g (12 oz) snow peas (mangetout), topped and tailed

salt

1 small bunch (20 g/²/₃ oz) fresh chives, snipped

DRESSING

50 g (1³/₄ oz) pickled ginger, shredded

1 tablespoon light olive oil

1 teaspoon sesame oil

freshly ground black pepper

METHOD

1 Put snow peas in a pan of salted boiling water and cook 1–2 minutes, until tender but still crisp. Drain and set aside.
2 To make the dressing, put pickled ginger, olive oil, sesame oil and pepper to taste in a salad bowl and mix well.
3 Add snow peas and toss to coat with the dressing. Scatter chives over the salad and serve.

NUTRIENTS PER SERVING

251 kJ, 60 kcal, 5 g protein, 1 g fat (0.6 g saturated fat), 7 g carbohydrate

VARIATION

You can substitute 1 tablespoon green peppercorns in brine, rinsed and drained but left whole, for the ginger.

COOK'S TIP

Finely sliced pickled ginger, sometimes called sushi ginger, is served with Japanese dishes and may be found in Asian food stores, larger supermarkets and specialty food and health food shops. It teams well with slices of cold ham.

MIXED LEAF, CUCUMBER AND RED ONION SALAD

TIME **10 MINUTES** SERVES **4**

INGREDIENTS

1 curly endive or frisée

1 witlof (Belgian endive)

1 rosso or treviso radicchio

250 g (8 oz) cucumber, peeled and finely sliced

1 small red onion, finely sliced

¹/₂ cup (50 g) walnut halves

DRESSING

1 clove garlic, crushed

2 tablespoons walnut oil

3 teaspoons white wine vinegar

salt and freshly ground black pepper

METHOD

1 Put the leaves of the curly endive or frisée, witlof and radicchio in a large salad bowl and gently mix together.
2 Put cucumber and onion in the bowl, then add the walnuts.
3 To make the dressing, put garlic in a small bowl. Pour in walnut oil and vinegar, add salt and pepper to taste, then whisk well together.
4 Just before serving, trickle the dressing over the salad and toss through gently.

NUTRIENTS PER SERVING

783 kJ, 187 kcal, 4 g protein, 17 g fat (2 g saturated fat), 5 g carbohydrate

CARROT AND GINGER SALAD

TIME **30 MINUTES** SERVES **4**

INGREDIENTS

1 cup (125 g) sultanas (golden raisins)
400 g (14 oz) young carrots, grated
salt
$\frac{1}{2}$ teaspoon honey or sugar
$\frac{1}{2}$ cup (60 g) chopped pecans, peanuts
    (groundnuts) or walnuts

DRESSING

5 cm (2 inch) piece fresh ginger, grated
grated zest and juice of $\frac{1}{2}$ lemon
grated zest and juice of $\frac{1}{2}$ orange
1 cup (250 g) sour cream or natural
    (plain) yogurt

METHOD

1 Put sultanas in a small bowl,
  then cover with boiling water
  and set aside.
2 To make the dressing, put ginger,
  lemon and orange zest and juice
  in a small mixing bowl. Stir in
  sour cream or yogurt until well
  blended, then set aside.
3 Put carrots in a serving bowl.
  Drain sultanas and add to
  the carrots.
4 Stir dressing through carrot and
  sultana mixture. Season with salt,
  add honey or sugar, and pecans,
  peanuts or walnuts, and stir. Serve
  immediately.

NUTRIENTS PER SERVING

1318 kJ, 315 kcal, 7 g protein, 18 g fat
(8 g saturated fat), 35 g carbohydrate

Right Mixed leaf, cucumber and red onion
salad (top); Snow pea and pickled ginger
salad (middle); Carrot and ginger salad (bottom)

CUCUMBER, RADISH AND MELON SALAD

TIME 20 MINUTES SERVES 4

500 g (1 lb) watermelon or honeydew
   melon, peeled and seeds removed,
   diced
100 g (3¹/₂ oz) cucumber, diced
salt
2 teaspoons olive oil
¹/₄ cup (25 g) flaked almonds
100 g (3¹/₂ oz) bean sprouts, trimmed
150 g (5 oz) radishes, quartered
4 spring onions (scallions), sliced
1 bunch (250 g/8 oz) watercress, trimmed

DRESSING

1¹/₂ teaspoons honey
2 tablespoons walnut oil
3 teaspoons cider vinegar
freshly ground black pepper

METHOD

1 Put melon and cucumber in a colander, add a little salt and toss together.
  Place a saucer on top and leave to drain.
2 Heat olive oil in a frying pan and fry almonds until golden, then drain on
  paper towel. Set aside.
3 Put bean sprouts, radishes and spring onions in a large bowl and mix
  together.
4 To make the dressing, whisk honey, walnut oil and vinegar together in a
  small bowl. Season with pepper, then pour over the salad.
5 Arrange watercress in a shallow serving dish. Add melon and cucumber
  to the salad, toss gently, then spoon over the watercress. Scatter almonds
  over the top just before serving.

NUTRIENTS PER SERVING

967 kJ, 231 kcal, 4 g protein, 18 g fat (2 g saturated fat), 15 g carbohydrate

CAESAR SALAD
TIME **25 MINUTES** SERVES **4**

METHOD

1 Put lettuce leaves in a salad bowl.
2 Heat peanut oil and 2 tablespoons olive oil in a frying pan. Add garlic and cubes of bread and fry, stirring, until the croutons are crisp. Drain on paper towel.
3 Cook egg in a small saucepan of boiling water 1 minute. Remove egg from the water and set aside.
4 Put lemon juice, remaining olive oil and salt and pepper to taste in a small bowl, then whisk in the egg.
5 Pour dressing over lettuce and toss, then add anchovies and croutons and toss again. Scatter over parmesan shavings and serve.

INGREDIENTS

2 cos (romaine) lettuces
2 tablespoons peanut (groundnut) oil
6 tablespoons olive oil
2 cloves garlic, crushed
5 thick slices white bread, crusts
    discarded, cut into small cubes
1 large egg
1 tablespoon lemon juice
salt and freshly ground black pepper
8 anchovy fillets, roughly chopped
100 g (3½ oz) parmesan, shaved

NUTRIENTS PER SERVING
2272 kJ, 543 kcal, 18 g protein, 41 g fat (9 g saturated fat), 27 g carbohydrate

SPICY THREE-BEAN SALAD
TIME **25 MINUTES** SERVES **4**

METHOD

1 Cook green beans in a saucepan of salted boiling water 3–5 minutes, then drain and rinse under cold running water. Drain again and tip into a large bowl.

2 Put oil, vinegar, curry powder or paprika, garlic, salt and pepper to taste in a screw-top jar. Shake well to blend.

3 Tip kidney beans and cannellini beans or black-eyed peas into the bowl together with spring onions and mozzarella. Toss with the dressing.

4 Lay tomato slices on a large serving plate and spoon dressed beans and mozzarella on top. Scatter with parsley or coriander. If you have time, chill before serving.

NUTRIENTS PER SERVING

1374 kJ, 328 kcal, 20 g protein, 18 g fat (7 g saturated fat), 20 g carbohydrate

VARIATION

Instead of mozzarella, use cubes of fetta, stilton or cheddar. Add an avocado, cut into chunks.

INGREDIENTS

125 g (4 oz) green beans, halved

2 tablespoons olive oil

2 tablespoons white wine vinegar

1 teaspoon mild curry powder or smoked paprika

1 clove garlic, crushed

$1/2$ teaspoon sea salt

freshly ground black pepper

400 g (14 oz) can red kidney beans, rinsed and drained

400 g (14 oz) cannellini beans or black-eyed peas, rinsed and drained

6 spring onions (scallions), chopped

150 g (5 oz) firm mozzarella, diced or cut into sticks

2 large or 4 medium ripe tomatoes, thinly sliced

4 tablespoons roughly chopped fresh flat-leaf (Italian) parsley or coriander (cilantro) leaves

SUMMER BEEF SALAD

TIME **25 MINUTES** SERVES **4**

INGREDIENTS

$^1/_2$ teaspoon salt

1 small red onion, halved and thinly sliced

100 g (3$^1/_2$ oz) radishes, sliced

1 thick-cut lean rump (round) steak
(about 350 g/12 oz), trimmed of fat,
patted dry

1 tablespoon olive oil

$^1/_4$ teaspoon mixed dried herbs

freshly ground black pepper

2 tablespoons walnut oil

1 tablespoon balsamic vinegar

4 celery stalks, sliced diagonally

125 g (4 oz) rocket (arugula) or mixed
salad leaves

METHOD

1 Stir salt into a bowl of cold water until dissolved. Add onion and radishes and leave to soak while cooking the steak (this will take away some of the heat and sharpness and prevent radishes from discolouring).

2 Heat a chargrill pan or non-stick frying pan until hot. Rub steak on both sides with 2 teaspoons olive oil, then season with herbs and some pepper. Cook steak 2$^1/_2$–3$^1/_2$ minutes on each side, depending on whether you like it medium-rare or medium. Transfer steak to a board and leave it to rest a few minutes.

3 Whisk together remaining olive oil, walnut oil and vinegar in a small bowl.

4 Cut steak into slices about 5 mm ($^1/_4$ inch) thick. Pour any meat juices that have collected into the dressing.

5 Drain onion and radishes well and put in a salad bowl. Add dressing, celery and beef slices. Gently toss everything together. Divide rocket or salad leaves among four plates, then spoon over beef mixture and serve immediately.

NUTRIENTS PER SERVING

1035 kJ, 247 kcal, 20 g protein, 17 g fat (3 g saturated fat), 3 g carbohydrate

VARIATION

You could make a horseradish dressing for the beef salad: whisk together 4 tablespoons light olive oil, the juice of 1 small lemon and 2 teaspoons grated horseradish from a jar.

LAMB, POTATO AND SUN-DRIED TOMATO SALAD

TIME **30 MINUTES** SERVES **4**

INGREDIENTS

4 lamb steaks (about 125 g/4 oz each)

olive oil, for brushing

salt and freshly ground black pepper

750 g (1¹/₂ lb) small new potatoes, halved

350 g (12 oz) green beans, topped and
    tailed, cut into small lengths

5 spring onions (scallions), finely chopped

¹/₃ cup (50 g) semi-dried (sun-blushed)
    tomatoes, coarsely chopped

3 tablespoons chopped fresh mint

5 tablespoons extra virgin olive oil

1 tablespoon balsamic vinegar

1 tablespoon lemon juice

1 teaspoon dijon mustard

1 teaspoon honey

METHOD

1   Brush lamb steaks lightly with oil and season with salt and black pepper.
    Heat a heavy-based frying pan over medium heat and add lamb. Cook
    5–8 minutes depending on thickness, turning once, until slightly pink in
    the centre. Remove from heat, cover lightly with foil and leave to rest
    5 minutes.
2   Meanwhile, cook potatoes in a saucepan of lightly salted boiling water
    10–12 minutes, or until tender. Add beans for the final 4 minutes of
    cooking time.
3   Drain potatoes and beans and put in a large serving dish with spring
    onions and semi-dried tomatoes. Slice lamb and add to the vegetables,
    reserving any meat juices.
4   Put 2 tablespoons mint, the oil, vinegar, lemon juice, mustard and honey
    in a screw-top jar. Shake together until well mixed. Add meat juices, then
    pour over meat and vegetables. Toss lightly to coat evenly, sprinkle with
    the remaining mint and serve warm.

NUTRIENTS PER SERVING

2349 kJ, 561 kcal, 36 g protein, 31 g fat (6 g saturated fat), 33 g carbohydrate

VARIATION

Instead of potatoes, use 350 g (12 oz) pasta shapes, such as penne or fusilli,
cooked following the instructions on the packet. Toss in the dressing while
still warm.

SIZZLING CHICKEN SALAD WITH DATES AND MINTED YOGURT

TIME **20 MINUTES** SERVES **4**

INGREDIENTS

4 boneless, skinless chicken breasts
  (about 125 g/4 oz each)
salt and freshly ground black pepper
2 cloves garlic, crushed
1 teaspoon ground mace or nutmeg
3 tablespoons olive oil
1 cos (romaine) or iceberg lettuce,
  torn into pieces
150 g (5 oz) rocket (arugula)
4 spring onions (scallions), sliced
400 g (14 oz) can or jar artichoke hearts,
  drained and halved
8 sprigs fresh mint, leaves chopped,
  plus extra, to garnish
200 g (7 oz) low-fat natural (plain) yogurt
4 tablespoons mixed seeds, such
  as sunflower, sesame, pepitas
  (pumpkin) and linseed
100 g (3½ oz) dried stoned dates, sliced

METHOD

1 Preheat grill (broiler) to high. Put chicken in a shallow ovenproof dish or the grill pan. Sprinkle with a little salt and pepper, the garlic, mace or nutmeg and oil, then turn the chicken over a few times to distribute the seasonings.

2 Slide dish or pan under the grill and cook chicken 10 minutes, turning once, until well browned on both sides and cooked through. Test by piercing the thickest part with the point of a knife; the juices should run clear and the flesh should be white, not pink. Remove from heat and leave in the dish or pan.

3 Meanwhile, mix lettuce, rocket, spring onions and artichokes. Divide among four large plates. Mix mint into yogurt. Set aside.

4 Turn chicken over and sprinkle with seeds, pressing them on with a spoon. Grill 10–20 seconds to heat and brown the seeds. Add dates and stir them with the seeds and juices around the chicken.

5 Slice chicken and arrange with the dates and seeds on top of each salad. Spoon over cooking juices, drizzle with mint and yogurt dressing, and serve immediately, garnished with extra mint.

NUTRIENTS PER SERVING

2106 kJ, 503 kcal, 27.5 g protein, 38 g fat (5 g saturated fat), 26 g carbohydrate

VARIATION

Replace dates with dried figs, and use turkey instead of chicken.

SALMON AND ASPARAGUS SALAD

TIME **25 MINUTES** SERVES **4**

INGREDIENTS

1 tablespoon olive or vegetable oil
4 salmon fillets (about 750 g/1¹/₂ lb in
 total), skinned, bones discarded, diced
200 g (7 oz) asparagus spears, trimmed,
 cut into 5 cm (2 inch) pieces
1 large celery stalk, finely sliced
250 g (8 oz) mixed salad leaves

DRESSING

2 large mangoes, stoned and peeled,
 diced
4 fresh chives, snipped
100 g (3¹/₂ oz) natural (plain) yogurt
1 teaspoon wholegrain mustard
1 tablespoon pernod or ouzo
freshly ground black pepper

METHOD

1 Heat oil in a frying pan and stir-fry salmon 2–3 minutes, until just cooked
 through and lightly browned. Drain on paper towel.
2 Blanch asparagus in a large saucepan of boiling water 2 minutes. Rinse
 under cold water and drain.
3 To make the dressing, put mangoes, chives, yogurt, mustard and pernod or
 ouzo in a food processor or blender and process until dressing is smooth.
 Add pepper to taste.
4 Put celery in a salad bowl with salmon and asparagus. Pour dressing over
 the top, holding a little back in case there is more than you need. Toss
 gently, taking care not to break up the salmon.
5 Arrange salad leaves on four individual plates and top with salmon salad.

NUTRIENTS PER SERVING

2452 kJ, 586 kcal, 48 g protein, 29 g fat (5 g saturated fat), 33 g carbohydrate

VARIATION

You can use dry vermouth as a substitute for the aniseed flavour of the
pernod or ouzo.

COOK'S TIP

You need about 500 g (1 lb) diced mango flesh for the dressing. The dressing
can be made and the fish cooked in advance and both put in the refrigerator,
leaving the salad to be assembled at the last minute.

WARM BROAD BEAN AND FETTA SALAD
TIME **20 MINUTES** SERVES **4**

METHOD

1 Put broad beans in a saucepan of boiling water and cook about 3 minutes, until just tender. Drain well.
2 Meanwhile, heat oil in a large non-stick frying pan. Add tomatoes and garlic and gently cook 2–3 minutes, or until softened. Remove pan from heat.
3 Add fetta to frying pan with cooked beans, parsley, olives, lemon juice and a few grinds of black pepper. Stir together, then serve warm.

NUTRIENTS PER SERVING
1364 kJ, 326 kcal, 18 g protein, 24 g fat (9 g saturated fat), 11 g carbohydrate

COOK'S TIP
Double-peel broad beans for the best flavour and texture. To do this, leave boiled beans until they are cool enough to handle, then, using a pinching motion, slip off the thick grey-green skins to reveal the bright green, tender bean within. Reheat briefly in hot water if you are serving them warm.

INGREDIENTS
500 g (1 lb) shelled fresh or frozen
    broad (fava) beans
2 tablespoons olive oil
250 g (8 oz) small tomatoes, such as
    roma (plum) tomatoes, cut into wedges
2 cloves garlic, crushed
200 g (7 oz) fetta, diced
2 tablespoons chopped fresh parsley
12 pitted kalamata olives or other pitted
    black olives
1 tablespoon lemon juice
freshly ground black pepper

VEGETARIAN COUSCOUS SALAD

TIME **20 MINUTES** SERVES **4**

INGREDIENTS

3 tablespoons oil from the jar of
　sun-dried tomatoes
250 g (8 oz) smoked tofu, diced
1 tablespoon olive oil
4 spring onions (scallions), sliced
1 clove garlic, crushed
450 ml (15 fl oz) vegetable stock
250 g (8 oz) couscous
75 g (2^1/$_2$ oz) sultanas (golden raisins)
1 pinch ground cinnamon
2 teaspoons red wine vinegar
2 teaspoons harissa paste
6 sun-dried tomatoes in oil, chopped
freshly ground black pepper
50 g (1^3/$_4$ oz) toasted flaked almonds
1 tablespoon chopped fresh flat-leaf
　(Italian) parsley, to garnish

METHOD

1　Heat 1 tablespoon sun-dried tomato oil in a frying pan. Add tofu and stir-fry about 2 minutes, or until golden brown. Remove and drain on paper towel.

2　Heat olive oil in pan. Add spring onions and garlic and stir-fry over medium heat 2 minutes. Add stock and bring to a boil. Remove from heat and stir in couscous, sultanas and cinnamon. Cover and leave 3 minutes, then stir in tofu. Cover and leave 2 minutes.

3　Whisk together remaining sun-dried tomato oil, vinegar, harissa, sun-dried tomatoes and pepper in a small bowl.

4　Drizzle dressing over couscous, then mix and fluff up with a fork. Spoon onto plates and scatter with almonds and parsley.

NUTRIENTS PER SERVING

2521 kJ, 602 kcal, 17 g protein, 29 g fat
(4 g saturated fat), 68 g carbohydrate

MIDDLE EASTERN SALAD

TIME **20 MINUTES** SERVES **4**

INGREDIENTS

2 large white or sesame seed pitas
4 tablespoons olive oil
juice of 1 lemon
salt and freshly ground black pepper
2 tablespoons chopped fresh
　coriander (cilantro) leaves
2 tablespoons chopped fresh mint,
　plus extra leaves, to garnish

^{1}/$_2$ Lebanese or other small
　cucumber, diced
4 large tomatoes, quartered, cored
　and chopped
4 spring onions (scallions), sliced
　diagonally
400 g (14 oz) can black-eyed peas or
　chickpeas, rinsed and drained

METHOD

1　Warm pitas in the toaster 1 minute to make them easier to open up, then split each in half using a knife. Toast the four halves 1 minute, or until crisp and lightly browned. Tear into bite-sized pieces.

2　Put oil and lemon juice in a small jug and whisk together with a fork. Season with salt and pepper to taste and stir in coriander and chopped mint.

3　Put cucumber, tomatoes, spring onions and black-eyed peas or chickpeas in a large bowl. Drizzle over the dressing, then toss together until well mixed. Immediately before serving, add pita pieces and toss through. Garnish with mint leaves.

NUTRIENTS PER SERVING

1586 kJ, 379 kcal, 10 g protein, 19 g fat (2.5 g saturated fat), 41 g carbohydrate

VARIATION

Instead of spring onions, use a finely chopped small red onion. Replace the black-eyed peas or chickpeas with a 200 g (7 oz) can French-style green (puy) lentils, drained and rinsed.

Right Middle Eastern salad

SPINACH AND BABY CORN SALAD
TIME **15 MINUTES** SERVES **4**

INGREDIENTS

100 g (3¹/₂ oz) baby corn,
 halved crosswise
salt
100 g (3¹/₂ oz) rocket (arugula)
250 g (8 oz) baby spinach leaves

DRESSING

1 avocado (about 125 g/4 oz)
1 clove garlic, crushed
2 tablespoons extra virgin olive oil
3 teaspoons white wine vinegar
1 teaspoon sugar
1 teaspoon Tabasco sauce
salt

METHOD

1 Put baby corn in a small saucepan of salted boiling water and simmer
 1 minute, then drain.
2 To make the dressing, scoop avocado flesh into a large salad bowl. Add
 garlic, oil, vinegar, sugar and Tabasco. Season to taste with salt, then stir
 together: some of the avocado will merge into the oil, but some small
 chunks should remain.
3 Add corn, rocket and spinach leaves to the dressing and toss well. Serve as
 soon as possible.

NUTRIENTS PER SERVING

728 kJ, 174 kcal, 3 g protein, 15 g fat (3 g saturated fat), 8 g carbohydrate

VARIATION

Peppery watercress makes a good substitute for the rocket.

THAI CHICKEN SALAD
TIME **25 MINUTES** SERVES **4**

METHOD

1 Preheat grill (broiler) to medium. Grill chicken 5–6 minutes, turning once, then cut into fine strips.
2 Put chicken in a bowl and pour over lime juice, sweet chilli sauce and fish sauce. Toss to combine well. Add spring onions, lemongrass and mint and toss again to combine well.
3 Arrange salad leaves and avocado on four individual plates. Sprinkle avocado with lemon juice to prevent discoloration. Spoon chicken mixture over the salad just before serving.

NUTRIENTS PER SERVING
1006 kJ, 240 kcal, 14 g protein, 17 g fat (4 g saturated fat), 4 g carbohydrate

VARIATION
Instead of chicken, you can use lamb fillets; if you do, omit the fish sauce.

COOK'S TIP
You could brush the chicken with a little oil and cook on a hot chargrill pan or plate, turning once.

INGREDIENTS

2 boneless, skinless chicken breasts
$1/3$ cup (80 ml) lime juice
1 tablespoon sweet chilli sauce
1 tablespoon fish sauce
6 spring onions (scallions), white part only
3 lemongrass stems, white part only, finely chopped
4 tablespoons chopped fresh mint
250 g (8 oz) mixed salad leaves
1 large avocado, sliced
1 teaspoon lemon juice

CHAPTER 4

Pasta & Noodles

SPICY NAPOLITANA SPAGHETTI

TIME **30 MINUTES** SERVES **4**

INGREDIENTS

2 tablespoons olive oil

1 large onion, finely chopped

1 good pinch caster (superfine) sugar

2 x 410 g (15 oz) cans tomatoes

1/4 teaspoon dried red chilli flakes, or to taste

freshly ground black pepper

400 g (14 oz) spaghetti

400 g (14 oz) roasted red or mixed capsicums (bell peppers), from a jar, drained and sliced

50 g (1 3/4 oz) stuffed green olives, rinsed, drained and halved

grated parmesan or Italian-style hard cheese, to serve

METHOD

1 Heat oil in a frying pan, add onion and sugar, and cook gently 5 minutes, or until just softened. Meanwhile, tip tomatoes into a food processor or blender and purée.

2 Add tomatoes and chilli flakes to onion in the pan and season well with pepper (the olives will probably add enough salt to the dish). Bring to a boil, reduce heat to medium and boil gently 20 minutes, stirring occasionally.

3 Meanwhile, cook spaghetti in a large saucepan of salted boiling water, following packet instructions.

4 Drain pasta and tip into a large warmed serving bowl. Spoon over sauce, add capsicums and olives, and toss gently to combine. Serve immediately with grated parmesan or Italian-style hard cheese.

NUTRIENTS PER SERVING

2491 kJ, 595 kcal, 19 g protein, 21 g fat (5 g saturated fat), 81 g carbohydrate

VARIATION

Instead of the capsicums, use 200 g (7 oz) frozen broad (fava) beans, boiled 4 minutes, or following packet instructions, or a 280 g (10 oz) jar or can of artichoke hearts, drained and cut into quarters.

FETTUCCINE WITH CRAB
AND FRESH ASPARAGUS
TIME **30 MINUTES** SERVES **4**

METHOD

1 Cook fettuccine in a large saucepan of salted boiling water 2–3 minutes, until al dente.
2 Meanwhile, blanch asparagus in a separate saucepan of boiling water 3 minutes. Drain and set aside.
3 When pasta is ready, drain and return to the cooking pot. Add asparagus, crabmeat, oil, parsley and sage; toss well.
4 Spoon pasta into heated bowls and top with parmesan and a generous grinding of black pepper.

NUTRIENTS PER SERVING

1635 kJ, 391 kcal, 21 g protein, 20 g fat (6 g saturated fat), 33 g carbohydrate

COOK'S TIP

Dried fettuccine can be used if fresh is difficult to find. Follow packet instructions, but allow two to three times the cooking time, and start taste-testing after 5 minutes.

INGREDIENTS

500 g (1 lb) fresh fettuccine

2 bunches asparagus (about 300 g/10 oz in total), trimmed and sliced diagonally in half

200 g (7 oz) fresh cooked crabmeat

3 tablespoons olive oil

$1/2$ cup finely chopped fresh flat-leaf (Italian) parsley

1 tablespoon finely chopped fresh sage

75 g ($2^1/2$ oz) parmesan, shaved

freshly ground black pepper

SPEEDY MACARONI WITH PEAS AND GOAT'S CHEESE

TIME **15 MINUTES** SERVES **4**

INGREDIENTS

500 g (1 lb) fresh egg macaroni
   or dry macaroni
1²/₃ cups (250 g) frozen peas
grated zest of 1 lemon
juice of ¹/₂ lemon
salt and freshly ground black pepper
125 g (4 oz) creamy goat's cheese,
   crumbled or diced

METHOD

1 Cook macaroni in a saucepan of boiling salted water 4 minutes, or following packet instructions. Add peas for the final 3 minutes of cooking time. Drain, reserving about 5 tablespoons of the cooking water. Tip pasta and peas into a warmed serving bowl.

2 Put reserved cooking water, lemon zest and juice, and salt and pepper to taste in a bowl. Stir to combine thoroughly, then pour over the pasta and peas.

3 Add goat's cheese to bowl and toss gently to combine the ingredients, Serve immediately.

NUTRIENTS PER SERVING

2262 kJ, 540 kcal, 24 g protein, 7 g fat
(4 g saturated fat), 93 g carbohydrate

COOK'S TIP

Serve this macaroni dish with a tomato and mixed leaf salad.

FARFALLE WITH BROCCOLI AND ANCHOVIES

TIME **25 MINUTES** SERVES **4**

INGREDIENTS

400 g (14 oz) farfalle or other
   pasta shapes
300 g (10 oz) broccoli florets,
   thick stalks discarded, cut into
   small florets
45 g (1¹/₂ oz) can anchovy fillets,
   drained
2 tablespoons low-fat milk
2 tablespoons olive oil

4 large cloves garlic, crushed
1 small bunch (20 g/²/₃ oz) fresh
   flat-leaf (Italian) parsley, leaves
   chopped
¹/₄ teaspoon dried red chilli flakes
freshly ground black pepper
20 g (²/₃ oz) unsalted butter
grated parmesan, to serve (optional)

METHOD

1 Cook pasta in a large saucepan of salted boiling water, following packet instructions. Add broccoli to pasta for the final minute of cooking. Reserve 100 ml (3¹/₂ fl oz) cooking water, then drain pasta and broccoli thoroughly and set aside.

2 While pasta is cooking, soak anchovies in milk 5 minutes to remove some of the salt. Drain, then chop.

3 Heat oil in the warm pasta pan and add anchovies, garlic, parsley and dried red chilli flakes. Stir over medium heat 2 minutes.

4 Add pasta and broccoli to pan with reserved cooking water. Toss gently and season with plenty of pepper. Add butter and toss until melted. Transfer to warmed serving bowls and serve immediately with parmesan, if you like.

NUTRIENTS PER SERVING

2278 kJ, 544 kcal, 22 g protein, 19 g fat (7 g saturated fat), 70 g carbohydrate

VARIATION

Add 1 tablespoon drained capers or ¹/₃ cup (50 g) semi-dried (sun-blushed) tomatoes, chopped, to the pan with the anchovies and flavourings in step 3.

Right Farfalle with broccoli and anchovies

PAPPARDELLE WITH CHICKEN LIVERS AND PORT

TIME **25 MINUTES** SERVES **4 AS A STARTER**

INGREDIENTS

500 g (1 lb) fresh chicken livers

2 tablespoons olive oil

1 small onion, chopped

2 cloves garlic, crushed

2 tablespoons chopped fresh parsley

1 teaspoon chopped fresh sage

250 g (8 oz) fresh pappardelle or tagliatelle or 175 g (6 oz) dried pasta

2 teaspoons vegetable oil

4 tablespoons port

1 tablespoon butter

salt and freshly ground black pepper

METHOD

1 Cut away any discoloured areas and tough sinews from chicken livers, then slice into large pieces and set aside.

2 Heat olive oil in a frying pan over low heat. Add onion and garlic and fry gently, 5 minutes, or until transparent. Stir in parsley and sage and fry gently.

3 Meanwhile, cook pasta in a large saucepan of salted boiling water with the vegetable oil until al dente, following packet instructions. Fresh pasta will take about 3 minutes, dried pasta will take 10–12 minutes. Drain and keep warm.

4 Meanwhile, increase heat under saucepan with onion. Add chicken livers and stir-fry until nicely browned. Pour in port and boil vigorously until liquid has reduced by half.

5 Stir in butter and season with salt and pepper. Add chicken livers to the pasta, toss gently together and serve.

NUTRIENTS PER SERVING

1817 kJ, 434 kcal, 28 g protein, 21 g fat (6 g saturated fat), 31 g carbohydrate

VARIATION

Duck livers can be used instead of chicken livers, and Marsala instead of the port.

COOK'S TIP

For a main course, serve with crusty bread and a green salad.

GNOCCHI WITH TOMATO AND HERB SAUCE

TIME **30 MINUTES** SERVES **4**

INGREDIENTS

1 1/2 tablespoons olive oil

2 cloves garlic, crushed

6 spring onions (scallions), thinly sliced

1/2 teaspoon caster (superfine) sugar

1 teaspoon balsamic vinegar

410 g (15 oz) can chopped tomatoes

2 sprigs fresh herbs, such as rosemary and oregano (optional)

salt and freshly ground black pepper

2 tablespoons red capsicum (bell pepper) pesto

500 g (1 lb) gnocchi

1/3 cup (50 g) pistachios, roughly chopped

1/4 cup (25 g) grated parmesan

METHOD

1 Heat 1 tablespoon oil in a large saucepan. Add garlic and spring onions. Cook gently 2–3 minutes, or until tender. Sprinkle over sugar and vinegar, then add tomatoes and fresh herbs, if using. Cook uncovered 10 minutes, or until thick and pulpy. Season to taste with salt and pepper, then stir through pesto.

2 When the sauce is almost ready, simmer gnocchi in a large pan of salted boiling water with the remaining olive oil 2–3 minutes, or following packet instructions, stirring gently once or twice during cooking. The gnocchi are cooked when they rise to the surface.

3 Drain gnocchi and stir into sauce. Spoon onto warmed plates, scatter with pistachios and parmesan, and serve.

NUTRIENTS PER SERVING

1827 kJ, 436 kcal, 11 g protein, 18 g fat (3 g saturated fat), 58 g carbohydrate

Left Pappardelle with chicken livers and port

SPAGHETTI WITH ARTICHOKES AND BROAD BEANS

TIME **20 MINUTES** SERVES **4**

INGREDIENTS

400 g (14 oz) spaghetti

250 g (8 oz) frozen small broad (fava) beans

400 g (14 oz) can or jar artichoke hearts, drained

50 g (1³/₄ oz) semi-dried (sun-blushed) tomatoes, chopped

4 tablespoons pesto

freshly ground black pepper

grated parmesan, to serve

METHOD

1 Cook spaghetti in a large saucepan of salted boiling water, following packet instructions. Add broad beans to the pan for the final 5 minutes of cooking time.

2 While pasta is cooking, cut each artichoke heart into six pieces. Drain pasta and beans, reserving about 100 ml (3¹/₂ fl oz) cooking water. Transfer pasta and beans to a large warmed serving bowl. Add artichoke hearts and tomatoes.

3 Combine pesto with reserved cooking water and spoon over the pasta. Season with plenty of pepper, then toss gently to combine all ingredients. Serve immediately with a bowl of grated parmesan.

NUTRIENTS PER SERVING

2296 kJ, 548 kcal, 26 g protein, 15 g fat (5 g saturated fat), 76 g carbohydrate

COOK'S TIP

If you have time to prepare them, you can use fresh broad beans for this recipe. You will need 1 kg (2 lb) fresh beans in their pods.

CHILLI PENNE WITH BUTTERNUT PUMPKIN

TIME **30 MINUTES** SERVES **4**

INGREDIENTS

350 g (12 oz) penne

1 kg (2 lb) butternut pumpkin (squash), peeled and cut into chunks

1 tablespoon olive oil

¹/₄ teaspoon dried red chilli flakes, or to taste

¹/₄ teaspoon cumin seeds, or to taste

150 g (5 oz) soft goat's cheese, crumbled

salt and freshly ground black pepper

¹/₂ cup (50 g) grated parmesan or Italian-style hard cheese

METHOD

1 Cook penne and pumpkin in a large saucepan of salted boiling water 10–12 minutes, or until pumpkin is soft and pasta is tender. Reserve 100 ml (3¹/₂ fl oz) cooking water, then drain well.

2 Warm oil in a frying pan over low heat. Stir in chilli flakes and cumin seeds. Cook 1 minute, then remove pan from heat.

3 Return pasta and pumpkin to pan and add reserved cooking water. Combine gently. Add crumbled goat's cheese, season to taste and toss well. Divide among warmed serving bowls and top with the parmesan or Italian-style hard cheese. Serve immediately.

NUTRIENTS PER SERVING

2588 kJ, 618 kcal, 28 g protein, 22 g fat (12 g saturated fat), 77 g carbohydrate

COOK'S TIP

Butternut pumpkin will keep uncut for several weeks as long as the skin is not damaged. Store in a cool, dark place and check its condition often.

Right Chilli penne with butternut pumpkin

PASTA WITH RUSTIC SAUCE
TIME 25 MINUTES SERVES 4

INGREDIENTS

1 tablespoon olive oil

1 onion, roughly chopped

1 clove garlic, crushed

500 g (1 lb) lean pork sausages

2 tablespoons brandy, white wine
   or chicken stock

410 g (15 oz) can chopped tomatoes

salt and freshly ground black pepper

500 g (1 lb) fresh penne or
   350 g (12 oz) dried penne

1 cup (150 g) frozen peas

1 small bunch (20 g/²⁄₃ oz) chives,
   snipped, to garnish

grated parmesan, to serve

METHOD

1 Heat oil in a large frying pan. Add onion and garlic and cook over medium heat about 4 minutes, stirring occasionally, until onion is soft.

2 Meanwhile, coarsely chop sausages, or remove skins and break up meat with a fork. Add sausages to the frying pan and stir over high heat 7 minutes, or until well browned all over.

3 Add brandy, wine or stock and tomatoes, and season to taste with salt and pepper. Bring to a boil, reduce heat and simmer 10 minutes, stirring occasionally.

4 Meanwhile, cook fresh pasta and peas in a large saucepan of salted boiling water 4–5 minutes, or following packet instructions, until pasta is al dente. If using dried pasta, cook 6–7 minutes before adding peas.

5 Drain pasta and peas and toss through tomato sauce. Taste and adjust the seasoning, garnish with chives and serve with parmesan.

NUTRIENTS PER SERVING

2812 kJ, 672 kcal, 36 g protein, 23 g fat (8 g saturated fat), 80 g carbohydrate

COOK'S TIP

The choice of sausage is crucial to the success of this dish. Use a really meaty, coarse-cut variety, or a very high-quality sausage meat from an Italian butcher.

PAGLIA E FIENO WITH SMOKED SALMON
TIME 25 MINUTES SERVES 6 AS A STARTER

METHOD

1 Bring wine or vermouth to a boil in a frying pan and boil 1–2 minutes, until the liquid has reduced by half. Stir in onion and cook about 4 minutes, until softened, then reduce heat to very low.

2 Cook pasta in a large saucepan of salted boiling water, following packet instructions, until al dente. Fresh pasta will take 4–5 minutes, dried pasta will take 10–12 minutes.

3 Meanwhile, add smoked salmon to the onion and wine and heat through very gently. Stir in dill and capers.

4 As soon as pasta is cooked, drain well and transfer to a large serving bowl.

5 Season salmon mixture with pepper to taste (it won't need any salt), then spoon over the pasta. Stir through gently and serve.

NUTRIENTS PER SERVING

1042 kJ, 249 kcal, 21 g protein, 4 g fat (<1 g saturated fat), 31 g carbohydrate

COOK'S TIP

Serve the pasta as a starter for six people, or make it into a substantial main course for four by adding a mixed green side salad or a plate of thinly sliced tomatoes with fennel, black olives and lemon and olive oil dressing.

INGREDIENTS

6 tablespoons white wine or dry vermouth

1 small onion, chopped

375 g (13 oz) fresh paglia e fieno or other narrow yellow and green pasta, such as linguine or fettuccine, or 300 g (10 oz) dried yellow and green pasta

350 g (12 oz) smoked salmon or smoked salmon trimmings, cut into small strips

4 tablespoons chopped fresh dill

2 teaspoons capers, rinsed and squeezed dry, roughly chopped

freshly ground black pepper

CHARGRILLED VEGETABLE, PESTO AND FETTA PASTA
TIME 30 MINUTES SERVES 4

INGREDIENTS

1 large or 2 medium zucchini (courgettes), sliced crosswise

1 eggplant (aubergine), sliced crosswise

1 red and 1 yellow capsicum (bell pepper), seeds removed, thickly sliced

1 red onion, cut into thin wedges

100 ml (3 1/2 fl oz) olive oil

2 cloves garlic, crushed

freshly ground black pepper

50 g (1 3/4 oz) pine nuts or walnuts

400 g (14 oz) tagliatelle

4 tablespoons pesto

200 g (7 oz) fetta, cubed

METHOD

1 Preheat grill (broiler) to medium–high. Put zucchini, eggplant, capsicums and onion in a large bowl and drizzle with oil. Add garlic and season with black pepper. Mix well, then spread vegetables in the grill pan. Grill 20 minutes, or until softened and lightly charred, turning occasionally and removing any vegetables that are cooked before the others. Alternatively, cook vegetables on a medium–hot chargrill pan or plate until softened and lightly charred, turning occasionally.

2 While vegetables are grilling, put pine nuts or walnuts in a small dry frying pan and toast over medium heat, tossing regularly, 2–3 minutes, or until golden brown. Tip onto a plate and set aside.

3 Towards the end of grilling, cook tagliatelle in a saucepan of salted boiling water 8 minutes, or following packet instructions, until al dente. Drain thoroughly and return to the pan.

4 Add chargrilled vegetables, pesto, fetta and reserved nuts to the pasta. Gently toss everything together and serve at once.

NUTRIENTS PER SERVING

3653 kJ, 873 kcal, 26 g protein, 52 g fat (13 g saturated fat), 75 g carbohydrate

FUSILLI WITH HAM AND GORGONZOLA
TIME **25 MINUTES** SERVES **4**

INGREDIENTS
250 g (8 oz) button mushrooms, sliced
1 cup (250 ml) thick (heavy/double) cream
1/4 teaspoon freshly grated nutmeg
freshly ground black pepper
500 g (1 lb) fresh fusilli or other small
    pasta shapes
60 g (2 oz) gorgonzola cheese, crumbled
200 g (7 oz) thick slices smoked ham,
    fat and rind discarded, diced
3 tablespoons chopped fresh flat-leaf
    (Italian) parsley
1 1/2 teaspoons poppyseeds

METHOD
1 Put mushrooms, cream, nutmeg and some pepper in a heavy-based medium saucepan. Bring to a boil, reduce heat to medium and cook, stirring often, until cream starts to thicken.
2 Meanwhile, boil pasta in a large saucepan of salted boiling water 3–5 minutes, until al dente.
3 When cream is thick enough to coat the back of a spoon, remove pan from heat, add gorgonzola cheese and stir until it melts.
4 Add ham, return pan to heat and warm through gently. Stir in parsley. Set aside to keep warm.
5 Drain pasta, transfer to a warmed serving bowl and sprinkle with poppyseeds. Pour over the sauce, toss gently and serve.

NUTRIENTS PER SERVING
2733 kJ, 653 kcal, 25 g protein, 39 g fat (22 g saturated fat), 56 g carbohydrate

COOK'S TIP
Grating fresh nutmeg straight into a dish gives the food far more flavour than using the ready-ground variety.

SPAGHETTI ALLA VONGOLE
TIME **30 MINUTES** SERVES **4**

INGREDIENTS
1 1/2 tablespoons olive oil
1 large clove garlic, crushed
410 g (15 oz) can chopped tomatoes
2 kg (4 lb) fresh clams (vongole),
    rinsed well, or 290 g (10 oz) can
    clams, drained

3 tablespoons dry white wine
350 g (12 oz) spaghetti
salt and freshly ground black pepper
2 tablespoons chopped fresh parsley,
    to garnish (optional)

METHOD
1 Heat oil in a saucepan. Add garlic and fry briefly, then add tomatoes and cook over medium heat, stirring occasionally, 20 minutes, or until reduced to a thick sauce.
2 If using fresh clams in their shells, add to sauce for the final 5 minutes and cook, covered, shaking pan occasionally, until clams open (discard any unopened clams). Remove from heat as soon as the clams open.
3 Meanwhile, cook spaghetti in a large saucepan of salted boiling water, following packet instructions.
4 If using canned clams, stir clams into the sauce and heat through gently, without allowing it to boil. Season the clam sauce with salt and pepper.
5 Drain spaghetti, transfer to a serving bowl or individual plates and spoon over the clam sauce. Sprinkle with parsley, if using.

NUTRIENTS PER SERVING
1737 kJ, 415 kcal, 18 g protein, 8 g fat (1 g saturated fat), 70 g carbohydrate

COOK'S TIP
If using fresh clams, look for shells that are closed, or that close when tapped, and have a pleasant fresh sea smell. Check with your fishmonger to make sure that they have been purged.

Left Spaghetti alla vongole (top); Fusilli with ham and gorgonzola (bottom)

PASTA WITH BROAD BEANS, ARTICHOKES AND SPINACH

TIME **30 MINUTES** SERVES **4**

INGREDIENTS

2 tablespoons olive oil

1 onion, chopped

1 large clove garlic, crushed

1 red capsicum (bell pepper), halved, seeds removed, sliced

410 g (15 oz) can chopped tomatoes

1 pinch dried oregano

1/2 teaspoon soft brown sugar

freshly ground black pepper

200 g (7 oz) pasta shapes, such as farfalle, shells or rigatoni

1 ciabatta or other crusty Italian loaf, to serve

1 2/3 cups (250 g) frozen broad (fava) beans

350 g (12 oz) English spinach or silverbeet (Swiss chard), stalks discarded

400 g (14 oz) can artichoke hearts, drained and quartered

parmesan, to serve

METHOD

1 Preheat oven to its lowest setting. Heat oil in a large saucepan. Add onion and garlic and fry gently 5 minutes, until soft. Add capsicum and fry a further 2 minutes.

2 Stir in tomatoes, oregano, sugar and some pepper. Bring to a boil, then partially cover and simmer about 10 minutes.

3 Meanwhile, cook pasta in a large saucepan of salted boiling water, following packet instructions.

4 Put ciabatta in the oven to heat through.

5 Add broad beans to the tomato sauce and simmer 3 minutes. Add spinach or silverbeet leaves and cook a further minute.

6 Drain pasta. Add pasta and artichokes to the sauce and heat through 1–2 minutes. Turn into a warmed serving bowl, grate or shave some parmesan over the top and serve with the hot bread.

NUTRIENTS PER SERVING

3185 kJ, 761 kcal, 26 g protein, 32 g fat (6 g saturated fat), 92 g carbohydrate

COOK'S TIP

You can use canned artichoke bottoms (fonds d'artichaut), the nutty-tasting chunk from the bottom of the artichoke that has no leaves attached, instead of artichoke hearts, if you prefer. Cut them into slices instead of quarters and add in step 6.

GARLIC SEAFOOD PASTA

TIME **30 MINUTES** SERVES **4**

INGREDIENTS

400 g (14 oz) linguine

2 tablespoons olive oil

3 cloves garlic, crushed

4 tablespoons dry white wine
   or vermouth

250 g (8 oz) red cherry tomatoes,
   quartered

500 g (1 lb) mixed seafood
   (marinara mix)

3 tablespoons crème fraîche or
   light sour cream

salt and freshly ground black pepper

25 g (1 oz) fresh flat-leaf (Italian)
   parsley, leaves roughly chopped

METHOD

1 Cook linguine in a large saucepan of salted boiling water, following packet instructions.
2 While pasta is cooking, heat oil in a frying pan. Add garlic and stir in wine or vermouth. Simmer gently 1 minute, then stir in tomatoes. Add seafood and return to a simmer. Cook, stirring occasionally, 4 minutes, or until tomatoes have started to soften, prawns (shrimp) have turned pink and fish flakes easily. Stir in crème fraîche or sour cream, heat through gently and season to taste.
3 Drain pasta and transfer to a large warmed serving bowl. Spoon sauce over pasta. Add parsley and gently toss until thoroughly combined. Serve immediately.

NUTRIENTS PER SERVING

2592 kJ, 619 kcal, 33 g protein, 18 g fat (7 g saturated fat), 76 g carbohydrate

COOK'S TIP

Mixed seafood usually contains a combination of prawns, mussels, calamari or squid, fish and scallops.

Left Garlic seafood pasta

SEAFOOD AND CHILLI NOODLES

TIME **20 MINUTES** SERVES **4**

INGREDIENTS

2 tablespoons olive oil

500 g (1 lb) mixed seafood (marinara mix)

200 g (7 oz) frozen soybeans

3 spring onions (scallions), cut into
   short lengths

2 cloves garlic, chopped

1 red chilli, seeds removed, finely chopped,

3 cm (1¼ inch) piece fresh ginger, grated

1 tablespoon soy sauce

100 ml (3½ fl oz) vegetable stock

400 g (14 oz) dried medium egg noodles
   or 300 g (10 oz) wok-ready hokkien
   (egg) or udon (rice) noodles

METHOD

1 Heat oil in a frying pan and stir-fry mixed seafood 1 minute. Add soybeans and cook 1 minute. Add spring onions, garlic, chilli and ginger and cook 2 minutes.
2 Stir in soy sauce and vegetable stock. Cook a further 2 minutes, or until prawns (shrimp) have turned pink, fish has started to flake and vegetables are tender.
3 Meanwhile, cook dried egg noodles in boiling water, following packet instructions. Drain, then toss through the sauce and serve. Alternatively, add the wok-ready hokkien or udon noodles directly to the sauce. Stir-fry 1–2 minutes, or until hot.

NUTRIENTS PER SERVING

2813 kJ, 672 kcal, 51 g protein, 18 g fat (3 g saturated fat), 75 g carbohydrate

VEGETABLE PRIMAVERA
TIME 30 MINUTES SERVES 4

INGREDIENTS

200 g (7 oz) baby carrots, cut into
   small lengths

150 g (5 oz) baby corn, cut into
   small lengths

200 g (7 oz) small green beans, topped
   and tailed, cut into small lengths

400 g (14 oz) fresh ricotta and spinach
   tortellini

3 teaspoons olive oil

250 g (8 oz) small zucchini (courgettes),
   sliced

juice of $1/2$ lemon

1 tablespoon wholegrain mustard

salt and freshly ground black pepper

2 tablespoons chopped fresh parsley
   or chervil

METHOD

1 Plunge carrots, corn and beans into a saucepan of boiling water. Add salt, bring back to a boil, then simmer 4–5 minutes, until cooked but still slightly crisp.

2 Lift cooked vegetables out of the boiling water with a slotted spoon, put in a bowl and keep warm. Bring water back to a boil, topping up with more if necessary. Add pasta and cook gently 5–6 minutes.

3 Meanwhile, heat oil in a large saucepan. Add zucchini and fry, stirring continuously, 2–3 minutes. Add lemon juice, the drained vegetables, mustard, salt and pepper to taste. Toss gently.

4 Drain pasta and mix through the vegetables. Transfer to a warmed serving dish, sprinkle over parsley or chervil, and serve hot.

NUTRIENTS PER SERVING

1674 kJ, 400 kcal, 18 g protein, 12 g fat (5 g saturated fat), 55 g carbohydrate

VARIATION

You can substitute thin young asparagus spears for the green beans and, for a creamy finish, stir in 1–2 tablespoons sour cream or natural (plain) yogurt just before serving.

TAGLIATELLE WITH BREADCRUMBS

TIME **30 MINUTES** SERVES **4**

INGREDIENTS

350 g (12 oz) crusty white bread

4 tablespoons chopped fresh flat-leaf (Italian) parsley

1½ tablespoons chopped fresh oregano

1½ tablespoons snipped fresh chives

½ cup (125 ml) extra virgin olive oil

3 cloves garlic, crushed

⅓ cup (50 g) pine nuts

salt and freshly ground black pepper

500 g (1 lb) fresh tagliatelle

⅔ cup (65 g) grated parmesan, to serve

METHOD

1 Remove and discard crusts from the bread. Break bread into pieces and process in a food processor or blender to make soft breadcrumbs. Add parsley, oregano and chives and process briefly to combine thoroughly.

2 Heat 3 tablespoons oil in a frying pan over medium heat. Add garlic and pine nuts; stir in breadcrumb mixture. Season to taste and cook, stirring constantly, 5–6 minutes, until breadcrumbs are lightly browned but still soft. Remove from heat and keep warm.

3 Meanwhile, cook pasta in a large saucepan of salted boiling water 3–4 minutes, or until al dente.

4 Drain pasta and place in a large serving bowl with remaining oil. Toss well, then add breadcrumb mixture and toss again. Serve with parmesan either scattered over or in a separate bowl.

NUTRIENTS PER SERVING

4089 kJ, 977 kcal, 29 g protein, 52 g fat (9 g saturated fat), 106 g carbohydrate

COOK'S TIP

A simple tomato salad seasoned with freshly ground black pepper and scattered with torn fresh basil would go well with this dish.

QUICK SPAGHETTI BOLOGNESE

TIME **30 MINUTES** SERVES **4**

INGREDIENTS

2 tablespoons olive oil

500 g (1 lb) minced (ground) lean beef

1 large onion, finely chopped

1 carrot, finely chopped

2 celery stalks, finely chopped

4 cloves garlic, crushed

410 g (15 oz) can chopped tomatoes

500 g (1 lb) tomato passata
(puréed tomatoes)

1 good pinch dried oregano, or to taste

salt and freshly ground black pepper

400 g (14 oz) spaghetti

grated parmesan, to serve

METHOD

1 Heat oil in a wok or large deep frying pan. Crumble beef into pan and stir-fry over high heat 2 minutes to break up meat and brown it.

2 Add onion, carrot, celery and garlic. Stir over medium heat 1 minute. Add chopped tomatoes and passata. Stir well; add oregano and a few grinds of pepper (you may not need salt due to the salt content of the canned tomatoes and passata). Simmer on medium heat 15 minutes, or until thick, stirring occasionally.

3 While sauce is cooking, cook spaghetti in a large saucepan of salted boiling water, following packet instructions. Drain and transfer to a warmed serving bowl.

4 Taste sauce and adjust seasoning, then pour over the hot pasta. Toss gently and serve immediately with grated parmesan.

NUTRIENTS PER SERVING

3025 kJ, 723 kcal, 45 g protein, 23 g fat (8 g saturated fat), 82 g carbohydrate

EGG AND BACON SPAGHETTI

TIME **25 MINUTES** SERVES **4**

INGREDIENTS

400 g (14 oz) spaghetti

²/₃ cup (100 g) frozen peas

100 g (3¹/₂ oz) pancetta or rindless bacon (bacon strips), cut into thin strips

6 spring onions (scallions), sliced

4 eggs

¹/₂ cup (50 g) grated parmesan, plus extra, to serve

100 g (3¹/₂ oz) crème fraîche or light sour cream

freshly ground black pepper

METHOD

1 Cook spaghetti in a large saucepan of salted boiling water, following packet instructions. Add peas to pan for final 3 minutes of cooking.

2 While pasta is cooking, put pancetta or bacon in a frying pan and fry without any additional fat over medium heat 4–5 minutes, or until lightly browned and crisp, stirring occasionally. If necessary, drain off excess fat, leaving about 1 teaspoon. Add spring onions and cook gently 1 minute, or until just soft. Set aside.

3 Combine eggs, parmesan and crème fraîche or sour cream in a bowl. Season with pepper and beat together with a fork.

4 Drain spaghetti and peas; return to the hot pan with pancetta and spring onions. With the pan off the heat, add egg mixture and toss thoroughly so that the eggs thicken in the residual heat to make a creamy sauce to coat the pasta. Transfer to warmed serving bowls and serve sprinkled with more parmesan.

NUTRIENTS PER SERVING

2621 kJ, 626 kcal, 30 g protein, 24 g fat (13 g saturated fat), 72 g carbohydrate

VARIATION

Instead of frying pancetta or bacon and spring onions, use 125 g (4 oz) smoked salmon, cut into thin strips (or use smoked salmon trimmings), and add 2 tablespoons snipped fresh chives.

COOK'S TIP

You can buy bacon pieces in vacuum packs, or loose from the deli section of the supermarket, to save time on chopping.

Right Egg and bacon spaghetti

PAPPARDELLE WITH CHICKEN AND CHERRY TOMATOES

TIME **30 MINUTES** SERVES **4**

INGREDIENTS

2 tablespoons olive oil

1 red onion, halved and thinly sliced

2 cloves garlic, crushed

500 g (1 lb) boneless, skinless
  chicken breast, cubed

400 g (14 oz) red cherry tomatoes,
  halved

400 g (14 oz) pappardelle

150 g (5 oz) rocket (arugula)

salt and freshly ground black pepper

METHOD

1 Heat oil in a frying pan with a lid. Add onion and garlic; cook gently 2 minutes. Add chicken and stir-fry over medium heat until lightly coloured. Reduce heat slightly and stir in tomatoes. Cover pan and simmer, stirring occasionally, 8–10 minutes, or until tomatoes are very soft and chicken is cooked through.

2 Meanwhile, cook pappardelle in a large saucepan of salted boiling water, following packet instructions. Drain.

3 Stir rocket into the sauce and season to taste. Transfer pasta to a large warmed serving bowl. Spoon over the sauce and toss gently to combine thoroughly. Serve immediately.

NUTRIENTS PER SERVING

2582 kJ, 617 kcal, 36 g protein, 20 g fat (4 g saturated fat), 73 g carbohydrate

COOK'S TIP

Capers, bacon, pancetta, olives, cheese and many canned ingredients (including tomatoes, anchovies and tuna) can be quite salty. If using such ingredients in a pasta sauce, don't add extra salt during cooking. Taste the finished sauce, then adjust the seasoning if necessary.

Left Pappardelle with chicken and cherry tomatoes

SPICY SAUSAGES WITH FARFALLE

TIME **30 MINUTES** SERVES **4**

INGREDIENTS

2 tablespoons olive oil

4 large or 6 medium spicy sausages
  (about 400 g/14 oz in total),
  each cut into 5 pieces

1 onion, chopped

2 cloves garlic, crushed

125 g (4 oz) Swiss brown or porcini or
  large flat mushrooms, halved

410 g (15 oz) can chopped tomatoes

400 g (14 oz) farfalle

280 g (10 oz) jar roasted mixed capsicums
  (bell peppers), drained and thickly sliced

1/4 teaspoon dried red chilli flakes,
  or to taste

freshly ground black pepper

METHOD

1 Heat oil in a frying pan that has a lid. Add sausages and fry, stirring frequently, 4 minutes, or until lightly browned. Add onion and garlic and cook, stirring, 1 minute. Add mushrooms and stir-fry 2 minutes, then stir in tomatoes. Bring to a boil, cover and simmer gently 5–10 minutes.

2 Meanwhile, cook farfalle in a large saucepan of salted boiling water, following packet instructions.

3 Add capsicums, chilli flakes and plenty of pepper to the sauce and heat through, stirring, 1 minute.

4 Drain pasta and transfer to a warmed serving bowl. Taste the sauce and adjust seasoning, then pour over pasta and toss gently to combine. Serve immediately.

NUTRIENTS PER SERVING

3118 kJ, 745 kcal, 25 g protein, 37 g fat (13 g saturated fat), 77 g carbohydrate

FETTUCCINE WITH BROCCOLI

TIME **20 MINUTES** SERVES **4**

INGREDIENTS

2 tablespoons dijon mustard

125 g (4 oz) softened butter

10 fresh basil leaves, finely chopped

3 tablespoons finely chopped fresh parsley

2 spring onions (scallions), white part
   sliced, green part finely sliced

2 small cloves garlic, crushed

2 teaspoons olive oil

500 g (1 lb) fresh fettuccine or tagliatelle

600 g (1 lb 5 oz) broccoli florets

salt and freshly ground black pepper

10 red cherry tomatoes, halved, to garnish

METHOD

1   Blend mustard and butter in a bowl. Stir in basil, parsley, white part of spring onions and garlic, crushing them against the bottom of the bowl to release their flavours. Set aside.

2   Put oil, pasta and broccoli in a large saucepan of salted boiling water and cook 4 minutes, or until pasta is al dente.

3   Thoroughly drain pasta and broccoli. Quickly melt flavoured butter in the pasta pan. Return pasta and broccoli to the pan and toss gently in the butter over medium heat until pasta is well coated, but do not allow it to fry.

4   Transfer pasta to a heated serving platter, season with salt and pepper to taste, and garnish with green spring onions and tomatoes.

NUTRIENTS PER SERVING

1842 kJ, 440 kcal, 12 g protein, 30 g fat (18 g saturated fat), 32 g carbohydrate

COOK'S TIP

You will need two large heads of broccoli to give 600 g (1 lb 5 oz) florets.

FARFALLE WITH PESTO AND BACON

TIME **30 MINUTES** SERVES **4**

METHOD

1 Cook pasta in a large saucepan of salted boiling water, following packet instructions. Add peas for the final 4 minutes of cooking time, until pasta is al dente.

2 Meanwhile, cook potatoes in a separate large saucepan of salted boiling water, partially covered, over medium heat 7 minutes, or until tender. Drain and keep hot.

3 Meanwhile, heat half the oil in a frying pan. Add bacon and fry over high heat, stirring frequently, 2–3 minutes, until cooked. Transfer to a plate and set aside.

4 Heat remaining oil in the same pan, add onion and cook gently 5 minutes, until soft but not brown. Return bacon to the pan and stir in pesto and sour cream or yogurt. Season well with pepper, then cover and keep warm.

5 Drain pasta and peas and return to their pan. Add potatoes and gently stir in the bacon and pesto mixture.

6 Serve pasta on individual warmed plates, sprinkled with parmesan and garnished with basil leaves.

NUTRIENTS PER SERVING

3579 kJ, 855 kcal, 33 g protein, 48 g fat (21 g saturated fat), 75 g carbohydrate

COOK'S TIP

If you find it difficult to buy bacon in a piece, you can substitute smoked ham or ham steaks. Dice ham as directed. Eliminate step 3 and add the ham to the onions in step 4 to heat through gently.

INGREDIENTS

250 g (8 oz) farfalle or other small pasta shapes

175 g (6 oz) frozen peas

500 g (1 lb) boiling (waxy) potatoes, such as long white, peeled and diced

1 tablespoon olive oil

300 g (10 oz) smoked bacon, in one piece, rind and fat discarded, diced

1 onion, finely chopped

$1/3$ cup (90 g) pesto

$1 1/4$ cups (310 g) sour cream or natural (plain) yogurt

freshly ground black pepper

$1/2$ cup (50 g) grated parmesan

fresh basil leaves, to garnish

FIVE-SPICE NOODLES

TIME **15 MINUTES** SERVES **4**

INGREDIENTS

2 tablespoons vegetable oil

2 cloves garlic, chopped

1 large onion, finely sliced

2 teaspoons grated fresh ginger

500 g (1 lb) ready-sliced stir-fry
vegetables

2 tablespoons soy sauce

1/2 teaspoon Chinese five-spice

300 g (10 oz) wok-ready hokkien
(egg) noodles

125 g (4 oz) roasted peanuts
(groundnuts) or cashew nuts

METHOD

1 Heat oil in a wok or frying pan. Add garlic, onion and ginger, and
stir-fry 2 minutes. Add vegetables and stir-fry 5 minutes.

2 Add soy sauce and Chinese five-spice, then stir in hokkien noodles
and cook, following packet instructions. When noodles are thoroughly
heated, top with roasted peanuts or cashew nuts.

NUTRIENTS PER SERVING

1805 kJ, 431 kcal, 15 g protein, 25 g fat (3 g saturated fat), 35 g carbohydrate

SPAGHETTI WITH FRESH TOMATO AND CHILLI SAUCE

TIME **20 MINUTES** SERVES **4**

INGREDIENTS

350 g (12 oz) spaghetti

8 large ripe tomatoes, roughly chopped

2 cloves garlic, crushed

2 tablespoons chopped fresh flat-leaf
(Italian) parsley

2 tablespoons olive oil

freshly ground black pepper

dried red chilli flakes, to taste

grated parmesan, to serve

METHOD

1 Cook spaghetti in a large saucepan
of salted boiling water, following
packet instructions.

2 Drain, then toss with tomatoes,
garlic, parsley and oil. Season to
taste with pepper and chilli flakes,
then serve with grated parmesan.

NUTRIENTS PER SERVING

1997 kJ, 477 kcal, 18 g protein, 15 g fat
(4 g saturated fat), 67 g carbohydrate

PESTO PASTA WITH SMOKED TROUT

TIME **15 MINUTES** SERVES **4**

INGREDIENTS

350 g (12 oz) tagliatelle or linguine

4 tablespoons good-quality pesto

200 g (7 oz) hot-smoked trout
or salmon, flaked

freshly ground black pepper

grated parmesan, to serve

METHOD

1 Cook pasta in a large saucepan of salted boiling water, following packet
instructions. Drain pasta, reserving 100 ml (3 1/2 fl oz) cooking water.

2 Mix reserved cooking water with pesto, then toss through the pasta. Top
with smoked trout or salmon, season with black pepper and serve with
grated parmesan.

NUTRIENTS PER SERVING

2078 kJ, 496 kcal, 29 g protein, 15 g fat (5 g saturated fat), 60 g carbohydrate

COOK'S TIP

Cool unused pasta sauces quickly, then chill and store in the fridge for up
to 2 days, or pour into a freezer-proof container and freeze for up to a month.
To use, thaw, reheat and simmer 10 minutes.

FARFALLE WITH ANCHOVY AND CHERRY TOMATOES

TIME **15 MINUTES** SERVES **4**

INGREDIENTS

350 g (12 oz) farfalle

45 g (1 1/2 oz) can anchovy fillets,
    drained

2 cloves garlic, chopped

250 g (8 oz) red cherry tomatoes,
    halved

freshly ground black pepper or dried
    red chilli flakes

2 tablespoons chopped fresh flat-leaf
    (Italian) parsley

METHOD

1 Cook farfalle in a large saucepan
   of salted boiling water, following
   packet instructions. Drain.

2 Meanwhile, heat a non-stick frying
   pan and add anchovy fillets, garlic
   and cherry tomatoes. Gently sauté
   3–4 minutes, occasionally stirring
   and crushing anchovies. Season
   with pepper or chilli flakes and
   parsley, then toss with the hot
   pasta and serve.

NUTRIENTS PER SERVING

1308 kJ, 213 kcal, 12 g protein, 2 g fat
(0 g saturated fat), 61 g carbohydrate

COOK'S TIP

Long pasta includes spaghetti,
spaghettini, linguine and angel hair.
Pappardelle, fettuccine and tagliatelle
are types of ribbon pasta. The tube
pastas include penne, macaroni and
rigatoni. Pasta shapes include farfalle
and conchiglie. Flat pasta sheets are
used for lasagne. If you can't find the
specified pasta, substitute another of
the same type of pasta.

PAD THAI WITH CHICKEN
TIME **20 MINUTES** SERVES **4**

METHOD

1 Soak rice noodles in a heatproof bowl of hot water 10 minutes, or following packet instructions. Stir gently with a fork or chopsticks to separate. Drain thoroughly and set aside.

2 Meanwhile, heat oil in a wok or large frying pan. When very hot, add garlic, onion and chilli; stir-fry 1 minute. Add chicken slices and stir-fry 2 minutes, or until lightly coloured.

3 Push chicken to one side of wok to make room for the eggs. Pour eggs into wok and stir gently until lightly scrambled. Add drained noodles and 3 tablespoons water. Add bean sprouts, soy sauce, fish sauce and lime juice; stir-fry with noodles, chicken and eggs 2 minutes.

4 Remove wok from heat. Taste, then add pepper or more fish sauce or soy sauce if necessary. If you like, add some chilli flakes. Transfer to a warmed serving dish and scatter over chives and peanuts. Serve immediately, with lime halves to garnish, if using.

NUTRIENTS PER SERVING
2221 kJ, 530 kcal, 29 g protein, 21 g fat (4 g saturated fat), 56 g carbohydrate

VARIATION
Instead of chicken, use pork stir-fry strips and cook 5 minutes. Or use 250 g (8 oz) raw prawns (uncooked shrimp), adding them with the fish sauce in step 3. Cook 3 minutes if fresh and 4 minutes if frozen, or until they turn pink.

INGREDIENTS

250 g (8 oz) dried rice stick noodles

2 tablespoons vegetable oil

2–4 cloves garlic, crushed

1 small onion, finely chopped

1 red or green chilli, seeds removed, finely chopped

350 g (12 oz) boneless, skinless chicken breast, thinly sliced

2 eggs, beaten

200 g (7 oz) bean sprouts, trimmed

1 tablespoon soy sauce, or to taste

2 tablespoons fish sauce, or to taste

1 tablespoon lime juice

freshly ground black pepper

dried red chilli flakes, to taste (optional)

1 bunch (20 g/^{2}/$_3$ oz) fresh chives, snipped

30 g (1 oz) chopped roasted peanuts (groundnuts)

lime halves, to serve (optional)

SPECIAL PORK CHOW MEIN
TIME 20 MINUTES SERVES 4

INGREDIENTS

2 tablespoons vegetable oil

2/3 cup (100 g) cashew nuts

4 cloves garlic, crushed

5 cm (2 inch) piece fresh ginger, peeled
and finely chopped

500 g (1 lb) ready-sliced stir-fry vegetables

250 g (8 oz) cooked pork, cut into strips

300 g (10 oz) wok-ready Singapore or
hokkien (egg) noodles

2 tablespoons soy sauce

1 tablespoon Chinese rice wine or
dry sherry

salt and freshly ground black pepper

2 teaspoons sesame oil

METHOD

1 Heat 1 tablespoon oil in a wok or large frying pan over medium heat. Add cashew nuts and stir-fry 2 minutes, or until golden. Transfer to a plate and set aside. Wipe the wok clean.

2 Heat remaining oil in the wok over medium heat and stir-fry garlic and ginger 10 seconds. Increase heat and add vegetable mixture. Stir-fry 1 minute. Stir in pork and stir-fry 3 minutes to heat through.

3 Add noodles, soy sauce and rice wine or sherry to the wok. Season to taste. Stir-fry 3 minutes, or until piping hot, then add sesame oil and toss well to mix. Transfer to a warmed serving bowl, scatter with toasted cashew nuts and serve immediately.

NUTRIENTS PER SERVING

2468 kJ, 589 kcal, 35 g protein, 27 g fat (4 g saturated fat), 49 g carbohydrate

COOK'S TIP

Look for packs of ready-sliced stir-fry vegetables that contain bok choy, capsicum (bell pepper), water chestnuts, bamboo shoots, broccoli and carrots for this dish.

DUCK CHOW MEIN

TIME **30 MINUTES** SERVES **4**

INGREDIENTS

250 g (8 oz) dried fine egg noodles

3–4 boneless, skinless duck breasts (about
    400 g/14 oz in total), cut into strips

2 tablespoons soy sauce

2 tablespoons peanut (groundnut) oil

1 clove garlic, chopped

3 large spring onions (scallions), sliced

300 g (10 oz) mixed vegetables, such as
    Chinese cabbage, carrots, broccoli,
    red capsicums (bell peppers) and leeks,
    cut into matchsticks

125 g (4 oz) baby corn

2 tablespoons hoisin sauce

1 cup (250 ml) hot vegetable or
    chicken stock

1 teaspoon cornflour (cornstarch)

50 g (1¾ oz) bean sprouts, trimmed

METHOD

1 Put noodles in a bowl of boiling water and soak 6 minutes, or cook following packet instructions. Drain and rinse, then set aside to drain thoroughly.

2 Put duck and 1 tablespoon soy sauce in a bowl and toss gently.

3 Heat 1 tablespoon oil in a large wok or frying pan. Add duck and stir-fry 4–5 minutes. Transfer to a dish and keep warm.

4 Heat remaining oil in the wok or frying pan. Add garlic, spring onions, mixed vegetables and corn, and stir-fry 15 seconds in the wok, or 30 seconds in the pan.

5 Return duck to the wok or pan, add hoisin sauce and hot stock and simmer a further 3–4 minutes.

6 Blend cornflour with 1 teaspoon cold water and stir into the wok with bean sprouts. Cook, stirring, 1–2 minutes, then add noodles and remaining soy sauce. Toss well, reheat 3–5 minutes, then serve.

NUTRIENTS PER SERVING

3202 kJ, 765 kcal, 25 g protein, 50 g fat (13 g saturated fat), 59 g carbohydrate

COOK'S TIP

The strips of duck should be about 1 x 7.5 cm (½ x 3 inches). Boneless, skinless chicken breast, or a mixture of beef and chicken strips, can be used instead of the duck.

NOODLES WITH PLUM AND GINGER DUCK

TIME **30 MINUTES** SERVES **4**

INGREDIENTS

2 tablespoons soy sauce

2 tablespoons Chinese rice wine
  or dry sherry

1 good pinch ground sichuan peppercorns
  or Chinese five-spice, or to taste

400 g (14 oz) boneless, skinless duck
  breast, sliced thinly crosswise

2 tablespoons olive oil

3 spring onions (scallions), cut into
  short lengths

3 cm (1$^1/4$ inch) piece fresh ginger, grated

300 g (10 oz) sugarsnap peas or snow
  peas (mangetout), topped and tailed

4 tablespoons plum sauce

$^2/3$ cup (150 ml) chicken or
  vegetable stock

375 g (13 oz) wok-ready Singapore
  or hokkien (egg) noodles

fresh coriander (cilantro) sprigs,
  to garnish (optional)

METHOD

1 Combine soy sauce, rice wine or sherry and ground peppercorns or five-spice in a bowl. Add duck and toss gently so that it is thoroughly coated in the marinade.

2 Heat oil in a wok or frying pan. Drain duck, reserving marinade. Add duck to wok and stir-fry over high heat 1 minute. Stir in spring onions and ginger, followed by sugarsnap peas or snow peas. Stir-fry 1 minute, then add the reserved marinade, plum sauce and stock. Stir well and leave to cook over medium heat 3–4 minutes.

3 Meanwhile, cook noodles in a saucepan of boiling water, following packet instructions.

4 Drain noodles and add to the wok. Toss gently to combine all ingredients. Transfer to warmed serving bowls and garnish with sprigs of coriander, if you like.

NUTRIENTS PER SERVING

1871 kJ, 447 kcal, 25 g protein, 17 g fat (4 g saturated fat), 49 g carbohydrate

VARIATION

NOODLES WITH CHICKEN AND OYSTER MUSHROOMS

Thinly slice 300 g (10 oz) boneless, skinless chicken breast. Add 2 tablespoons soy sauce, 2 tablespoons Chinese rice wine or dry sherry and 1 teaspoon grated fresh ginger (if time, let the chicken marinate in the refrigerator for up to 8 hours). Heat 2 tablespoons vegetable oil in a wok or frying pan, add 2 thinly sliced cloves garlic and 1 mild red chilli, seeds removed, cut into rings, and stir-fry 1 minute. Add chicken and marinade, and stir-fry 3 minutes. Add 175 g (6 oz) sliced oyster mushrooms, 4 tablespoons plum sauce and 100 ml (3$^1/2$ fl oz) chicken or vegetable stock. Cook 3–4 minutes. Meanwhile, boil 375 g ($^3/4$ lb) wok-ready Singapore or udon (rice) noodles until just warmed through, then add to the wok and stir to combine all ingredients thoroughly.

COOK'S TIP

If you cook Chinese dishes regularly, you will find Chinese rice wine a useful ingredient to have on hand. Sherry is a good alternative and has other culinary uses too, such as in baking or to enrich soups.

PORK WITH EGG NOODLES
TIME 20 MINUTES SERVES 4

INGREDIENTS

500 g (1 lb) pork fillet, trimmed of any
    fat or tissue, cut into thin strips
freshly ground black pepper
1 tablespoon olive oil
300 g (10 oz) celery, sliced
8 spring onions (scallions), sliced
300 g (10 oz) button mushrooms, sliced
250 g (8 oz) wok-ready hokkien
    (egg) noodles
2 tablespoons wholegrain mustard
200 g (7 oz) crème fraîche or sour cream
salt

METHOD

1 Season pork with pepper.
2 Heat half the oil in a wok or frying pan over high heat and stir-fry pork
   4–5 minutes. Remove from wok and keep warm.
3 Add remaining oil, celery and half the spring onions to the wok and stir-fry
   5 minutes. Add mushrooms and cook until soft.
4 Meanwhile, cook noodles in a saucepan of boiling water, following packet
   instructions. Drain well and keep warm.
5 Stir mustard and crème fraîche into the vegetables and bring the mixture
   to a boil. Add the reserved pork, heat through, then season to taste with
   salt and pepper.
6 Spoon the pork mixture over the noodles, sprinkle with remaining spring
   onions and serve.

NUTRIENTS PER SERVING
2812 kJ, 672 kcal, 40 g protein, 37 g fat (16 g saturated fat), 48 g carbohydrate

VARIATION
Beef fillet or boneless, skinless chicken breast can be used instead of the pork.

CHICKEN, BABY CORN AND SNOW PEAS WITH NOODLES
TIME **30 MINUTES** SERVES **4**

METHOD
1 Cook noodles in a saucepan of boiling water, following packet instructions, until just tender. Drain well and toss with 1 teaspoon sesame oil. Set aside.
2 Meanwhile, put chicken in a bowl, add eggwhite, cornflour and remaining sesame oil and mix together.
3 Heat vegetable oil in a wok or large frying pan. When very hot, add chicken and stir-fry 2 minutes, or until lightly coloured. Add spring onions, baby corn, snow peas and capsicums and stir-fry 3–4 minutes, or until just softened. Add soy sauce and stock; mix thoroughly. Reduce heat so the liquid simmers gently, then cook about 2 minutes, or until the vegetables are just tender and the chicken is thoroughly cooked.
4 Stir noodles into chicken and vegetables, toss to combine all the ingredients and cook briefly to reheat the noodles. As soon as they are hot, transfer to warmed serving bowls and serve immediately.

NUTRIENTS PER SERVING
1365 kJ, 326 kcal, 26 g protein, 13 g fat (3 g saturated fat), 26 g carbohydrate

VARIATION
Instead of chicken, use peeled raw prawns (uncooked shrimp), added with the soy sauce at step 3. Cook 3 minutes if fresh, or 4 minutes if frozen, or until they turn pink.

COOK'S TIP
Replace the capsicums with ready-sliced stir-fry vegetables to cut down on preparation time, if you prefer.

INGREDIENTS
250 g (8 oz) wok-ready hokkien (egg) noodles
2 teaspoons sesame oil
350 g (12 oz) boneless, skinless chicken breast, thinly sliced
1 eggwhite
2 teaspoons cornflour (cornstarch)
1 tablespoon vegetable oil
3 spring onions (scallions), cut diagonally into 2.5 cm (1 inch) pieces
250 g (8 oz) baby corn, halved lengthwise if large
250 g (8 oz) snow peas (mangetout), topped and tailed
1 red and 1 yellow capsicum (bell pepper), seeds removed, thinly sliced
2 tablespoons soy sauce
2/3 cup (150 ml) vegetable or chicken stock

CHINESE NOODLES WITH PRAWNS AND BEAN SPROUTS

TIME **20 MINUTES** SERVES **4**

INGREDIENTS

200 g (7 oz) dried medium egg noodles
  or wok-ready hokkien (egg) noodles
2 teaspoons sesame oil
3 tablespoons vegetable oil
5 spring onions (scallions), chopped
2 large cloves garlic, crushed
1 large green chilli, halved, seeds removed,
  thinly sliced
250 g (8 oz) ready-sliced stir-fry vegetables
300 ml (10 fl oz) chicken or
  vegetable stock
150 g (5 oz) button mushrooms, sliced
150 g (5 oz) fresh lentil, mung bean or
  other sprouts, trimmed
2 tablespoons soy sauce
300 g (10 oz) peeled cooked prawns
  (shrimp)
3 eggs, beaten
salt and freshly ground black pepper

METHOD

1 Cook or soak noodles, following packet instructions. Drain, toss with sesame oil and set aside.
2 Heat 1 tablespoon vegetable oil in a wok or large frying pan and stir-fry spring onions, garlic, chilli and ready-sliced vegetables 3 minutes. Stir in stock and bring to a boil. Add mushrooms and sprouts and cook a further 2–3 minutes.
3 Stir in soy sauce, then add prawns and cook 1–2 minutes if fresh, or 3 minutes if frozen. Add noodles, toss to combine all the ingredients and cook to reheat the noodles.
4 Heat remaining oil in a small frying pan. Season eggs with salt and pepper and pour into pan. Fry, gently stirring to scramble the eggs slightly, until lightly set into large soft curds. Mix into the noodles and serve immediately.

NUTRIENTS PER SERVING

2153 kJ, 514 kcal, 34 g protein, 22 g fat (4 g saturated fat), 43 g carbohydrate

VARIATION

For a vegetarian version, omit the prawns and add $2/3$ cup (100 g) roughly chopped cashew nuts.

TOFU STIR-FRY WITH CASHEW NUTS

TIME **30 MINUTES** SERVES **4**

INGREDIENTS

300 g (10 oz) fresh tofu, drained

2 tablespoons peanut (groundnut) oil

1 cm ($^1/_2$ inch) piece fresh ginger, peeled and finely chopped

150 g (5 oz) snow peas (mangetout), topped and tailed

100 g ($3^1/_2$ oz) shiitake mushrooms, thinly sliced

1 large red or yellow capsicum (bell pepper), halved, seeds removed, thinly sliced

400 g (14 oz) Chinese cabbage or cos (romaine) lettuce, thickly sliced

5 spring onions (scallions), sliced

250 g (8 oz) fine dry egg noodles

salt

$^2/_3$ cup (100 g) roasted cashew nuts

MARINADE

2 cloves garlic, crushed

1 tablespoon Japanese soy sauce (shoyu)

$1^1/_2$ tablespoons dry sherry

$1^1/_2$ teaspoons sesame oil

1 teaspoon soft brown sugar

freshly ground black pepper

METHOD

1 To make the marinade, combine garlic, soy sauce, sherry, sesame oil, sugar and pepper in a bowl. Cut tofu into oblongs 1 cm ($^1/_2$ inch) thick, add to the marinade and leave to marinate.

2 Heat 1 tablespoon peanut oil in a wok or frying pan over medium heat. Drain tofu, reserving the marinade. Stir-fry tofu 3 minutes, then remove and keep warm.

3 Heat the remaining oil in the wok. Add ginger, snow peas and mushrooms and stir-fry 2 minutes. Add capsicum, stir-fry 2 minutes, then add cabbage or lettuce and spring onions and stir-fry a further 2 minutes.

4 Put noodles in a large heatproof bowl, add a little salt, pour over boiling water to cover and leave to soak, following packet instructions. Stir gently with a fork or chopsticks to separate.

5 While noodles are soaking, pour reserved marinade into the vegetables, add cashew nuts and stir 1–2 minutes until hot.

6 Add tofu and stir. Drain noodles, add to the wok and stir with the vegetables and tofu. Serve immediately.

NUTRIENTS PER SERVING

2402 kJ, 574 kcal, 24 g protein, 30 g fat (7 g saturated fat), 58 g carbohydrate

SINGAPORE NOODLES WITH PRAWNS

TIME **25 MINUTES** SERVES **4**

INGREDIENTS

1 tablespoon vegetable oil

1 onion, finely chopped

3 cloves garlic, crushed

1 tablespoon laksa paste or Thai yellow curry paste, or to taste

400 ml (14 fl oz) can coconut milk

1 cup (250 ml) vegetable or fish stock

250 g (8 oz) dried rice stick noodles

200 g (7 oz) peeled large raw prawns (uncooked shrimp)

4 spring onions (scallions), roughly chopped

300 g (10 oz) bean sprouts, trimmed

juice of 1 lime

salt and freshly ground black pepper

lime wedges, to garnish

METHOD

1 Heat oil in a wok or frying pan. Add onion and garlic and cook 2 minutes, stirring frequently. Add laksa or curry paste and fry, stirring, 2 minutes, then stir in coconut milk and stock. Bring to a boil, then simmer 5 minutes.

2 Meanwhile, put noodles in a large heatproof bowl, pour over boiling water to cover and leave to soak 5 minutes, or following packet instructions. Separate noodles gently using a fork or chopsticks.

3 Add prawns to wok and cook, stirring frequently, 3 minutes, or until prawns have turned pink. Stir in spring onions and bean sprouts. Add lime juice and season to taste.

4 Drain noodles and divide among four bowls. Ladle over prawns and sauce and serve, garnished with lime wedges.

NUTRIENTS PER SERVING

2434 kJ, 581 kcal, 18 g protein, 27 g fat (19 g saturated fat), 66 g carbohydrate

Left Tofu stir-fry with cashew nuts

CHICKEN NOODLES WITH PEANUT DRESSING

TIME **25 MINUTES** SERVES **4**

INGREDIENTS

100 g (3½ oz) broccoli, cut into
   small florets
1 orange and 1 yellow capsicum
   (bell pepper), halved, seeds removed,
   sliced lengthwise
250 g (8 oz) dried medium egg noodles
4 tablespoons crunchy peanut butter
juice of 1 small lemon
2 tablespoons soy sauce
1 pinch caster (superfine) sugar
2 cooked boneless, skinless chicken
   breasts, shredded
100 g (3½ oz) Chinese cabbage,
   shredded

METHOD

1. Drop broccoli and capsicums into a large pan of boiling water. Add dried egg noodles and return to a boil, then remove from heat, cover with a lid and leave 4 minutes. Reserve 5 tablespoons cooking liquid.
2. Tip noodles and vegetables into a colander and drain. Gently cool noodles and vegetables under cold running water and drain again. Transfer to a serving bowl.
3. Whisk together peanut butter, reserved cooking liquid, lemon juice, soy sauce and caster sugar in a small bowl.
4. Add chicken to noodles and vegetables with Chinese cabbage and half the peanut dressing. Gently toss together to mix. Drizzle over remaining dressing and serve.

NUTRIENTS PER SERVING

2791 kJ, 667 kcal, 56 g protein, 26 g fat (6 g saturated fat), 51 g carbohydrate

COOK'S TIP

Most noodles take about 4 minutes to cook, and some need only to be soaked in hot water. To cook noodles, heat plenty of boiling water to a rolling boil. Add the noodles, and when the water returns to a boil, begin timing according to the packet instructions. Move the noodles gently once or twice with a fork during cooking to separate them. Drain well.

CHICKEN AND SOBA NOODLES

TIME **30 MINUTES** SERVES **4**

INGREDIENTS

¾ cup (180 ml) salt-reduced chicken
   stock
2 cloves garlic, crushed
½ teaspoon ground ginger
¼ teaspoon dried red chilli flakes
375 g (¾ lb) skinless, boneless
   chicken breasts
300 g (10 oz) soba noodles
   (buckwheat noodles)
250 g (8 oz) green beans, halved
2 carrots, cut into matchsticks
1½ tablespoons dark brown sugar
1 tablespoon salt-reduced soy sauce
1 tablespoon peanut or other vegetable oil
2 cups (150 g) finely shredded cabbage

METHOD

1 Put the stock, garlic, ginger and
chilli flakes into a large non-stick
frying pan and bring to the boil.
Reduce the heat to low, add the
chicken, cover, and simmer for
5 minutes. Turn the chicken over
and cook for a further 5 minutes,
or until cooked through. Remove
the chicken to a plate, reserving
the cooking liquid. When it is
cool enough to handle, shred
the chicken.

2 Meanwhile, cook the noodles
in a large saucepan of boiling
water according to the packet
instructions. Blanch the beans
and carrots for the last minute
of cooking time until just tender.
Drain well.

3 Whisk together the sugar, soy sauce, peanut oil and the reserved cooking
liquid in a large bowl. Add the shredded chicken, noodles, beans, carrots
and the cabbage, tossing to combine. Divide among serving bowls and
serve the noodles at room temperature or chilled.

NUTRIENTS PER SERVING

2003 kJ, 479 kcal, 32 g protein, 10 g fat (2 g saturated fat), 62 g carbohydrate

CHINESE BEEF NOODLE SOUP WITH SHIITAKE MUSHROOMS

TIME **20 MINUTES** SERVES **4**

INGREDIENTS

2 tablespoons soy sauce

1 tablespoon sesame oil

2 tablespoons Chinese rice wine
or dry sherry

300 g (10 oz) lean rump steak,
very thinly sliced

4 cups (1 litre) beef stock

4 spring onions (scallions), sliced

150 g (5 oz) shiitake mushrooms,
thickly sliced

200 g (7 oz) baby bok choy,
halved crosswise

250 g (8 oz) dried fine egg noodles

1 tablespoon vegetable oil

freshly ground black pepper

METHOD

1 Combine soy sauce, sesame oil and Chinese rice wine or sherry in a bowl. Add beef and toss until well mixed. Leave to marinate until needed.

2 Heat stock in a large saucepan or flameproof casserole dish. Add spring onions, mushrooms and bok choy and simmer 2 minutes.

3 Add noodles and stock and cook 2–4 minutes, or until tender.

4 While noodles are cooking, heat vegetable oil in a wok or frying pan and stir-fry beef 2 minutes, or until browned. Tip beef and pan juices into the simmering stock. Return to a boil. Add black pepper to taste, then ladle into four serving bowls and serve.

NUTRIENTS PER SERVING

1997 kJ, 477 kcal, 32 g protein, 14 g fat (3 g saturated fat), 53 g carbohydrate

VARIATION

Instead of beef, use boneless, skinless chicken breast. Also replace the beef stock with chicken stock.

COOK'S TIP

Dried shiitake mushrooms are useful to keep in the pantry, but you will need time to soak them before they can be added to a recipe. Soak in water about 3 minutes, then rinse to remove any grit. Soak in warm water a further 30 minutes to soften. Cut off the stalks and discard, then continue as for fresh shiitake. (The soaking liquid can be strained and added to the stock.)

CHAPTER 5

Rice, Beans & Grains

SEAFOOD AND BACON PAELLA

TIME **30 MINUTES** SERVES **4**

INGREDIENTS

2 tablespoons olive oil

1 large onion, chopped

1 green capsicum (bell pepper),
    seeds removed, chopped

2 large cloves garlic, chopped

200 g (7 oz) bacon pieces or rindless
    bacon (bacon strips), cut into thin strips

1 large tomato, chopped, or 200 g (7 oz)
    canned chopped tomatoes

300 g (10 oz) paella rice or arborio rice

$1/2$ teaspoon saffron threads, crushed

5 cups (1.25 litres) hot chicken or
    fish stock

400 g (14 oz) mixed seafood
    (marinara mix)

lime wedges, to serve (optional)

METHOD

1 Heat oil in a large non-stick frying pan. Add onion, capsicum, garlic and bacon and cook over low heat 5 minutes. Add tomato and cook 2 minutes.

2 Add rice and stir to coat in the oil. Add saffron threads and heat for a few seconds, then pour in hot stock. Bring to a boil, stir lightly and simmer 5 minutes.

3 Stir in seafood, return to a gentle simmer and cook 10 minutes, or until rice is tender and liquid is absorbed, stirring occasionally. Serve with lime wedges, if you like.

NUTRIENTS PER SERVING

2346 kJ, 560 kcal, 36 g protein, 16 g fat (4 g saturated fat), 68 g carbohydrate

VARIATION

GOLDEN CHICKPEA PAELLA Cook a mixture of chopped vegetables in the oil in step 1, such as 1 bulb fennel or 3 celery stalks, 1 yellow capsicum (bell pepper), with 1 chopped onion and 1 crushed clove garlic. Omit the bacon. Add the tomato, rice and saffron as in steps 1 and 2, and 1 teaspoon ground paprika. Add 1 chopped zucchini (courgette), $3^{1}/2$ cups (875 ml) hot vegetable stock and $1/2$ cup (125 ml) white wine, and cook 5 minutes as for step 2. Add a 400 g (14 oz) can chickpeas, rinsed and drained, instead of seafood, and simmer 10 minutes as for step 3.

COOK'S TIP

Always use saffron threads; powdered saffron loses its flavour more quickly, and can also be adulterated with cheaper spices such as turmeric. Although saffron is expensive, just a pinch is enough to flavour a dish. Stored in a dry, dark place, the threads will never go off.

1 Keep stock gently simmering in a saucepan. Heat butter and oil in a large saucepan or flameproof casserole dish. Add onion and garlic and cook over medium heat 4–5 minutes until softened.

2 Meanwhile, snap off and discard any woody stems from asparagus spears at the point where they break easily. Separate asparagus tips and stalks, and slice the stalks into bite-sized pieces.

3 Put rice in the saucepan of buttery onions and use a wooden spoon to stir until rice is well coated. Add wine and simmer until it has almost evaporated. Stir in asparagus stalks and a ladleful of stock. Cook, stirring occasionally, until stock is absorbed into rice.

4 Keep adding hot stock a ladleful at a time, stirring occasionally, about 12 minutes. Add asparagus tips and zucchini and stir. Keep adding the hot stock a ladleful at a time, stirring occasionally, a further 8 minutes, or until risotto is tender and creamy. Stir in broad beans or soybeans with last ladle of stock. Stir in parsley or chives, then season with pepper. Scatter over parmesan and serve.

FRESH GREEN VEGETABLE RISOTTO
TIME **30 MINUTES** SERVES **4**

INGREDIENTS

4 cups (1 litre) hot vegetable stock
50 g (1¾ oz) butter
1 tablespoon olive oil
1 onion, chopped
1 clove garlic, crushed
250 g (8 oz) asparagus spears
1⅓ cups (300 g) arborio rice
⅔ cup (150 ml) dry white wine

1 zucchini (courgette), thinly sliced
125 g (4 oz) baby broad (fava) beans
   or frozen soybeans, thawed
2 tablespoons chopped fresh parsley
   or snipped fresh chives
freshly ground black pepper
50 g (1¾ oz) shaved parmesan

NUTRIENTS PER SERVING
2305 kJ, 551 kcal, 16 g protein, 20 g fat
(11 g saturated fat), 69 g carbohydrate

COOK'S TIP
Quickly thaw the frozen soybeans by putting them in a colander and pouring boiling water over.

CHICKEN AND SPINACH RISOTTO

TIME **30 MINUTES** SERVES **4**

INGREDIENTS

900 ml (30 fl oz) hot chicken stock

50 g (1¾ oz) butter

1 tablespoon olive oil

1 onion, chopped

1 clove garlic, crushed

1⅓ cups (300 g) arborio rice

⅔ cup (150 ml) dry white wine

200 g (7 oz) baby spinach leaves

300 g (10 oz) chopped barbecued chicken

2 tablespoons mascarpone cheese

2 tablespoons chopped fresh parsley

freshly ground black pepper

freshly grated nutmeg

50 g (1¾ oz) shaved parmesan

METHOD

1 Keep stock gently simmering in a saucepan. Heat butter and oil in a large saucepan or flameproof casserole dish. Add onion and garlic and cook over medium heat 4–5 minutes until softened.

2 Using a wooden spoon, stir in rice until coated with buttery onions. Add wine and simmer until it has almost evaporated. Stir in a ladleful of hot stock. Cook, stirring occasionally, until stock has been absorbed into the rice.

3 Keep adding hot stock a ladleful at a time, stirring occasionally, about 20 minutes, or until risotto is tender and creamy. Five minutes before the end of cooking time, increase heat and stir in baby spinach. Lower heat when the risotto starts to bubble again. Two minutes before the end of cooking time, stir in chicken and mascarpone cheese. When the risotto is tender and creamy, stir in parsley, pepper to taste and a little nutmeg. Scatter with parmesan.

NUTRIENTS PER SERVING

2936 kJ, 701 kcal, 32 g protein, 31 g fat (16 g saturated fat), 66 g carbohydrate

PRAWN, SUN-DRIED TOMATO AND PEA RISOTTO

TIME **30 MINUTES** SERVES **4**

INGREDIENTS

4 cups (1 litre) hot vegetable stock

50 g (1¾ oz) butter

1 tablespoon olive oil

1 onion, chopped

1 clove garlic, crushed

1⅓ cups (300 g) arborio rice

⅔ cup (150 ml) dry white wine

6–8 sun-dried tomatoes, chopped

250 g (8 oz) peeled cooked prawns (shrimp)

200 g (7 oz) fresh or frozen peas, thawed if frozen

2 tablespoons chopped fresh parsley or snipped fresh chives

freshly ground black pepper

50 g (1¾ oz) shaved parmesan

METHOD

1 Keep stock gently simmering in a saucepan. Heat butter and oil in a large saucepan or flameproof casserole dish. Add onion and garlic and cook over medium heat 4–5 minutes until softened.

2 Using a wooden spoon, stir in rice until coated with buttery onions. Add wine and simmer until it has almost evaporated. Stir in sun-dried tomatoes and a ladleful of stock. Cook, stirring occasionally, until stock is absorbed into rice.

3 Keep adding hot stock a ladleful at a time, stirring occasionally, about 20 minutes, or until risotto is tender and creamy. Stir in the prawns and peas for the final 2 minutes of cooking time. Stir in parsley or chives, and season with pepper. Scatter with parmesan.

NUTRIENTS PER SERVING

2569 kJ, 614 kcal, 29 g protein, 21 g fat (11 g saturated fat), 70 g carbohydrate

EMERALD RISOTTO
TIME **30 MINUTES** SERVES **4**

5 cups (1.25 litres) vegetable stock,
   or 5 cups (1.25 litres) hot water with
   3 tablespoons vegetable stock
   (bouillon) powder
4 tablespoons white wine
3 tablespoons virgin olive oil
1 small onion, finely chopped
2 cloves garlic, finely chopped
2 cups (440 g) arborio rice
250 g (8 oz) baby spinach leaves
salt and freshly ground black pepper
freshly grated nutmeg

METHOD

1 Put stock or hot water and stock powder into a large saucepan and bring to a boil. Add wine, reduce heat and leave to simmer.
2 Heat oil in a separate large saucepan or flameproof casserole dish. Add onion and garlic and fry gently 2–3 minutes, until soft but not brown. Using a wooden spoon, stir in rice until the grains are translucent and coated with oil.
3 Add a ladleful of hot stock, adjust the heat to maintain a gentle boil, and stir until most of the liquid has been absorbed. Keep adding hot stock, a ladleful at a time, stirring constantly, about 15 minutes, or until the rice is almost cooked.
4 Add spinach and more stock and stir until the rice is cooked — it should retain a bite, but the risotto should be of a soft, dropping consistency.
5 Season to taste with salt, pepper and nutmeg. Serve straight from the pan.

NUTRIENTS PER SERVING
1875 kJ, 448 kcal, 8 g protein, 14 g fat (2 g saturated fat), 73 g carbohydrate

COOK'S TIP
Italian risotto rice, such as arborio, is a fat grain that absorbs the cooking liquid. Never wash the rice before cooking, because it is the starch in the grains that gives risotto its lovely creamy texture.

COUSCOUS WITH PRAWNS AND MINT

TIME **25 MINUTES** SERVES **4**

INGREDIENTS

2 tablespoons olive oil

2 French shallots (eschalots), chopped

1 clove garlic, chopped

350 g (12 oz) small zucchini (courgettes), thinly sliced

salt and freshly ground black pepper

1¾ cups (435 ml) hot fish or chicken stock

1¼ cups (130 g) couscous

250 g (8 oz) peeled cooked prawns (shrimp)

4 tablespoons chopped fresh mint

harissa paste (optional), to serve

METHOD

1 Heat 1½ tablespoons oil in a frying pan, add shallots, garlic and zucchini, stir to coat with oil, then fry 4 minutes, until slightly soft. Season with salt and pepper.

2 Add hot stock, bring to a boil, then stir in couscous. Remove from heat, cover and leave to stand 10 minutes, until the stock is absorbed.

3 Heat remaining oil in a small frying pan. Stir in prawns and heat through gently.

4 Add prawns and mint to the couscous, stir and season to taste with extra salt and pepper. Serve accompanied by a side dish of harissa paste, if you like.

NUTRIENTS PER SERVING

1168 kJ, 279 kcal, 18 g protein, 10 g fat (1 g saturated fat), 31 g carbohydrate

COOK'S TIP

If you like spicy food, you will enjoy harissa paste, a fiery sauce made with red chillies, garlic and olive oil. Harissa paste can be found in Middle Eastern food stores, some Asian food stores, and larger supermarkets.

SPANISH RICE WITH CHORIZO AND SAGE
TIME **30 MINUTES** SERVES **4**

METHOD

1 Heat oil in a wide frying pan. Add onion and garlic and cook over medium–high heat about 3 minutes, stirring frequently, until onion is soft. Add capsicum, rice and turmeric and stir-fry 3 minutes.

2 Add stock and tomatoes, and season to taste with salt and black pepper. Bring to a boil, reduce heat, cover pan and simmer about 5 minutes, stirring occasionally.

3 Stir in chorizo and cook a further 5 minutes. Add sage and peas. Return to a boil, then reduce heat and simmer 5 minutes until the rice is tender and has absorbed most of the liquid. If the mixture dries out before the rice is cooked, add a little more stock or some dry white wine. Serve hot, straight from the cooking pan.

NUTRIENTS PER SERVING
1745 kJ, 417 kcal, 15 g protein, 14 g fat (4 g saturated fat), 53 g carbohydrate

VARIATION
Cabanosi or a spicy salami, cut into thick slices, can be used instead of chorizo, if you wish.

INGREDIENTS

2 tablespoons olive oil

1 red onion, chopped

1 clove garlic, chopped

1 red capsicum (bell pepper), halved, seeds removed, roughly chopped

1⅓ cups (265 g) long-grain rice

1 teaspoon ground turmeric

1¼ cups (310 ml) hot chicken stock

410 g (15 oz) can chopped tomatoes

salt and freshly ground black pepper

200 g (7 oz) chorizo, cut into thick chunks

1 small bunch (20 g/⅔ oz) fresh sage, leaves roughly chopped

1⅓ cups (200 g) frozen peas

PRAWN PILAF
TIME **30 MINUTES** SERVES **4**

INGREDIENTS

1 tablespoon butter

1¹⁄₂ tablespoons olive oil

1 small onion, finely sliced

1 clove garlic, sliced

2 dried red chillies, crumbled

1¹⁄₂ cups (300 g) long-grain rice,
    such as basmati

1 pinch saffron threads

3 cups (750 ml) hot fish stock

3 bay leaves

500 g (1 lb) peeled raw prawns
    (uncooked shrimp)

salt and freshly ground black pepper

2 tablespoons chopped fresh flat-leaf
    (Italian) parsley or dill

METHOD

1 Heat butter and oil in a large saucepan. Add onion and cook over medium heat about 3 minutes, stirring occasionally.

2 Add garlic and chillies and stir-fry 3–4 minutes. Add rice and stir until it is coated in the oil.

3 Add saffron and hot stock to the pan, bring to a boil, then add bay leaves, prawns and some salt. Cover, reduce heat and simmer 10 minutes, then remove from the heat and stand, covered, 4 minutes.

4 Spoon the prawn pilaf onto a serving dish, season with salt and pepper to taste, and garnish with parsley or dill.

NUTRIENTS PER SERVING

1674 kJ, 400 kcal, 27 g protein, 12 g fat (4 g saturated fat), 46 g carbohydrate

COOK'S TIP

Never keep rice warm once it is cooked, as bacteria can develop. Cook and serve it immediately, then quickly cool any that is left over in the refrigerator if you want to keep it.

INDONESIAN SPICY RICE SALAD
TIME **30 MINUTES** SERVES **4**

METHOD

1 Add rice to a large saucepan of lightly salted boiling water. Stir, return to a boil, then reduce heat and simmer 25 minutes.
2 Meanwhile, put olive oil, lime or lemon juice, garlic, chilli, soy sauce, honey and vinegar in a large salad bowl. Season with black pepper and whisk to blend.
3 Add spring onions, celery, bean sprouts and nuts to the bowl. Toss well.
4 When rice is just tender, drain in a colander, then rinse under cold running water until warm. Drain well, then add to salad bowl and toss to mix. Serve in shallow bowls lined with torn Chinese cabbage and spinach.

NUTRIENTS PER SERVING
2115 kJ, 505 kcal, 13 g protein, 23 g fat (4 g saturated fat), 60 g carbohydrate

VARIATION
For a spicy chilli flavour without the bother of chopping, simply add a whole chilli, slit lengthwise, seeds removed. Discard before serving. Or use $^1/_2$–1 teaspoon dried red chilli flakes.

COOK'S TIP
You can cook rice ahead of time or make up a double batch to use later, but remember that it must be used within 2 days. Although you can freeze rice, the texture becomes a little brittle when it is thawed. Frozen rice must be used within 3 months.

INGREDIENTS

1$^1/_4$ cups (250 g) brown rice, rinsed
salt
2 tablespoons olive oil
2 tablespoons lime or lemon juice
1 large clove garlic, crushed
1 large red chilli, seeds removed
   if you like, thinly sliced
2 tablespoons soy sauce
2 teaspoons honey, or to taste
2 tablespoons rice vinegar or
   white wine vinegar
freshly ground black pepper
4 spring onions (scallions), thinly sliced
2 celery stalks, thinly sliced
250 g (8 oz) bean sprouts, trimmed
100 g (3$^1/_2$ oz) unsalted cashew nuts
   or peanuts (groundnuts)
Chinese cabbage and baby spinach
   leaves, to serve

BABY LEEK AND MUSHROOM QUINOA
TIME **30 MINUTES** SERVES **4**

INGREDIENTS

4 tablespoons mixed seeds, such
   as pepitas (pumpkin seeds) and
   sunflower seeds
30 g (1 oz) butter
150 g (5 oz) baby leeks, sliced diagonally
   into 2.5 cm (1 inch) pieces
175 g (6 oz) baby button mushrooms
1 clove garlic, crushed
225 g (8 oz) quinoa or brown rice, rinsed
3 cups (750 ml) vegetable stock
$1/2$ teaspoon mixed dried herbs
grated zest and juice of 1 small lemon
3 tablespoons chopped fresh parsley
salt and freshly ground black pepper

METHOD

1 Gently toast seeds in a large dry saucepan over a medium heat
   2–3 minutes. Tip onto a plate and set aside.
2 Add butter to the pan and, when melted, stir in leeks, mushrooms and
   garlic. Stir over medium–high heat 1 minute.
3 Add quinoa or brown rice to the pan and stir, then add stock and dried
   herbs. Bring to a boil, then reduce heat, stir and cover the pan. Simmer
   gently 15 minutes (or 20–25 minutes if using rice), or until most of the
   stock has been absorbed and the grain and vegetables are tender.
4 Stir lemon zest and juice and parsley into the quinoa and season to taste.
   Serve scattered with toasted seeds.

NUTRIENTS PER SERVING
1568 kJ, 375 kcal, 13 g protein, 16 g fat (5 g saturated fat), 46 g carbohydrate

COOK'S TIP
Toasted seeds add a delicious crunch to all kinds of dishes, from rice and
grains to toppings for breakfast cereals and desserts. You can buy them ready-
toasted or prepare your own. Once toasted, spread them out and allow to
cool completely, then store in an airtight jar. They will keep their freshly
toasted flavour for up to 2 weeks.

EGG FRIED RICE

TIME **30 MINUTES** SERVES 4

INGREDIENTS

2 cups (400 g) long-grain rice,
    such as basmati

salt

2 tablespoons vegetable oil

4 eggs, lightly beaten

250 g (8 oz) rindless bacon (bacon strips),
    fat discarded, cut into strips

3 carrots, diced

8 spring onions (scallions), sliced

2 cloves garlic, crushed

1⅓ cups (200 g) frozen baby peas

200 g (7 oz) bean sprouts, trimmed

250 g (8 oz) peeled cooked prawns
    (shrimp)

3 tablespoons soy sauce

3 tablespoons sake or dry sherry

3 tablespoons mirin (sweet rice wine)
    or 1 teaspoon honey

1 tablespoon sesame oil

METHOD

1 Put rice in a large saucepan with
   a little salt, add 3 cups (750 ml)
   boiling water and 1 teaspoon
   vegetable oil. Bring to a boil,
   reduce heat, cover the pan and
   simmer 10–15 minutes.

2 Meanwhile, heat 1 tablespoon
   vegetable oil in a wok or large
   frying pan. Pour beaten eggs into
   the wok, tipping the mixture to
   make a thin omelette. Cook over
   medium heat until set, then turn
   omelette onto a plate and set aside
   to cool.

3 Add remaining oil to the wok
   and fry bacon over medium heat
   until crisp.

4 Add carrots, reduce heat and fry
   gently, 5 minutes. Add spring
   onions, garlic and peas and stir-fry
   2 minutes.

5 Add bean sprouts. Increase heat, stir-fry 1 minute, then add prawns and
   stir-fry a further 1 minute, or to heat through.

6 Transfer half the mixture to another wok or large frying pan. Drain rice.
   Slice omelette into thin strips. Divide rice and omelette strips equally
   between the two woks.

7 Add half the soy sauce, half the sake or sherry and half the mirin or
   honey to each pan. Then add half the sesame oil to each. Mix together
   thoroughly and stir-fry over high heat 5 minutes, or until the mixture is
   dry. Serve immediately.

NUTRIENTS PER SERVING

3081 kJ, 736 kcal, 44 g protein, 28 g fat (5.5 g saturated fat), 68 g carbohydrate

BASMATI PILAF WITH TANDOORI-SPICED CHICKEN

TIME **30 MINUTES** SERVES **4**

METHOD

1 Mix chicken, half the garlic and half the spice mix or curry powder in a bowl. Leave to marinate while you cook the pilaf, turning chicken strips in the marinade after about 10 minutes.

2 Heat oil in a large non-stick saucepan, add onion and remaining garlic, and cook gently 3 minutes. Stir in basmati rice, then sprinkle in the remaining spice mix or curry powder. Mix well.

3 Pour hot stock into rice; add raisins and salt. Bring to a boil, then reduce heat to a low simmer. Cover and cook 10 minutes without lifting the lid. The liquid should have been absorbed and small steam holes should have appeared in the rice. If necessary, cover and cook a further 2 minutes. Add coriander and tomatoes, stir through to heat briefly, then remove pan from heat and leave 5 minutes. Add pine nuts and use a fork to gently mix them through the rice.

4 While rice is cooking, preheat grill (broiler) or a chargrill pan. Cook chicken strips under the grill or in the chargrill pan 6–8 minutes, or until just firm, turning once. Spoon pilaf into a large warmed serving dish and top with chicken. Serve with lemon wedges.

INGREDIENTS

500 g (1 lb) boneless, skinless chicken breast, thickly sliced

1 large clove garlic, chopped

1 tablespoon tandoori spice mix or mild curry powder

2 tablespoons vegetable oil

1 onion, sliced

1¼ cups (250 g) basmati rice, rinsed

600 ml (21 fl oz) hot vegetable or chicken stock

50 g (1¾ oz) raisins

½ teaspoon salt

1 tablespoon chopped fresh coriander (cilantro) leaves

100 g (3½ oz) red cherry tomatoes, halved

30 g (1 oz) toasted pine nuts

lemon wedges, to serve

NUTRIENTS PER SERVING

2451 kJ, 585 kcal, 34 g protein, 21 g fat (4 g saturated fat), 63 g carbohydrate

VARIATION

Instead of chicken, use salmon fillets (left whole) or lamb cutlets. Grill for 3–4 minutes each side. Make a ginger marinade for the salmon or lamb by blending 1 teaspoon grated ginger into the spice mix.

COOK'S TIP

If you like, make a quick raita while the rice and chicken are cooking. Finely chop ½ Lebanese or other small cucumber and mix with ½ cup (125 g) natural (plain) yogurt, 1 tablespoon chopped fresh mint and ¼ teaspoon ground cumin.

SAFFRON PILAF WITH RAISINS AND NUTS

TIME **30 MINUTES** SERVES **4**

INGREDIENTS

2 cups (400 g) long-grain rice
2 tablespoons butter
1 red onion, chopped
2 cloves garlic, chopped
1 teaspoon ground coriander
2 teaspoons ground cumin
1 cinnamon stick
1 pinch saffron threads
$1/3$ cup (40 g) raisins
salt and freshly ground black pepper
500 g (1 lb) frozen broad (fava) beans
$2/3$ cup (150 g) natural (plain) yogurt
3 tablespoons chopped fresh coriander
   (cilantro) leaves
1–2 tablespoons chilli-flavoured olive oil
   (optional)
$1/2$ cup (90 g) flaked almonds,
   lightly toasted

METHOD

1 Put rice in a bowl, cover with cold water and leave to soak, to remove some of the starch.

2 Melt butter in a large heavy-based saucepan over very low heat. Add onion and garlic, increase heat and fry 1–2 minutes, or until the onion softens. Stir in ground coriander and cumin and reduce heat to very low.

3 Pour rice into a sieve and rinse. Add to the onion, then stir in $1^1/2$ cups (375 ml) boiling water. Add cinnamon stick, saffron threads, raisins, and salt and pepper to taste. Bring to a fast boil, then reduce heat until barely simmering. Cover and cook 15 minutes; do not lift the lid.

4 Meanwhile, put broad beans in a separate saucepan of boiling water and bring back to a boil. Reduce heat, cover and simmer 5–6 minutes.

5 Put yogurt and fresh coriander in a bowl, stir together and set aside.

6 Drain broad beans and drizzle with the oil, if using.

7 Remove rice from the heat and leave to stand, still covered, 3 minutes. Discard cinnamon stick. Add almonds and broad beans, stir through and fluff up with a fork. Serve the rice accompanied by the bowl of yogurt and coriander.

NUTRIENTS PER SERVING
2704 kJ, 646 kcal, 18 g protein, 27 g fat (9 g saturated fat), 84 g carbohydrate

EGG-TOPPED KEDGEREE

TIME **30 MINUTES** SERVES **4**

INGREDIENTS

2 cups (400 g) long-grain rice

3 tablespoons butter

1 small onion, chopped

250 g (8 oz) skinned smoked
   haddock fillets

1 tablespoon Indian curry powder

1 tablespoon white wine vinegar

4 large eggs

125 g (4 oz) peeled cooked prawns
   (shrimp)

salt and freshly ground black pepper

3 tablespoons chopped fresh parsley

8 anchovy fillets, chopped

20 capers, rinsed and squeezed dry,
   chopped

1 tablespoon lemon juice

METHOD

1 Put rice in a saucepan, add salt
   and enough boiling water to cover
   well. Return to a boil, cover and
   cook gently 15 minutes.

2 Meanwhile, melt butter in a large
   saucepan. Fry onion 3–4 minutes
   until soft.

3 Place haddock in a shallow dish
   and cover with boiling water.
   Leave to stand 2–3 minutes, then
   drain well. Flake fish into chunks,
   removing any bones, then add to
   the onion, along with the curry
   powder. Cook 5 minutes.

4 Fill a frying pan with about 6 cm
   (2½ inches) water, add vinegar
   and bring to a gentle boil. Poach
   eggs about 3 minutes, or until set
   but still soft in the centre. Remove
   from pan and keep warm.

5 Drain rice thoroughly. Stir into
   the fish mixture in the pan, add
   prawns and heat through gently.
   Season with salt and pepper.

6 Spoon out the kedgeree onto individual serving plates or shallow bowls.
   Sprinkle with parsley, anchovies, capers and lemon juice. Make a hollow
   in each serving and top with a poached egg.

NUTRIENTS PER SERVING

2394 kJ, 572 kcal, 33 g protein, 23 g fat (11 g saturated fat), 58 g carbohydrate

Above Saffron pilaf with raisins and nuts (top); Egg-topped kedgeree (bottom)

HOT AND SPICY CAPSICUM, RICE AND BEANS

TIME **30 MINUTES** SERVES **4**

INGREDIENTS

2 tablespoons vegetable oil

1 large onion, chopped

1 red capsicum (bell pepper), seeds removed, chopped

2 large cloves garlic, crushed

1–2 red chillies, seeds removed, chopped, to taste

150 g (5 oz) chorizo or other spicy cured sausage, cubed

1¼ cups (250 g) basmati rice, rinsed

400 ml (14 fl oz) can coconut milk

600 ml (21 fl oz) hot water or chicken stock

salt and freshly ground black pepper

2 sprigs fresh thyme, plus extra, to garnish

1 bay leaf

400 g (14 oz) can cannellini beans, black-eyed peas or red kidney beans, rinsed and drained

METHOD

1 Heat oil in a large heavy-based saucepan, and cook onion, capsicum, garlic and chillies 5 minutes, or until just softened.

2 Add chorizo or spicy sausage and rice, and stir-fry 1–2 minutes. Add coconut milk and water or stock. Season and bring to a boil. Stir in thyme and bay leaf, then cover and simmer gently 10 minutes.

3 Stir in beans or peas and cook a further 5 minutes, or until rice is tender and beans are heated through. Serve sprinkled with a little thyme.

NUTRIENTS PER SERVING

2525 kJ, 603 kcal, 17 g protein, 29 g fat (15 g saturated fat), 70 g carbohydrate

Left Hot and spicy capsicum, rice and beans

FENNEL, MUSHROOMS AND CANNELLINI BEANS

TIME **30 MINUTES** SERVES **4**

INGREDIENTS

2 tablespoons olive oil

1 onion, halved and sliced

3 bulbs fennel (about 750 g/1½ lb in total), thinly sliced

2½ tablespoons paprika

300 g/10 oz button or Swiss brown or porcini mushrooms, halved

410 g (15 oz) can chopped tomatoes with herbs

2 tablespoons sun-dried tomato paste (concentrated purée)

300 ml (10 fl oz) vegetable stock

400 g (14 oz) can cannellini beans, rinsed and drained

salt and freshly ground black pepper

Greek-style yogurt, to serve

METHOD

1 Heal oil in a large heavy-based saucepan and cook onion over medium heat 5 minutes, or until softened.

2 Add fennel and paprika and stir briefly, then add mushrooms, tomatoes, sun-dried tomato paste and stock.

3 Stir in cannellini beans and season with salt and pepper, then bring to a boil and stir. Cover pan, reduce heat and simmer 20 minutes, or until the vegetables are tender. Serve with yogurt.

NUTRIENTS PER SERVING

967 kJ, 231 kcal, 11 g protein, 11 g fat (1 g saturated fat), 24 g carbohydrate

COOK'S TIP

Serve this dish with rice or slices of crusty bread.

STIR-FRIED RICE WITH
VEGETABLES AND CASHEW NUTS

TIME **30 MINUTES** SERVES **4**

INGREDIENTS

1¼ cups (250 g) basmati rice, rinsed

2 tablespoons soy sauce

1 tablespoon dry sherry

2 teaspoons sesame oil

2 tablespoons vegetable oil

250 g (8 oz) carrots, halved lengthwise
and thinly sliced

300 g (10 oz) leeks, white part only,
thinly sliced

150 g (5 oz) savoy cabbage, thinly sliced

1 large clove garlic, crushed

1 large fresh red chilli, seeds removed,
sliced, or ½ teaspoon dried red
chilli flakes

75 g (2½ oz) cashew nuts

salt and freshly ground black pepper

75 g (2½ oz) mixed toasted seeds

METHOD

1 Add rice to a saucepan of boiling water and boil 10 minutes, or until tender. Drain.

2 While rice is cooking, mix together soy sauce, sherry and sesame oil in a small bowl and set aside.

3 Heat vegetable oil in a wok or large frying pan and stir-fry carrots and leeks 2–3 minutes, or until softened. Add cabbage, garlic and chilli, and stir-fry 2–3 minutes. Stir in soy sauce mixture and cashew nuts. Season to taste with salt and pepper.

4 Mix hot rice into the wok. Sprinkle with seeds and use a fork to mix them evenly through the rice.

NUTRIENTS PER SERVING

2473 kJ, 591 kcal, 16 g protein, 31 g fat (4 g saturated fat), 61 g carbohydrate

VARIATION

You can vary the vegetables depending on what is available. Try strips of zucchini (courgette), eggplant (aubergine), capsicum (bell pepper) or fennel. Or use 600 g (1 lb 5 oz) ready-sliced stir-fry vegetables.

THAI COCONUT RICE WITH LIME AND CORIANDER PRAWNS

TIME 30 MINUTES SERVES 4

METHOD

1 Heat 1 tablespoon oil in a large non-stick frying pan. Add French shallot or onion, garlic and chilli, and cook 3 minutes, or until softened. Stir in rice, stock and coconut cream. Season lightly.

2 Bring rice mixture to a boil. Stir once, then reduce heat to a gentle simmer. Cover and cook 10 minutes without lifting the lid. The liquid should have been absorbed and small steam holes should have appeared. If necessary, cover and cook the rice mixture a further 2 minutes. Add cucumber and cook, covered, a further 1 minute, then remove the pan from the heat and leave to stand 5 minutes.

3 While rice is standing, heat remaining oil in a wok or large frying pan and stir-fry prawns 3 minutes, or until they turn pink. Stir in cumin and cook for a few seconds, then add lime juice and chopped coriander and stir.

4 Divide rice among four plates and top with the prawns. Garnish with coriander sprigs and serve with lime wedges, if you like.

NUTRIENTS PER SERVING

2742 kJ, 655 kcal, 29 g protein, 22 g fat (11 g saturated fat), 84 g carbohydrate

COOK'S TIP

You can use cooked peeled prawns (shrimp) if you prefer. Add in step 3 and just heat them through 1–2 minutes.

INGREDIENTS

2 tablespoons vegetable oil

1 large French shallot (eschalot) or small onion, chopped

2 cloves garlic, crushed

1 large red chilli, seeds removed, sliced

1³⁄₄ cups (350 g) jasmine rice or long-grain rice

600 ml (21 fl oz) hot vegetable or chicken stock

200 ml (7 fl oz) coconut cream

salt and freshly ground black pepper

¹⁄₂ cucumber, halved lengthwise and sliced

400 g (14 oz) peeled raw large prawns (uncooked large shrimp)

1 teaspoon ground cumin

juice of 1 lime

3 tablespoons chopped fresh coriander (cilantro) leaves and stems, plus extra sprigs, to garnish

lime wedges, to serve (optional)

VEGETABLE COUSCOUS
TIME 30 MINUTES SERVES 2

INGREDIENTS

15 g (¹/₂ oz) butter

3 teaspoons olive oil

1 small onion, chopped

2 small carrots, cut into small chunks

¹/₂ small swede (rutabaga), cut into
  small chunks

1 parsnip, cut into small chunks

1 pinch cayenne pepper

1 pinch ground turmeric

¹/₂ teaspoon ground ginger

¹/₂ teaspoon ground cinnamon

1 pinch saffron threads (optional)

salt and freshly ground black pepper

¹/₂ cup (90 g) dried apricots, chopped

¹/₃ cup (40 g) frozen baby peas

¹/₃ cup (60 g) canned chickpeas,
  rinsed and drained

²/₃ cup (125 g) couscous

2 sprigs fresh coriander (cilantro),
  to garnish

METHOD

1 Heat butter and oil in a large heavy flameproof casserole dish. Add onion and fry gently 5 minutes until soft.

2 Add carrots, swede and parsnip, then stir in cayenne, turmeric, ginger, cinnamon and saffron threads, if using, and season to taste with salt and black pepper.

3 Add apricots, peas, chickpeas and 300 ml (10 fl oz) boiling water and bring back to a boil. Reduce heat, cover and simmer 15 minutes.

4 Meanwhile, pour 1 cup (250 ml) boiling water into a saucepan, add couscous and stir, then turn off heat and leave to stand, covered, until the vegetables are ready.

5 When the vegetables are cooked, season the couscous to taste with salt and pepper. Separate and fluff up the grains with a fork, then transfer couscous to a serving dish. Spoon the vegetables over the top, garnish with coriander and serve.

NUTRIENTS PER SERVING

2511 kJ, 600 kcal, 20 g protein, 17 g fat (5 g saturated fat), 95 g carbohydrate

VARIATION

Other fresh root vegetables, such as celeriac (celery root), potatoes or turnips, make excellent substitutes for the carrots, swede or parsnip.

LAMB WITH APRICOT AND PINE NUT COUSCOUS
TIME **20 MINUTES** SERVES **4**

METHOD

1 Put couscous and apricots in a heatproof bowl and mix in 400 ml (14 fl oz) stock, 1 tablespoon oil and 1 teaspoon salt. Set aside so that the liquid can be absorbed.

2 When couscous has been soaking for 10 minutes, heat remaining oil in a large non-stick frying pan and stir-fry lamb with garlic, chilli, cumin and paprika 7 minutes, or until nicely browned and just tender. Add remaining stock and bring to a boil, stirring to loosen the residue on the base of the pan. Season to taste with salt and pepper, add lemon juice, then mix in crème fraîche or sour cream.

3 Using a fork, rake through couscous quite briskly to separate the grains and fluff them up. Mix in pine nuts and coriander. Divide among four plates and top with the lamb. Garnish with extra pine nuts and a sprinkle of paprika.

NUTRIENTS PER SERVING

2775 kJ, 663 kcal, 36 g protein, 37 g fat (11 g saturated fat), 48 g carbohydrate

VARIATION

CURRIED VEGETABLES AND COUSCOUS This is a great way to use up left-over vegetables and meat from a roast dinner. Dice all the lean meat from a cooked joint. Cut any left-over vegetables (roast potatoes, carrots, parsnips) into small chunks (allow about 100 g/3¹/2 oz per person). Soak the couscous and apricots as for step 1. Heat 1 tablespoon olive oil in a wok and add the meat with 1 crushed clove garlic, a 2.5 cm (1 inch) piece fresh ginger, grated, and 1 large red chilli, seeds removed, chopped. Sprinkle in 1 tablespoon mild curry powder or curry paste. Stir-fry 2–3 minutes, then toss in the vegetables and cook until hot. Season, then mix into the couscous.

INGREDIENTS

200 g (7 oz) couscous

1/3 cup (60 g) dried apricots, chopped

550 ml (19 fl oz) beef or chicken stock, boiling

2 tablespoons olive oil

1 teaspoon salt

400 g (14 oz) lamb stir-fry strips or leg steaks, thinly sliced

2 large cloves garlic, crushed

1 large red chilli, seeds removed, thinly sliced

1 teaspoon ground cumin

1 teaspoon paprika, plus extra for dusting

salt and freshly ground black pepper

juice of 1 lemon

4 tablespoons low-fat crème fraîche or light sour cream

4 tablespoons toasted pine nuts, plus extra, to garnish

2 tablespoons chopped fresh coriander (cilantro) leaves

COUSCOUS WITH CHARGRILLED HALOUMI AND VEGETABLES

TIME 30 MINUTES SERVES 4

INGREDIENTS

2 zucchini (courgettes), sliced lengthwise

1 eggplant (aubergine), halved lengthwise
   and thinly sliced

1 red capsicum (bell pepper), seeds
   removed, cut into wide strips

8 red cherry tomatoes

3 tablespoons olive oil

1 clove garlic, crushed

1 teaspoon fresh thyme

salt and freshly ground black pepper

250 g (8 oz) haloumi cheese

250 g (8 oz) couscous

400 ml (14 fl oz) vegetable stock, boiling

METHOD

1 Put all the vegetables into a bowl. Mix oil with garlic and thyme. Season, then drizzle 2 tablespoons over the vegetables and toss gently.

2 Heat a non-stick or ridged chargrill pan until hot. Cook the vegetables, in batches if necessary, 2 minutes on each side, or until they are seared golden brown. Keep warm.

3 Slice haloumi into eight pieces and put in the pan. Cook 1–2 minutes on each side, or until lightly coloured. Arrange on a serving plate with the vegetables.

4 While cheese is cooking, put couscous in a heatproof serving bowl and pour over stock. Stir gently, then cover and leave to absorb the liquid 5 minutes. Stir in the remaining oil mixture and serve with haloumi and vegetables.

NUTRIENTS PER SERVING

2275 kJ, 543 kcal, 23 g protein, 25 g fat (9 g saturated fat), 55 g carbohydrate

VARIATION

Instead of the Mediterranean vegetables, use baby corn, asparagus and mushrooms. You can also replace the couscous with chargrilled garlic bread made with ciabatta slices.

VEGETABLE DAL

TIME **30 MINUTES** SERVES **4**

METHOD

1 Put lentils in a bowl and pour over enough cold water to cover them by about 1 cm ($\frac{1}{2}$ inch). Leave to soak.

2 Heat oil in a large heavy-based saucepan. Add onion and gently cook 5 minutes, or until almost soft, stirring occasionally. Add garlic, ginger, cumin and turmeric. Cook 1 minute, stirring constantly.

3 Drain lentils and add to pan with coconut milk, stock and salt and pepper to taste. Bring to a boil, then reduce heat, partially cover the pan with a lid and simmer 5 minutes.

4 Meanwhile, put tomatoes in a heatproof bowl and pour over boiling water to cover. Leave 1 minute, then remove with a slotted spoon and rinse briefly under cold water. Peel off skins and dice the flesh.

5 Add tomatoes and lime or lemon juice to lentil mixture. Cover pan and simmer a further 10 minutes. Stir in zucchini and cook, stirring occasionally, a further 5 minutes, or until lentils are tender and dal is thick and creamy. Taste and adjust the seasoning if necessary, then stir in the coriander before serving, if you like.

NUTRIENTS PER SERVING

1214 kJ, 290 kcal, 7 g protein, 21 g fat (12 g saturated fat), 18 g carbohydrate

VARIATION

Instead of lentils and zucchini, use 2 x 400 g (14 oz) cans red kidney beans, rinsed and drained. Purée 1 can with 100 ml ($3\frac{1}{2}$ fl oz) vegetable stock, and add to the pan with the coconut milk in step 3. Stir in the beans from the second can. Add 250 g (8 oz) shredded spinach leaves with the tomatoes, then simmer uncovered 8–10 minutes. Serve sprinkled with poppyseeds.

COOK'S TIP

The dal can be made up to 24 hours beforehand, then stored in the fridge, or frozen for up to 3 months. Thaw if frozen, reheat with an extra 2 tablespoons vegetable stock or water, and simmer 1–2 minutes.

INGREDIENTS

1 cup (250 g) red lentils, rinsed and drained

2 tablespoons peanut (groundnut) oil

1 onion, finely chopped

2 cloves garlic, crushed

2.5 cm (1 inch) piece fresh ginger, grated

2 teaspoons ground cumin

2 teaspoons ground turmeric

400 ml (14 fl oz) can light coconut milk

400 ml (14 fl oz) hot vegetable stock

salt and freshly ground black pepper

4 tomatoes

juice of $\frac{1}{2}$ lime or 1 tablespoon lemon juice

2 zucchini (courgettes), diced

3 tablespoons chopped fresh coriander (cilantro) leaves (optional)

TOFU AND VEGETABLES WITH TAHINI SAUCE

TIME **30 MINUTES** SERVES **2**

INGREDIENTS

3 tablespoons soy sauce

3 tablespoons olive oil

350 g (12 oz) small zucchini (courgettes),
or a mixture of zucchini and baby
eggplant (aubergine), sliced crosswise

125 g (4 oz) medium cup mushrooms,
thickly sliced

250 g (8 oz) firm tofu, cut into
bite-sized pieces

TAHINI SAUCE

3 tablespoons tahini

1 large clove garlic, crushed

2 tablespoons chopped fresh parsley

1/2 teaspoon sesame oil

1 teaspoon dijon mustard

salt and freshly ground black pepper

METHOD

1 Preheat grill (broiler) to medium.

2 Blend soy sauce and olive oil thoroughly in a large bowl. Add zucchini, eggplant if using, mushrooms and tofu and stir gently until well coated.

3 Spread vegetables and tofu in a single layer in the grill tray or on a baking tray (sheet). Grill 20 minutes, or until cooked and browned, shaking the vegetables occasionally to prevent sticking.

4 Meanwhile, make the tahini sauce. Pour tahini into a jug, add garlic, then briskly stir in just enough water to give the sauce the consistency of pouring (light) cream. Stir in parsley, sesame oil and mustard, and season to taste with salt and pepper.

5 When vegetables and tofu are cooked, transfer to a warmed serving plate and pour over the tahini sauce. Serve hot or warm.

NUTRIENTS PER SERVING

2453 kJ, 586 kcal, 29 g protein, 49 g fat (9 g saturated fat), 8 g carbohydrate

COOK'S TIP

You could cook the vegetables and tofu on a hot chargrill pan or plate until cooked and browned, turning occasionally.

POLENTA AND TOMATO TART

TIME **30 MINUTES** SERVES **4**

INGREDIENTS

3 cups (750 ml) hot chicken stock

1 cup (150 g) coarse polenta
  or cornmeal

3 tablespoons parmesan

3 tablespoons unsalted butter

$^1/_4$ cup (60 ml) virgin olive oil

6 vine-ripened tomatoes, finely sliced

4 tablespoons torn fresh basil

freshly ground black pepper

1 tablespoon caster (superfine) sugar

4 slices prosciutto

METHOD

1 Bring stock to a boil in a large saucepan then gradually pour in polenta or cornmeal, stirring with a large wooden spoon. Cook over low heat about 10 minutes, stirring constantly, until polenta is smooth and thick. Remove from heat.

2 Stir in parmesan and butter, and press the mixture into a lightly oiled 23 cm (9 inch) flan or quiche dish. Brush the top with a little oil and refrigerate 10 minutes. Preheat grill (broiler) to medium.

3 When the polenta has firmed, place dish under the grill and cook 5 minutes, until golden. Remove dish but leave the grill on.

4 Arrange tomatoes on top of the polenta and scatter over basil. Season with pepper, sprinkle with sugar, drizzle over remaining oil and top with prosciutto. Put the tart back under the grill 5 minutes, or until prosciutto is crisp. Cut into wedges and serve immediately.

NUTRIENTS PER SERVING

1925 kJ, 460 kcal, 12 g protein, 30 g fat (12 g saturated fat), 34 g carbohydrate

COOK'S TIP

Good-quality, coarsely ground polenta should be used; instant polenta will not give the same result.

Left Polenta and tomato tart (top); Polenta with provolone cheese (bottom)

POLENTA WITH PROVOLONE CHEESE

TIME **20 MINUTES** SERVES **4**

INGREDIENTS

$1^1/_3$ cups (200 g) instant polenta
  or cornmeal

1 small bunch (20 g/$^2/_3$ oz) fresh sage,
  oregano, basil or parsley, leaves
  finely chopped

200 g (7 oz) provolone or gruyère cheese,
  grated or diced

2 teaspoons black or mixed peppercorns,
  crushed

1 teaspoon salt

8–10 pitted black olives, finely chopped

METHOD

1 Put polenta or cornmeal in a saucepan with $3^1/_2$ cups (875 ml) water. Place over high heat, bring to a boil, then reduce heat and simmer about 10 minutes, stirring frequently with a large wooden spoon or paddle to remove any lumps.

2 When the polenta becomes thick and starts to stiffen, stir in sage, oregano, basil or parsley, cheese, peppercorns, salt and olives. Beat vigorously until the cheese is incorporated and the mixture begins to leave the side of the saucepan when stirred.

3 Serve immediately, or leave to stand 5–10 minutes to stiffen further. It will remain hot.

NUTRIENTS PER SERVING

1096 kJ, 262 kcal, 9 g protein, 2 g fat (1 g saturated fat), 46 g carbohydrate

COOK'S TIP

Serve the polenta with a green leaf salad or steamed vegetables, such as snow peas (mangetout) or fennel, or roasted vegetables.

SUMMER SQUASH WITH POLENTA

TIME 30 MINUTES SERVES 4

INGREDIENTS

1½ cups (225 g) instant polenta
   or cornmeal
2 tablespoons olive oil
1 small onion, finely chopped
1 clove garlic, crushed
500 g (1 lb) mixed yellow and green baby
   (pattypan) squash, quartered, and/or
   young green and yellow zucchini
   (courgettes), sliced crosswise
4 sprigs fresh thyme
salt and freshly ground black pepper
200 g (7 oz) grated cheddar or
   cheshire cheese
1 tablespoon butter
2 large tomatoes, diced
grated zest of 1 lemon
3 tablespoons finely chopped fresh parsley

METHOD

1 Put polenta or cornmeal in a large saucepan with 3 cups (750 ml) water. Bring to a boil, reduce heat and simmer 8 minutes. Stir occasionally to remove any lumps.
2 Meanwhile, slowly heat oil in a shallow pan over medium heat. Add onion and garlic and fry 5–8 minutes, until soft. Add baby squash and/or zucchini, thyme, salt and pepper to taste, and cook 10 minutes.
3 When polenta comes away cleanly from the side of the pan, remove from heat. Beat cheese and butter into the polenta, then season to taste, cover and keep warm.
4 Add tomatoes to the pan of vegetables and cook 5 minutes. Add lemon zest and parsley. Remove and discard the thyme.
5 Serve the stewed vegetables on individual plates, with a portion of polenta on the side.

NUTRIENTS PER SERVING

2030 kJ, 485 kcal, 18 g protein, 29 g fat (14 g saturated fat), 39 g carbohydrate

VARIATION

For extra flavour, add eggplant (aubergine) or red and yellow capsicums (bell peppers), or enrich the stew with a little crème fraîche or sour cream.

BUCKWHEAT CAULIFLOWER CHEESE
TIME **30 MINUTES** SERVES **4**

INGREDIENTS

150 g (5 oz) buckwheat grains

400 ml (14 fl oz) boiling water or stock

salt and freshly ground black pepper

200 ml (7 fl oz) low-fat milk mixed with
    200 ml (7 fl oz) water

1 cauliflower, cut into small florets

1 large leek, white part only, thinly sliced

100 g (3¹/₂ oz) baby spinach leaves

2¹/₂ tablespoons cornflour (cornstarch)

15 g (¹/₂ oz) butter

150 g (5 oz) mature cheddar, grated

12 red cherry tomatoes, halved

METHOD

1 Put buckwheat and water or stock in a large saucepan and add ¹/₂ teaspoon salt and black pepper to taste. Bring to a boil, then cover and simmer gently 10 minutes, or until liquid has been absorbed. Remove from heat and allow to stand, still covered, 5 minutes, then rake through the grains with a fork.

2 While buckwheat is cooking, put milk and water and a little salt in a saucepan. Add cauliflower and leek, and cook 7 minutes, or until just tender. Using a slotted spoon, transfer vegetables to a large, shallow, warmed ovenproof dish. Mix buckwheat and spinach into the cauliflower and leek. Preheat grill (broiler) to high.

3 Blend cornflour with 3 tablespoons cold water to make a paste and stir briskly into the hot milk mixture in the pan. Stir over medium heat until sauce starts to thicken. Add butter and simmer 1 minute, then remove from heat and stir in two-thirds of the cheese until melted. Check the seasoning, then pour over the vegetables and grains, mixing in lightly.

4 Dot surface with tomatoes and scatter with the remaining cheese. Grill until the top is browned and bubbling. Serve hot.

NUTRIENTS PER SERVING
1681 kJ, 401 kcal, 21 g protein, 17 g fat (10 g saturated fat), 42 g carbohydrate

VARIATION
For non-vegetarians, add some slices of crisp pancetta, or dry-fry 125 g (4 oz) bacon pieces until crisp. Scatter pancetta or bacon on top of the vegetables, then pour over the sauce.

COOK'S TIP
Buckwheat can be cooked, cooled quickly and frozen for up to 1 month. To use, reheat in the microwave, partially covered in a bowl, 4–5 minutes on High, raking through the grains with a fork once. To use in a salad, leave to thaw at room temperature 2–3 hours, or thaw in the microwave on High 3–4 minutes. Then stir in chopped vegetables and toss with vinaigrette.

ITALIAN CHEESE POLENTA WITH QUICK RATATOUILLE

TIME **30 MINUTES** SERVES **4**

INGREDIENTS

2 tablespoons olive oil

1 red onion, cut into thin wedges

2 cloves garlic, crushed

1 red or yellow capsicum (bell pepper),
   seeds removed, sliced

1 medium–large zucchini (courgette),
   cut into small chunks

1 small eggplant (aubergine), cut into
   small chunks

1 large red chilli, seeds removed, sliced

salt and freshly ground black pepper

4 cups (1 litre) boiling water

1⅓ cups (200 g) polenta or cornmeal

150 g (5 oz) fontina or dolcelatte cheese,
   cubed

410 g (15 oz) can chopped tomatoes
   with basil

15 g (½ oz) fresh basil leaves, torn,
   plus extra leaves, to garnish (optional)

METHOD

1 Heat oil over medium heat in a large frying pan that has a lid. Add onion, garlic, capsicum, zucchini, eggplant and chilli, cover pan and cook, stirring occasionally, 10 minutes, or until vegetables begin to soften. Add salt and pepper to taste.

2 Meanwhile, put boiling water in a large non-stick saucepan, return to a boil and add 1 teaspoon salt. Pour in polenta in a steady stream while stirring continuously with a wooden spoon.

3 Lower heat and continue stirring briskly until polenta begins to thicken and bubble slowly. It should be free from lumps. Half-cover pan and cook 5 minutes, stirring often. Remove from heat and mix in cheese. Season with pepper, then cover and set aside.

4 Stir tomatoes into ratatouille and cook a further 10 minutes, or until vegetables are tender. Add torn basil. Spoon polenta onto serving plates, top with ratatouille and garnish with basil leaves, if you like.

NUTRIENTS PER SERVING

1863 kJ, 445 kcal, 17 g protein, 22 g fat (9 g saturated fat), 44 g carbohydrate

COOK'S TIP

Make a double quantity of polenta, use half with the ratatouille and pour the remainder into a baking tray, spreading it level. Cool until set, then cover and chill. Next day, cut into wedges or squares. Brush with 2 tablespoons oil or melted butter, then grill (broil) at high temperature until browned and crisp. Serve with a vegetable or meat sauce.

BURGHUL PILAF WITH MUSHROOMS
TIME **30 MINUTES** SERVES **4**

INGREDIENTS
125 g (4 oz) butter

1 onion, finely chopped

2 cups (350 g) burghul (bulgur)

3¹/₂ cups (875 ml) hot vegetable stock

3 teaspoons olive oil

250 g (8 oz) mixed mushrooms, such as
    button, oyster and shiitake mushrooms

salt and freshly ground black pepper

¹/₃ cup (30 g) flaked almonds

¹/₃ cup (40 g) chopped hazelnuts

1 small bunch (20 g/²/₃ oz) fresh parsley,
    leaves finely chopped

METHOD
1 Heat half the butter in a flameproof casserole dish. Add onion and fry about 5 minutes, until translucent.

2 Add burghul and cook, stirring frequently, 3 minutes. Add stock, bring to a boil, then reduce heat, cover casserole dish and simmer gently about 10–15 minutes, or until all the stock has been absorbed.

3 Meanwhile, heat oil in a frying pan, add mushrooms and fry 3 minutes, or until softened. Season with salt and pepper. Pour mushrooms and any juices over the partially cooked burghul, cover the casserole dish and leave to continue cooking.

4 Add almonds to the frying pan and cook over medium heat, shaking, 1–2 minutes. Add hazelnuts and cook both until lightly browned.

5 When stock is absorbed and burghul cooked, stir in remaining butter, toasted nuts and parsley. Taste for seasoning, adding more salt and pepper if necessary, and serve the pilaf straight from the casserole dish.

NUTRIENTS PER SERVING
3064 kJ, 732 kcal, 15 g protein, 44 g fat (17 g saturated fat), 73 g carbohydrate

COOK'S TIP
Burghul, traditionally used in Middle Eastern dishes such as tabouleh, is hulled, parboiled cracked wheat. It is also sold as bulgur and bulgar.

STUFFED CAPSICUMS WITH CHICKEN AND COUSCOUS
TIME **25 MINUTES** SERVES **4**

METHOD

1 Put couscous, currants and garlic in a heatproof bowl and pour over the boiling stock. Cover and leave to stand.

2 Meanwhile, cook capsicums in a large saucepan of boiling water 5 minutes. Drain well and put into a grill (broiler) pan, cut side up.

3 Preheat grill to medium. Stir chicken and oregano into the couscous. Season with salt and pepper to taste, then divide the mixture among the capsicums, pressing down firmly with a spoon. Top with fetta.

4 Grill slowly 10 minutes, or until hot and golden, then serve.

NUTRIENTS PER SERVING
1509 kJ, 360 kcal, 14 g protein, 22 g fat (7 g saturated fat), 35 g carbohydrate

COOK'S TIP
Serve these stuffed capsicums with a green salad. They are a good way to use up the leftovers from a roast chicken. Alternatively, you could use store-bought barbecue chicken, or grill some boneless, skinless chicken breast.

INGREDIENTS

150 g (5 oz) couscous

2 tablespoons currants

1 clove garlic, chopped

300 ml (10 fl oz) vegetable stock, boiling

4 red and/or green capsicums (bell peppers), halved lengthwise, seeds removed

250 g (8 oz) cooked chicken, diced

1 tablespoon chopped fresh oregano

salt and freshly ground black pepper

100 g (3 1/2 oz) fetta, crumbled

QUINOA WITH BALSAMIC VEGETABLE SKEWERS

TIME **30 MINUTES** SERVES **4**

INGREDIENTS

¾ cup (150 g) quinoa or brown rice,
    rinsed
400 ml (14 fl oz) hot vegetable stock
salt and freshly ground black pepper
1 red onion, cut into wedges
1 red capsicum (bell pepper), seeds
    removed, cut into chunks
2 small zucchini (courgettes),
    cut into chunks
200 g (7 oz) pumpkin (winter squash),
    cut into chunks
2 tablespoons vegetable oil
1–2 teaspoons fresh thyme
200 g (7 oz) can corn, drained
15 g (½ oz) butter
125 g (4 oz) frozen peas or sliced
    green beans
250 g (8 oz) marinated tofu, cut into
    bite-sized cubes
1 teaspoon mild chilli powder or a few
    shakes of Tabasco sauce, to taste
3 tablespoons chopped fresh parsley
2 tablespoons balsamic vinegar

METHOD

1 Preheat oven to 200°C (400°F/Gas 6). Put quinoa or brown rice and stock in a large saucepan and add ½ teaspoon salt and black pepper to taste. Bring to a boil, then cover and simmer gently 10 minutes for quinoa, or 20 minutes for brown rice.

2 Meanwhile, push onion, capsicum, zucchini and pumpkin chunks onto eight metal skewers, making sure each has a good mix of vegetables. Brush with oil and scatter with thyme. (The vegetables can also be cooked on wooden skewers; these need to be soaked 15–30 minutes beforehand so that they do not burn in the oven.) Place in a shallow roasting pan (baking dish) and season. Roast 10–12 minutes, or until vegetables begin to soften.

3 Stir corn into the saucepan of quinoa, then add butter, peas or beans and tofu. Add chilli powder or Tabasco to taste. Cover again and cook gently a further 5 minutes. Remove from heat and leave 5 minutes. Add parsley and rake through with a fork.

4 Drizzle balsamic vinegar over skewers and return them to the oven to roast a further 5 minutes, or until just tender. Serve with the quinoa.

NUTRIENTS PER SERVING
1760 kJ, 420 kcal, 18 g protein, 20 g fat (4 g saturated fat), 43 g carbohydrate

COOK'S TIP
Always rinse quinoa well before using, as it has a natural coating, called saponin, which can give the grain a bitter taste.

CHEESY CHICKPEA ENCHILADAS
TIME **30 MINUTES** SERVES **4**

INGREDIENTS

1 tablespoon vegetable oil

1 red onion, thinly sliced

1 teaspoon ground cumin

1 clove garlic, crushed

1 small red chilli, seeds removed, sliced

500 g (1 lb) tomatoes, chopped

400 g (14 oz) can chickpeas, rinsed
  and drained

salt and freshly ground black pepper

4 x 20 cm (8 inch) soft flour tortillas

1 small iceberg lettuce, shredded

100 g (3^1/$_2$ oz) mature cheddar, grated

Greek-style yogurt or sour cream, to serve

METHOD

1 Heat oil in a frying pan and cook onion over medium–high heat, stirring occasionally, 5 minutes, or until softened and lightly browned.

2 Add cumin and stir to coat, then add garlic, chilli, tomatoes and chickpeas. Cook over medium heat, stirring occasionally, 5–8 minutes, until most of the liquid has evaporated, then season with salt and pepper to taste.

3 Preheat grill (broiler) to high. Place tortillas on a flat surface and divide lettuce among them. Spoon chickpea mixture down the centre of each, fold the sides over and place in a flameproof dish. Sprinkle with cheese and cook under the grill until the cheese melts.

4 Serve the enchiladas with yogurt or sour cream.

NUTRIENTS PER SERVING

2285 kJ, 546 kcal, 27 g protein, 23 g fat (7 g saturated fat), 61 g carbohydrate

VARIATION

You can use ordinary pancakes as a substitute for the tortillas.

COOK'S TIP

Enchiladas, a Mexican dish of soft tortillas stuffed with beans, meat or cheese and topped with a hot sauce, are traditionally baked, but grilling is faster.

CURRIED CHICKPEA SALAD
TIME **25 MINUTES** SERVES **4**

METHOD

1 In a salad bowl, toss avocado in 1 teaspoon lemon juice. Add salad leaves, cherry tomatoes and cucumber and mix.
2 Heat oil in a large non-stick frying pan and cook onion 5 minutes, or until tender and beginning to brown. Stir in cumin, coriander, turmeric and chickpeas. Cook, stirring constantly, 1–2 minutes, or until the spices give off a rich aroma. Remove from heat and stir in remaining lemon juice. Cool 2 minutes.
3 Meanwhile, make the yogurt dressing. Stir yogurt and mint sauce together in a small bowl.
4 Add chickpea mixture to salad and toss together until well mixed. Drizzle yogurt dressing over the salad and serve with warmed naan.

NUTRIENTS PER SERVING
1112 kJ, 266 kcal, 8 g protein, 19 g fat (4 g saturated fat), 16 g carbohydrate

INGREDIENTS
1 large ripe avocado, diced
3 teaspoons lemon juice
150 g (5 oz) crisp mixed salad leaves, such as frisée, baby spinach leaves and rocket (arugula)
300 g (10 oz) red cherry tomatoes, halved
1/4 cucumber, diced
1 1/2 tablespoons olive oil
1 red onion, thinly sliced
1/2 teaspoon ground cumin
1 teaspoon ground coriander
1 pinch ground turmeric
400 g (14 oz) can chickpeas, rinsed and drained
warmed naan, to serve

YOGURT DRESSING
2 teaspoons ready-made mint sauce
150 g (5 oz) natural (plain) yogurt

SWEET AND SPICY CHICKPEAS
TIME 20 MINUTES SERVES 4

INGREDIENTS

400 g (14 oz) can chickpeas, rinsed
   and drained

finely grated zest and juice of 1 lime

1 teaspoon caster (superfine) sugar

1 teaspoon garam masala

$1/2$ teaspoon ground cinnamon

1 teaspoon dried oregano

2 tablespoons vegetable oil

2 small onions, halved and thickly sliced

1 red and 1 yellow capsicum (bell pepper),
   seeds removed, thickly sliced

12 red cherry tomatoes, halved

METHOD

1 Combine chickpeas, lime zest and juice, sugar, garam masala, cinnamon
   and oregano in a bowl. Stir to coat the chickpeas in the spicy mixture.
   Set aside for a few minutes.

2 Heat oil in a large frying pan or wok. When hot, add onions and stir-fry
   4 minutes, or until just beginning to colour. Reduce heat and add
   capsicums. Cook a further 3–4 minutes, stirring occasionally, until the
   vegetables are almost tender.

3 Stir in tomatoes, then add chickpea mixture. Cook 2 minutes, or until the
   vegetables are tender and everything is hot.

NUTRIENTS PER SERVING

715 kJ, 172 kcal, 5 g protein, 11 g fat (1 g saturated fat), 14 g carbohydrate

MIXED BEANS WITH PANCETTA
TIME **30 MINUTES** SERVES **4**

METHOD

1. Put stock or white wine in a small saucepan with bouquet garni. Bring to a boil, then simmer until the liquid has reduced by half.
2. Meanwhile, fry pancetta or bacon in a large frying pan 1–2 minutes until crisp, then drain on paper towel and set aside.
3. Add onion to the pan and fry in the remaining fat over medium heat 5 minutes, until golden.
4. Add green beans and cannellini beans and the reduced stock. Bring to a boil, cover, then reduce heat and simmer about 10 minutes, until the green beans are tender. To test, cool a bean under cold running water, then bite into it. When the beans are ready, there should be almost no liquid left in the pan.
5. Add crème fraîche or sour cream and warm through, then add the reserved pancetta, tarragon or parsley, and salt and pepper to taste. Stir and warm through again, then serve.

INGREDIENTS

1 cup (250 ml) chicken stock
   or white wine
bouquet garni
250 g (8 oz) pancetta or rindless dry-cured
   smoked bacon (bacon strips), diced
1 red or white onion, chopped
350 g (12 oz) small green beans, topped
   and tailed, cut into bite-sized pieces
400 g (14 oz) can cannellini beans, rinsed
   and drained
1 tablespoon crème fraîche or sour cream
3 tablespoons chopped fresh tarragon
   or parsley
salt and freshly ground black pepper

NUTRIENTS PER SERVING
1348 kJ, 322 kcal, 20 g protein, 19 g fat (2 g saturated fat), 19 g carbohydrate

SPICED CARROT AND CHICKPEA FRITTERS

TIME **20 MINUTES** SERVES **4**

INGREDIENTS

400 g (14 oz) can chickpeas, rinsed
   and drained
1 clove garlic, chopped
4 tablespoons chopped fresh coriander
   (cilantro) leaves
1½ teaspoons ground cumin
1½ teaspoons ground coriander
350 g (12 oz) carrots, coarsely grated
1 large egg
2 tablespoons flour
1–2 tablespoons vegetable oil
4 hamburger buns

METHOD

1 Put chickpeas in a food processor
  or blender with the garlic, fresh
  coriander, ground cumin and
  ground coriander. Process to a
  rough paste, then add carrot, egg
  and flour, and process briefly until
  evenly mixed but still slightly
  chunky. Divide the mixture into
  eight flat fritters.
2 Heat oil in a frying pan. Fry the
  fritters in two batches 2–3 minutes
  on each side, until golden, then
  drain on paper towel. Serve in the
  hamburger buns.

NUTRIENTS PER SERVING

1942 kJ, 464 kcal, 21 g protein, 14 g fat
(2 g saturated fat), 66 g carbohydrate

COOK'S TIP

Serve these burgers with the salad of
your choice. The fritters can be made
smaller and served as a snack or as
an entrée or party dish, accompanied
by some of your favourite chutney.

BEAN AND MUSHROOM BURGERS

TIME **30 MINUTES** SERVES **4**

INGREDIENTS

400 g (14 oz) can red kidney beans
1 red onion, quartered
200 g (7 oz) cup mushrooms
2 tablespoons olive oil
1 clove garlic, crushed
1 tablespoon garam masala
2 tablespoons wholemeal
  (whole-wheat) flour
2 tablespoons chopped fresh mint

salt and freshly ground black pepper
4 pitas, to serve

RED ONION RELISH

1 tablespoon olive oil
1 red onion (about 100 g/3½ oz
  in total), thinly sliced
2 tablespoons red wine vinegar
2 tablespoons soft brown sugar

METHOD

1 Rinse red kidney beans well and spread on a clean tea towel (dish
  towel) to drain.
2 To make the red onion relish, heat oil in a saucepan. Add onion,
  vinegar and sugar, and bring to a boil, stirring, then reduce heat and
  simmer, uncovered, 15–20 minutes, stirring occasionally, or until
  softened and slightly sticky. Remove from heat and keep warm.
3 Meanwhile, put onion and mushrooms in a food processor or blender
  and process until finely chopped. Alternatively, chop onion and
  mushrooms finely by hand.
4 Heat 1 tablespoon oil in a frying pan, add onion and mushroom
  mixture and cook over medium–high heat 5–8 minutes, stirring
  occasionally, until golden and dry. Stir in garlic, garam masala and
  flour, and cook 1 minute. Remove pan from heat, stir in mint and
  season well with salt and pepper.
5 Dry kidney beans on the tea towel and tip into a deep plate. Dry the
  kidney beans thoroughly before adding them to the mushroom mixture;
  if the beans retain too much liquid, the burgers will be difficult to
  handle. Mash the beans firmly with a potato masher, then stir in the
  cooled mushroom mixture. Divide mixture into four and, with lightly
  floured hands, shape each portion into a burger.
6 Heat remaining oil in a large frying pan, add burgers and cook over
  medium–high heat 6–8 minutes, turning carefully once, until browned.
  Meanwhile, warm pitas.
7 Arrange burgers on a warmed dish or individual plates and spoon some
  onion relish over the top of each. Serve with the warm pitas.

NUTRIENTS PER SERVING

1930 kJ, 461 kcal, 15 g protein, 13 g fat (2 g saturated fat), 73 g carbohydrate

Right Bean and mushroom burgers (top); Spiced carrot and chickpea fritters (bottom)

CHAPTER 6

Fish & Seafood

HONEY AND MUSTARD SALMON WITH CRUSHED BUTTERBEANS AND SPINACH

TIME **15 MINUTES** SERVES **4**

INGREDIENTS

1 tablespoon vegetable oil

1 tablespoon soy sauce

2 teaspoons honey

2 teaspoons wholegrain mustard

grated zest and juice of 1 lemon

4 skinless salmon fillets
    (about 125 g/4 oz each)

175 g (6 oz) baby spinach leaves, rinsed

2 x 400 g (14 oz) cans butterbeans
    (lima beans), rinsed and drained

1 large clove garlic, crushed

2 tablespoons extra virgin olive oil

1 pinch dried red chilli flakes

12 vine-ripened red cherry tomatoes

salt and freshly ground black pepper

METHOD

1 In a shallow dish, mix together vegetable oil, soy sauce, honey, mustard and 1 tablespoon lemon juice. Add salmon and coat with marinade. Set aside.

2 Heat a frying pan or chargrill pan until hot. Meanwhile, tip spinach into a dry saucepan with only the water that clings to its leaves and stir over low heat 2 minutes, or until wilted. Drain and set aside.

3 While spinach is wilting, put butterbeans, garlic, olive oil, remaining lemon juice, zest and dried red chilli flakes in a separate saucepan and heat gently.

4 Cook salmon in the heated pan 2–3 minutes on each side, or until just firm and pink. Add tomatoes for the last 1–2 minutes of cooking time.

5 Roughly crush butterbeans with a vegetable masher or fork. Stir through spinach and season to taste. Divide butterbean and spinach mixture among four serving plates. Put a salmon fillet on top of each and add tomatoes. Serve immediately.

NUTRIENTS PER SERVING

1635 kJ, 391 kcal, 25 g protein, 23 g fat (4 g saturated fat), 15 g carbohydrate

COOK'S TIP

If you have time, leave the salmon to marinate, covered, in the fridge overnight, ready to cook the next day. Use frozen spinach if fresh is not available, and cook following the packet instructions.

BASQUE-STYLE FISH
TIME 25 MINUTES SERVES 4

INGREDIENTS
2 tablespoons olive oil

1 onion, halved and thinly sliced

2 large red and 2 large green
capsicums (bell peppers),
seeds removed, thinly sliced
into short strips

2 sprigs fresh oregano

3 cloves garlic, crushed

400 g (14 oz) large ripe tomatoes,
diced

1 teaspoon sugar

1 good pinch chilli powder

50 g (1³/₄ oz) pitted black olives,
halved

1 tablespoon white wine vinegar

salt and freshly ground black pepper

400 g (14 oz) skinless thick white fish
fillet, such as snapper, bream,
flathead or barramundi

1¹/₂ cups (30 g) fresh flat-leaf
(Italian) parsley, chopped,
to garnish

METHOD
1 Heat oil in a large frying pan. Add onion, capsicums, oregano and
garlic. Cook, stirring frequently, 5 minutes, or until vegetables are
slightly softened.
2 Add tomatoes, sugar, chilli powder, olives and vinegar to the pan.
Cook over medium–high heat, stirring frequently, 3 minutes, or until
tomatoes are slightly softened. Season to taste.
3 Cut fish into four equal portions and add to pan, shuffling them down
into the vegetables. Reduce heat so that the vegetables bubble gently.
Cover with a piece of foil and cook about 5 minutes. The fish should
be firm, succulent and opaque, with flakes that just separate.
4 Sprinkle parsley over fish and vegetables, and serve in large bowls.

NUTRIENTS PER SERVING
1041 kJ, 249 kcal, 23 g protein, 14 g fat (2 g saturated fat), 8 g carbohydrate

COOK'S TIP
Drained roasted capsicums (bell peppers) from a jar save cooking time.
Use a 410 g (15 oz) can chopped tomatoes instead of fresh tomatoes.

Left Basque-style fish

FISH PARCELS WITH CHORIZO
TIME 30 MINUTES SERVES 4

INGREDIENTS
vegetable oil, for greasing

4 skinless thick white fish fillets (about
125 g/4 oz each), such as snapper,
bream, flathead or barramundi

1 chorizo (about 60 g/2 oz), thinly sliced

1 red and 1 yellow capsicum (bell pepper),
seeds removed, sliced

2 teaspoons balsamic or sherry vinegar

freshly ground black pepper

1 tablespoon chopped fresh parsley
(optional)

METHOD
1 Preheat oven to 200°C (400°F/
Gas 6). Cut four 30 cm (12 inch)
squares of foil and lightly grease
with a little oil.
2 Put a fish fillet in the centre of
each square of foil. Scatter with
chorizo and capsicum slices, and
sprinkle each mound of filling
with ¹/₂ teaspoon vinegar. Season
with pepper.
3 Bring up edges of foil and fold
together loosely to make four
parcels. Put parcels in a roasting
pan (baking dish) or a shallow
ovenproof dish and bake in the
oven 20–25 minutes, or until the
fish is tender and flakes easily.
4 Serve fish parcels opened on
serving plates and sprinkle with
parsley, if you like.

NUTRIENTS PER SERVING
874 kJ, 209 kcal, 27 g protein, 10 g fat
(2 g saturated fat), 3 g carbohydrate

VARIATION
Instead of fresh fish fillets, use frozen
fillets and cook 25–30 minutes.

CRAB AND AVOCADO SALAD

TIME **30 MINUTES** SERVES **4**

INGREDIENTS

4 cooked crabs

1 small red chilli, seeds removed,
    finely chopped

1 small bunch (20 g/²/₃ oz) fresh
    coriander (cilantro), leaves chopped,
    plus extra sprigs, to garnish

1 clove garlic, crushed

2 cm (³/₄ inch) piece fresh ginger,
    peeled and finely chopped

2 spring onions (scallions), finely chopped

3 lemongrass stems, white part only,
    finely chopped

juice of 4 limes

¹/₄ cup (60 ml) fish sauce

¹/₄ cup (60 ml) sherry vinegar

1 tablespoon sugar

3 tablespoons light soy sauce

2 ripe firm avocados, sliced

lime wedges, to garnish

METHOD

1 Cut crabs in half and clean. Place in a large bowl and set aside.
2 Put chilli, chopped coriander, garlic, ginger, spring onions, lemongrass, lime juice, fish sauce, vinegar, sugar and soy sauce in a food processor or blender and process 10–15 seconds.
3 Pour marinade over crab and allow to marinate 10 minutes.
4 Arrange crab and avocado on four serving plates and spoon over the remaining marinade. Serve immediately, garnished with coriander sprigs and lime wedges.

NUTRIENTS PER SERVING

1579 kJ, 377 kcal, 13 g protein, 31 g fat (7 g saturated fat), 7 g carbohydrate

SALMON PIZZAS WITH YOGURT AND DILL
TIME **30 MINUTES** SERVES **4**

METHOD

1 Preheat oven to 220°C (425°F/Gas 7).

2 Place pizza bases on baking trays (sheets). Cover with tomatoes and onion. Arrange salmon on top and season with salt and pepper to taste.

3 Bake 15–20 minutes, or until lightly browned, swapping the trays around in the oven halfway through.

4 Mix yogurt, dill and some pepper in a small bowl.

5 Remove pizzas from oven, spoon some yogurt mixture over each and garnish with dill sprigs. Cut each pizza into quarters and serve, accompanied by mango chutney, if using.

NUTRIENTS PER SERVING
2130 kJ, 509 kcal, 25 g protein, 29 g fat (15 g saturated fat), 37 g carbohydrate

INGREDIENTS

2 x 25 cm (10 inch) thin ready-made
   pizza bases

2 large tomatoes, finely chopped

1 small white or red onion, finely chopped

2 small skinless salmon fillets
   (about 350 g/12 oz in total),
   bones discarded, diced

salt and freshly ground black pepper

$\frac{1}{2}$ cup (125 g) natural (plain) yogurt

3 tablespoons finely chopped fresh dill,
   plus extra sprigs, to garnish

4 tablespoons mango chutney,
   to serve (optional)

SCALLOPS WITH TARRAGON

TIME **15 MINUTES** SERVES **4**

INGREDIENTS

24 scallops on the shell,
    plus 24 shucked scallops
1 clove garlic, crushed
1 small red chilli, seeds removed,
    finely chopped
60 g (2 oz) unsalted butter
grated zest and juice of 1 lemon
2 tablespoons chopped fresh tarragon
    or 1 tablespoon dried tarragon
1½ cups (375 ml) dry vermouth
freshly ground black pepper
lemon wedges, to garnish
fresh tarragon or dill sprigs, to garnish

METHOD

1 Preheat oven to 200°C (400°F/ Gas 6). Arrange scallop shells on baking trays (sheets) and place an extra scallop on each.
2 Put garlic, chilli and butter in a medium saucepan and stir over medium heat. Add lemon zest and juice, tarragon, vermouth and a generous grinding of pepper. Cook, stirring, 3–4 minutes, until reduced and slightly thickened.
3 Spoon sauce over scallops. Bake 6–8 minutes, until scallops have turned opaque and are cooked through.
4 Remove from oven, arrange on four warmed plates, garnish with lemon wedges and tarragon or dill sprigs, and serve immediately.

NUTRIENTS PER SERVING

1320 kJ, 315 kcal, 20 g protein, 14 g fat (9 g saturated fat), 17 g carbohydrate

WARM SALAD OF SCALLOPS WITH GARLIC AND LEMONGRASS

TIME **20 MINUTES** SERVES **4**

INGREDIENTS

1 bunch (125 g/4 oz) rocket
    (arugula), trimmed
1 rosso or treviso radicchio, trimmed
1 witlof (Belgian endive), trimmed
1 red capsicum (bell pepper), seeds
    removed, finely sliced
2 tablespoons olive oil
2 lemongrass stems, white part only,
    finely chopped
2 cloves garlic, finely chopped
3 kaffir lime (makrut) leaves,
    shredded

1 kg (2 lb) shucked scallops
lime wedges, to garnish
fresh coriander (cilantro) sprigs,
    to garnish

DRESSING

1 clove garlic, crushed
1 stalk lemongrass, white part only,
    finely chopped
grated zest and juice of 1 lime
1 teaspoon sweet chilli sauce
4 tablespoons olive oil

METHOD

1 To make the dressing, put garlic, lemongrass, lime zest and juice, sweet chilli sauce and oil in a screw-top jar. Shake well and set aside.
2 Arrange rocket, radicchio and witlof leaves and capsicum on four individual serving plates.
3 Heat oil in a large heavy-based frying pan or wok and add lemongrass, garlic and kaffir lime leaves. Stir-fry over medium heat 30 seconds. Add scallops and stir-fry a further 3–4 minutes, until the scallops are opaque and cooked through.
4 Remove scallops from the pan with a slotted spoon and divide among the four plates, arranging them on top of the salad. Spoon over the dressing and garnish with lime wedges and coriander sprigs. Serve immediately.

NUTRIENTS PER SERVING

2234 kJ, 534 kcal, 56 g protein, 31 g fat (6 g saturated fat), 5 g carbohydrate

Right Scallops with tarragon (top); Warm salad of scallops with garlic and lemongrass (bottom)

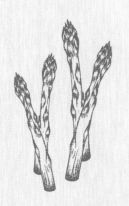

STEAMED SCALLOP PARCELS

TIME **25 MINUTES** SERVES **4**

INGREDIENTS

8 spring onions (shallots), sliced

300 g (10 oz) scallops, with or without roe

2 tablespoons dry sherry

1 tablespoon light soy sauce

1 tablespoon sesame oil

250 g (8 oz) snow peas (mangetout)

200 g (7 oz) asparagus tips, trimmed

2.5 cm (1 inch) piece fresh ginger,
   peeled and finely chopped

METHOD

1 Cut four 30 cm (12 inch) squares of foil. Prepare a saucepan of boiling water with a steamer basket on top.

2 Put half the spring onions in a bowl and add scallops, sherry, soy sauce and sesame oil. Mix well and set aside to marinate briefly.

3 Divide snow peas and asparagus among the squares of foil. Sprinkle with ginger and remaining spring onions. Fold up the foil to form deep nests around the vegetables, turning the edges in slightly to enclose them in open-topped bundles. Put in the steamer basket and cook 5 minutes.

4 Add scallops to vegetables, dividing them evenly among the parcels. Pour the marinade mix into the parcels. Cover the steamer basket and cook a further 3–5 minutes, or until the scallops are just firm. Serve.

NUTRIENTS PER SERVING

571 kJ, 136 kcal, 13 g protein, 5 g fat (1 g saturated fat), 7 g carbohydrate

COOK'S TIP

If you don't have a steamer basket, stand a heatproof bowl or soufflé dish in a large lidded saucepan. Pour boiling water into the saucepan until it comes to about 2.5 cm (1 inch) below the rim of the dish. Bring the water to a simmer. Stand a heatproof plate on top of the bowl and place the parcels on this to steam, covering the pan with a close-fitting lid. Alternatively, the parcels can be steamed in a bamboo steamer over a wok. Pour in enough boiling water to come to about 1 cm (1/2 inch) below the steamer in the wok.

SCALLOPS WITH NOODLE STIR-FRY AND WATERCRESS

TIME **20 MINUTES** SERVES **4**

INGREDIENTS

200 g (7 oz) dried fine egg noodles

300 g (10 oz) scallops, with or without roe

1 clove garlic, crushed

grated zest of 1 lemon

1 teaspoon English mustard

2 tablespoons chopped fresh tarragon

3 tablespoons olive oil

500 g (1 lb) ready-sliced stir-fry vegetables, such as capsicums (bell peppers), broccoli, zucchini (courgettes) and cabbage

150 g (5 oz) watercress, trimmed

METHOD

1 Put noodles in a large bowl and cover generously with boiling water. Cover with a lid and set aside 5 minutes, or until softened.

2 Meanwhile, cut scallops into thick slices and put in a bowl. Add garlic, lemon zest, mustard, tarragon and 2 tablespoons oil. Mix well and set aside.

3 Heat remaining oil in a large frying pan or wok. Add vegetables and stir-fry 5 minutes.

4 Drain noodles, wipe bowl with paper towel and return noodles to the warm bowl. Add vegetables and mix well. Set aside.

5 Add scallops to the pan, scraping in all the marinade too, and cook quickly 2–3 minutes, turning the scallops once. Divide vegetable and noodle mixture among four large plates. Arrange scallops on the plates and add watercress to one side.

6 Add 4 tablespoons boiling water to the pan and bring to a boil, stirring to loosen all the cooking residue. Boil hard for a few seconds. Spoon the boiling juices over the watercress and serve immediately.

NUTRIENTS PER SERVING
1728 kJ, 413 kcal, 19 g protein, 16 g fat (2 g saturated fat), 46 g carbohydrate

SPICY STIR-FRIED CALAMARI
TIME 20 MINUTES SERVES 4

INGREDIENTS

300 g (10 oz) calamari (squid), cleaned
   by the fishmonger, cut into rings
1/4–1/2 teaspoon chilli powder
1 tablespoon ground coriander
2 tablespoons vegetable oil
250 g (8 oz) sugarsnap peas
5 cm (2 inch) piece fresh ginger,
   peeled and chopped
2 cloves garlic, sliced
2 celery stalks, sliced
1 red capsicum (bell pepper), seeds
   removed, sliced into short strips
salt and freshly ground black pepper
3/4 cup (25 g) fresh basil leaves
3/4 cup (25 g) fresh coriander
   (cilantro) leaves
6 spring onions (scallions), sliced
1/2 cup (125 ml) dry sherry

METHOD

1 Put calamari in a bowl and season with chilli powder and ground coriander. Mix well and set aside.
2 Heat 1 tablespoon oil in a wok or large frying pan. Add sugarsnap peas and stir-fry over high heat 1 minute, or until they are bright green. Add ginger, garlic, celery, capsicum and season to taste, then stir-fry 3–4 minutes. Remove from heat. Stir in basil, coriander and spring onions, then divide vegetables among four large pasta bowls or deep plates.
3 Heat the remaining oil in the wok. Stir-fry calamari 2 minutes, or until it is just firm (do not overcook the pieces or they will become rubbery). Season, then arrange the rings on the vegetables. Pour sherry into the wok and cook over high heat 1 minute, stirring to loosen any residue from the wok. Pour cooking juices over calamari and vegetables, and serve immediately.

NUTRIENTS PER SERVING

957 kJ, 229 kcal, 16 g protein, 11 g fat (1 g saturated fat), 10 g carbohydrate

VARIATION

Instead of calamari (squid) rings, use peeled raw prawns (uncooked shrimp) or chunks of skinless thick firm fish fillet — try swordfish, salmon or tuna.

CALAMARI WITH OLIVES AND CAPERS
TIME **25 MINUTES** SERVES **4**

METHOD

1 Heat oil in a large heavy-based saucepan. Add calamari and garlic. Cook, stirring, over medium heat until garlic is golden.

2 Add anchovies, wine, capers, tomatoes and sugar. Simmer gently over low heat 15 minutes.

3 When calamari is cooked, add olives, parsley and pepper to taste. Stir through, then serve immediately.

NUTRIENTS PER SERVING

1836 kJ, 438 kcal, 44 g protein, 20 g fat (2 g saturated fat), 4 g carbohydrate

COOK'S TIP

Good crusty bread is essential to soak up the rich juices in this dish. If you like, you can also serve some simply cooked pasta.

INGREDIENTS

$^{1}/_{2}$ cup (125 ml) olive oil

1 kg (2 lb) calamari (squid), cleaned by the fishmonger, cut into rings

2 cloves garlic, peeled and finely chopped

6 anchovy fillets, finely chopped

1 cup (250 ml) dry white wine

2 tablespoons capers, rinsed and squeezed dry

2 x 410 g (15 oz) cans chopped tomatoes

1 pinch sugar

1 cup (185 g) black olives

$^{1}/_{2}$ cup (20 g) finely chopped fresh flat-leaf (Italian) parsley

freshly ground black pepper

CHARGRILLED BABY OCTOPUS

TIME **30 MINUTES** SERVES **4**

INGREDIENTS

2 red capsicums (bell peppers)

¹/₂ cup (75 g) sun-dried tomatoes, drained and finely chopped

grated zest and juice of 1 lime

grated zest and juice of 1 lemon

2 tablespoons chopped fresh thyme

1 kg (2 lb) baby octopus, cleaned and debeaked by the fishmonger

¹/₂ cup (125 ml) olive oil

1 bunch (125 g/4 oz) rocket (arugula), trimmed

2 tablespoons extra virgin olive oil

sea salt and freshly ground black pepper

lime or lemon wedges, to garnish

METHOD

1 Preheat oven to 260°C (500°F/Gas 9). Preheat chargrill pan or barbecue to very hot.

2 Slice capsicums across the stem end to remove the base, then remove the seeds with your fingertips. Arrange capsicums on a baking tray (sheet) and roast in the oven 10–12 minutes, until the skin is charred. Remove and set aside to cool.

3 Meanwhile, combine sun-dried tomatoes, lime zest and juice, lemon zest and juice and thyme in a bowl with octopus and olive oil. Marinate 10–15 minutes.

4 When capsicums are cool, remove skin and slice flesh into wide strips.

5 Put octopus on the chargrill pan and cook over high heat 5–6 minutes, spooning marinade over regularly.

6 Arrange capsicum, rocket leaves and octopus on four serving plates. Drizzle each with 2 teaspoons extra virgin olive oil, season with salt and pepper, and garnish with lime or lemon wedges.

NUTRIENTS PER SERVING

2620 kJ, 626 kcal, 45 g protein, 48 g fat (6 g saturated fat), 7 g carbohydrate

COOK'S TIP

The octopus can be marinated for up to 24 hours in the refrigerator. Remove from the refrigerator about 10–15 minutes before cooking.

KING PRAWNS WITH SUN-DRIED TOMATOES
TIME **20 MINUTES** SERVES **4**

METHOD

1 Heat olive oil in a large heavy-based frying pan. Add prawns and cook over medium–high heat 1–2 minutes.

2 Add sun-dried tomatoes and sweet chilli sauce and cook, stirring, a further 3–4 minutes, or until prawns are opaque.

3 Add lime zest and juice and season with pepper. Remove pan from heat and set aside.

4 To make the dressing, combine lime juice, virgin olive oil, soy sauce and sugar in a small bowl.

5 Arrange rocket and avocado on four individual plates and spoon over the dressing. Pile prawns, with their pan juices, on top of the salad and serve immediately.

NUTRIENTS PER SERVING
1734 kJ, 414 kcal, 18 g protein, 34 g fat (6 g saturated fat), 7 g carbohydrate

INGREDIENTS

3 tablespoons olive oil

500 g (1 lb) raw king prawns (uncooked large shrimp), peeled and deveined

⅔ cup (100 g) sun-dried tomatoes, drained and finely chopped

2 tablespoons sweet chilli sauce

finely grated zest and juice of 1 lime

freshly ground black pepper

1 bunch (125 g/4 oz) rocket (arugula), trimmed

1 avocado, sliced

DRESSING

2 teaspoons lime juice

1 tablespoon virgin olive oil

1 tablespoon light soy sauce

1 pinch sugar

MUSSELS WITH TOMATO AND GARLIC

TIME **30 MINUTES** SERVES **4**

INGREDIENTS

2 kg (4 lb) mussels

2 tablespoons olive oil

3 cloves garlic, finely chopped

500 g (1 lb) very ripe tomatoes,
    roughly chopped

5 spring onions (scallions), white part only,
    finely chopped

1 cup (250 ml) white wine

1 cup (250 g) ready-made tomato sauce

1 pinch sugar

$^{1}/_{2}$ cup (15 g) chopped fresh basil or
    flat-leaf (Italian) parsley

freshly ground black pepper

crusty bread, to serve

METHOD

1 Prepare mussels by rinsing well under cold running water. Thoroughly scrub with a scourer to remove any mud or seaweed and remove the beards by pulling firmly. Discard any broken mussels, or any open mussels that don't close when tapped.

2 Heat oil in a large heavy-based pan with a tight-fitting lid. Add garlic, tomatoes and spring onions and cook, stirring, 2–3 minutes.

3 Add wine, tomato sauce and sugar and simmer a further 2–3 minutes.

4 Add mussels to the pan, along with basil or parsley and a generous grinding of pepper. Cover with lid and cook over high heat 5 minutes, shaking the pan from time to time.

5 Discard any mussels that have not opened and divide the remainder among four serving bowls. Spoon over the sauce and serve immediately with lots of crusty bread to soak up the sauce.

NUTRIENTS PER SERVING

1327 kJ, 317 kcal, 35 g protein, 15 g fat (3 g saturated fat), 12 g carbohydrate

VARIATION

You can use a mixture of seafood, such as prawns (shrimp) and fish pieces, instead of the mussels.

COOK'S TIP

Ready-made tomato sauce — a mixture of chopped tomatoes with onion, garlic, oil, salt and pepper — can be made in minutes on top of the stove. If time is limited, however, you can substitute a good-quality store-bought Italian pasta sauce or tomato passata (puréed tomatoes).

STIR-FRIED PRAWNS WITH GINGER AND SPRING ONIONS

TIME 20 MINUTES SERVES 4

INGREDIENTS

2 tablespoons vegetable or peanut
   (groundnut) oil
24 raw king prawns (uncooked large
   shrimp), peeled and deveined
5 spring onions (scallions),
   sliced diagonally
3 cm (1¼ inch) piece fresh ginger,
   peeled and finely chopped
2 cloves garlic, finely chopped
¼ cup (45 g) soft brown sugar
½ cup (125 ml) chicken stock
2 tablespoons sweet chilli sauce
grated zest and juice of 1 lime
lime wedges, to garnish
large red chillies, sliced, to garnish

METHOD

1 Heat oil in a wok or large heavy-
   based frying pan. Add prawns and
   stir-fry over medium heat until
   they change colour and are just
   cooked. Remove from the wok
   with a slotted spoon and set aside.

2 Add spring onions, ginger and
   garlic to the wok and stir-fry over
   low heat, 3–4 minutes.

3 Increase heat and add sugar,
   stock, sweet chilli sauce and lime
   zest and juice. Cook, stirring, until
   the liquid is reduced and slightly
   thickened.

4 Reduce heat, return prawns to the
   wok and heat through. Garnish
   with lime wedges and chilli slices
   and serve immediately.

NUTRIENTS PER SERVING
1139 kJ, 272 kcal, 27 g protein, 10 g fat (2 g saturated fat), 11 g carbohydrate

COOK'S TIP
Serve these stir-fried prawns with a bowl of steaming rice or boiled noodles.

STIR-FRIED SESAME PRAWNS
TIME **15 MINUTES** SERVES **4**

METHOD

1 Pat prawns dry on paper towel, then put in a bowl with sesame oil and soy sauce, and toss together to coat. Tip into a sieve placed over another bowl to catch the marinade (there will not be much).

2 Heat a wok or large non-stick frying pan until very hot, then add oil and swirl to coat the base. Add prawns and stir-fry 1½ minutes.

3 Add chilli, garlic, lemongrass and ginger to the wok. Stir-fry a further 30–60 seconds, or until prawns have turned pink and are just cooked through (take care not to overcook or they will be tough). Remove from heat and stir in reserved marinade, sugar, sesame seeds and coriander. Serve with sweet chilli dipping sauce.

NUTRIENTS PER SERVING

885 kJ, 211 kcal, 20 g protein, 12 g fat (1 g saturated fat), 4 g carbohydrate

VARIATION

Instead of all the oils and flavourings, stir 2 tablespoons red curry paste in 2 tablespoons vegetable oil 30 seconds before adding the prawns. Stir-fry 1½ minutes, as for step 2, then stir in 2 tablespoons coconut milk. Stir-fry a further 30–60 seconds, or until the prawns are cooked.

INGREDIENTS

40 peeled raw prawns (uncooked shrimp) (about 350 g/12 oz in total), thawed if frozen

1 tablespoon sesame oil

1½ tablespoons dark soy sauce

1 tablespoon vegetable oil

1 large medium–hot red chilli, seeds removed, finely chopped

1 clove garlic, crushed

1 stalk lemongrass, white part only, finely chopped

2 teaspoons crushed ginger, from a jar, or grated fresh ginger

1 teaspoon soft brown sugar

1 tablespoon sesame seeds

2 tablespoons chopped fresh coriander (cilantro) leaves

sweet chilli dipping sauce, to serve

PRAWNS MASALA
TIME 20 MINUTES SERVES 4

INGREDIENTS

2 tablespoons vegetable oil

1 onion, chopped

2 cloves garlic, finely chopped

5 cm (2 inch) piece fresh ginger,
    finely chopped

2 teaspoons ground coriander

2 teaspoons ground cumin

1 teaspoon ground turmeric

400 g (14 oz) peeled raw prawns
    (uncooked shrimp)

200 ml (7 fl oz) coconut cream

salt and freshly ground black pepper

1 small bunch (20 g/²/₃ oz) fresh
    coriander (cilantro), leaves chopped,
    plus extra sprigs, to garnish

METHOD

1 Heat oil in a heavy-based frying pan. Add onion and garlic and fry
   3–4 minutes until softened. Then add ginger and ground coriander, cumin
   and turmeric and cook a further 1–2 minutes, until spices have released
   their fragrance.

2 Add prawns and coconut cream, and season to taste with salt and pepper.
   Bring the mixture to a boil, reduce heat and simmer 2–3 minutes.

3 Pour the prawn mixture into a serving dish. Just before serving, scatter
   chopped coriander over the top and garnish with coriander sprigs.

NUTRIENTS PER SERVING

1510 kJ, 361 kcal, 26 g protein, 26 g fat (16 g saturated fat), 7 g carbohydrate

VARIATION

The prawns could be replaced by chunks of firm white fish.

COOK'S TIP

This light dish could be served with steamed long-grain rice or some warmed
naan. Or you could also add a vegetable curry and a dal to make a more
substantial meal.

CURRY-DUSTED SCALLOPS
WITH LEMONY LENTILS
TIME **30 MINUTES** SERVES **4**

INGREDIENTS

200 g (7 oz) French-style green
    (puy) lentils
400 ml (14 fl oz) water or vegetable
    or fish stock, boiling
1 small carrot, diced
1/2 small bulb fennel, diced
1 French shallot (eschalot), chopped
1 teaspoon mild curry powder
sea salt and freshly ground black pepper
400 g (14 oz) scallops, rinsed and
    patted dry
2 tablespoons extra virgin olive oil
1 teaspoon grated lemon zest
2 tablespoons lemon juice
3 tablespoons chopped fresh parsley
250 g (8 oz) mixed salad leaves,
    such as baby spinach leaves, rocket
    (arugula) and watercress

METHOD

1 Put lentils in a saucepan with boiling water or stock, carrot, fennel and French shallot. Return to a boil, cover and simmer gently 12–15 minutes, or until lentils are just tender and most of the liquid has been absorbed. Drain lentils, leaving just enough liquid to moisten.

2 Meanwhile, put curry powder and a little fine sea salt onto a plate and roll scallops in the mixture to coat lightly.

3 Season lentils with salt and pepper and mix with 1 tablespoon oil, lemon zest, juice and parsley. Divide lentils among four warmed plates and scatter salad leaves on top.

4 Heat remaining oil in a large non-stick frying pan and arrange scallops in a circle in the pan. Cook 1–2 minutes, then turn scallops over in the same order in which you placed them (to ensure even cooking). Cook a further 1 minute, then immediately remove and place on top of the lentils. Serve.

NUTRIENTS PER SERVING

1194 kJ, 285 kcal, 25 g protein, 11 g fat (2 g saturated fat), 23 g carbohydrate

COOK'S TIP

French-style green lentils (also known as puy lentils or lentilles vertes de Puy) come from a defined area in France and have their own appellation contrôlée. This recipe also works well with the slightly larger green or brown lentils, which take a little longer to cook (up to 25 minutes).

LOBSTER TAILS WITH LEMON SAUCE
TIME 25 MINUTES SERVES 4

METHOD

1 Preheat oven to 200°C (400°F/Gas 6). Cut lobster tails in half lengthwise and clean, if necessary. Place the halves flesh side up in a small roasting pan (baking dish).

2 Put garlic, butter, parsley, lemon zest and juice, and a generous grinding of pepper in a medium saucepan. Heat gently until butter has melted.

3 Brush lobster tails with the butter mixture. Bake 10–15 minutes, until lobster tails are cooked.

4 Garnish with lemon halves and serve immediately.

NUTRIENTS PER SERVING
2384 kJ, 569 kcal, 22 g protein, 53 g fat (36 g saturated fat), 3 g carbohydrate

COOK'S TIP
Choose salad leaves such as mizuna or rocket (arugula) to accompany this dish. Toss with 1 tablespoon virgin olive oil just before serving.

INGREDIENTS

2 raw (uncooked) lobster tails

1 clove garlic, crushed

250 g (8 oz) unsalted butter

2 tablespoons finely chopped fresh
flat-leaf (Italian) parsley

grated zest and juice of 3 lemons

freshly ground black pepper

lemon halves wrapped in muslin
(cheesecloth), to garnish

SCALLOP BROCHETTES WITH PROSCIUTTO

TIME **30 MINUTES** SERVES **4**

INGREDIENTS

24 scallops with roe (about 350 g/
   12 oz in total)
16 thin slices prosciutto or parma ham
   (about 150 g/5 oz in total), halved
freshly ground black pepper

MARINADE

2 large cloves garlic, crushed
2 tablespoons chopped fresh basil, plus
   extra sprigs, to garnish (optional)
2 tablespoons chopped fresh coriander
   (cilantro) leaves
2 tablespoons chopped fresh parsley
juice of $^1/_2$ lemon
2 tablespoons virgin olive oil

METHOD

1 Rinse and dry scallops with paper towel. Separate the roe from the white meat and put both in a bowl.
2 To make the marinade, add garlic, basil, coriander and parsley to the scallops in the bowl. Add lemon juice and oil, stir and leave to marinate at room temperature 15 minutes.
3 Preheat grill (broiler) to high. Gather a piece of ham into a ruffle, thread it onto a metal skewer, then thread on a scallop and a piece of roe. Repeat twice and finish with ham. Prepare seven more skewers.
4 Place skewers across the grill tray, baste with some marinade and grill 5 minutes, turning and basting again halfway through, until the ham is crisp and the scallops are just cooked.
5 Serve on skewers, or remove and pile the scallops and ham onto individual serving plates. Spoon over the tray juices, then top with pepper and garnish with sprigs of basil, if using.

NUTRIENTS PER SERVING

1318 kJ, 315 kcal, 30 g protein, 20 g fat (6 g saturated fat), 4 g carbohydrate

VARIATION

Peeled raw tiger prawns (uncooked large shrimp) or cubes of firm white fish can be used instead of the scallops.

COOK'S TIP

Always use fresh scallops. Frozen scallops are too watery and this will dilute the marinade too much.

SARDINES IN A PEPPERCORN CRUST

TIME **30 MINUTES** SERVES **4**

INGREDIENTS

8 large fresh sardines (about 500 g/
    1 lb in total)

1 teaspoon mixed peppercorns, crushed

1 small bunch (20 g/⅔ oz) fresh dill,
    chopped

1 clove garlic, crushed

grated zest of 1 lemon

salt

2 tablespoons olive oil

8 small sprigs fresh rosemary

4 crisp lettuce leaves, finely shredded

8 sprigs watercress, trimmed

lemon wedges, to garnish

METHOD

1 Preheat grill (broiler) to high. Cut
along belly of each sardine with
kitchen scissors, then pull out the
insides. Rinse sardines inside and
out, gently rubbing off the scales
with your fingers, then dry the fish
on paper towel.

2 Put peppercorns, dill, garlic,
lemon zest, salt and oil in a small
bowl. Mix thoroughly.

3 Put a sprig of rosemary inside
each fish, then brush both sides
with the peppercorn paste; reserve
any paste that is left over. Leave
fish to marinate 5–10 minutes.

4 Meanwhile, arrange lettuce and
watercress on four serving plates.
Garnish each with a lemon wedge.

5 Thread each sardine lengthwise
onto a metal skewer, then grill
2–3 minutes on each side.

6 Slide sardines off skewers and
arrange two on each plate on top
of the salad. Spoon over the
reserved peppercorn paste and
serve immediately.

NUTRIENTS PER SERVING
1109 kJ, 265 kcal, 24 g protein, 19 g fat (4 g saturated fat), 1 g carbohydrate

COOK'S TIP

As an alternative to grilling, cook the skewered sardines on a very hot
chargrill pan or a barbecue.

Above Sardines in a peppercorn crust (top); Scallop brochettes with prosciutto (bottom)

CREAMY SEAFOOD WRAPS WITH ZUCCHINI AND CUCUMBER SALAD

TIME 30 MINUTES SERVES 4

METHOD

1 Heat 2 tablespoons olive oil in a frying pan. Add mixed seafood and stir-fry 2–3 minutes, or until prawns have turned pink and fish is white and flakes easily. Tip into a bowl and set aside.

2 Preheat oven to 200°C (400°F/Gas 6). In a bowl, mix together spring onions, tomatoes, cream cheese and a little pepper.

3 Lay out tortillas on a flat surface and spread with cream cheese mixture. Divide seafood mixture evenly among tortillas, spreading it over the centre of each, then roll up tortillas tightly. Put in a large ovenproof dish or a roasting pan (baking dish). Brush with remaining olive oil. Sprinkle cheese over the top and cover loosely with foil. Bake 20 minutes, or until heated through. Uncover for the last 5 minutes to lightly brown the cheese.

4 Meanwhile, toss zucchini, cucumber and rocket together in a bowl. Divide among four large plates. Grate zest from lime, or use a zester, and sprinkle it over the salads. Trickle a little chilli oil over the top. Cut lime into eight wedges and add two to each plate.

5 Cut the wraps in half and arrange beside the salad. Serve immediately.

INGREDIENTS

3 tablespoons olive oil

250 g (8 oz) mixed seafood (marinara mix)

4 spring onions (scallions), finely sliced

4 large tomatoes, diced

150 g (5 oz) low-fat cream cheese with garlic and herbs

freshly ground black pepper

4 large soft flour tortillas

1/2 cup (60 g) grated mature cheddar

2 small zucchini (courgettes), thinly sliced

1/2 Lebanese or other small cucumber, thinly sliced

150 g (5 oz) rocket (arugula)

1 lime

chilli oil, for drizzling

NUTRIENTS PER SERVING

2037 kJ, 487 kcal, 29 g protein, 29 g fat (7 g saturated fat), 27 g carbohydrate

COOK'S TIP

Various crushed or puréed herbs and spices — such as basil, chilli, coriander (cilantro), galangal, garlic, ginger, lemongrass and parsley — are available in jars and tubes from supermarkets. Keep them on hand for when you don't have time to buy or prepare fresh herbs.

SALMON PUFFS WITH TZATZIKI

TIME 30 MINUTES SERVES 4

INGREDIENTS

375 g (13 oz) ready-rolled puff pastry,
    thawed if frozen
150 g (5 oz) skinless salmon fillet,
    cut into small squares
3/4 cup (115 g) frozen broad (fava) beans
1/2 cup (30 g) fresh fennel fronds
    or dill, chopped
1/2 cup (25 g) snipped fresh chives
salt and freshly ground black pepper
1 egg, beaten
100 g (3 1/2 oz) ricotta

TZATZIKI

1/2 Lebanese or other small
    cucumber, grated
1 clove garlic, crushed (optional)
3/4 cup (185 g) Greek-style yogurt

METHOD

1 Preheat oven to 240°C (460°F/Gas 8). If time allows, leave pastry, still wrapped, at room temperature 20 minutes (this makes it easier to unroll without cracking, but isn't essential). Put salmon in a bowl and add broad beans, fennel or dill, and chives. Season to taste and mix well.

2 Unroll pastry, leaving it on its paper, then cut it into four 17.5 x 9 cm (7 x 3 1/2 inch) pieces. Lightly brush pastry all over with some beaten egg. Divide salmon mixture among pastry pieces, mounding it in the centre, leaving a border of pastry at the top and bottom and keeping the long ends clear on either side. Place ricotta in small dollops on each mound of filling. Fold long ends of pastry up to meet over the filling and pinch them together at the top. Press sides together to seal in filling.

3 Transfer pastries to a non-stick baking tray (sheet) or a baking tray lined with baking (parchment) paper. Brush with the remaining egg, then bake 20 minutes, or until puffed and golden.

4 Meanwhile, make the tzatziki. Put cucumber in a sieve and press out excess moisture over sink. Mix cucumber and garlic, if using, into yogurt. Transfer tzatziki to a serving bowl and serve with hot salmon puffs.

NUTRIENTS PER SERVING

2258 kJ, 539 kcal, 22 g protein, 33 g fat (17 g saturated fat), 38 g carbohydrate

VARIATION

Instead of salmon, use cooked peeled prawns (shrimp) or flaked smoked trout. Replace broad beans with frozen baby peas or corn, and the fennel or dill with watercress.

COOK'S TIP

To save time, buy good-quality tzatziki instead of making your own.

BAKED ROSEMARY FISH WITH TOMATOES AND LIME
TIME **30 MINUTES** SERVES **4**

METHOD

1 Preheat oven to 200°C (400°F/Gas 6). Cut four pieces of foil, each large enough to enclose a piece of fish. Brush foil with a little oil.

2 Put one fish fillet on each piece of foil. Make small cuts all over the fish. Push pieces of garlic and small sprigs of rosemary into slits in the fish.

3 Grate lime zest over the fish. Trim off ends of lime, then cut it into four thick slices. Squeeze a few drops of juice from the lime slices over the fish, then lay lime slices on top. Dot with butter and season to taste.

4 Put tomatoes, cut side up, alongside the fish. Fold up the foil to enclose fish and tomatoes completely and seal the edges.

5 Put the parcels on a baking tray (sheet) and bake 10 minutes. Open the foil and bake a further 10 minutes, or until fish is opaque and cooked through. Test with the point of a knife. Transfer fish and tomatoes to individual serving plates. Pour over the juices from the parcels and serve immediately.

INGREDIENTS

1 tablespoon olive oil

4 firm white fish fillets (about 125 g/ 4 oz each)

2 large cloves garlic, quartered lengthwise

2 sprigs fresh rosemary, broken into small sprigs

1 lime

30 g (1 oz) butter

salt and freshly ground black pepper

4 tomatoes, halved

NUTRIENTS PER SERVING

1049 kJ, 251 kcal, 28 g protein, 13 g fat (5 g saturated fat), 6 g carbohydrate

VARIATION

Instead of white fish, use tuna, swordfish or salmon. You could also replace the lime with lemon.

GRILLED SOLE WITH BUTTERY ZUCCHINI

TIME **30 MINUTES** SERVES **4**

INGREDIENTS

600 g (1 lb 5 oz) zucchini (courgettes)

salt and freshly ground black pepper

4 whole sole or flounder (about 500 g/1 lb
    each), dark skin and heads removed,
    rinsed and dried with paper towel

1 tablespoon chopped fresh dill, plus
    4 sprigs, to garnish

1 tablespoon chopped snipped chives

1 tablespoon chopped fresh parsley

4 tablespoons butter

oil, for greasing

juice of 1/2 lemon

lemon wedges, to garnish

METHOD

1 Preheat grill (broiler) to high. Shred zucchini coarsely in a food processor or blender, or grate coarsely by hand. Put in a colander with a little salt, toss gently together and set aside to drain thoroughly.

2 Make three diagonal cuts through the white skin of each sole or flounder.

3 Put chopped dill, chives and parsley in a small bowl with 2 tablespoons butter, season well with pepper, and mash with a fork until well mixed. Divide herb butter into four and set aside.

4 Melt remaining butter in a frying pan. Fry zucchini over medium heat 10 minutes, until cooked but still slightly firm. Shake pan gently from time to time.

5 Meanwhile, lightly oil a large grill tray and place sole in it, white skin side up. Grill 5 minutes, then turn and sprinkle with lemon juice. Cook 2–3 minutes, until the flesh flakes easily.

6 Place a portion of herb butter on each sole and warm under the grill for a few seconds until butter starts to melt. Serve on individual plates, accompanied by zucchini, dill sprigs and lemon wedges.

NUTRIENTS PER SERVING

2319 kJ, 554 kcal, 84 g protein, 23 g fat (10 g saturated fat), 2 g carbohydrate

COOK'S TIP

If your grill tray is not big enough for four sole, you can cook them on a large baking tray (sheet) in the oven instead. Preheat oven to 220°C (425°F/Gas 7), then bake the fish, white skin side up, 15–20 minutes.

SMOKED HADDOCK WITH RICE VERMICELLI
TIME **30 MINUTES** SERVES **4**

METHOD

1 Put rice vermicelli in a bowl, cover with boiling water, leave to stand 5 minutes, then drain and set aside.

2 Heat peanut oil in a wok or large frying pan with a lid. Add garlic and chilli and sweat over low heat 2 minutes to flavour the oil.

3 Add carrots, beans and asparagus, and increase heat. Stir in fish sauce or soy sauce, wine and honey.

4 Place smoked haddock fillets on top of the vegetables, cover and cook 5 minutes. Remove fish with a slotted spoon and keep warm.

5 Add drained vermicelli to the pan, toss with vegetables and pan juices, then stir in sesame oil. Toss the mixture a further 1–2 minutes to warm the vermicelli through.

6 Divide vegetables and vermicelli among four serving plates and arrange a haddock fillet on top of each.

NUTRIENTS PER SERVING
1929 kJ, 461 kcal, 38 g protein, 7 g fat (1 g saturated fat), 59 g carbohydrate

COOK'S TIP
Fish sauce is known as *nam pla* in Thailand and *nuoc nam* in Vietnam. It is available from Asian food stores and larger supermarkets.

INGREDIENTS

250 g (8 oz) dried rice vermicelli

1 tablespoon peanut (groundnut) oil

1 clove garlic, crushed

1 green chilli, seeds removed, chopped

100 g (3½ oz) baby carrots

100 g (3½ oz) small green beans, trimmed

250 g (8 oz) thin asparagus, trimmed, cut into lengths

1–2 tablespoons fish sauce or soy sauce

2 tablespoons white wine

3 teaspoons honey

4 smoked haddock fillets (about 175 g/ 6 oz each), skin removed

1 teaspoon sesame oil

GRILLED LEMON FISH WITH GOLDEN
COUSCOUS AND FENNEL
TIME **20 MINUTES** SERVES **4**

INGREDIENTS

200 g (7 oz) couscous

1 teaspoon ground turmeric

2 tablespoons olive oil

4 flat fish fillets, such as flounder or dory
(about 150 g/5 oz each)

2 bulbs fennel

2 spring onions (scallions), sliced

2 tablespoons capers, rinsed and
squeezed dry

1 lemon

40 g (1½ oz) butter

salt and freshly ground black pepper

METHOD

1 Put couscous in a heatproof bowl and stir in turmeric. Pour in boiling water to cover couscous by just under 1 cm (½ inch). Do not stir. Cover bowl and set aside.

2 Preheat grill (broiler) to high. Brush the grill tray lightly with a little oil. Lay fish fillets, skin side up, in the tray. Brush skin lightly with a little olive oil. Set aside.

3 Prepare fennel while grill heats up: reserve any fronds for garnish, cut bulbs in half, discard any tough core and slice finely. Separate slices into thin shreds and put in a bowl. Add spring onions, capers and remaining oil. Mix well.

4 Grill fish 3–4 minutes, or until skin begins to brown. Turn using a spatula. Grate zest from lemon, or use a zester, and sprinkle over fish. Cut lemon into eight wedges and arrange in grill pan. Dot butter over fish and season. Grill 1–2 minutes, or until fish is firm and just cooked.

5 Toss couscous with fennel mixture and divide it among four warmed plates. Add fish and hot lemon wedges. Pour over the cooking juices and serve immediately, garnished with reserved fennel fronds.

NUTRIENTS PER SERVING

2164 kJ, 517 kcal, 40 g protein, 21 g fat (8 g saturated fat), 41 g carbohydrate

VARIATION

Instead of flat fish fillets, try trout fillets (you will need 2 per portion if they are small), or portions of skinless salmon fillet, allowing 2–3 minutes cooking on the second side.

MUSTARD–MAYO FISH WITH TARRAGON–ORANGE ZUCCHINI

TIME **15 MINUTES** SERVES **4**

INGREDIENTS

1 tablespoon olive oil

4 zucchini (courgettes), halved
lengthwise then crosswise

4 flat fish fillets, such as flounder or dory
(about 125 g/4 oz each)

4 tablespoons mayonnaise

2 teaspoons dijon mustard

1 tablespoon fresh tarragon

grated zest of 1 orange

orange wedges, to serve

METHOD

1 Preheat grill (broiler) to high.
Brush an ovenproof dish with a
little oil and lay zucchini inside,
cut side down. Brush with a little
oil and grill 3 minutes. Turn
zucchini, brush with oil and grill
a further 4–5 minutes, or until
browned and tender. Set aside in
their dish and keep warm.

2 Meanwhile, prepare fish. Brush
the grill tray with remaining oil
and put fillets in, skin side down.
Mix mayonnaise and mustard,
then spread over fish. Grill about
5 minutes, or until the topping is
golden and fish is firm and cooked
through. If it begins to brown too
quickly, lower the grill tray so it is
further away from the heat.

3 Sprinkle tarragon and orange
zest over zucchini. Transfer fish
to warmed serving plates and add
zucchini. Garnish with orange
wedges and serve.

NUTRIENTS PER SERVING

1127 kJ, 269 kcal, 26 g protein, 14 g fat
(2 g saturated fat), 10 g carbohydrate

VARIATION

Instead of flat fish fillets, use whiting fillets. If they are fairly thick, grill, skin
side up, 2 minutes, then turn them over and spread with mayonnaise mixture.
Finish cooking as for the basic recipe.

FISH PARCELS WITH CREAMY BROCCOLI
TIME 30 MINUTES SERVES 4

METHOD

1 Preheat oven to 180°C (350°F/Gas 4). Brush fish cutlets with 1 tablespoon oil and season well.
2 Cut four pieces of foil, each large enough to enclose a cutlet. Put one cutlet on each piece of foil, fold the edges together to make a roomy parcel and crimp to seal. Place parcels on a baking tray (sheet) and bake 15 minutes.
3 Meanwhile, heat remaining oil in a medium frying pan and fry French shallot until softened and translucent.
4 Add broccoli to the frying pan, stems down, with 150 ml ($^2/_3$ cup) water. Bring to a boil, then cover and simmer 4–5 minutes, until broccoli is just tender. Remove lid, raise heat and cook until only 1–2 tablespoons water remain in the pan. Do not let broccoli burn.
5 Add tarragon and cream to broccoli and stir to heat through. Season to taste with salt and pepper and keep warm.
6 Remove foil parcels from the oven. Unwrap parcels and transfer the fish to four warmed plates. Serve broccoli alongside the fish and garnish with tarragon sprigs.

NUTRIENTS PER SERVING

2063 kJ, 493 kcal, 37 g protein, 37 g fat (18 g saturated fat), 3 g carbohydrate

COOK'S TIP

Serve the cutlets sitting on top of individual portions of Sweet Potato Rösti (see page 421), as photographed.

INGREDIENTS

4 thick firm white fish cutlets, such as snapper, ling, hake or cod (about 175 g/6 oz each), patted dry
2 tablespoons extra virgin olive oil
salt and freshly ground black pepper
1 French shallot (eschalot), grated
350 g (12 oz) broccoli, divided into small florets
2 tablespoons chopped fresh tarragon, plus 4 sprigs, to garnish
1 cup (250 ml) thick (heavy/double) cream

BAKED FISH PLAKI
TIME **30 MINUTES** SERVES **4**

INGREDIENTS

2 tablespoons olive oil

1 onion, thinly sliced

1 green capsicum (bell pepper),
   seeds removed, thinly sliced

6 roma (plum) tomatoes, sliced

1 clove garlic, crushed

750 g (1¹/₂ lb) skinless firm white
   fish fillet, cut into 5 cm (2 inch) pieces

juice of ¹/₂ lemon, plus 1 lemon,
   thinly sliced

3 tablespoons dry white wine

3 tablespoons tomato paste
   (concentrated purée)

salt and freshly ground black pepper

4 tablespoons finely chopped fresh parsley

METHOD

1 Slowly heat oil in a large flameproof casserole dish. Put onion, capsicum, tomatoes and garlic in the dish, then cover and cook over high heat 6–8 minutes, shaking occasionally so the vegetables do not stick.

2 Meanwhile, sprinkle fish with lemon juice and set aside.

3 Stir wine and tomato paste into the vegetables. Arrange lemon slices in a single layer on top.

4 Put fish on top of the lemon slices. Season with salt and pepper and sprinkle over parsley. Reduce heat to medium, cover and simmer 15 minutes; uncover for the last 5 minutes if the sauce seems too liquid. The fish is cooked when the flesh turns opaque and flakes easily.

NUTRIENTS PER SERVING

1154 kJ, 276 kcal, 35 g protein, 10 g fat (1 g saturated fat), 11 g carbohydrate

VARIATION

Any type of firm white fish can be used in this recipe, as long as the fillets are not too thin. If fresh roma tomatoes are not available, use canned whole roma tomatoes or canned chopped tomatoes, drained.

COOK'S TIP

Serve the fish with plenty of crusty bread or a big bowl of steamed rice for soaking up the juices. Add a green salad tossed with fetta or soft goat's cheese and black olives on the side.

AROMATIC STEAMED FISH WITH VEGETABLES
TIME **25 MINUTES** SERVES **4**

METHOD

1 Cook potatoes in a saucepan of boiling water 10 minutes, or until tender. Drain and keep warm. Meanwhile, prepare a large saucepan of boiling water with a large steamer basket on top. Cut four pieces of foil, each large enough to enclose a folded fish fillet.

2 Arrange leeks and carrots in the steamer basket, in one layer if possible, then set aside. Grate zest from the lime, or use a zester, and set aside. Cut lime into quarters.

3 Lay a fish fillet, skin side down, on each piece of foil. At the wide end of each fillet, lay 3 cucumber slices and a bay leaf. Season to taste. Lightly squeeze a little juice from a lime quarter over each fillet and fold the narrow end over. Top each with a squeezed lime quarter. Drizzle oil over fillets. Bring foil up to enclose fillets in neat parcels that will fit inside the steamer basket. Set the parcels aside.

4 Cook leeks and carrots in the steamer basket 5 minutes. Put zucchini, cut sides up, on top of the partly cooked vegetables, then add foil parcels. Steam 10 minutes, or until vegetables are tender and fish is cooked.

5 Open foil parcels and sprinkle the reserved lime zest and shredded rocket into each. Divide potatoes and steamed vegetables among four plates. Transfer fish to plates using a spatula, then pour juices from the foil over. Serve immediately.

INGREDIENTS

500 g (1 lb) small new potatoes

2 leeks, white part only, sliced

250 g (8 oz) baby carrots

1 lime

4 thin white fish fillets, such as whiting, garfish, dory or flounder (about 100 g/3^1/$_2$ oz each)

12 thin slices cucumber

4 bay leaves

salt and freshly ground black pepper

2 tablespoons olive oil

4 small zucchini (courgettes), halved lengthwise

^{3}/$_4$ cup (30 g) fresh rocket (arugula), finely shredded

NUTRIENTS PER SERVING
1304 kJ, 311 kcal, 26 g protein, 12 g fat (2 g saturated fat), 25 g carbohydrate

VARIATION
Instead of rocket, use fresh parsley, or a mixture of fresh parsley, dill and a little tarragon. Or for a stronger flavour, use watercress.

FRESH TROUT WITH WALNUT DRESSING

TIME **25 MINUTES** SERVES **4**

INGREDIENTS

2 teaspoons vegetable oil

4 trout fillets (about 175 g/6 oz each)

salt

$1/4$ teaspoon paprika

10 walnut halves

125 g (4 oz) rocket (arugula), watercress
or mixed salad leaves

DRESSING

1 French shallot (eschalot) or 2 spring
onions (scallions), finely chopped

2–3 tablespoons chopped fresh dill
or celery leaves

$1^1/_2$ tablespoons spiced rice vinegar
or sherry vinegar

4 tablespoons walnut oil

salt and freshly ground black pepper

METHOD

1 Preheat grill (broiler) to high. To make the dressing, put French shallot or spring onions, dill or celery leaves, vinegar, walnut oil, salt and pepper in a small bowl. Mix well and set aside.

2 Grease the grill tray with 1 teaspoon vegetable oil and place trout fillets on top, skin side down. Season with salt and paprika. Grill trout 5–8 minutes, on one side only, until the flesh is opaque in the centre and delicately brown at the edges.

3 Meanwhile, heat remaining vegetable oil in a small frying pan and gently fry walnuts, shaking and stirring constantly so that they colour but do not burn. Drain on paper towel, then chop roughly.

4 Arrange rocket, watercress or salad leaves on four plates. Place a fillet of trout on each. Stir the dressing, spoon over the fish and scatter walnuts on top.

NUTRIENTS PER SERVING

1888 kJ, 451 kcal, 37 g protein, 33 g fat (4 g saturated fat), 1 g carbohydrate

COOK'S TIP

Tiny new potatoes go well with the clear flavours of this dish. Put them on to boil before you start grilling the trout.

HASTY TASTY FISH ON TOMATO AND RED ONION SALSA

TIME **20 MINUTES** SERVES **4**

INGREDIENTS

1 red onion, halved and very thinly sliced

4 tomatoes, halved, cores removed,
    thinly sliced

¼ teaspoon dried red chilli flakes

1 tablespoon chopped glacé ginger

1 teaspoon sugar

1 tablespoon tomato passata
    (puréed tomatoes)

1 tablespoon red wine vinegar

salt and freshly ground black pepper

3 tablespoons olive oil

4 thick skinless firm white fish fillets
    (about 125 g/4 oz each)

mustard and cress, to garnish

METHOD

1 Separate onion slices into shreds and put in a bowl. Add tomatoes, chilli flakes, ginger and sugar, then stir in tomato passata and vinegar and season to taste. Stir in 2 tablespoons oil and set aside.

2 Preheat grill (broiler) to high. Lightly oil the grill tray, then add fish fillets, skin side up, and brush with a little oil. Cook 3 minutes. Turn fish, brush with remaining oil and cook a further 3 minutes, or until cooked through.

3 Divide salsa among four plates and lay fish portions on top. Garnish with mustard and cress and serve.

NUTRIENTS PER SERVING

1200 kJ, 287 kcal, 27 g protein, 16 g fat (3 g saturated fat), 8 g carbohydrate

VARIATION

TUNA WITH CUCUMBER AND WATERCRESS SALSA For a green salsa, dice ½ Lebanese or other small cucumber, dice 2 celery stalks, seed and chop 1 green chilli, and shred 50 g (1¾ oz) watercress. Mix with grated zest and juice of 1 lime and 2 tablespoons extra virgin olive oil. Grill or barbecue 4 tuna steaks instead of the white fish. Serve with the green salsa.

COOK'S TIP

This recipe will also work with thin fillets; reduce the cooking time slightly.

SPICE-CRUSTED FISH WITH PEA PURÉE
TIME **30 MINUTES** SERVES 2

METHOD

1 Preheat oven to 200°C (400°F/Gas 6). If using the leatherjacket tail, remove the skin and trim off any fins and tough outer membrane. Place fillets or tail on a rack on a baking tray (sheet).

2 Put garlic, chilli, oil, cumin, coriander, sugar and lemon juice in a small bowl and stir to make a thick paste. Spread evenly over both sides of fish fillets or tail, then bake 20 minutes, or until just cooked.

3 Meanwhile, make the pea purée. Put peas in a saucepan with vegetable stock and bring to a boil. Add garlic and simmer, uncovered, 5 minutes, skimming off any scum that comes to the surface.

4 When peas are tender, drain stock into a measuring jug. Blend peas with cream and ²/₃ cup (150 ml) stock to make a textured purée. Season to taste with salt and pepper and keep warm.

5 When fish is cooked, remove from oven. If using leatherjacket tail, cut fillets from both sides of the central bone. Pour the purée onto two warmed plates, put one white fish fillet, or two fillets from the tail, on top of each serve and garnish with mint sprigs.

NUTRIENTS PER SERVING
1203 kJ, 287 kcal, 37 g protein, 13 g fat (3 g saturated fat), 10 g carbohydrate

INGREDIENTS

2 skinless firm white fish fillets
   (about 175 g/6 oz each) or
   1 large leatherjacket tail
   (about 500 g/1 lb)
1 clove garlic, crushed
1 red chilli, seeds removed, finely chopped
1 tablespoon olive oil
1 teaspoon ground cumin
1 teaspoon ground coriander
¹/₂ teaspoon sugar
1 teaspoon lemon juice
2 sprigs fresh mint, to garnish

PEA PURÉE

1 cup (150 g) frozen peas
1¹/₂ cups (375 ml) vegetable stock
1 clove garlic, crushed
1 tablespoon cream
salt and freshly ground black pepper

BAKED FISH WITH PESTO

TIME **30 MINUTES** SERVES **4**

INGREDIENTS

650 g (1 lb 7 oz) boiling (waxy)
   potatoes, such as long white
   or desiree, diced

salt and freshly ground black pepper

4 thick white fish fillets or cutlets,
   such as gemfish or blue-eye cod
   (about 175 g/6 oz each)

1 tablespoon basil or sun-dried
   tomato pesto

1 tablespoon olive oil

1 clove garlic, crushed

2 tablespoons butter

3 tablespoons cream

4 sprigs fresh basil, to garnish

METHOD

1 Preheat oven to 200°C (400°F/Gas 6). Boil potatoes in a saucepan of
   salted boiling water 10–15 minutes, until cooked.

2 Meanwhile, line a small roasting pan (baking dish) with foil. Wipe fish
   with paper towel and place in the roasting pan. Spread pesto evenly over
   each piece of fish and season with salt and pepper. Drizzle over oil and
   bake fish on the top shelf of the oven 15–20 minutes, or until the flesh
   flakes easily.

3 Drain potatoes and return to the pan. Add garlic and mash roughly. Stir
   in butter and cream and reheat gently.

4 Serve fish resting on a bed of mashed potato, garnished with basil.

NUTRIENTS PER SERVING

1804 kJ, 431 kcal, 37 g protein, 22 g fat (10 g saturated fat), 23 g carbohydrate

COOK'S TIP

Accompany with a simply cooked vegetable dish, such as steamed beans or
chargrilled vegetables.

CRISP FISH AND PRAWN GRATIN WITH BABY SPINACH
TIME **30 MINUTES** SERVES **4**

METHOD

1 Preheat oven to 220°C (425°F/Gas 7). Spread out spinach in a deep ovenproof dish large enough to hold the fish in one layer. Cut fish into four equal pieces and put on top of spinach.

2 Put cornflour in a saucepan and stir in a little of the milk to make a smooth, thin paste. Gradually stir in remaining milk, then cook over low heat, whisking continuously, until sauce boils and thickens. (The sauce will seem too thick but it will thin down when baked with the cheese, fish and prawns.)

3 Whisk in three-quarters of the cheese and all the spring onions with a little nutmeg. Season to taste. Remove from heat and stir in frozen prawns and parsley. Immediately pour sauce over fish and spinach to cover evenly.

4 Sprinkle grissini pieces over sauce and press in gently so they are almost submerged. Sprinkle with remaining cheese. Bake 15 minutes, or until bubbling hot and golden.

INGREDIENTS

300 g (10 oz) baby spinach leaves

250 g (8 oz) skinless firm white fish fillet

4 tablespoons cornflour (cornstarch)

2½ cups (625 ml) low-fat milk

⅔ cup (85 g) grated mature cheddar

4 spring onions (scallions), chopped

freshly grated nutmeg

salt and freshly ground black pepper

200 g (7 oz) frozen peeled cooked prawns (shrimp)

¾ cup (25 g) chopped fresh parsley

6 plain or sesame-flavoured grissini (thin breadsticks), coarsely crumbled

NUTRIENTS PER SERVING
1468 kJ, 351 kcal, 38 g protein, 10 g fat (5 g saturated fat), 27 g carbohydrate

VARIATION
Instead of firm white fish, use salmon or smoked trout or smoked salmon. Or soften frozen fish fillets or steaks in the microwave for a few seconds, then cut them into chunks and distribute over the spinach. Or use drained canned tuna or salmon instead of the fish or prawns (use the liquid from the canned salmon in the sauce).

SALMON WITH LIME HERB BUTTER

TIME 30 MINUTES SERVES 4

INGREDIENTS

5 cm (2 inch) piece fresh ginger,
  peeled and sliced
8 sprigs fresh coriander (cilantro),
  plus extra sprigs, to garnish
grated zest and juice of 1 lime, plus
  1 lime, cut into wedges, to garnish

125 g (4 oz) butter
salt and freshly ground black pepper
cayenne pepper
2 tablespoons vegetable oil
4 salmon fillets (about 175 g/
  6 oz each)

METHOD

1 Preheat oven to 220°C (425°F/Gas 7). Add ginger, 8 coriander sprigs, lime zest and juice, butter, salt, pepper and cayenne pepper to a food processor or blender, and blend.
2 Shape butter into a sausage, wrap in foil and chill in the freezer.
3 Meanwhile, brush a baking tray (sheet) with a little oil, place salmon fillets on it and brush with remaining oil. Sprinkle with salt and bake 8 minutes, or until the flesh flakes easily.
4 Cut butter into thick rounds. Transfer fish to four serving plates, place a round of butter on each and garnish with lime wedges and coriander.

NUTRIENTS PER SERVING

2695 kJ, 644 kcal, 26 g protein, 59 g fat (33 g saturated fat), 2 g carbohydrate

FISH CUTLETS WITH HORSERADISH BUTTER

TIME 25 MINUTES SERVES 4

INGREDIENTS

2 tablespoons snipped fresh chives
1½ tablespoons horseradish cream,
  from a jar
125 g (4 oz) butter, plus 2 teaspoons extra
4 firm white fish cutlets (about 175 g/
  6 oz each), patted dry
salt and freshly ground black pepper
2 teaspoons vegetable oil

METHOD

1 Mix chives, horseradish cream and 125 g (4 oz) butter in a bowl.
2 Shape butter into a sausage, wrap in foil and chill in the freezer.
3 Season fish with salt and pepper. Heat remaining butter and oil in a pan. Cook fish over high heat 4–6 minutes, until it flakes easily.
4 Cut butter into rounds. Transfer fish to four serving plates and place a round of butter on each.

NUTRIENTS PER SERVING

1833 kJ, 438 kcal, 38 g protein, 31 g fat (18 g saturated fat), 1 g carbohydrate

TUNA WITH WASABI BUTTER

TIME 25 MINUTES SERVES 4

INGREDIENTS

1 teaspoon sesame seeds
1 teaspoon lemon juice
3–4 sprigs each fresh basil, chives,
  coriander (cilantro) and parsley
125 g (4 oz) unsalted butter
1 tablespoon wasabi
  (Japanese horseradish)
1 tablespoon soy sauce
3 drops Tabasco sauce
4 tuna steaks (about 175 g/6 oz each)
1 tablespoon olive or vegetable oil

METHOD

1 Cook sesame seeds in a small dry frying pan until lightly coloured.
2 Put sesame seeds and lemon juice in a bowl. Finely chop herbs, reserving a few sprigs of basil for a garnish. Stir chopped herbs into sesame seeds along with butter, wasabi, soy sauce and Tabasco sauce. Beat until smooth.
3 Shape butter into a sausage, wrap in foil and chill in the freezer.
4 Heat a chargrill pan or frying pan over medium–high heat. Brush both sides of tuna steaks with oil and fry 3–4 minutes on each side.
5 Cut butter into rounds. Transfer steaks to four serving plates, place a round of butter on each and garnish with the herb sprigs.

NUTRIENTS PER SERVING

2185 kJ, 522 kcal, 42 g protein, 39 g fat (19 g saturated fat), 1 g carbohydrate

Right Fish cutlets with horseradish butter (top left); Tuna with wasabi butter (middle); Salmon with lime herb butter (bottom)

STEAMED WHOLE FISH CHINESE-STYLE

TIME **30 MINUTES** SERVES **4**

METHOD

1 Rinse fish and pat dry with paper towel. Make three or four diagonal slashes down to the bone on each side of the fish and gently rub with salt, inside and out. Set aside 10 minutes.
2 Meanwhile, stir soy sauce and sesame oil together in a small bowl and set aside. Fill a steamer or wok with water to a level of 5–7.5 cm (2–3 inches) and bring to a boil. If using a wok, put a trivet or wire rack in the bottom.
3 Rinse salt from fish under cold running water, then dry with paper towel. Place fish on a heatproof plate and lower into the steamer basket or wok; do not let the plate touch the water. Cover, reduce heat and steam gently 15–20 minutes, or until fish is cooked.
4 Meanwhile, heat peanut oil in a small frying pan and cook ginger and chilli over high heat, until softened. Set aside.
5 Transfer fish to a warmed serving dish and sprinkle with spring onions, ginger and chilli. Pour soy sauce and sesame oil mixture over the top, garnish with coriander sprigs and serve immediately.

INGREDIENTS

1 whole round fish, such as bream or snapper (about 1 kg/2 lb), cleaned by the fishmonger

salt

2 tablespoons soy sauce

1 tablespoon sesame oil

2 tablespoons peanut (groundnut) or vegetable oil

5 cm (2 inch) piece fresh ginger, peeled and cut into thin matchsticks

1 small red chilli, seeds removed, thinly sliced

4 spring onions (scallions), cut into 7.5 cm (3 inch) lengths and finely shredded

fresh coriander (cilantro) sprigs, to garnish

NUTRIENTS PER SERVING

1599 kJ, 382 kcal, 50 g protein, 19 g fat (2 g saturated fat), 2 g carbohydrate

COOK'S TIP

If you do not have a wok or steamer large enough to hold a whole fish, use a roasting pan (baking dish) with a wire rack. Pour water into the roasting pan, place the fish on its plate on the rack and cover the pan with foil, tucking it under the rim to keep the steam in.

FISH WITH WALNUT, GARLIC AND LEMON CRUST

TIME 25 MINUTES SERVES 4

INGREDIENTS

2 slices wholemeal (whole-wheat) bread
   with crusts, diced
3 tablespoons low-fat milk
1 tablespoon olive oil
1 lemon
2 spring onions (scallions), chopped
1–2 large cloves garlic, crushed
50 g (1¾ oz) walnut pieces, chopped
¾ cup (25 g) chopped fresh flat-leaf
   (Italian) parsley
4 skinless firm white fish fillets
   (about 125 g/4 oz each)
salt and freshly ground black pepper

METHOD

1 Preheat oven to 220°C (425°F/
   Gas 7). Put bread in a bowl and
   pour over milk and oil evenly.
   Grate zest from lemon, or use a
   zester, and add to bread mixture.
   Add spring onions, garlic, walnuts
   and parsley. Stir, pressing with the
   back of the spoon to moisten the
   bread evenly.
2 Put fish in a shallow ovenproof
   dish that holds them fairly snugly.
   Season lightly. Divide the bread
   mixture among fillets, piling it up
   and pressing it on quite firmly to
   keep it in place. Bake 15 minutes,
   or until crust is well browned and
   crisp, and fish is cooked through.
   Test the middle of one piece with
   the point of a knife — the fish
   should flake easily and look firm,
   succulent and white.
3 Cut lemon into wedges. Transfer
   fish to serving plates and garnish
   with lemon wedges.

NUTRIENTS PER SERVING

1250 kJ, 299 kcal, 29 g protein, 16 g fat
(2 g saturated fat), 8 g carbohydrate

MARMALADE-GLAZED MACKEREL WITH APPLES

TIME 25 MINUTES SERVES 4

INGREDIENTS

4 teaspoons olive oil
4 mackerel fillets (about 90 g/
   3 oz each)
2 apples, peeled
1 sprig fresh rosemary
3 tablespoons orange marmalade
   (preferably seville orange)
3 tablespoons cider vinegar

METHOD

1 Use tweezers to remove any fine bones that remain in the mackerel.
   Preheat grill (broiler) to high. Brush a shallow flameproof dish (such as
   a lasagne dish) with a little oil and put mackerel fillets in it, skin side
   up. (The mackerel can be cooked in the grill pan, but a dish is more
   convenient.) Make three cuts across each fillet, scoring the skin to
   prevent it from curling up during cooking.
2 Cut apples into quarters, remove cores, then cut each quarter into three
   or four slices. Put in the dish around the mackerel. Brush apples and
   fish with remaining oil. Sprinkle rosemary leaves over the fish.
3 Grill mackerel 2–3 minutes, or until the skin is browned in places.
   Meanwhile, stir marmalade and vinegar together in a bowl. Turn over
   mackerel fillets and apple slices. Brush a little marmalade mixture
   over apples, then spoon the remainder evenly over mackerel. Grill
   2 minutes, or until mackerel and apples are well browned in places.
   The fish should be firm and cooked, with flakes that separate easily
   and look opaque. Serve immediately.

NUTRIENTS PER SERVING

1659 kJ, 396 kcal, 15 g protein, 28 g fat (7 g saturated fat), 23 g carbohydrate

VARIATION

Instead of mackerel, use skinless salmon fillets, but omit the apples and
rosemary. Replace the marmalade with plum jam, and use halved stoned
plums instead of apples.

COOK'S TIP

Fish fillets, even if they are sold as boneless, can sometimes have the odd
small bone. Feel for bones by running a finger over the fillet, especially
down the middle. Use tweezers to easily remove any bones you find.

Right Marmalade-glazed mackerel with apples

1 Cook potatoes in a saucepan of boiling water 10–15 minutes, or until tender. Drain thoroughly, return to pan with butter and mash until it is a very smooth consistency.

2 Add horseradish, parsley, spring onions and corn to the mashed potato and stir thoroughly, then add tuna and season to taste. Allow mixture to cool slightly.

3 Shape mixture into eight thick flat cakes, each about 7.5 cm (3 inches) in diameter. Dust them on both sides with flour.

4 Heat oil in a large non-stick frying pan. Add the fishcakes and cook over medium heat 3–4 minutes on each side, or until well browned, turning them carefully with a spatula. If you don't have a large enough pan, cook in two batches, keeping the first batch warm while you cook the second. Serve hot with lemon mayonnaise and lemon wedges.

NUTRIENTS PER SERVING
1462 kJ, 349 kcal, 15 g protein, 18 g fat (5 g saturated fat), 31 g carbohydrate

VARIATION
Add 1 chopped green chilli, grated zest of 1 lime and 2 tablespoons chopped fresh coriander (cilantro) leaves.

COOK'S TIP
If you have time, leave the fishcakes to chill in the fridge for 30 minutes before cooking, as this will make them easier to handle.

TASTY TUNA AND CORN FISHCAKES
TIME **30 MINUTES** SERVES **4**

INGREDIENTS

600 g (1 lb 5 oz) potatoes, cut into chunks
25 g (1 oz) butter
1 tablespoon horseradish cream, from a jar
2 tablespoons chopped fresh parsley
3 spring onions (scallions), chopped
200 g (7 oz) canned corn, drained

180 g (6 oz) can tuna chunks, drained
salt and freshly ground black pepper
2 tablespoons plain (all-purpose) flour
2 tablespoons vegetable oil
lemon mayonnaise and lemon wedges,
   to serve

SMOKED FISH SALAD
TIME **25 MINUTES** SERVES **4**

METHOD

1 Put eggs in a saucepan of boiling water and cook 10 minutes. Drain and put in a bowl of cold water to cool.

2 Arrange mixed salad leaves on a serving platter or four individual plates. Top with smoked fish.

3 Toss apple in 2 teaspoons lemon juice and scatter over salad and fish. Peel eggs, cut into quarters and add to salad.

4 Mix mayonnaise with remaining lemon juice and drizzle over salad. Grind over a little pepper and serve.

NUTRIENTS PER SERVING

1682 kJ, 402 kcal, 20 g protein, 30 g fat (7 g saturated fat), 14 g carbohydrate

COOK'S TIP

Choose a salad mix with a combination of slightly bitter leaves such as frisée or curly endive, chicory and radicchio. Serve the salad with triangles of wholemeal (whole-wheat) bread and butter.

INGREDIENTS

2 eggs

200 g (7 oz) mixed salad leaves

350 g (12 oz) smoked mackerel or other smoked fish, skin removed, separated into large flakes

1 red apple, quartered, cored and chopped

1 tablespoon lemon juice

6 tablespoons good-quality mayonnaise

freshly ground black pepper

BLACKENED WHITE FISH

TIME 20 MINUTES SERVES 4

INGREDIENTS

1 teaspoon black peppercorns

1 teaspoon each fennel seeds, dried
   oregano and dried thyme

$1/2$–1 teaspoon cayenne pepper

salt

3 cloves garlic, crushed

2 tablespoons polenta or cornmeal

4 firm white fish fillets (about 175–250 g/
   6–8 oz each), skin removed

2 tablespoons peanut (groundnut) oil

1 lemon, cut into wedges, to garnish

METHOD

1 Crush peppercorns and put in a large bowl. Add fennel seeds and dried herbs, cayenne pepper, some salt, garlic and polenta or cornmeal and stir thoroughly.

2 Put fish fillets in the bowl and press herb and spice mixture onto the fish firmly to coat well.

3 Heat oil in a large heavy-based frying pan until it starts to smoke. Add fish and fry $1^{1}/2$ minutes on each side, or until fillets are lightly browned and cooked through.

4 Drain cooked fish on paper towel, then transfer to a warmed serving dish, garnish with lemon wedges and serve.

NUTRIENTS PER SERVING

1080 kJ, 258 kcal, 34 g protein, 10 g fat (2 g saturated fat), 9 g carbohydrate

COOK'S TIP

Any round firm white fish fillets are suitable for this dish. Fish cutlets can be used too, but allow them a little longer to cook — they will need about 6–8 minutes in total. Flat fish, such as sole and flounder, are too thin and too delicate to be cooked this way.

SEARED TUNA WITH CAPSICUM SAUCE

TIME 30 MINUTES SERVES 4

INGREDIENTS

2 red capsicums (bell peppers), seeds removed, halved lengthwise

1 onion, halved crosswise

2 cloves garlic, unpeeled

1 small red chilli, seeds removed, chopped

1 large slice wholemeal (whole-wheat) bread, diced

3 teaspoons tomato paste (concentrated purée)

3 tablespoons olive oil

grated zest and juice of 1 lime

salt and freshly ground black pepper

4 tuna or swordfish steaks (about 175 g/6 oz each)

METHOD

1 Preheat grill (broiler) or chargrill pan to high. Put capsicums and onion under the grill, skin sides up, with the unpeeled garlic cloves. Grill 10 minutes, or until the skins are slightly charred. Alternatively, brush vegetables with a little oil and chargrill on the hot pan until cooked and skins are lightly charred.

2 When grilled vegetables are cool enough to handle, remove skin and put flesh in a food processor or blender with chilli, bread, tomato paste and 2 tablespoons oil. Add half the lime zest and juice. Process mixture to a purée, then season to taste with salt and pepper. Transfer sauce to a bowl and set aside.

3 Brush the chargrill pan or a large heavy-based frying pan with the remaining oil and place over very high heat. Lightly season fish steaks and fry 4–6 minutes, until golden brown on the outside and cooked through, turning once.

4 Sprinkle fish with the remaining lime zest and juice and serve with the capsicum sauce, either spooned around the fish or offered separately in a serving bowl.

NUTRIENTS PER SERVING

1712 kJ, 409 kcal, 44 g protein, 20 g fat (4 g saturated fat), 14 g carbohydrate

COOK'S TIP

This dish is suitable for barbecuing. Barbecue the capsicums, onion and garlic, then finish off the sauce while the tuna is cooking on the barbecue.

Right Seared tuna with capsicum sauce (top); Blackened white fish (bottom)

PAN-FRIED OCEAN TROUT WITH LEEKS AND CREAM
TIME 20 MINUTES SERVES 4

INGREDIENTS

2 tablespoons unsalted butter

4 leeks, white part only, finely chopped

4 ocean trout fillets (about 150 g/
   5 oz each)

1/2 cup (125 ml) white wine

1/2 cup (125 ml) thick (heavy/double)
   cream

1 small bunch (20 g/2/3 oz) fresh chives,
   snipped

freshly ground black pepper

steamed spinach, to serve

METHOD

1 Heat butter gently in a large heavy-based frying pan. Add leeks and sauté 4–5 minutes, until just tender.

2 Add trout and cook 2–3 minutes on each side, until just cooked. Remove fish from pan and keep warm.

3 Add wine, cream and most of the chives to the pan and season with pepper. Increase heat and cook, stirring, 3–4 minutes, until the sauce has reduced and thickened.

4 Place some steamed spinach on four individual plates and pour over a little sauce. Top each with a trout fillet, drizzle over some more sauce and scatter over the remaining chives.

NUTRIENTS PER SERVING
2049 kJ, 489 kcal, 30 g protein, 37 g fat (13 g saturated fat), 4 g carbohydrate

COOK'S TIP
Offset the creaminess of the sauce with some crispy sautéed potatoes.

SMOKED SALMON WITH STIR-FRIED VEGETABLES

TIME **25 MINUTES** SERVES **4**

METHOD

1 Arrange salad leaves on a serving plate.
2 Heat olive oil and sesame oil in a large frying pan. Add garlic and chilli and stir-fry over medium heat 1 minute. Add beans and carrots and stir-fry a further 1–2 minutes.
3 Add French shallots and asparagus and stir-fry 1 minute. Then add sherry, cover pan and cook 1 minute.
4 Add smoked salmon strips to pan, cover and cook 1 minute. Stir in soy sauce and caster sugar and heat through.
5 Spoon smoked salmon mixture over the salad leaves and garnish with coriander. Serve immediately.

NUTRIENTS PER SERVING

732 kJ, 175 kcal, 10 g protein, 10 g fat (1 g saturated fat), 5 g carbohydrate

INGREDIENTS

250 g (8 oz) mixed salad leaves
1 tablespoon olive oil
1 tablespoon sesame oil
1 clove garlic, crushed
1 green chilli, seeds removed, sliced
100 g (3¹⁄₂ oz) small green beans, topped and tailed
100 g (3¹⁄₂ oz) baby carrots, topped and tailed, halved lengthwise if thick
100 g (3¹⁄₂ oz) French shallots (eschalots), halved or quartered if large
100 g (3¹⁄₂ oz) thin asparagus spears, trimmed, cut into bite-sized pieces
100 ml (3¹⁄₂ fl oz) dry sherry
125 g (4 oz) smoked salmon trimmings or slices, cut into strips
1 tablespoon light soy sauce
¹⁄₂ teaspoon caster (superfine) sugar
fresh coriander (cilantro) sprigs, to garnish

CHAPTER 7

Poultry

ONE-POT CHICKEN CASSEROLE
WITH CREAMY SHERRY SAUCE
TIME **30 MINUTES** SERVES **4**

INGREDIENTS

2 tablespoons olive oil

8 boneless, skinless chicken thighs
(about 650 g/1 lb 7 oz in total)

salt and freshly ground black pepper

250 g (8 oz) button mushrooms

175 g (6 oz) baby leeks

4 small turnips, quartered

500 g (1 lb) small new potatoes

2¹/₂ cups (625 ml) chicken stock

4 tablespoons sherry

200 g (7 oz) green beans

1 tablespoon cornflour (cornstarch)

³/₄ cup (185 g) low-fat natural
(plain) yogurt

grated zest of 1 lemon

METHOD

1 Heat oil in a large saucepan or flameproof casserole dish. Add chicken, season lightly with salt and pepper and cook over high heat 2 minutes, turning to brown both sides. Remove from pan and set aside on a plate.

2 Add mushrooms to pan and cook over high heat, stirring, 1 minute. Reduce heat, move mushrooms to the sides of the pan and lay leeks across the middle of the pan. Add turnips and potatoes in an even layer.

3 Pour in stock and sherry. Bring to a boil. Put chicken on top of vegetables, adding any juices from the plate. Reduce heat so that the stock bubbles steadily without boiling too fiercely. Cover and cook 10 minutes.

4 Add green beans, cover and continue to bubble a further 5 minutes, or until chicken and vegetables are cooked. Using a slotted spoon, divide ingredients among four warmed plates or transfer them to a serving dish. Keep warm while finishing the sauce.

5 Boil cooking stock hard, over high heat, in the open pan 5 minutes to reduce it slightly and concentrate the flavour. Meanwhile, mix cornflour with yogurt and lemon zest in a heatproof bowl to make a smooth paste.

6 Gradually add a little of the reduced stock to the yogurt mixture, stirring. Then gradually stir in the remaining stock. Pour it back into the pan; bring to a boil, stirring, to thicken the sauce slightly. (The cornflour stabilises the yogurt and stops it curdling.) Taste for seasoning. Pour a little sauce over the chicken and vegetables, and serve the rest separately.

NUTRIENTS PER SERVING

2156 kJ, 515 kcal, 43 g protein, 22 g fat (5 g saturated fat), 32 g carbohydrate

CHICKEN BREASTS WITH APPLES AND CIDER
TIME **30 MINUTES** SERVES **2**

METHOD

1 Heat oil and butter in a frying pan or flameproof casserole dish over low heat. Add French shallots, increase heat to medium and fry 3–4 minutes, stirring occasionally, until soft.

2 Add apples and sprinkle with brown sugar. Raise heat to medium–high and fry until the mixture starts to turn a golden caramel colour. Lift shallots and apples from the pan with a slotted spoon and set aside.

3 Add a little more oil to the pan, if necessary. Add chicken and fry over medium–high heat about 6 minutes, turning once, until golden brown.

4 Pour cider over chicken. Bring to a boil and simmer, uncovered, about 8–10 minutes, stirring occasionally and turning the chicken once, until cooked. The chicken is ready if the juices run clear when it is pierced with the tip of a knife.

5 Stir in worcestershire sauce and crème fraîche or sour cream, and season to taste with salt and pepper. Return shallots and apple slices to the pan and warm through 1–2 minutes, but do not allow the sauce to boil.

INGREDIENTS

3 teaspoons olive oil

3 teaspoons butter

2 French shallots (eschalots), finely chopped

2 crisp red dessert apples (about 175 g/ 6 oz each), quartered, cored and sliced

2 teaspoons soft brown sugar

2 boneless, skinless chicken breasts (about 175 g/6 oz each)

2/3 cup (150 ml) dry alcoholic (hard) cider

1 teaspoon worcestershire sauce

2 tablespoons crème fraîche or sour cream

salt and freshly ground black pepper

NUTRIENTS PER SERVING

2072 kJ, 495 kcal, 40 g protein, 23 g fat (11 g saturated fat), 28 g carbohydrate

VARIATION

The sauce can be made with a dry white wine or richly flavoured chicken stock instead of cider, if you prefer, but you must always use red dessert apples as green cooking apples lose their shape. This dish can also be made very successfully with tender veal escalopes instead of chicken breasts.

COOK'S TIP

Serve these succulent chicken breasts with jacket potatoes cooked in salted boiling water or a microwave oven, or with some boiled rice or buttered noodles, with a green salad or vegetable on the side.

CREAMY CHICKEN AND ALMOND CURRY

TIME **30 MINUTES** SERVES **4**

INGREDIENTS

2 tablespoons vegetable oil

1 onion, chopped

2 cloves garlic, chopped

2 tablespoons plain (all-purpose) flour

2 tablespoons korma curry powder

750 g (1¹/₂ lb) boneless, skinless chicken breast, cut into bite-sized pieces

1 tablespoon chopped fresh coriander (cilantro) leaves, plus extra leaves, to garnish

2 tablespoons raisins

1¹/₂ cups (375 ml) hot chicken or vegetable stock

¹/₄ cup (25 g) flaked almonds, toasted

juice of ¹/₂ lemon

2 tablespoons natural (plain) yogurt

2 tablespoons thick (heavy/double) cream

salt and freshly ground black pepper

METHOD

1 Heat oil in a large frying pan. Add onion and garlic and fry gently about 5 minutes, until soft.

2 Mix flour and curry powder in a large bowl, then toss chicken in the mixture until evenly coated. Add chicken and flour mixture to pan and fry, stirring, 3 minutes.

3 Add chopped coriander, raisins and hot stock. Bring to a boil, stirring, then reduce heat and simmer 10 minutes.

4 When chicken is cooked, remove pan from heat and stir in almonds, lemon juice, yogurt, cream and salt and pepper to taste. Reheat very gently, but do not allow to boil. Garnish with reserved coriander leaves.

NUTRIENTS PER SERVING

2126 kJ, 508 kcal, 46 g protein, 26 g fat (8 g saturated fat), 22 g carbohydrate

COOK'S TIP

Serve the curry with basmati rice, cooked while the chicken is simmering.

BARBECUED CHICKEN BREASTS

TIME **25 MINUTES** SERVES **4**

INGREDIENTS

1 tablespoon vegetable oil

2 tablespoons dijon mustard

2 tablespoons tomato passata
(puréed tomatoes)

1 tablespoon sugar

2 cloves garlic, crushed

1 pinch chilli powder

4 boneless, skinless chicken breasts
(about 125 g/4 oz each)

salt and freshly ground black pepper

4 spring onions (scallions)

METHOD

1 Put oil, dijon mustard, tomato passata, sugar and garlic in a small bowl. Add a good pinch of chilli powder (or more, to taste) and stir to mix well.

2 Cut three slashes in each chicken breast. Put chicken breasts in a shallow ovenproof dish and coat both sides with mustard mixture. Season well.

3 Barbecue chicken breasts, or cook on a chargrill pan, over medium heat 15–20 minutes, turning often. You may need to brush them with oil to keep moist. Alternatively, preheat grill (broiler) to medium and grill about 4 minutes on each side. Cook whole spring onions on the barbecue or under the grill, alongside the chicken, and serve.

NUTRIENTS PER SERVING

1047 kJ, 250 kcal, 28 g protein, 12 g fat (3 g saturated fat), 7 g carbohydrate

COOK'S TIP

Serve with crusty bread or baked potatoes and salad. This chicken is also good cold.

CHICKEN WITH TOASTED ALMONDS

TIME **30 MINUTES** SERVES **4**

INGREDIENTS

4 tablespoons plain (all-purpose) flour

salt and freshly ground black pepper

1 pinch paprika and/or mace

4 boneless, skinless chicken breasts
(about 125 g/4 oz each)

50 g (1¾ oz) slivered or flaked almonds

2 tablespoons olive oil

lemon wedges, to serve

METHOD

1 Mix flour, salt, pepper and paprika and/or mace in a bowl. Roll chicken breasts in the flour until well coated.

2 Heat a dry frying pan and toast almonds 2–3 minutes, until golden. Shake the pan and stir the almonds frequently so they do not burn. Remove from pan and set aside.

3 Heat oil in the pan. Add chicken and cook over medium heat about 4 minutes on each side, or until browned and cooked through. Sprinkle over the toasted almonds and serve with lemon wedges to squeeze over the chicken.

NUTRIENTS PER SERVING

1538 kJ, 367 kcal, 31 g protein, 23 g fat (4 g saturated fat), 9 g carbohydrate

CHICKEN WITH MUSHROOM SAUCE

TIME **30 MINUTES** SERVES **4**

INGREDIENTS

4 boneless, skinless chicken breasts
   (about 175 g/6 oz each)
freshly ground black pepper
1 tablespoon olive oil
1 tablespoon butter
4 spring onions (scallions), sliced
2 cloves garlic, finely chopped
350 g (12 oz) button or oyster
   mushrooms, sliced
1 tablespoon plain (all-purpose) flour
$^2/_3$ cup (150 ml) chicken stock
$^2/_3$ cup (150 ml) cream
2 tablespoons chopped fresh parsley
2 teaspoons chopped fresh thyme
2 teaspoons dijon mustard

METHOD

1　Season chicken with pepper.
2　Heat oil and butter in a frying pan until sizzling. Add chicken and cook 2–3 minutes on each side until golden, then reduce heat to low, cover and continue cooking 8–10 minutes, turning once. The chicken is ready when the juices run clear when it is pierced with the tip of a knife. Transfer to a plate, cover and keep warm.
3　Add spring onions, garlic and mushrooms to pan and fry over medium heat 3–4 minutes, or until softened.
4　Stir in flour and cook 1 minute, then add stock and bring to a boil, stirring constantly. Cook 2–3 minutes, then reduce heat, add cream, parsley, thyme and mustard, and stir well. Return chicken and any juices to the pan and heat gently a further 2–3 minutes.
5　Remove cooked chicken breasts from pan with a slotted spoon and put on four warmed plates, then spoon over mushroom sauce.

NUTRIENTS PER SERVING

1594 kJ, 381 kcal, 41 g protein, 22 g fat (10 g saturated fat), 4 g carbohydrate

VARIATION

This sauce also goes beautifully with escalopes of veal or pork.

COOK'S TIP

New potatoes and green beans or a green salad would make a good accompaniment to the chicken.

CHICKEN BREASTS WITH TARRAGON
TIME **30 MINUTES** SERVES **4**

INGREDIENTS

4 boneless, skinless chicken breasts
   (about 175 g/6 oz each), trimmed
   of fat and patted dry
2 tablespoons plain (all-purpose) flour
salt and freshly ground black pepper
1 tablespoon unsalted butter
1¹/₂ tablespoons vegetable oil
2 French shallots (eschalots), chopped
1 cup (250 ml) dry white wine
4 sprigs fresh tarragon, leaves roughly
   chopped, tips reserved, to garnish
1¹/₂ cups (375 ml) chicken stock
4 tablespoons crème fraîche or sour cream

METHOD

1 Dust chicken with flour and season lightly with salt and pepper.
2 Heat butter and 1 tablespoon oil in a frying pan over medium heat and cook chicken about 6 minutes on each side. Transfer to a plate, cover and keep warm.
3 Add the remaining oil and French shallots to the pan and fry, stirring, 1 minute. Add wine and half the chopped tarragon. Boil until the wine has reduced by half. Add chicken stock and boil to reduce by half again.
4 Stir in crème fraîche or sour cream and remaining chopped tarragon, then return chicken to the pan and warm through 1 minute on each side. Adjust seasoning and serve, garnished with tarragon tips.

NUTRIENTS PER SERVING
1737 kJ, 415 kcal, 40 g protein, 22 g fat (10 g saturated fat), 5 g carbohydrate

COOK'S TIP
A selection of steamed vegetables would offset this dish beautifully.

LIME CHICKEN WITH WATER CHESTNUTS
TIME **25 MINUTES** SERVES **4**

METHOD

1 Put rice vermicelli in a large bowl, cover with boiling water and leave to stand 10 minutes.

2 Meanwhile, pour oil into a wok or large frying pan with a lid. Add ginger, chilli, garlic and lime zest and stir-fry over high heat. When very hot, add chicken and stir-fry 2 minutes.

3 Add lime juice, sugar and water chestnuts. Stir well, then cover and cook over medium heat 3–5 minutes, until chicken is cooked through.

4 Drain rice vermicelli thoroughly. Add to the chicken with spring onions and coconut milk, and toss together to heat through. Add fish sauce or soy sauce to taste and serve immediately.

NUTRIENTS PER SERVING
1352 kJ, 323 kcal, 30 g protein, 8 g fat (2 g saturated fat), 32 g carbohydrate

VARIATION
You can substitute some boneless duck breasts for the chicken, or use 300 g (10 oz) peeled raw prawns (uncooked shrimp).

COOK'S TIP
Known as *nam pla* in Thailand and *nuoc nam* in Vietnam, fish sauce is available from Asian food stores and larger supermarkets.

INGREDIENTS

125 g (4 oz) dried rice vermicelli

1 tablespoon peanut (groundnut) oil

3 cm (1¼ inch) piece fresh ginger, peeled and finely chopped

1 green chilli, seeds removed, finely chopped

2 cloves garlic, crushed

grated zest of 2 limes and juice of 3 limes

500 g (1 lb) boneless, skinless chicken breast, cut into thick strips

½ teaspoon sugar

230 g (8 oz) can water chestnuts, drained and halved

5 spring onions (scallions), thinly sliced

½ cup (125 ml) coconut milk

fish sauce or soy sauce, to taste

RICOTTA CHICKEN WITH TOMATO SALSA
TIME 25 MINUTES SERVES 4

INGREDIENTS

4 boneless, skinless chicken breasts
  (about 175 g/6 oz each)
100 g (3^1/$_2$ oz) ricotta
5 tablespoons pesto
2 teaspoons olive oil
freshly ground black pepper
2 large tomatoes, finely chopped
1 small red onion, finely chopped
1 clove garlic, finely chopped
3 tablespoons torn fresh basil,
  plus extra leaves, to garnish
4 slices crusty Italian bread

METHOD

1 Preheat grill (broiler) to medium–high. Cut a deep slit lengthwise down the side of each chicken breast to make a pocket.
2 Put ricotta in a small bowl with 1 tablespoon pesto and mix together. Spoon a quarter of the mixture into the pocket in each chicken breast, then fold the chicken over to enclose the filling.
3 Place chicken in an oiled grill tray, brush well with oil and season with pepper. Grill 7–8 minutes each side, until cooked through. Transfer to a plate, cover and keep warm.
4 Meanwhile, mix together tomatoes, onion, garlic and torn basil in a bowl, then season generously with pepper.
5 Spread slices of bread with remaining pesto. Lightly toast under the grill.
6 Arrange chicken on the toast on individual plates. Spoon some salsa alongside and garnish with basil leaves.

NUTRIENTS PER SERVING
1758 kJ, 420 kcal, 53 g protein, 21 g fat (7 g saturated fat), 21 g carbohydrate

VARIATION
If ricotta is not available, use cream cheese or, if necessary, some finely grated hard cheese, such as gruyère or a mild cheddar.

COOK'S TIP
Use a food processor or blender to speed up the chopping of the tomatoes, onion and garlic, but take care to process each of them for no more than a few seconds, to leave some texture in the salsa.

GRILLED ROSEMARY CHICKEN

TIME **30 MINUTES** SERVES **4**

INGREDIENTS

8 x 5 cm (2 inch) sprigs rosemary

8 large chicken thighs (about 800 g/
    1³/₄ lb in total)

500 g (1 lb) new potatoes

salt and freshly ground black pepper

4 tablespoons olive oil

2 large cloves garlic, crushed

6 tablespoons mayonnaise

METHOD

1 Preheat grill (broiler) to high. Insert a sprig of rosemary under the skin of each chicken thigh.

2 Cook potatoes in a large saucepan of salted boiling water 15 minutes, until tender.

3 Meanwhile, arrange chicken, skin side down, on the grill rack. Brush with 1 tablespoon oil, sprinkle with salt and pepper and cook, about 10 cm (4 inches) below the heat, 10 minutes. Turn chicken over, brush with 1 tablespoon oil, season with more salt and pepper and cook a further 10 minutes, until skin is golden and crisp. Turn off grill, but leave chicken on the rack to keep warm.

4 While chicken is cooking, put the remaining oil in a small saucepan. Add garlic and cook, shaking, over medium heat until it starts to sizzle; do not let it colour. Turn off heat and beat in mayonnaise with 2 tablespoons hot water until well amalgamated, then cover and keep warm.

5 Drain potatoes. Slice thickly, then return to saucepan to reheat gently.

6 Arrange chicken thighs and potatoes on four individual plates. Spoon a little mayonnaise alongside each portion, then sprinkle with pepper and serve immediately.

NUTRIENTS PER SERVING

2352 kJ, 562 kcal, 31 g protein, 41 g fat (7 g saturated fat), 19 g carbohydrate

Above Grilled rosemary chicken (top); Ricotta chicken with tomato salsa (bottom)

CHICKEN AND PRAWN JAMBALAYA

TIME **30 MINUTES** SERVES **4**

INGREDIENTS

100 g (3^1/$_2$ oz) chorizo, cut into chunks

300 g (10 oz) boneless, skinless chicken breast, cut into bite-sized pieces

1^3/$_4$ cups (350 g) long-grain rice

3^2/$_3$ cups (900 ml) hot chicken or vegetable stock

1 bay leaf

^{3}/$_4$ cup (185 g) tomato salsa, from a jar

200 g (7 oz) peeled raw prawns (uncooked shrimp)

3 tablespoons chopped fresh parsley

salt and freshly ground black pepper

Tabasco sauce (optional)

METHOD

1 Heat a large deep frying pan over medium heat. Add chorizo and fry 2–3 minutes, or until just starting to brown. Remove from pan using a slotted spoon and set aside. Cook chicken in pan 1–2 minutes, stirring until lightly coloured. Remove and set aside.

2 Add rice to pan and cook, stirring, 1 minute. Pour in hot stock and add bay leaf. Bring to a boil, then reduce heat, cover pan with a lid and simmer gently 5 minutes.

3 Stir chorizo and chicken into rice. Cover and simmer 10 minutes. Stir in salsa, prawns and parsley. Cook a further 3–4 minutes, or until prawns are just cooked, most of the liquid has been absorbed and rice is tender.

4 Remove bay leaf. Season with salt and pepper, sprinkle with a dash of Tabasco, if you like, then serve.

NUTRIENTS PER SERVING

2370 kJ, 566 kcal, 39 g protein, 10 g fat (4 g saturated fat), 77 g carbohydrate

Left Chicken and prawn jambalaya

CHICKEN THAI GREEN CURRY

TIME **30 MINUTES** SERVES **4**

INGREDIENTS

4 boneless, skinless chicken breasts (about 125 g/4 oz each)

4 tablespoons green curry paste

2–3 tablespoons vegetable oil

2 onions, sliced

2 cloves garlic, crushed

1 red capsicum (bell pepper), seeds removed, sliced

250 g (8 oz) long thin eggplant (aubergine), halved

salt and freshly ground black pepper

2 cups (500 ml) boiling water

200 g (7 oz) baby zucchini (courgettes), stalks trimmed

4 large sprigs fresh basil, leaves roughly chopped

4 large sprigs fresh coriander (cilantro), leaves roughly chopped

METHOD

1 Put chicken in a dish and add curry paste. Turn chicken over several times to coat with paste.

2 Heat 2 tablespoons oil in a large frying pan over medium–high heat. Add chicken and lightly brown 1 minute on each side. Remove from pan and set aside.

3 Add remaining oil if necessary, then add onions, garlic, capsicum and eggplant to the pan. Cook, stirring, 1 minute. Return the chicken breasts to the pan, shuffling them in among the vegetables, and scrape in any juices and curry paste from the dish.

4 Season to taste with salt and pepper. Pour in boiling water. Heat until simmering, then reduce heat so that the liquid bubbles steadily. Cover tightly with a lid or foil and simmer 10 minutes.

5 Add baby zucchini to the pan, cover and cook a further 5 minutes. Taste for seasoning, remove from heat and stir in basil and coriander. Serve immediately.

NUTRIENTS PER SERVING

1560 kJ, 373 kcal, 30 g protein, 25 g fat (2 g saturated fat), 8 g carbohydrate

VARIATION

Replace baby zucchini and thin eggplant with regular zucchini and large eggplant cut into matchsticks.

CHICKEN AND SPINACH CURRY

TIME 25 MINUTES SERVES 4

INGREDIENTS

2 tablespoons vegetable oil

1 small onion, chopped

1 clove garlic, crushed

1 teaspoon peeled and finely chopped
  fresh ginger

$1/2$ teaspoon ground turmeric

$1/2$ teaspoon ground cumin

$1/2$ teaspoon ground coriander

$1/4$ teaspoon chilli powder

$1/4$ teaspoon garam masala

2 ripe tomatoes, roughly chopped

4 boneless, skinless chicken breasts
  (about 175 g/6 oz each), cut into
  bite-sized pieces

salt and freshly ground black pepper

$2/3$ cup (150 ml) thick (heavy/double)
  cream

4 large naan

200 g (7 oz) baby spinach leaves

METHOD

1 Heat oil in a large saucepan over medium heat. Add onion and fry 4 minutes, then stir in garlic and fry 1 minute.

2 Add ginger, turmeric, cumin, coriander, chilli and garam masala and cook, stirring, 1 minute. Add tomatoes and fry over gentle heat 7 minutes, until cooked down to a pulp.

3 Increase heat to high, add chicken and stir-fry until all the pieces have turned white. Season with salt and pepper, then pour in cream and simmer a further 6 minutes.

4 Meanwhile, preheat grill to high. Put naan under grill to heat through.

5 Add spinach to the curry, press down and stir continuously until it wilts. Bring to a boil, then remove pan from heat immediately. Serve the curry with the warmed naan.

NUTRIENTS PER SERVING

4227 kJ, 1010 kcal, 55 g protein, 53 g fat (14 g saturated fat), 85 g carbohydrate

CINNAMON–MUSTARD CHICKEN WITH SWEET POTATOES

TIME **30 MINUTES** SERVES **4**

METHOD

1 Preheat oven to 240°C (460°F/Gas 8). Mix mustard, cinnamon and apple juice in a large ovenproof dish or roasting pan (baking dish). Add chicken, turning pieces over several times to coat them in the marinade. Set aside.

2 Put sweet potato wedges in a large saucepan, pour over boiling water to cover and boil 5 minutes.

3 Drain sweet potatoes, then add to chicken with onions and capsicums. Turn all vegetables in the marinade to coat evenly, then turn chicken once more.

4 Season chicken and vegetables with salt and pepper to taste and drizzle over oil. Roast 20 minutes, or until cooked and well browned. Test chicken is cooked by piercing the thickest part with the point of a knife; the juices should run clear, not pink. Serve at once.

NUTRIENTS PER SERVING

2144 kJ, 512 kcal, 37 g protein, 21 g fat (5 g saturated fat), 44 g carbohydrate

VARIATION

Use mango juice instead of apple juice and add a peeled, stoned and sliced firm mango to the roasting pan halfway through cooking.

INGREDIENTS

2 tablespoons wholegrain mustard

2 teaspoons ground cinnamon

$3/4$ cup (180 ml) apple juice

8 boneless, skinless chicken thighs (about 650 g/1 lb 7 oz in total)

4 orange sweet potatoes (kumara) (about 800 g/1$3/4$ lb in total), cut into chunky wedges

4 onions, quartered

2 red and 2 yellow capsicums (bell peppers), seeds removed, quartered lengthwise

salt and freshly ground black pepper

2 tablespoons olive oil

SPANISH-STYLE CHICKEN
TIME 30 MINUTES SERVES 4

INGREDIENTS

2 tablespoons olive oil

8 boneless, skinless chicken thighs
  (about 750 g/1¹/₂ lb in total), halved

1 red onion, thinly sliced

1 clove garlic, crushed

1 large red and 1 large yellow capsicum
  (bell pepper), halved, seeds removed,
  sliced crosswise

410 g (15 oz) can chopped tomatoes,
  drained

²/₃ cup (150 ml) dry white wine

1 tablespoon paprika

100 g (3¹/₂ oz) chorizo, thickly sliced

2 tablespoons pitted black olives, halved

salt and freshly ground black pepper

1 small bunch (20 g/²/₃ oz) fresh parsley,
  leaves chopped

crusty white bread, to serve

METHOD

1 Heat oil in a large flameproof casserole dish or heavy-based saucepan. Add chicken and fry over high heat, 4–5 minutes, turning frequently, until golden.

2 Add onion, garlic and capsicums to the dish and fry, 5 minutes, until lightly browned and slightly softened.

3 Stir in tomatoes, wine and paprika and bring to a boil. Add chorizo, reduce heat and simmer 15 minutes, or until chicken is cooked.

4 Add olives, season to taste with salt and pepper and stir to heat through. Scatter parsley over chicken and serve with some crusty bread.

NUTRIENTS PER SERVING
2452 kJ, 586 kcal, 44 g protein, 23 g fat (5 g saturated fat), 49 g carbohydrate

CHICKEN WITH GARLIC SAUCE AND NOODLES
TIME **30 MINUTES** SERVES **4**

METHOD

1 Put garlic, mustard, tomato paste, vinegar and stock or water in a bowl and stir to combine. Set aside

2 Heat 1^1/$_2$ tablespoons oil in a frying pan over high heat. Add chicken and stir-fry 1–2 minutes, until it turns white.

3 Stir reserved garlic mixture into pan and add white parts of spring onions. Bring to a boil, cover and simmer gently about 5 minutes.

4 Meanwhile, cook egg noodles in a large saucepan of salted boiling water 3 minutes, or following packet instructions, then drain well and toss in remaining oil.

5 Blend cornflour with a little cream in a bowl, then stir into chicken. Add green parts of spring onions, reserving some for a garnish, then add the remaining cream and season to taste. Stir over medium heat 2–3 minutes, until the sauce thickens.

6 Serve the chicken and sauce over the noodles on individual plates, and garnish with the reserved spring onions.

NUTRIENTS PER SERVING
2440 kJ, 583 kcal, 36 g protein, 24 g fat (9 g saturated fat), 56 g carbohydrate

INGREDIENTS

4–6 cloves garlic, crushed

2 tablespoons dijon mustard

1 tablespoon tomato paste (concentrated purée)

2 tablespoons white wine vinegar

4 tablespoons chicken stock or water

2 tablespoons olive oil

500 g (1 lb) boneless, skinless chicken breast, cut diagonally into long thin strips

4 spring onions (scallions), green and white parts separated, finely sliced

250 g (8 oz) dried fine egg noodles

salt and freshly ground black pepper

2 teaspoons cornflour (cornstarch)

1 cup (250 ml) cream

CHICKEN ARRABBIATA
TIME **30 MINUTES** SERVES **4**

INGREDIENTS

2 tablespoons olive oil

500 g (1 lb) skinless, boneless chicken
    breast, diced

1 onion, chopped

2 cloves garlic, chopped

2 celery stalks, diced

2 green chillies, seeds removed, chopped,
    or 1 teaspoon dried red chilli flakes

2 x 410 g (15 oz) cans chopped tomatoes

salt and freshly ground black pepper

grated parmesan, to serve

METHOD

1 Heat oil in a large saucepan. Add chicken, onion, garlic, celery and chilli
  or chilli flakes. Cook over medium heat, stirring occasionally, 5 minutes,
  or until chicken is golden brown and onion is softened and translucent.

2 Stir in tomatoes and season to taste with salt and pepper. Bring mixture
  to a boil, then reduce heat, partially cover the pan with a lid and simmer
  gently 15 minutes.

3 Serve chicken on individual plates with a bowl of parmesan alongside.

NUTRIENTS PER SERVING

1259 kJ, 301 kcal, 37 g protein, 21 g fat (5 g saturated fat), 28 g carbohydrate

VARIATION

Serve the chicken with rigatoni or penne, accompanied by a green leaf salad
for a complete meal.

CHICKEN BREASTS WITH HOT SALSA
TIME **30 MINUTES** SERVES **4**

METHOD

1 Preheat grill (broiler) to high. Put capsicums, skin side up, on the grill rack. Add chilli and grill 15 minutes, or until skins are blistered and brown, but not burnt. Turn chilli over halfway through.
2 Meanwhile, pour 2 teaspoons oil into a large bowl and the remaining oil into a small salad bowl. Divide garlic between the two bowls.
3 Put chicken breasts in the large bowl and turn in the oil until evenly coated. Season with pepper. Put chicken, skin side up, on the grill rack alongside capsicums. Grill 7–8 minutes, until chicken is golden and blistered, then turn and cook a further 7–8 minutes.
4 When capsicums and chilli are blistered, transfer to a bowl. Cover and set aside until cool enough to handle.
5 While chicken finishes cooking, put lime or lemon juice in the salad bowl, with salt and pepper to taste.
6 Remove capsicum skin and finely dice flesh. Remove chilli skin, then halve chilli, remove seeds and finely dice flesh. Stir capsicums and chilli into the dressing.
7 Serve chicken on individual plates with the salsa alongside.

INGREDIENTS

1 red and 1 yellow capsicum (bell pepper), quartered, seeds removed
1 green chilli
4 tablespoons extra virgin olive oil
2 small cloves garlic, crushed
4 boneless, skinless chicken breasts (about 175 g/6 oz each)
salt and freshly ground black pepper
juice of 1/2 lime or 1/2 lemon

NUTRIENTS PER SERVING

1515 kJ, 362 kcal, 39 g protein, 21 g fat (4 g saturated fat), 5 g carbohydrate

VARIATION

The salsa also goes well with grilled fish and can be made 1–2 days ahead and stored in the refrigerator.

CREAMY CHICKEN KORMA

TIME **30 MINUTES** SERVES 4

INGREDIENTS

1 tablespoon vegetable oil

1 onion, chopped

1 teaspoon finely chopped
  fresh ginger

2 tablespoons korma or other mild
  curry paste or powder

600 g (1 lb 5 oz) boneless, skinless
  chicken breast, thickly sliced

²/₃ cup (150 ml) hot chicken stock

400 ml (14 fl oz) can coconut milk

salt and freshly ground black pepper

50 g (1¾ oz) almond meal
  (ground almonds)

2 tablespoons chopped fresh
  coriander (cilantro) leaves
  (optional)

METHOD

1 Heat oil in a heavy-based saucepan or flameproof casserole dish and
   lightly cook onion and ginger 4–5 minutes, or until softened. Stir in
   curry paste or powder and cook over low heat 1 minute, taking
   care that it does not burn.

2 Add chicken slices to the pan, stirring to coat them in the spicy onions.
   Add stock and coconut milk, and bring to a boil. Season. Simmer on
   the stovetop 20 minutes.

3 Stir in almond meal to thicken the sauce. Scatter coriander on top,
   if you like, and serve.

NUTRIENTS PER SERVING

2151 kJ, 514 kcal, 38 g protein, 36 g fat (15 g saturated fat), 10 g carbohydrate

COOK'S TIP

If you don't need this dish in a hurry, preheat oven to 180°C (350°F/
Gas 4), and if using a heavy-based saucepan, transfer mixture to a warmed
ovenproof dish after seasoning in step 2. Cover with a tight-fitting lid, put
in the oven and leave to cook 45–60 minutes, then continue with step 3.

Left Creamy chicken korma

TANDOORI CHICKEN WITH MUSHROOMS

TIME **30 MINUTES** SERVES 4

INGREDIENTS

8 boneless, skinless chicken thighs
  (about 650 g/1 lb 7 oz in total)

3 tablespoons tandoori spice mix

3 tablespoons vegetable oil

500 g (1 lb) button mushrooms,
  stalks discarded

4 green capsicums (bell peppers),
  seeds removed, cut into chunks

4 tablespoons chopped fresh coriander
  (cilantro) leaves

lemon wedges, to garnish

METHOD

1 Preheat grill (broiler) to high. Put
   chicken in the grill tray or a large
   shallow ovenproof dish, keeping
   the pieces close together in the
   middle. Sprinkle spice mix over
   chicken. Drizzle with 1 tablespoon
   oil, then use a spoon and fork to
   turn chicken pieces over several
   times to coat them evenly in the
   spices and oil.

2 Grill chicken, skinned side up,
   5 minutes, then turn over. Add
   mushrooms, gill side down, and
   capsicums, skin side up. Brush
   vegetables with 1 tablespoon oil.
   Grill 5 minutes, or until lightly
   browned. Turn chicken and
   vegetables over. Brush remaining
   oil over vegetables and cook a
   further 4–5 minutes.

3 Transfer chicken and vegetables to
   individual plates, spooning all the
   cooking juices over them. Sprinkle
   with coriander and garnish with
   lemon wedges, then serve.

NUTRIENTS PER SERVING

1734 kJ, 414 kcal, 37 g protein, 27 g fat
(5 g saturated fat), 8 g carbohydrate

CHICKEN AND CASHEW NUT STIR-FRY

TIME **25 MINUTES** SERVES **4**

INGREDIENTS

2 tablespoons olive oil

500 g (1 lb) boneless, skinless chicken
    breast, cut into strips

¹/₃ cup (50 g) cashew nuts

1 large yellow capsicum (bell pepper),
    seeds removed, sliced

4 celery stalks, thinly sliced

4 spring onions (scallions), sliced

2 zucchini (courgettes), halved lengthwise,
    seeds removed, thinly sliced

¹/₄ cup (45 g) dried apricots, sliced

4 tablespoons dry sherry

grated zest and juice of 1 lime

1 teaspoon sesame oil

salt and freshly ground black pepper

¹/₂ Chinese cabbage, finely shredded

³/₄ cup (25 g) fresh basil leaves

METHOD

1 Heat olive oil in a large frying pan or wok. Add chicken and cashew
    nuts and stir-fry 2–3 minutes, or until chicken is cooked and nuts are
    lightly browned.

2 Add capsicum, celery and spring onions and stir-fry 1–2 minutes to soften
    the vegetables slightly. Stir in zucchini and apricots; stir-fry 1–2 minutes.
    The vegetables should be lightly cooked but still crisp.

3 Add sherry and lime zest and juice to the vegetables, then sesame oil.
    Add salt and pepper to taste and boil, stirring, 30–60 seconds to cook off
    the alcohol and coat all the ingredients. Finally, add Chinese cabbage and
    basil and stir briskly. Remove from heat and serve immediately.

NUTRIENTS PER SERVING

1708 kJ, 408 kcal, 32 g protein, 24 g fat (5 g saturated fat), 13 g carbohydrate

COOK'S TIP

When shopping, look for ingredients such as chicken and dried apricots that
are already sliced or chopped, to save cutting them up (and to reduce the
washing up). Look in your supermarket for ready-sliced stir-fry vegetable
mixtures, either fresh or frozen. These can be used instead of the capsicum,
zucchini, celery and spring onions. Allow about 500 g (1 lb) prepared
vegetables for four people.

CHICKEN SKEWERS WITH ZESTY MAYONNAISE

TIME **25 MINUTES** SERVES **4**

INGREDIENTS

2 tablespoons olive oil

2 teaspoons ground turmeric

2 cloves garlic, crushed

salt and freshly ground black pepper

4 boneless, skinless chicken breasts
(about 125 g/4 oz each), cut into
bite-sized chunks

3 nectarines, halved and stoned

12 baby capsicums (bell peppers),
halved, seeds removed

2 spring onions (scallions), chopped

grated zest of $1/2$ lemon

100 g ($3^1/2$ oz) mayonnaise

75 g ($2^1/2$ oz) low-fat natural (plain) yogurt

1 pinch cayenne pepper or chilli powder
(optional)

lemon juice, to taste

METHOD

1 Put oil, turmeric, garlic and plenty of salt and black pepper in a bowl. Add chicken to the bowl and toss to coat thoroughly with mixture. Set aside.

2 Preheat grill (broiler) to high. Cut each nectarine half into four wedges, to give 24 pieces in total. Thread chicken, nectarine and capsicum pieces onto eight metal skewers, nestling nectarine wedges inside (or close to) the capsicum halves and alternating them with chunks of chicken. Put skewers in a large shallow ovenproof dish or the grill tray.

3 Grill skewers 5 minutes on each side. The chicken pieces should be cooked through; the capsicums and edges of the nectarines should be well browned, with a hint of charring in places.

4 Meanwhile, in a small bowl, mix spring onions, lemon zest, mayonnaise and yogurt. Season with a hint of cayenne or chilli powder, if you like, and add lemon juice to taste. Serve dollops of the dressing beside the skewers.

NUTRIENTS PER SERVING

2043 kJ, 488 kcal, 31 g protein, 34 g fat (6 g saturated fat), 16 g carbohydrate

VARIATION

Instead of chicken, use boneless, skinless turkey or duck breasts. Replace nectarines with papaya or mango. Select fruit that is just ripe but firm; peel it, discard the seeds or stone, then cut into large chunks. Use 2 large capsicums, cut into bite-sized chunks, instead of the baby capsicums.

BLUE-BRIE CHICKEN POCKETS
WITH CABBAGE AND WALNUTS

TIME **30 MINUTES** SERVES **4**

INGREDIENTS

2.5 cm (1 inch) piece fresh ginger, grated

1 apple, peeled, quartered, cored
   and grated

2 thick boneless, skinless chicken breasts
   (about 300 g/10 oz each)

150 g (5 oz) blue brie, cut into 4 wedges

3 tablespoons olive oil

salt and freshly ground black pepper

500 g (1 lb) savoy cabbage,
   finely shredded

8 spring onions (shallots), sliced

1/2 cup (50 g) walnuts, chopped

boiled small new potatoes, to serve

METHOD

1   Preheat oven to 240°C (460°F/Gas 8). Mix ginger and apple in a bowl.
    Cut each chicken breast in half crosswise, then cut a pocket in the middle
    of each piece of meat. Take care not to cut right through. Divide ginger
    and apple mixture among pockets, then push a wedge of cheese into each.
    Press meat together, moulding it back into shape and pushing the filling
    evenly into the pockets.

2   Put chicken pockets in a shallow ovenproof dish, large enough to hold
    them neatly in one layer. Brush with 1 tablespoon oil and sprinkle with salt
    and pepper to taste. Bake 15 minutes, or until chicken is browned on top
    and cooked through, and filling is running out in places.

3   Meanwhile, heat remaining oil in a large saucepan and add cabbage,
    spring onions and walnuts. Cook over medium heat, stirring most of the
    time, about 5 minutes, or until cabbage is reduced in volume and lightly
    cooked. Season to taste.

4   Transfer chicken to plates using a large serving spoon, spooning over the
    escaping cheese and juices. Add some cabbage to each plate and serve
    immediately with new potatoes.

NUTRIENTS PER SERVING

2644 kJ, 632 kcal, 46 g protein, 44 g fat (14 g saturated fat), 15 g carbohydrate

CHICKEN BURGERS
TIME **25 MINUTES** SERVES **4**

METHOD

1 Put chicken in a bowl. Add spring onions, mixed dried herbs, mace or nutmeg, tomato paste and plenty of salt and pepper. Mix together until thoroughly combined.

2 Divide mixture into four portions. Roll one portion into a ball, then press flat into a fairly thin burger, about 10 cm (4 inches) in diameter. Set aside on a plate or board. Repeat with remaining mixture.

3 Heat a large frying pan over high heat, then add oil and tilt pan to coat it evenly. Add burgers, reduce heat to medium and press them flat with a spatula. Cook 4–5 minutes, or until well browned underneath. Turn over, press flat and cook a further 4–5 minutes, or until well browned on the other side.

4 Meanwhile, slice rolls in half crosswise and spread bottom layer with mayonnaise. Add 2 lettuce leaves to each. When cooked, put a burger on each and add a little onion, if you like. Replace top of roll and serve with a pile of cherry tomatoes.

NUTRIENTS PER SERVING
1776 kJ, 424 kcal, 32 g protein, 19 g fat (4 g saturated fat), 31 g carbohydrate

VARIATION
Make the burgers with minced (ground) turkey instead of chicken.

COOK'S TIP
The bread rolls can be toasted until golden on the sliced side, if you prefer.

INGREDIENTS
500 g (1 lb) minced (ground) chicken

4 spring onions (scallions), thinly sliced

2 teaspoons mixed dried herbs

1 teaspoon ground mace or nutmeg

1 tablespoon tomato paste
    (concentrated purée)

salt and freshly ground black pepper

1 tablespoon vegetable oil

4 large bread rolls

2 tablespoons mayonnaise

8 lettuce leaves

$^1/_2$ onion, thinly sliced (optional)

about 20 red cherry tomatoes, to serve

GLAZED CHICKEN AND GREEN VEGETABLES

TIME 30 MINUTES SERVES 4

INGREDIENTS

2 tablespoons hoisin sauce

2 tablespoons sherry or white wine vinegar

2 tablespoons dark soy sauce

1 tablespoon honey

2 teaspoons sesame oil

300 g (10 oz) boneless, skinless chicken
    breast, cut into thick strips

1¹/₂ tablespoons vegetable oil

200 g (7 oz) broccoli, cut into small florets

1 leek, white part only, finely sliced

100 g (3¹/₂ oz) small snow peas
    (mangetout)

METHOD

1 Preheat grill (broiler) to medium–
   high and line the grill tray with
   lightly oiled foil. Mix together
   hoisin sauce, sherry or vinegar,
   dark soy sauce, honey and sesame
   oil. Put chicken in the grill tray in
   a single layer and brush with two-
   thirds of the hoisin glaze. Cook
   3–4 minutes, turning halfway
   through cooking time (the chicken
   should be just cooked through; cut
   a piece in half to check).

2 Meanwhile, heat vegetable oil
   in a wok or large heavy-based
   non-stick frying pan. Add broccoli
   and stir-fry 2 minutes. Add leek
   and stir-fry 1 minute, then add
   snow peas and stir-fry a further
   2 minutes.

3 Blend the remaining glaze with
   4 tablespoons water and add to
   wok. Cook 2–3 minutes, stirring
   frequently, until vegetables are
   tender and everything is hot.

NUTRIENTS PER SERVING

1085 kJ, 259 kcal, 20 g protein, 14 g fat
(2 g saturated fat), 12 g carbohydrate

MANDARIN CHICKEN WITH BEAN SPROUT AND WATERCRESS SALAD

TIME 20 MINUTES SERVES 4

INGREDIENTS

4 boneless, skinless chicken breasts
    (about 150 g/5 oz each)

2 tablespoons chopped fresh
    rosemary

1 teaspoon dried red chilli flakes

1 tablespoon coriander seeds,
    coarsely crushed

2 tablespoons olive oil

salt and freshly ground black pepper

4 mandarins

400 g (14 oz) bean sprouts, trimmed

75 g (2¹/₂ oz) watercress, trimmed

8 spring onions (scallions), sliced

1 tablespoon sugar

¹/₂ cup (125 g) mayonnaise

cayenne pepper (optional)

METHOD

1 Put chicken breasts in a shallow dish. Sprinkle with rosemary, chilli
   flakes, coriander seeds and 1 tablespoon oil. Season with salt and
   pepper and turn chicken over a few times to coat it in the mixture.

2 Peel mandarins. Slice in half across the middle and discard any pips.

3 Mix bean sprouts, watercress and spring onions, and divide among
   four individual plates.

4 Heat a chargrill pan or frying pan over high heat. Brush chicken with
   remaining oil. Cook over high heat 1¹/₂–2 minutes on each side, or until
   well browned and cooked through; when cut, the juices should run
   clear, not pink. Transfer the chicken to the plates.

5 Add mandarin halves to pan, cut side down, and cook 30–60 seconds,
   or until browned on the surface and hot. Transfer the mandarins to the
   plates, browned side up, and sprinkle each half with ¹/₂ teaspoon sugar.
   Add a dollop of mayonnaise to each plate and sprinkle with a little
   cayenne pepper, if you like. Serve.

NUTRIENTS PER SERVING

2056 kJ, 491 kcal, 36 g protein, 28 g fat (5 g saturated fat), 25 g carbohydrate

VARIATION

Instead of chicken, buy skinless, boneless turkey or duck breasts. Use a
meat mallet to beat them out thinly between pieces of baking (parchment)
paper or greaseproof (wax) paper. Or use thin pork loin steaks or chops.

Right Mandarin chicken with bean sprout and watercress salad

CHICKEN AND VEGETABLE STEAMBOAT

TIME **30 MINUTES** SERVES **4**

INGREDIENTS

500 g (1 lb) boneless, skinless
    chicken breast, cut into thin strips
$^1/_2$ teaspoon Chinese five-spice
2 tablespoons light soy sauce
3 cm (1$^1/_4$ inch) piece fresh ginger,
    peeled and chopped
1 celery stalk, thinly sliced
1 clove garlic, thinly sliced
1 lemongrass stem or strip of
    lemon zest
6 cups (1.5 litres) chicken stock

1 large red capsicum (bell pepper),
    seeds removed, cut into chunks
250 g (8 oz) baby corn
200 g (7 oz) broccolini,
    cut into florets
2 spring onions (scallions),
    thinly sliced
250 g (8 oz) fresh rice noodles or
    wok-ready noodles
250 g (8 oz) bok choy, quartered
    lengthwise

METHOD

1 Put chicken in a bowl. Add Chinese five-spice and soy sauce and mix well. Set aside.
2 Put ginger in a large saucepan with celery, garlic, lemongrass or lemon zest and stock. Bring to a boil, then reduce heat. Cover and simmer 5 minutes.
3 Add chicken to stock, then add capsicum, baby corn and broccolini. Return to a boil and simmer 3 minutes, or until chicken is cooked and vegetables are just tender.
4 Add spring onions and noodles, stir gently and briefly to combine, then return to a boil. Lay bok choy over the top and simmer about 2 minutes, or until bok choy leaves are wilted and noodles are hot and cooked.
5 Take pan to the table and serve, ladling the cooked ingredients into warmed bowls with a little of the broth. Ladle out the last of the broth at the end of the meal.

NUTRIENTS PER SERVING

2083 kJ, 498 kcal, 40 g protein, 8 g fat (3 g saturated fat), 63 g carbohydrate

VARIATION

Instead of noodles, use Chinese dumplings (pot-stickers) or won tons from Chinese and Asian supermarkets. There are several types, with different fillings. Follow the packet instructions for serving portions and cooking.

Left Chicken and vegetable steamboat

CHICKEN AND RICE SALAD

TIME **30 MINUTES** SERVES **4**

INGREDIENTS

1 cup (200 g) long-grain rice
300 g (10 oz) carrots, grated
juice of 1 large orange
2 teaspoons English mustard
2 tablespoons olive oil
6 tablespoons snipped fresh chives
salt and freshly ground black pepper
400 g (14 oz) cooked boneless,
    skinless chicken breast, cut into
    bite-sized chunks
4 tablespoons pistachios
200 g (7 oz) mixed salad leaves
orange wedges, to garnish (optional)

METHOD

1 Put rice in a large saucepan with plenty of boiling water. Return to a boil and stir once, then reduce heat to a simmer. Cover and cook 10–12 minutes, or until grains are just tender. Drain.
2 Meanwhile, put carrots in a large bowl. Add orange juice, mustard, oil and chives. Season to taste. Add chicken and pistachios and mix well.
3 Add rice to salad and mix lightly. The cold ingredients and dressing will quickly cool the rice to make a warm salad. Add mixed salad leaves and toss through, then garnish with orange wedges, if you like, and serve.

NUTRIENTS PER SERVING

2181 kJ, 521 kcal, 29 g protein, 22 g fat (4 g saturated fat), 51 g carbohydrate

VARIATION

Instead of rice, use orzo or risoni or small soup pasta shapes. Replace the chicken with diced cooked turkey or ham (or a mixture of both) or diced roast pork.

PAPRIKA AND LEMON CHICKEN
WITH HALOUMI EGGPLANT

TIME **20 MINUTES** SERVES **4**

INGREDIENTS

8 baby eggplant (aubergine)
    (about 350 g/12 oz in total)
150 g (5 oz) haloumi cheese,
    cut into 8 slices
4 boneless, skinless chicken breasts
    (about 125 g/4 oz each)
2 teaspoons paprika, or to taste
salt and freshly ground black pepper
grated zest of 1 lemon
2 tablespoons olive oil
lemon wedges, to garnish

METHOD

1 Leaving their stalks in place, slice eggplant in half lengthwise. Slice each half horizontally into two layers, leaving the slices attached at the stalk end. Cut haloumi slices in half crosswise to give pieces the right size for slipping into the eggplant later. Set aside.

2 Preheat grill (broiler) to high. Put chicken in a large, shallow ovenproof dish or the grill tray. Sprinkle with paprika and season with a little salt and pepper. Sprinkle with lemon zest, then drizzle 1 tablespoon oil evenly over the chicken. Turn the chicken pieces over a few times to distribute the seasoning evenly.

3 Put eggplant in the dish, cut side up, and drizzle remaining oil over. Grill 5 minutes, or until chicken is browned on one side. Turn chicken and eggplant over and grill a further 2 minutes.

4 Slide a piece of haloumi cheese between the layers of each eggplant half, then slip the top layer slightly to one side without breaking it off so that the cheese inside is exposed for grilling. Grill 3 minutes, or until chicken and eggplant are cooked and the edge of the haloumi is browned. Divide among individual serving plates and garnish with lemon wedges to squeeze over the chicken.

NUTRIENTS PER SERVING

1199 kJ, 286 kcal, 36 g protein, 14 g fat (7 g saturated fat), 4 g carbohydrate

COOK'S TIP

Haloumi cheese is salty, so do not salt the eggplant. If you can't find baby eggplant, buy 2 large eggplant, slice each into 8 horizontal slices, and lay the haloumi cheese on top of the slices. Then grill as directed.

PAN-FRIED CHICKEN WITH MUSHROOMS AND BLUEBERRIES
TIME 20 MINUTES SERVES 4

METHOD

1 Put flour in a shallow dish and season well with salt and pepper, then spread it out in the dish. Add chicken breasts and turn them over to coat in flour. Shake off excess.

2 Heat oil in a large frying pan over medium–high heat. Add chicken, reduce heat to medium and cook 2–3 minutes, or until well browned and crisp underneath. Turn over and cook a further 4–5 minutes to brown and crisp the other side. Reduce heat, if necessary, to prevent breasts from browning too quickly. Press occasionally with the back of a spatula to help them brown evenly. Pierce the middle of one breast with the point of a knife to check that the meat is cooked and not pink.

3 Transfer chicken to a serving dish and keep warm. Add bacon to the pan and cook, stirring, 2 minutes, or until cooked and the fat runs out. Add mushrooms and continue to cook over medium–high heat, stirring, 2 minutes. Do not overcook or they will become soggy.

4 Make some space in the middle of the pan. Add mustard and quickly stir with mushrooms and bacon for a few seconds until well mixed. Gently stir in blueberries. Add lemon juice and stir, then immediately remove pan from heat before blueberries begin to soften.

5 Sprinkle in chopped parsley, then spoon mushrooms and blueberries over chicken. Serve immediately, garnished with parsley sprigs and lemon wedges for extra juice to sharpen the blueberries, if you like.

INGREDIENTS

1 tablespoon plain (all-purpose) flour

salt and freshly ground black pepper

4 boneless, skinless chicken breasts, (about 125 g/4 oz each)

2 tablespoons olive oil

2 thick slices rindless bacon (bacon strips), cut into strips

250 g (8 oz) Swiss brown or porcini mushrooms, sliced

1 tablespoon dijon mustard

1⅓ cups (200 g) blueberries

juice of ½ lemon, plus lemon wedges, to garnish (optional)

3 tablespoons finely chopped fresh parsley, plus 4 sprigs, to garnish

NUTRIENTS PER SERVING

1446 kJ, 345 kcal, 35 g protein, 19 g fat (4 g saturated fat), 10 g carbohydrate

RED-HOT TURKEY WITH CASHEW NUTS
TIME 30 MINUTES SERVES 4

INGREDIENTS

2 cups (400 g) long-grain rice

3½ tablespoons peanut (groundnut) oil

salt

8–10 dried red chillies

1 clove garlic, crushed

2 tablespoons cornflour (cornstarch)

1 large eggwhite

500 g (1 lb) boneless, skinless turkey
   breast, diced

2 tablespoons honey

4 tablespoons soy sauce

2 tablespoons sake or dry sherry

230 g (8 oz) can water chestnuts,
   rinsed and drained, diced

8 spring onions (scallions), cut into pieces

⅔ cup (100 g) roasted salted
   cashew nuts

2 teaspoons rice vinegar or white
   wine vinegar

200 g (7 oz) bean sprouts, trimmed

METHOD

1 Put rice in a large saucepan and add 1 teaspoon oil, some salt and
   3 cups (750 ml) boiling water. Cover, bring back to a boil, then simmer
   10–15 minutes.

2 Meanwhile, put chillies in a separate pan of water, add 1 teaspoon oil,
   bring to a boil and simmer 10 minutes. Drain well.

3 Meanwhile, put garlic, cornflour and eggwhite in a bowl and stir. Add
   turkey to eggwhite mixture and coat well, then set aside.

4 Blend honey, soy sauce and sake or sherry with 3 tablespoons water in
   a separate bowl, and set aside.

5 Mix water chestnuts and spring onions together.

6 Heat 2 tablespoons oil in a wok or large frying pan over high heat until
   smoking. Add turkey and stir-fry until it begins to turn white. Add cashew
   nuts and drained chillies and stir-fry 30 seconds, then stir in vinegar. Use
   a slotted spoon to transfer turkey to a bowl.

7 Add remaining oil to the wok and heat until smoking. Add water chestnuts
   and spring onions and stir-fry 30 seconds. Return turkey mixture to the
   wok, along with bean sprouts. Stir 30 seconds, then pour in honey and soy
   sauce mixture and stir to heat through.

8 Drain rice and put in large individual bowls, with the turkey stir-fry on top.

NUTRIENTS PER SERVING

3394 kJ, 811 kcal, 43 g protein, 34 g fat (8 g saturated fat), 82 g carbohydrate

VARIATION

You can substitute boneless, skinless chicken breast or pork fillet for
the turkey.

SPICED TURKEY BURGERS
TIME **30 MINUTES** SERVES **4**

METHOD

1 Preheat grill (broiler) to medium. Put chillies, garlic, coriander and lime zest in a large bowl. Add minced turkey or chicken, soy sauce, sesame oil, cornflour, salt and pepper to taste and work together quickly with your hands, until well blended and compacted.

2 Divide mixture into four equal portions, shape each into a burger, then flatten on both sides using the blunt edge of a knife with a criss-cross movement. The burgers should be about 10 cm (4 inches) in diameter.

3 Brush one side of each burger with oil, then place, oiled side down, on the grill rack. Brush tops with remaining oil. Cook 10–12 minutes, turning once, until golden brown.

4 Meanwhile, bring some water to a boil in a steamer. Put snow peas in the steamer basket and sprinkle with salt. Cover and steam 3 minutes. Add bean sprouts, cover and steam a further 1–2 minutes.

5 Arrange snow peas and bean sprouts on warmed individual plates, position burgers on top and garnish with lime wedges. Serve immediately, with extra soy sauce as an accompaniment.

NUTRIENTS PER SERVING
1222 kJ, 292 kcal, 43 g protein, 9 g fat (2 g saturated fat), 9 g carbohydrate

INGREDIENTS

2 mild chillies, seeds removed, finely chopped

2 cloves garlic, crushed

3 tablespoons chopped fresh coriander (cilantro) leaves

grated zest of 1 lime, plus lime wedges, to garnish

750 g (1 1/2 lb) minced (ground) turkey or chicken

2 teaspoons soy sauce

2 teaspoons sesame oil

3 teaspoons cornflour (cornstarch)

salt and freshly ground black pepper

1 tablespoon vegetable oil

350 g (12 oz) snow peas (mangetout), topped and tailed

250 g (8 oz) bean sprouts, trimmed

extra soy sauce, to serve

CRISPY DUCK WITH ROAST POTATOES

TIME **30 MINUTES** SERVES 4

INGREDIENTS

600 g (1 lb 5 oz) small new potatoes

8 cloves garlic, peeled

2 tablespoons chopped fresh rosemary

salt and freshly ground black pepper

4 boneless duck breasts, with skin
  (about 200 g/7 oz each)

8 fresh bay leaves, plus extra leaves,
  to garnish (optional)

fruit jelly or preserve, such as crab apple
  or redcurrant, to serve

METHOD

1 Preheat oven to 240°C (460°F/ Gas 8). Put potatoes and garlic in a saucepan, add boiling water to cover and boil 5 minutes. Drain potatoes and put into a large shallow ovenproof dish. Sprinkle with rosemary, season with salt and pepper to taste and set aside.

2 Meanwhile, prick skin on duck breasts all over and put in a small roasting pan (baking dish), skin side up. Scrunch eight bay leaves, then rub over duck skin. Put two leaves under each duck breast. Season with salt and pepper to taste and roast 5 minutes.

3 Spoon a little duck fat over the potatoes and roll them in the dish to coat. Roast in oven with duck 20 minutes, or until both are well browned and cooked. Turn and baste duck twice. Add more duck fat to the potatoes, if necessary, and pour off any excess fat from the pan with the duck.

4 Discard bay leaves. Garnish with extra bay leaves, if you like, and serve with a fruit jelly or preserve.

NUTRIENTS PER SERVING

3619 kJ, 864 kcal, 29 g protein, 72 g fat (21 g saturated fat), 29 g carbohydrate

BRANDIED BLACKCURRANT DUCK WITH SAUTÉED PARSNIPS

TIME **30 MINUTES** SERVES 4

INGREDIENTS

250 g (8 oz) small parsnips, peeled
  and thinly sliced

2 onions, each cut into 8 wedges

4 boneless duck breasts, with skin
  (about 200 g/7 oz each)

1 tablespoon vegetable oil

salt and freshly ground black pepper

2/3 cup (150 ml) brandy

4 tablespoons blackcurrant syrup
  or cordial

juice of 1 lemon

fresh parsley sprigs, to garnish

METHOD

1 Put parsnips and onions in a large saucepan and add boiling water to cover. Return to a boil, cover, reduce heat and simmer 5 minutes. The parsnips should be tender but firm. Drain thoroughly, then return vegetables to the saucepan.

2 Meanwhile, prick skin on duck breasts all over without cutting into the meat. Heat oil in a frying pan over high heat; add duck breasts, skin side down. Reduce heat and cook, pressing duck occasionally (but not turning the pieces), 5 minutes, or until fat has run out of the duck and the skin is crisp and very well browned.

3 Drizzle 2 tablespoons duck fat over parsnips and onions, mix well, then set them over low–medium heat to brown lightly and slowly while duck finishes cooking. Stir and turn parsnips and onions occasionally, adding seasoning to taste. The parsnips should be firm and the onions should be tender but slightly crisp in places. Transfer to warmed plates.

4 Pour off remaining excess fat from frying pan and turn duck breasts over. Cook over low–medium heat 10–15 minutes, turning once more. Cook to your liking; after 10 minutes, they will be very pink and juicy in the middle; after 15 minutes, they should be cooked through but still pale pink in the middle and succulent. Season with salt and pepper during the last minute of cooking. Arrange duck, sliced if you prefer, over the vegetables on the plates.

5 Add brandy, blackcurrant syrup or cordial and lemon juice to the pan. Bring to a boil over high heat and boil about 30 seconds, stirring in all the sediment from the pan, to reduce the mixture to a sticky aromatic sauce. Spoon over duck, garnish with parsley and serve immediately.

NUTRIENTS PER SERVING

1848 kJ, 441 kcal, 36 g protein, 16 g fat (4 g saturated fat), 21 g carbohydrate

Right Brandied blackcurrant duck with sautéed parsnips

WARM DUCK BREAST SALAD WITH RED WINE AND APPLE
TIME **30 MINUTES** SERVES **4**

METHOD

1 Remove any skin and sinew from each duck breast. If they are uneven in size, cut larger ones in half horizontally. Season generously with salt and pepper and set aside.

2 To make the dressing, put mint or parsley, garlic, sugar, mustard, red wine and oil in a salad bowl. Season with salt and pepper, then whisk to a creamy emulsion.

3 Tear lettuces and radicchio into small pieces and add to the salad bowl. Add watercress, onion and apple and toss gently.

4 Heat oil in a frying pan, add duck and fry over medium heat 4–5 minutes on each side, until golden brown but still slightly pink in the centre. If you prefer duck well done, fry a further 3–4 minutes. Transfer to a board and leave to stand 2–3 minutes.

5 Pour off excess fat from frying pan and raise heat. Add red wine and bring to a boil, stirring and scraping the residue from the bottom of the pan.

6 Slice duck breasts thinly on the diagonal and add to the salad. Pour the pan juices over the salad, then toss well and serve.

NUTRIENTS PER SERVING
1704 kJ, 407 kcal, 36 g protein, 24 g fat (5 g saturated fat), 8 g carbohydrate

VARIATION
Boneless, skinless chicken breasts may be substituted for the duck; use white wine with the juices instead of red. Chicken needs to be cooked thoroughly, so allow a little longer for the cooking time.

INGREDIENTS
4 boneless duck breasts
  (about 200 g/7 oz each)
salt and freshly ground black pepper
2 oakleaf lettuces
50 g (1³/₄ oz) rosso or treviso radicchio
75 g (2¹/₂ oz) watercress, trimmed
1 small red onion, halved and thinly sliced
1 sweet red apple, quartered, cored
  and sliced
1 tablespoon olive oil
2–3 tablespoons red wine

DRESSING
4 tablespoons chopped fresh mint
  or parsley
1 clove garlic, crushed
1 teaspoon caster (superfine) sugar
2 teaspoons dijon or wholegrain mustard
1¹/₂ tablespoons red wine
2 tablespoons olive oil
salt and freshly ground black pepper

SWEET AND SOUR DUCK
TIME **30 MINUTES** SERVES **4**

INGREDIENTS

4 boneless duck breasts, with skin
    (about 200 g/7 oz each)
2 tablespoons soy sauce
2 tablespoons honey
1 tablespoon lime juice
1 tablespoon peanut (groundnut) oil
200 g (7 oz) sugarsnap peas
500 g (1 lb) wok-ready hokkien
    (egg) noodles
sweet chilli sauce, to serve

METHOD

1 Preheat oven to 200°C (400°F/Gas 6). Score a criss-cross pattern all over the duck skin and through the fat, without cutting into the meat. Heat a flameproof casserole dish or heavy-based frying pan over medium heat and add duck breasts, skin side down.

2 Blend soy sauce, honey and lime juice together, then brush a little over the meaty side of the duck. Fry 3–4 minutes, or until skin is well browned, then turn and cook a further 1 minute. Transfer duck to a plate; pour off fat in the dish or pan. If using a flameproof casserole dish, wipe it clean with paper towel, then return duck to dish, skin side up. If using a frying pan, transfer duck to a warmed ovenproof dish, skin side up.

3 Stir 2 tablespoons water into remaining soy sauce mixture and drizzle over duck. Put dish in oven and roast 8–10 minutes, or until duck is cooked through and sauce is thickened and reduced.

4 Meanwhile, heat oil in a wok or large frying pan over medium–high heat. Add sugarsnap peas and stir-fry 3–4 minutes, or until almost tender. If not quite cooked, add 2 tablespoons water, cover with a lid and steam a further 1–2 minutes.

5 Pour sauce from duck into the pan with the sugarsnap peas. Add noodles and stir-fry 5 minutes. Carve duck into thin slices, then add to noodles and toss over high heat a final few seconds. Serve immediately, accompanied by a bowl of sweet chilli sauce.

NUTRIENTS PER SERVING
4273 kJ, 1021 kcal, 31 g protein, 76 g fat (22 g saturated fat), 53 g carbohydrate

VARIATION
Instead of sugarsnap peas, use 200 g (7 oz) broccolini, cut into bite-sized pieces, or 150 g (5 oz) snow peas (mangetout), cut in half lengthwise, with 1 carrot, peeled and cut into fine matchsticks.

DUCK BREASTS WITH GINGER SAUCE

TIME **30 MINUTES** SERVES **4**

INGREDIENTS

4 boneless duck breasts, with skin
  (about 200 g/7 oz each)
3 tablespoons raspberry vinegar
2.5 cm (1 inch) piece fresh ginger,
  peeled and cut into thin matchsticks
1 piece stem ginger in syrup, chopped
2 tablespoons stem ginger syrup
1 cup (250 ml) green ginger wine
1 cup (250 ml) chicken stock
3 teaspoons butter
2 leeks, halved lengthwise,
  cut into matchsticks
salt and freshly ground black pepper

METHOD

1 Fry duck breasts, skin side down,
   in a large frying pan over medium
   heat about 8 minutes, then turn
   and cook a further 6 minutes.
   Transfer to a heatproof dish and
   keep warm.
2 Drain off all but 1 tablespoon
   of the duck fat from the pan.
   Add vinegar and bring to a boil,
   scraping up the brown residue
   from the pan, then add fresh and
   stem ginger, ginger syrup, ginger
   wine and stock. Bring back to a
   boil, then reduce heat and simmer
   8–10 minutes, until the liquid has
   reduced by half.
3 Meanwhile, melt butter in a small
   frying pan, add leeks, season with
   salt and pepper and stir-fry gently
   3–4 minutes, until just tender.
4 Add duck to the ginger sauce in
   the pan and reheat 2 minutes,
   then add salt and pepper to taste.
5 Arrange leeks on a serving dish,
   place duck on top and spoon over
   the sauce.

NUTRIENTS PER SERVING
3826 kJ, 914 kcal, 27 g protein, fat 78 g (23 g saturated fat), 15 g carbohydrate

VARIATION
If you prefer a thicker sauce, dissolve 1 teaspoon arrowroot in 3 tablespoons
cold water, then pour into the sauce and simmer 2 minutes before returning
the duck to the pan.

COOK'S TIP
Potato pancakes would complement the spicy flavour of the duck breasts.

GINGER DUCK WITH NOODLE SALAD AND SPICY PEANUT DRESSING

TIME **30 MINUTES** SERVES **4**

INGREDIENTS

3 tablespoons fish sauce or soy sauce,
   or a combination

2 tablespoons sesame oil

1 tablespoon soft dark brown sugar

5 cm (2 inch) piece fresh ginger,
   peeled and chopped

4 boneless duck breasts, with skin
   (about 200 g/7 oz each)

250 g (8 oz) baby corn

200 g (7 oz) dried medium egg noodles

400 g (14 oz) bean sprouts, trimmed

200 g (7 oz) bok choy, shredded

8 spring onions (scallions), sliced

1 red chilli, halved, seeds removed,
   thinly sliced

2 tablespoons smooth or crunchy
   peanut butter

grated zest and juice of 1 lime

1 clove garlic, crushed

METHOD

1 Preheat oven to 240°C (460°F/Gas 8). Mix 2 tablespoons fish or soy sauce with oil and sugar in a shallow ovenproof dish just large enough to hold the duck snugly in a single layer. Stir in half the ginger.

2 Score a criss-cross pattern all over duck skin and through the fat, without cutting into the meat. Put duck breasts into the dish and turn several times to coat with marinade. Roast, skin side up, 18–20 minutes, or until skin is crisp and very well browned (check after 15 minutes). The meat should be just cooked through, with a hint of pinkness in the middle.

3 Meanwhile, put baby corn in a large saucepan of boiling water and boil 2 minutes. Add noodles and boil a further 2 minutes. Drain and rinse under cold running water. Shake well to drain. Transfer to a large bowl. Add bean sprouts, bok choy, most of the spring onions and half the chilli. Mix well and divide among four large plates or pasta bowls.

4 Mix peanut butter with lime zest and juice, garlic and remaining fish sauce. Stir in 1 tablespoon water.

5 Transfer duck breasts to a plate. Carefully spoon off fat from juices in the dish, then stir 1 tablespoon boiling water into the juices. Slice duck breasts, if you have time. Drizzle peanut dressing over salads. Top with duck and spoon over the cooking juices (there will not be much, but it will have plenty of flavour). Sprinkle with remaining ginger, chilli and spring onions, and serve.

NUTRIENTS PER SERVING

4821 kJ, 1151 kcal, 41 g protein, 87 g fat (24 g saturated fat), 50 g carbohydrate

DUCK SKEWERS WITH HONEY AND ORANGE

TIME **20 MINUTES** SERVES **2**

INGREDIENTS

1 cup (200 g) long-grain or
    basmati rice

salt

1 bay leaf or cinnamon stick

2 boneless duck breasts (about
    350 g/12 oz in total), diced

Chinese garlic chives or chive
    flowers, to garnish

BASTING SAUCE

finely grated zest of 1 orange,
    plus 2 tablespoons orange juice

4 tablespoons thick honey

2 teaspoons soy sauce

METHOD

1 Put rice, a pinch of salt and bay leaf or cinnamon stick in a large
saucepan and add enough boiling water to reach 2.5 cm (1 inch) above
the surface of the rice. Bring water back to a boil, cover and simmer
gently 15 minutes, or until rice is tender.

2 Meanwhile, to make the basting sauce, put orange zest and juice, honey
and soy sauce in a small saucepan. Stir over low heat until combined.

3 Preheat grill (broiler) to high. Thread duck pieces onto two skewers.
Place skewers on the grill rack and baste with sauce. Grill 4–5 minutes,
then turn, baste with more sauce and any pan juices, and grill a further
4–5 minutes. The skewers are ready when the duck is cooked and the
skin is crispy at the edges.

4 Drain rice, removing the bay leaf or cinnamon stick, and serve on
warmed individual plates. Arrange skewers on top of the rice and
garnish with chives or chive flowers. Pour the juices from the grill tray
into the pan with the remaining basting sauce, heat through quickly,
then transfer to a jug to accompany the skewers.

NUTRIENTS PER SERVING

4646 kJ, 1110 kcal, 30 g protein, 66 g fat (19 g saturated fat), 101 g carbohydrate

VARIATION

Boneless, skinless chicken breasts can be used instead of the duck.

COOK'S TIP

The duck is rich and flavoursome, so a bowl of simply steamed snow peas
(mangetout), baby (pattypan) squash, carrots and zucchini (courgettes)
would be an ideal accompaniment.

Left Duck skewers with honey and orange (top); Pan-roasted quail with prosciutto (bottom)

PAN-ROASTED QUAIL WITH PROSCIUTTO

TIME **30 MINUTES** SERVES **4**

INGREDIENTS

8 fresh quail

8 slices prosciutto

8 fresh sage leaves, plus extra leaves,
    to garnish

2 tablespoons butter

1 tablespoon olive oil

4 cloves garlic, unpeeled

1 cup (250 ml) red wine

1 tablespoon quince paste or jelly

METHOD

1 Rinse quail inside and out under
cold running water, then pat dry
with paper towel. Place a slice of
prosciutto and a sage leaf inside
each quail.

2 Heat butter and oil in a large
heavy-based frying pan with a lid.
Add unpeeled garlic and quail to
the pan and sauté over medium
heat 3–4 minutes, until the birds
are golden all over and sealed.

3 Add red wine and quince paste or
jelly to the pan and cover with lid.
Reduce heat and simmer gently
20 minutes.

4 Remove quail from the pan and
keep warm. Increase heat and
cook juices, stirring continuously,
2–3 minutes, until reduced and
slightly thickened.

5 Put two quail on each plate, pour
over juices from the pan, garnish
with sage leaves and serve.

NUTRIENTS PER SERVING

1363 kJ, 326 kcal, 25 g protein, 17 g fat
(6 g saturated fat), 5 g carbohydrate

COOK'S TIP

These tasty birds need very simple
accompaniments, such as mashed
potatoes and steamed asparagus.

ROASTED QUAIL WITH BITTER MARMALADE

TIME **30 MINUTES** SERVES **4**

INGREDIENTS

8 fresh quail

1 clove garlic, crushed

1/2 cup (160 g) bitter orange marmalade
 or kumquat marmalade

1/2 cup (125 ml) medium dry sherry

2 tablespoons light soy sauce

2 tablespoons light olive oil

8 cumquats, halved

4 small sprigs watercress, to garnish

METHOD

1 Preheat oven to 200°C (400°F/Gas 6). Rinse quail under cold running
 water and pat dry with paper towel.

2 Combine garlic, marmalade, sherry, soy sauce and oil in a small bowl. Rub
 birds inside and out with this mixture.

3 Place quail in a lightly oiled roasting pan (baking dish). Roast 25 minutes,
 basting occasionally, until the juices from the thickest part of the thigh run
 clear and not pink when pricked with a skewer.

4 Meanwhile, sear cumquats in a hot frying pan 15–20 seconds.

5 Arrange quail and cumquat halves on warmed plates. Pour over pan juices
 and garnish each plate with watercress.

NUTRIENTS PER SERVING

1325 kJ, 316 kcal, 22 g protein, 12 g fat (1 g saturated fat), 21 g carbohydrate

COOK'S TIP

To maintain the Asian influences in the basting sauce, these roasted quail
are best served alongside some steamed jasmine rice rather than potatoes,
with maybe a small salad of bitter greens, such as rocket (arugula) and
watercress, on the side.

CHARGRILLED QUAIL WITH OLIVES
TIME **30 MINUTES** SERVES **4**

METHOD

1 Preheat chargrill pan or barbecue. Brush quail on both sides with
2 tablespoons oil and season generously with pepper. Grill or barbecue
about 15 minutes, until golden and tender.

2 Meanwhile, heat remaining oil in a small frying pan and cook garlic and
French shallots over low–medium heat about 2–3 minutes, until soft. Add
lemon juice, saffron threads and stock. Increase heat and cook, stirring,
about 5 minutes, until reduced by half. Stir in olives and heat through.

3 Serve quail on individual plates and spoon over the sauce.

NUTRIENTS PER SERVING
1063 kJ, 254 kcal, 21 g protein, 17 g fat (2 g saturated fat), 1 g carbohydrate

COOK'S TIP
This dish goes well with potato wedges sautéed with fresh rosemary leaves
in a little olive oil.

INGREDIENTS

8 fresh quail, halved

3 tablespoons olive oil

freshly ground black pepper

2 cloves garlic, chopped

4 French shallots (eschalots), chopped

2 tablespoons lemon juice

1 teaspoon saffron threads

1/2 cup (125 ml) chicken stock

1/2 cup (90 g) green olives, pitted

CHAPTER 8

Meat

PAN-FRIED STEAKS WITH ITALIAN SAUCE

TIME **30 MINUTES** SERVES **4**

INGREDIENTS

4 thin rump (round) or sirloin steaks
    (about 125 g/4 oz each),
    trimmed of fat
2 tablespoons olive oil
freshly ground black pepper
1 onion, finely chopped
2 cloves garlic, crushed
410 g (15 oz) can chopped tomatoes
100 ml (3¹/₂ fl oz) dry white or red wine
300 g (10 oz) tagliatelle
1 tablespoon capers, rinsed and
    squeezed dry
12 pitted green or black olives, halved
2 tablespoons chopped fresh basil,
    plus extra leaves, to garnish (optional)

METHOD

1 Rub steaks on both sides with 1 tablespoon oil and a little black pepper. Heat a large frying pan, then cook steaks, in two batches if necessary, about 2¹/₂ minutes on each side for rare, 4 minutes each side for medium, or 7 minutes each side for well done. Transfer to a plate using a slotted spoon and keep warm.

2 Heat the remaining oil in the pan, then add onion and garlic. Cook over low heat 5 minutes, or until softened. Stir in tomatoes and wine. Cook gently 5–10 minutes, stirring occasionally to break down the tomatoes.

3 While sauce is cooking, cook tagliatelle in a saucepan of salted boiling water 8 minutes, or following packet instructions, until al dente. Drain.

4 Stir capers, olives and basil into sauce, and season to taste (you may not need salt due to the salt content of the capers and tomatoes).

5 Return steaks to frying pan to heat through, spooning sauce over meat. Divide pasta among four plates and add some basil leaves, if you like. Serve with steak and sauce over the top.

NUTRIENTS PER SERVING

2407 kJ, 575 kcal, 35 g protein, 20 g fat (5 g saturated fat), 58 g carbohydrate

VARIATION

For a vegetarian version, serve the sauce with grilled (broiled) slices of haloumi cheese instead of the steak. Serve 2 slices haloumi per person; brush with oil before cooking under a hot grill or in a chargrill pan until golden.

COOK'S TIP

The sauce tastes great with grilled pork or lamb steaks and chops, and also goes very well with fish, so it's worth making a double batch and freezing half. Cool quickly after cooking, pack into a freezer container and freeze for up to 1 month. To use, thaw, reheat and simmer 3 minutes.

3 Meanwhile, slice beef fillet very thinly, then cut across the grain into thin strips (piling several slices on top of one another will speed up this process).

4 Add half the remaining oil to pan and increase heat to high. Add half the beef. Stir-fry 2–3 minutes, or until very lightly browned, then remove from pan. Heat remaining oil and cook the remaining beef in the same way.

5 Return onion, mushrooms and the first batch of beef with any juices to the frying pan. Add green peppercorns and salt to taste, and heat through 1–2 minutes.

6 Blend mustard and sour cream together and stir into beef along with cornichons. Heat through gently without boiling. Scatter chives over the top and serve immediately.

BEEF STROGANOFF
TIME **30 MINUTES** SERVES **4**

INGREDIENTS

2 tablespoons olive oil
1 large red onion, halved and thinly sliced
250 g (8 oz) small mushrooms, halved
600 g (1 lb 5 oz) beef fillet
2 teaspoons green peppercorns
  in brine, crushed

salt
2 tablespoons dijon mustard
1¼ cups (310 g) sour cream
100 g (3½ oz) cornichons (cocktail
  gherkins/pickles), drained
⅓ cup (20 g) snipped chives

METHOD

1 Heat 2 teaspoons oil in a large frying pan. Fry onion over medium heat 2–3 minutes, until slightly softened.

2 Add mushrooms, increase heat and cook, stirring, about 5 minutes, until mushrooms have softened and most of the liquid has evaporated. When cooked, tip mushrooms and onion into a large bowl and set aside.

NUTRIENTS PER SERVING
2356 kJ, 563 kcal, 35 g protein, 41 g fat
(16 g saturated fat), 14 g carbohydrate

VARIATION
The stroganoff can also be made with pork fillet, lean lamb fillet or boneless, skinless chicken breasts. You can use any type of mushroom and, if you prefer, the cornichons can be coarsely chopped.

COOK'S TIP
Serve with rice, mashed potatoes or noodles, which can be steamed or boiled while the beef is cooking, and a green side salad.

STIR-FRIED TERIYAKI STEAK SALAD
TIME **15 MINUTES** SERVES **4**

METHOD
1 Slice steak across the grain into thin strips.
2 Mix baby spinach or mixed salad leaves, rocket and capsicum in a bowl. Divide among four individual plates.
3 Heat a heavy-based non-stick frying pan until hot. Add oil and swirl to coat the base. Add steak strips and stir-fry 1 minute, or until browned on the outside but still pink inside. Add teriyaki marinade and 1 tablespoon water. Quickly swirl around pan to coat the meat, then spoon over the salad. Serve immediately.

NUTRIENTS PER SERVING
865 kJ, 207 kcal, 19 g protein, 10 g fat (3 g saturated fat), 14 g carbohydrate

COOK'S TIP
If time allows, toss the steak strips in 1 extra tablespoon teriyaki marinade at the end of step 1 and leave in the refrigerator to marinate 2 hours. Teriyaki marinade, made with soy sauce, rice wine and vinegar, can be bought from supermarkets. It has a very intense flavour, so don't be tempted to add more to this dish. If the pan is very hot and too much of the sauce evaporates and becomes very thick, add an extra 1–2 tablespoons of water in step 3.

INGREDIENTS
1 thick-cut sirloin or rump (round) steak (about 300 g/10 oz), trimmed of fat
75 g (2^1/$_2$ oz) baby spinach leaves or mixed salad leaves
75 g (2^1/$_2$ oz) rocket (arugula)
1 yellow capsicum (bell pepper), finely sliced
1 tablespoon olive oil
3 tablespoons teriyaki marinade

THAI BEEF WITH COCONUT
TIME 25 MINUTES SERVES 4

INGREDIENTS

2 tablespoons vegetable oil

3 French shallots (eschalots),
   finely chopped

2 cloves garlic, finely chopped

2.5 cm (1 inch) piece fresh ginger,
   peeled and finely chopped

500 g (1 lb) minced (ground) lean beef

1 tablespoon red curry paste

1 tablespoon fish sauce

1 tablespoon dark soy sauce

2–3 dried kaffir lime (makrut) leaves,
   crumbled

1/2 cup (125 ml) beef stock

3 tablespoons coconut cream

grated coconut, to garnish

2 tablespoons chopped fresh coriander
   (cilantro) leaves, to garnish

METHOD

1 Heat oil in a wok or large frying pan. Add French shallots, garlic and ginger and stir-fry 1 minute. Add beef and stir-fry over high heat 5 minutes, until lightly browned.

2 Stir in red curry paste, fish sauce, soy sauce and kaffir lime leaves and cook 2 minutes. Add stock and coconut cream and bring to a boil, then reduce heat and simmer 6 minutes. Sprinkle with grated coconut and coriander and serve.

NUTRIENTS PER SERVING

1499 kJ, 358 kcal, 28 g protein, 26 g fat (10 g saturated fat), 3 g carbohydrate

COOK'S TIP

Serve the beef with noodles or jasmine rice, cooked following the packet instructions.

SPICED STEAK WITH SPEEDY RATATOUILLE

TIME **30 MINUTES** SERVES **4**

INGREDIENTS

3 tablespoons olive oil

2–3 French shallots (eschalots), chopped

2 cloves garlic, chopped

500 g (1 lb) zucchini (courgettes), diced

300 g (10 oz) baby eggplant
(aubergine), diced

$^1/_2$ teaspoon dried thyme

$^1/_2$ teaspoon dried oregano

3 tablespoons red wine

410 g (15 oz) can chopped tomatoes

2 tablespoons tomato paste
(concentrated purée)

salt

1 teaspoon ground coriander

1 teaspoon ground cumin

1 teaspoon ground paprika

$^1/_2$ teaspoon cayenne pepper

4 sirloin or rump (round) steaks
(about 175 g–200 g/6–7 oz each)

METHOD

1　Heat 2 tablespoons oil in a large saucepan. Add French shallots and garlic and cook over medium heat 3–4 minutes.

2　Stir in zucchini, eggplant, thyme and oregano, and cook gently 5 minutes.

3　Add wine, tomatoes, tomato paste and a little salt, then cover and simmer gently about 15 minutes, stirring occasionally, until the vegetables have softened.

4　Meanwhile, put coriander, cumin, paprika and cayenne pepper in a small bowl, add a pinch of salt and mix well. Season steaks on both sides with spice mixture.

5　Heat the remaining oil in a large heavy-based frying pan until a faint haze rises, then cook steaks

on a medium–high heat 4–4$^1/_2$ minutes each side for rare, 5$^1/_2$–6 minutes for medium, or 6–8$^1/_2$ minutes for well done, depending on the thickness of the meat. Serve on individual plates, accompanied by the ratatouille.

NUTRIENTS PER SERVING

1703 kJ, 407 kcal, 46 g protein, 20 g fat (5 g saturated fat), 9 g carbohydrate

COOK'S TIP

Baby eggplant have tender skins that do not need peeling, but if you can get only larger ones, you will have to peel them first. You will also have to salt the flesh of the larger ones before cooking, which will take more time.

MEATBALLS WITH CREOLE SAUCE

TIME **30 MINUTES** SERVES **4**

INGREDIENTS

$^1/_2$ large onion, chopped

600 g (1 lb 5 oz) minced (ground) beef

1 large egg

2 tablespoons plain (all-purpose) flour

$^1/_4$ teaspoon cayenne pepper

$^1/_4$ teaspoon hot paprika

salt and freshly ground black pepper

2 tablespoons olive oil

CREOLE SAUCE

1 tablespoon olive oil

$^1/_2$ large onion, chopped

1 green and 1 red capsicum (bell pepper),
  seeds removed, chopped

2 cloves garlic, crushed

2 celery stalks, chopped

410 g (15 oz) can chopped tomatoes

1 bay leaf

1 teaspoon cayenne pepper

1 teaspoon hot paprika

1 teaspoon molasses or treacle

METHOD

1 Put onion, beef, egg, flour, cayenne pepper, paprika, salt and pepper to taste in a large bowl. Combine well, then set aside.

2 To make the creole sauce, heat oil in a large saucepan over medium heat and fry onion 5 minutes until softened. Stir in capsicums, garlic and celery and cook a further 2 minutes. Add tomatoes, bay leaf, cayenne pepper, paprika, molasses or treacle and 100 ml ($3^1/_2$ fl oz) water to the pan and bring to a boil. Reduce heat and simmer, uncovered, about 15 minutes, or until the sauce is thick but the vegetables still retain a little crunch.

3 Meanwhile, with wet hands, shape the meat mixture into 16 balls, each about the size of a golf ball. Heat oil slowly in a very large frying pan. Add meatballs and fry over high heat 10 minutes, until browned all over and just cooked on the inside.

4 Season the creole sauce to taste with salt and pepper and pour over the meatballs. Serve immediately.

NUTRIENTS PER SERVING

2326 kJ, 556 kcal, 35 g protein, 38 g fat (13 g saturated fat), 19 g carbohydrate

COOK'S TIP

A mix of steamed white rice and wild rice would be a good accompaniment to the meatballs.

CAJUN SPICED MEATBALLS
TIME **30 MINUTES** SERVES **4**

METHOD

1 Preheat oven to 220°C (425°F/Gas 7). Heat oil in a saucepan. Add onion and capsicum and fry 5 minutes. Remove from heat and set aside.
2 Put pork or beef, cajun spice blend, mint and pepper to taste in a large mixing bowl. Add onion and capsicum and mix together. Roll mixture roughly into walnut-sized balls and toss in breadcrumbs to coat.
3 Arrange meatballs on a baking tray (sheet) and bake in oven 15 minutes, or until golden brown.

NUTRIENTS PER SERVING

1127 kJ, 269 kcal, 28 g protein, 12 g fat (4 g saturated fat), 13 g carbohydrate

COOK'S TIP

Serve the meatballs with a fresh tomato and onion salsa and pasta, or oven-baked potato wedges, if you have time. If making wedges, put them on the top shelf of the oven before starting the meatballs, and they will be ready by the time the meatballs are cooked.

INGREDIENTS

$^1/_2$ tablespoon olive oil

1 onion, chopped

$^1/_2$ green capsicum (bell pepper), chopped

500 g (1 lb) minced (ground) lean pork
    or beef

2 teaspoons cajun spice blend

1 tablespoon chopped fresh mint

freshly ground black pepper

1 cup (100 g) dried fine white
    breadcrumbs

MEDITERRANEAN BURGERS

TIME **30 MINUTES** SERVES **4**

INGREDIENTS

250 g (8 oz) minced (ground) lean pork

250 g (8 oz) minced (ground) lean beef

2 cloves garlic, crushed

8 semi-dried (sun-blushed) tomatoes, chopped

2 tablespoons finely chopped pine nuts

2 tablespoons chopped fresh basil

freshly ground black pepper

1 tablespoon vegetable oil

4 hamburger buns

METHOD

1 In a bowl, combine pork, beef, garlic, semi-dried tomatoes, pine nuts, basil and pepper. Divide the mixture into four portions and shape each into a burger.

2 Brush burgers with a little oil and cook on a hot chargrill pan or plate, or under a hot grill (broiler), turning once, 10–12 minutes, or until golden brown. Serve in hamburger buns.

NUTRIENTS PER SERVING

1720 kJ, 411 kcal, 33 g protein, 16 g fat (4 g saturated fat), 31 g carbohydrate

BLUE CHEESE BEEFBURGERS

TIME **25 MINUTES** SERVES **4**

INGREDIENTS

500 g (1 lb) minced (ground) lean beef

1 onion, finely chopped

2 teaspoons dried thyme

2 teaspoons dijon mustard

salt and freshly ground black pepper

1 tablespoon crumbled roquefort or stilton cheese

1 tablespoon vegetable oil

4 hamburger buns

METHOD

1 In a bowl, combine beef, onion, thyme, mustard and salt and pepper to taste. Divide the mixture into eight equal portions. Shape each into a round and flatten slightly.

2 Top four of the rounds with roquefort or stilton cheese. Put the four remaining rounds of beef on top, pressing firmly around the edges to seal in the cheese completely.

3 Brush burgers with a little oil and cook in a hot frying pan or chargrill pan, or under a hot grill (broiler), turning once, 10–12 minutes, or until golden brown. Serve in hamburger buns.

NUTRIENTS PER SERVING

1581 kJ, 378 kcal, 34 g protein, 12 g fat (5 g saturated fat), 31 g carbohydrate

COOK'S TIP

Serve with rocket (arugula) and red cherry tomatoes. Beef and lamb burgers can be cooked until slightly pink inside, if you like, but pork and chicken must be cooked through. Shape burgers into equal-sized round patties about 9 cm (3^1/$_2$ inches) in diameter and 2 cm (³/₄ inch) thick.

PORK, SAGE AND ONION BURGERS

TIME **25 MINUTES** SERVES **4**

INGREDIENTS

350 g (12 oz) minced (ground) lean pork

150 g (5 oz) sausage mince (meat)

1 onion, finely chopped

1 tablespoon worcestershire sauce

2 tablespoons chopped fresh sage

salt and freshly ground black pepper

¹/₄ cup (35 g) plain (all-purpose) flour

1–2 tablespoons vegetable oil

4 hamburger buns

METHOD

1 In a bowl, combine pork, sausage mince, onion, worcestershire sauce and sage. Season and mix well, then divide the mixture into four portions and shape each into a burger. Dust lightly with a little flour.

2 Heat oil in a heavy-based frying pan and fry burgers over medium–high heat, turning once, 10–12 minutes, or until golden brown. Drain and serve in hamburger buns.

NUTRIENTS PER SERVING

1882 kJ, 450 kcal, 29 g protein, 22 g fat (8 g saturated fat), 32 g carbohydrate

Right Blue cheese beefburgers

BEEF BALTI

TIME **25 MINUTES** SERVES **4**

INGREDIENTS

2 tablespoons vegetable oil

1 onion, thinly sliced

500 g (1 lb) rump (round) or fillet steak,
    trimmed of fat and sliced into thin strips

1 clove garlic, crushed

4 cm (1 1/2 inch) piece fresh ginger, grated

1 small red chilli, seeds removed, chopped

1 green and 1 red capsicum (bell pepper),
    seeds removed, thinly sliced

3 teaspoons garam masala

1 teaspoon ground cumin

3 tomatoes, roughly chopped

juice of 1/2 lemon

salt

4 naan, to serve

2 tablespoons shredded coconut,
    to garnish

METHOD

1 Heat 1 tablespoon oil in a large balti pan, wok or frying pan. Add onion and fry over medium–high heat 3–4 minutes, stirring occasionally, until softened and lightly browned.

2 Add steak, garlic, ginger and chilli and cook over medium–high heat 5 minutes, stirring occasionally, until meat is lightly coloured. Remove from the pan and keep warm.

3 Add capsicums to the pan with the remaining oil, if necessary, and fry 3 minutes, stirring occasionally, until softened and lightly browned.

4 Stir in garam masala and cumin and cook, stirring continuously, 1 minute. Add tomatoes, lemon juice and some salt and simmer, stirring, about 3–4 minutes. If the mixture becomes dry, add a little water.

5 Meanwhile, preheat grill (broiler) to high. Sprinkle naan with water and grill about 1 minute each side.

6 Return beef to the pan and heat through. Sprinkle with shredded coconut and serve with the naan.

NUTRIENTS PER SERVING

3946 kJ, 942 kcal, 43 g protein, 48 g fat (12 g saturated fat), 90 g carbohydrate

COOK'S TIP

Naan is a flat, tear-shaped bread from India that is authentically baked on the walls of a tandoor oven. To approximate this at home, sprinkle each naan with water before grilling to help it puff up and become deliciously soft and light.

STEAK AND ONION SKEWERS
TIME **25 MINUTES** SERVES **4**

METHOD

1 Preheat grill (broiler) to high. Cut meat into 20 equal cubes. Cut onions in half crosswise, then cut each half into four wedges. Trim spring onions to 4 cm (1¹⁄₂ inch) lengths, then cut these in half lengthwise.

2 Thread five pieces of meat onto each of four metal skewers, about 35 cm (14 inches) long, alternating the meat with a combination of onion wedges and spring onion pieces. Place skewers across the grill tray or a small roasting pan (baking dish), balancing their ends on the rim.

3 Mix mustard, worcestershire sauce, vinegar, salt and pepper in a small bowl, then whisk in the oil.

4 Brush half the mixture over the skewers, then grill, close to the heat source, 3–5 minutes. Turn the skewers, brush with the remaining mixture and grill a further 3–5 minutes. If they start to burn, lower the grill tray a little.

5 The skewers can be served on their own, but taste even better accompanied by a sauce made from the pan juices. Put the skewers on a plate and keep warm. Pour wine into the grill tray and stir over medium heat, scraping up any residue. Cook until the liquid is reduced by half, then season to taste and pour the sauce over the skewers.

INGREDIENTS

750 g sirloin or rump (round) steak, trimmed of fat

2 red onions

4 thick spring onions (scallions)

3 teaspoons dijon mustard

1 teaspoon worcestershire sauce

¹⁄₂ teaspoon red wine vinegar

salt and freshly ground black pepper

3 tablespoons light olive oil

¹⁄₂ cup (125 ml) red wine (optional)

NUTRIENTS PER SERVING
1570 kJ, 375 kcal, 43 g protein, 20 g fat (5 g saturated fat), 8 g carbohydrate

COOK'S TIP
Serve with mashed potatoes and a steamed green vegetable.

COTTAGE PIE

METHOD

1 Heat a large heavy-based frying pan until hot, then add beef, onion, carrot and celery. Fry, stirring occasionally to break up any lumps, 5 minutes, or until lightly browned all over.

2 Meanwhile, stir tomato paste, worcestershire sauce and mixed dried herbs into the stock. Sprinkle flour over the beef and vegetables, then stir in flavoured stock. Bring to a boil, then reduce heat, cover and cook gently 15 minutes. Season to taste.

3 Meanwhile, cook potatoes in a saucepan of boiling water 10 minutes, or until tender. Drain, then mash with warmed milk and butter. Season to taste.

4 Preheat grill (broiler) to medium. Spoon mince into a large warmed ovenproof dish. Spread mashed potato over the top and fluff up with a fork. Put under the grill to brown lightly and crisp the top.

NUTRIENTS PER SERVING

1781 kJ, 425 kcal, 35 g protein, 14 g fat (7 g saturated fat), 38 g carbohydrate

VARIATION

BEEF-STUFFED TOMATOES Use a batch of the cooked minced beef, simmered 5 minutes, to make stuffed tomatoes. Slice the tops off 8 firm ripe tomatoes and set aside. Cut a small slice from the base of any tomatoes that don't sit upright. Scoop out the seedy centres using a teaspoon, and discard. Leave the tomato shells upside down to drain, then stand them in a roasting pan (baking dish) or a shallow ovenproof dish. Using a slotted spoon, fill the tomatoes with the mince mixture. Replace the tops and bake at 200°C (400°F/Gas 6) 15 minutes. Remove the tops and sprinkle with ½ cup (50 g) grated parmesan or mature cheddar. Replace the tops and bake uncovered a further 5 minutes, or until tomatoes are tender. Serve hot accompanied by rice and a salad.

COOK'S TIP

If you prefer, you can bake the pie at 200°C (400°F/Gas 6) 20 minutes, or until the topping is golden.

INGREDIENTS

500 g (1 lb) minced (ground) lean beef

1 onion, finely chopped

1 large carrot, grated

1 celery stalk, finely chopped

1 tablespoon tomato paste (concentrated purée)

1 teaspoon worcestershire sauce

1 teaspoon mixed dried herbs

1½ cups (375 ml) hot beef stock

1 tablespoon plain (all-purpose) flour

salt and freshly ground black pepper

1 kg (2 lb) boiling (waxy) potatoes, such as long white, peeled and diced

100 ml (3½ fl oz) low-fat milk, warmed

30 g (1 oz) butter

STIR-FRIED STEAK AND KIDNEY

TIME **30 MINUTES** SERVES **4**

INGREDIENTS

2 tablespoons vegetable oil

1 onion, thinly sliced

1 large red capsicum (bell pepper),
 seeds removed, thinly sliced

400 g (14 oz) rump (round) steak,
 trimmed of fat, sliced into thin strips

200 g (7 oz) lamb's or beef kidneys, cores
 removed, cut into bite-sized chunks

1/4 cup (60 ml) red wine

1–1 1/2 tablespoons grated horseradish,
 from a jar, to taste

1 tablespoon dark soy sauce

salt and freshly ground black pepper

METHOD

1 Heat 1 tablespoon oil in a wok
 or large frying pan and stir-fry
 onion and capsicum 3–4 minutes
 to soften slightly. Remove from
 pan and keep hot.

2 Heat the remaining oil in the wok
 and add steak and kidney. Stir-fry
 over high heat 4–5 minutes, or
 until evenly coloured, allowing
 the excess liquid to reduce by
 boiling.

3 Add red wine and boil rapidly,
 stirring, 1–2 minutes to reduce the
 liquid slightly. Stir in horseradish
 to taste and soy sauce, and season
 with salt and pepper to taste.

4 Return onion and capsicum to the
 pan, stir through and return to a
 boil, then serve.

NUTRIENTS PER SERVING

1244 kJ, 297 kcal, 32 g protein, 16 g fat
(4 g saturated fat), 4 g carbohydrate

VARIATION

Instead of red wine, use Guinness
or another strong brown ale, and
replace the dark soy sauce with
worcestershire sauce.

PEPPERED BEEF WITH PECANS

TIME **30 MINUTES** SERVES **4**

INGREDIENTS

500 g (1 lb) lean rump (round) steak

2 teaspoons black peppercorns

3/4 cup (75 g) pecans

1/2 tablespoon butter

2 tablespoons olive oil

1 onion, thinly sliced

350 g (12 oz) button mushrooms,
 sliced

salt

4 tablespoons brandy

2/3 cup (160 g) sour cream

75 g (2 1/2 oz) rocket (arugula)

METHOD

1 Slice steak into thin strips, trimming off any excess fat. Lightly crush
 peppercorns using a pestle and mortar (or use a rolling pin) and put
 into a large bowl. Toss steak strips with the peppercorns.

2 Put pecans in a large dry pan or wok and toast over medium–high heat,
 tossing regularly, 2–3 minutes. Chop roughly and set aside.

3 Heat butter and 1 tablespoon oil in the pan and stir-fry onion over
 medium heat 2–3 minutes to soften slightly. Add mushrooms and cook
 over high heat 3–4 minutes, or until slightly softened. Add a little salt
 to taste, then transfer mushrooms and onion to a plate.

4 Add remaining oil to the pan and stir-fry steak strips over medium–high
 heat 2–3 minutes, or until sealed.

5 Add brandy and bring to a boil. Boil about 30 seconds. Return onions
 and mushrooms to the pan and stir in sour cream. Heat, stirring, until
 blended. Add rocket and stir until wilted, then sprinkle over pecans and
 serve immediately.

NUTRIENTS PER SERVING

2397 kJ, 573 kcal, 34 g protein, 42 g fat (12 g saturated fat), 6 g carbohydrate

VARIATION

MUSTARD BEEF WITH WALNUTS Omit the peppercorns from the
basic recipe. Stir-fry beef strips in the oil and butter. Use 1 thinly sliced
red onion and 2 thinly sliced celery stalks instead of the mushrooms. Omit
the brandy and sour cream. Add 1/2 cup (125 ml) red wine and simmer
2–3 minutes to reduce slightly. Stir in 2 tablespoons wholegrain mustard
and 2/3 cup (150 ml) cream. Bring to a boil, season, add rocket, then
sprinkle over 2/3 cup (85 g) chopped walnuts.

COOK'S TIP

Serve with mashed potato or garlic mashed potato.

Right Peppered beef with pecans

BEEF AND BEAN CHILLI
TIME **30 MINUTES** SERVES **4**

METHOD

1 Heat oil in a large flameproof casserole dish and fry onion, capsicum, beef, paprika and cumin over medium heat, 5 minutes, or until the beef browns, stirring occasionally to break up any lumps

2 Add garlic, chilli, tomatoes, tomato paste, oregano, wine or stock, sugar and salt to taste. Bring to a boil, then reduce heat, cover with a lid and simmer 15 minutes.

3 Preheat grill (broiler) to high. Stir kidney beans into casserole dish and cook a further 5 minutes. Meanwhile, place tortillas under grill 1 minute until warmed through.

4 Transfer chilli to four serving dishes. Add 1 tablespoon sour cream to each, sprinkle spring onions over the top, and serve with warmed tortillas.

NUTRIENTS PER SERVING
2489 kJ, 594 kcal, 39 g protein, 24 g fat (8 g saturated fat), 53 g carbohydrate

COOK'S TIP
Tortillas are thin pancakes made from corn or wheat flour, which you can roll and stuff with a spicy meat or bean sauce. Corn tortillas can also be cut into small triangles, then deep-fried and sprinkled with salt to make corn chips.

INGREDIENTS

2 tablespoons vegetable oil

1 onion, chopped

1 small red capsicum (bell pepper), seeds removed, chopped

500 g (1 lb) minced (ground) lean beef

1 tablespoon paprika

1 tablespoon ground cumin

3 cloves garlic, crushed

1 small red chilli, seeds removed, chopped

410 g (15 oz) can chopped tomatoes

2 teaspoons tomato paste (concentrated purée)

1 teaspoon dried oregano

1/2 cup (125 ml) red wine or beef stock

1/2 teaspoon sugar

salt

400 g (14 oz) can red kidney beans, rinsed and drained

8 soft flour tortillas

4 tablespoons sour cream, or to taste

2 spring onions (scallions), chopped, to garnish

CHILLI BEEF AND TACO SALAD

TIME **30 MINUTES** SERVES **4**

INGREDIENTS

500 g (1 lb) minced (ground)
    premium beef
2 cloves garlic, crushed
1 teaspoon dried red chilli flakes
2 tablespoons sun-dried tomato paste
    (concentrated purée)
3 tablespoons chopped fresh oregano
    or 1 teaspoon dried oregano
juice of 1 lemon
salt and freshly ground black pepper
$^1/_4$ iceberg lettuce, torn
2 ripe avocados, sliced
1 red onion, thinly sliced
3 tomatoes, chopped
75 g (2$^1/_2$ oz) tortilla chips

METHOD

1 Heat a large heavy-based frying pan until hot, then add mince and fry 2–3 minutes, stirring to break up any lumps.

2 Add garlic and chilli flakes, then cook 6–8 minutes, or until lightly browned, stirring frequently. Stir in tomato paste, oregano and lemon juice and cook on low heat 2–3 minutes. Season to taste with salt and pepper.

3 Meanwhile, put lettuce, avocado, onion and tomatoes in a wide salad bowl. Add meat mixture and toss to mix evenly. Scatter some tortilla chips over and put the remainder in a separate bowl. Serve immediately.

NUTRIENTS PER SERVING

2153 kJ, 514 kcal, 31 g protein, 37 g fat (10 g saturated fat), 13 g carbohydrate

COOK'S TIP

Add more tortilla chips or some toasted chunks of pita to make the salad more substantial.

SPICY BEEF ROLLS

TIME **30 MINUTES** SERVES **4**

INGREDIENTS

500 g (1 lb) minced (ground)
    lean beef
1 onion, finely chopped
1 red or green capsicum (bell pepper),
    seeds removed, finely chopped
200 g (7 oz) tomatoes, chopped
1 tablespoon plain (all-purpose) flour
1 tablespoon tomato paste
    (concentrated purée)

$^2/_3$–$^3/_4$ cup (150–180 ml) beef stock
dash of Tabasco sauce
2 tablespoons chopped fresh basil
    or coriander (cilantro) leaves
salt and freshly ground black pepper
4 large white or wholemeal
    (whole-wheat) rolls, halved
shredded crisp lettuce, to serve
hot chilli sauce, to serve

METHOD

1 Heat a large heavy-based frying pan until hot, then add mince and onion. Fry over medium heat 7 minutes, or until browned all over, stirring occasionally to break up any lumps. Add capsicum and tomatoes, cook 3 minutes, then sprinkle over flour.

2 Stir tomato paste into stock in a small bowl, then add Tabasco sauce and basil or coriander. Stir $^2/_3$ cup (150 ml) stock into mince mixture. Bring to a boil, then reduce heat, cover and cook gently 10 minutes. Add a little extra stock if needed, and season.

3 When ready to serve, toast rolls lightly. Put some shredded lettuce on the base of each roll and spoon meat sauce on top. Each person can add chilli sauce to taste.

NUTRIENTS PER SERVING

1804 kJ, 431 kcal, 35 g protein, 12 g fat (4 g saturated fat), 46 g carbohydrate

Right Spicy beef rolls

VEAL BUTT FILLET WITH ROSEMARY AND REDCURRANT

TIME **25 MINUTES** SERVES **4**

INGREDIENTS

1 tablespoon butter

2 tablespoons olive oil

1 veal butt fillet or veal leg fillet
(about 800 g/1¾ lb in total),
cut into 4 pieces

2 sprigs fresh rosemary

freshly ground black pepper

1 cup (250 ml) medium dry sherry

1½ tablespoons redcurrant jelly

1 tablespoon unsalted butter

METHOD

1 Preheat oven to 220°C (425°F/Gas 7). Heat butter and oil in a roasting pan (baking dish) over medium heat on top of the stove.

2 Add veal and rosemary, season generously with pepper and cook about 5 minutes, until the meat is golden and sealed on all sides.

3 Transfer the pan to the oven and cook veal a further 10 minutes. Remove the pan from oven, place veal on a plate and keep warm.

4 Place the pan back on the stovetop and add sherry, redcurrant jelly and unsalted butter. Cook, stirring, over medium heat about 5 minutes, until the sauce has reduced and thickened slightly.

5 Cut veal into four pieces, arrange on individual plates and pour over sauce.

NUTRIENTS PER SERVING

2166 kJ, 517 kcal, 59 g protein, 21 g fat (8 g saturated fat), 7 g carbohydrate

VARIATION

You can use eye fillet of beef instead of the veal. To serve rare, it will take the same cooking time.

COOK'S TIP

Accompany this dish with a purée of parsnips and some steamed baby beans.

RACK OF VEAL ROASTED WITH GARLIC

TIME **30 MINUTES** SERVES 2

METHOD

1 Preheat oven to 220°C (425°F/Gas 7). Combine orange zest and juice, sage, marmalade, oil and pepper in a small bowl.

2 Place veal and unpeeled garlic in a lightly oiled roasting pan (baking dish). Baste veal with the orange mixture to coat thoroughly, then cook in the oven 20 minutes. Remove pan from oven, transfer veal to a serving platter and leave to rest in a warm place.

3 Place the pan with the garlic on the stovetop and add sherry and stock. Cook, stirring, over medium–high heat 2–3 minutes, until the sauce has reduced and thickened slightly.

4 To serve, carve the veal into individual chops and spoon over the garlic and sauce.

INGREDIENTS

grated zest and juice of 1 orange

6 fresh sage leaves, chopped

2 teaspoons bitter orange marmalade

1 tablespoon olive oil

freshly ground black pepper

1 veal rack with 2 thick chops
(about 350 g/12 oz in total)

8 cloves garlic, unpeeled

1/2 cup (125 ml) medium dry sherry

1/2 cup (125 ml) chicken stock

NUTRIENTS PER SERVING

1555 kJ, 371 kcal, 35 g protein, 15 g fat (2 g saturated fat), 9 g carbohydrate

VARIATION

A rack of lamb cutlets can be substituted for the veal; if you use lamb, add rosemary leaves to the basting mixture.

COOK'S TIP

Serve on a bed of wilted English spinach with steamed new potatoes.

VEAL PICCATA WITH SAGE AND LEMON
TIME 15 MINUTES SERVES 2

INGREDIENTS

1 tablespoon plain (all-purpose) flour

salt and freshly ground black pepper

2 veal escalopes (about 125 g/4 oz each)

6 fresh sage leaves

1 tablespoon oil

2 tablespoons butter

juice of $1/2$ lemon

4 tablespoons chicken stock or water

METHOD

1 Sprinkle flour onto a board or large plate and season well with salt and pepper. Cut each veal escalope into three equal pieces, press a sage leaf firmly onto each, then turn in flour to coat well.

2 Heat oil and half the butter in a large heavy-based frying pan until butter has melted. Add veal and cook 2 minutes on each side, then remove and keep warm.

3 Add lemon juice and stock or water to the pan and swirl over medium heat until the liquid has reduced by half. Add remaining butter and continue to swirl the mixture until all the butter has been absorbed into the sauce.

4 Return veal to the pan and cook a few seconds on each side to heat through. Transfer to individual plates and serve.

NUTRIENTS PER SERVING
1398 kJ, 334 kcal, 24 g protein, 25 g fat (12 g saturated fat), 4 g carbohydrate

COOK'S TIP
Serve the veal with boiled small new potatoes and a simply prepared green vegetable, such as steamed beans, peas or broccoli.

CALF'S LIVER WITH BALSAMIC VINEGAR
TIME **25 MINUTES** SERVES **4**

METHOD

1 Heat half the oil in a large frying pan over high heat and fry onion, stirring, 1 minute. Reduce heat, cover and cook 6 minutes, or until the onion is just tender and beginning to brown, then transfer to a plate and keep warm.

2 Season liver on both sides with pepper. Add the remaining oil to the pan and when very hot, fry liver 1–2 minutes on each side, until it changes colour. Transfer to a serving dish to keep warm.

3 To make the sauce, bring vinegar and 2 tablespoons water to a boil in the pan, stirring and scraping up the browned residue. Reduce heat and stir in mustard and cream.

4 Return liver and onions to the pan and reheat very gently in the sauce 1–2 minutes. Sprinkle with sage and serve.

NUTRIENTS PER SERVING
1218 kJ, 291 kcal, 25 g protein, 17 g fat (5 g saturated fat), 8 g carbohydrate

VARIATION
The sauce can also be served with lamb's fry, or fried chicken or pork.

COOK'S TIP
Serve with mashed potatoes. Put them on to cook before preparing the onion, and mash them while the liver is reheating.

INGREDIENTS
2 tablespoons olive oil

1 large red onion, halved and thinly sliced

4 slices calf's liver (about 125 g/ 4 oz each)

freshly ground black pepper

1 tablespoon chopped fresh sage

SAUCE
2 tablespoons balsamic vinegar

1 tablespoon dijon mustard

100 ml (3$\frac{1}{2}$ fl oz) cream

CHEESY VEAL SCHNITZEL

TIME **25 MINUTES** SERVES **4**

INGREDIENTS

$^1/_2$ cup (50 g) grated parmesan
1 tablespoon chopped fresh sage
1 cup (80 g) soft fresh breadcrumbs,
    made from day-old Italian bread
8 small veal escalopes (about 600 g/
    1 lb 5 oz in total), flattened to 3 mm
    ($^1/_8$ inch) thick
$^1/_2$ cup (75 g) plain (all-purpose) flour
2 eggs, lightly beaten
4 tablespoons olive oil
2 tablespoons butter
lemon slices, to serve

METHOD

1 Combine parmesan, sage and breadcrumbs in a bowl.
2 Coat veal with flour, then dip in beaten egg and then breadcrumbs.
3 Heat half the oil and half the butter in a large frying pan over medium heat. Add four escalopes and cook 1–2 minutes, until they are golden on both sides. Remove from the pan and keep warm while cooking the four remaining escalopes in the remaining oil and butter.
4 Put 2 escalopes on individual plates and serve with lemon slices.

NUTRIENTS PER SERVING

2707 kJ, 647 kcal, 47 g protein, 39 g fat (12 g saturated fat), 21 g carbohydrate

COOK'S TIP

Serve with sliced tomatoes and basil and a crisp green salad on the side.

CHARGRILLED VEAL CUTLETS

TIME **25 MINUTES** SERVES **4**

INGREDIENTS

125 g (4 oz) unsalted butter, softened
2 tablespoons chopped fresh
    tarragon, plus extra sprigs,
    to garnish
2 tablespoons lemon juice
sea salt and freshly ground
    black pepper
4 well-trimmed veal cutlets (about
    600 g/1 lb 5 oz in total)
2 tablespoons olive oil

METHOD

1 Preheat chargrill pan or grill (broiler) to high. Blend butter and chopped tarragon together in a small bowl, then beat in lemon juice and season well with salt and pepper. Shape butter into a sausage, wrap in plastic wrap and place in the freezer.
2 Brush veal cutlets with oil and season with a good grinding of pepper on both sides. Place on the chargrill pan or under the grill and cook 5–7 minutes each side, until golden brown outside and pink inside.
3 Slice tarragon butter into four rounds. Transfer the cutlets to four serving plates and place a round of tarragon butter on each. Garnish with tarragon sprigs and serve.

NUTRIENTS PER SERVING

2112 kJ, 504 kcal, 34 g protein, 40 g fat (19 g saturated fat), 3 g carbohydrate

COOK'S TIP

Chargrill sliced capsicum (bell pepper) and whole salad onions at the same time and serve with the veal cutlets. If you prefer, the cutlets can be cooked on a hot barbecue.

Right Cheesy veal schnitzel (top); Chargrilled veal cutlets (bottom)

LAMB CUTLETS WITH MIXED BEANS

TIME **30 MINUTES** SERVES **4**

INGREDIENTS

150 g (5 oz) small green beans, topped
  and tailed, cut into bite-sized pieces

salt and freshly ground black pepper

1 tablespoon olive oil

3 tablespoons butter

grated zest of 1 lemon and
  juice of $1/2$ lemon

2 sprigs fresh rosemary

8 lamb cutlets or lean lamb loin chops
  (about 90 g/3 oz each)

1 onion, chopped

2 cloves garlic, crushed

$1^{1}/_{2}$ x 400 g (14 oz) cans butterbeans
  (lima beans), rinsed and drained

$1^{1}/_{4}$ cups (310 ml) dry white wine

$2/_{3}$ cup (150 ml) hot lamb or
  chicken stock

3 tablespoons thick (heavy/double) cream

2 tablespoons capers, rinsed and
  squeezed dry

METHOD

1 Put green beans in a small saucepan of salted boiling water and cook
  5–6 minutes, until tender. Drain and set aside.

2 Meanwhile, heat oil and 1 tablespoon butter in a frying pan over medium
  heat. Add lemon zest and rosemary and increase heat.

3 Season lamb with pepper. When the butter in the pan starts to sizzle, add lamb, reduce heat to medium and fry 4–5 minutes on each side, until golden brown and cooked but still slightly pink in the centre.

4 Meanwhile, melt the remaining butter in a second frying pan. Add onion and fry over medium heat 5 minutes, until softened.

5 Add garlic and cook 30 seconds. Stir in reserved green beans and butterbeans and season to taste with salt and pepper. Reduce heat, then cook to heat through, stirring occasionally. Turn off the heat and keep warm.

6 When the lamb cutlets are cooked, transfer them and the rosemary to a plate and keep warm. Pour off any fat from the first frying pan, leaving the residue from the lamb. Add wine and lemon juice and boil rapidly until reduced by half.

7 Stir in stock, bring to a boil, then reduce heat and simmer. Stir in cream, then season with salt and pepper, add capers and heat through gently. Do not allow the sauce to boil or it will curdle.

8 Return lamb cutlets, rosemary and any juices to the sauce in the pan, and heat through.

9 To serve, spoon the beans onto warmed serving plates, top with the lamb cutlets and rosemary, and spoon over some sauce.

NUTRIENTS PER SERVING
4182 kJ, 999 kcal, 33 g protein, 74 g fat
(39 g saturated fat), 25 g carbohydrate

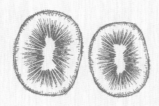

KIWI FRUIT AND LAMB SKEWERS
TIME **30 MINUTES** SERVES **4**

METHOD

1 Put lamb in a bowl. Add kiwi fruit, garlic, ginger and spices, and toss well to coat evenly. Cover and leave to marinate 5 minutes.

2 Preheat grill (broiler) to hot. Thread chunks of meat onto four long metal skewers, alternating with wedges of onion. Spoon over any remaining marinade and sprinkle with salt and pepper.

3 Grill the lamb skewers, turning occasionally, 8–10 minutes, or until golden and evenly cooked. Thread a wedge of lime onto the end of each skewer, then serve.

NUTRIENTS PER SERVING
1009 kJ, 241 kcal, 34 g protein, 9 g fat (4 g saturated fat), 6 g carbohydrate

VARIATION
Replace the ginger, coriander and cumin with 1 teaspoon each of dried thyme, tarragon and dill. Omit the lime and serve with horseradish cream from a jar.

COOK'S TIP
If you have time, prepare the lamb to the end of step 1 and leave in the refrigerator to marinate for up to 3 hours. This will tenderise the meat and improve its flavour.

INGREDIENTS

600 g (1 lb 5 oz) lean boned leg of lamb
   or lamb fillet, cut into bite-sized chunks
1 ripe kiwi fruit, peeled, chopped
   and mashed
1 clove garlic, crushed
1 tablespoon grated fresh ginger
1 teaspoon coriander seeds, crushed
1 teaspoon cumin seeds, crushed
2 small onions, each cut into 8 wedges
salt and freshly ground black pepper
1 lime, cut into wedges

LAMB STEAKS PROVENÇALE

TIME **25 MINUTES** SERVES **4**

INGREDIENTS

2 tablespoons olive oil

1 large red onion, diced

1 large green capsicum (bell pepper),
  seeds removed, diced

2 zucchini (courgettes), diced

1 small bulb fennel, chopped

2 cloves garlic, chopped

4 teaspoons herbes de provence

4 lean lamb leg steaks
  (about 125 g/4 oz each)

salt and freshly ground black pepper

4 large roma (plum) tomatoes, diced

2 tablespoons ready-made black
  olive tapenade

METHOD

1 Heat 1½ tablespoons oil in a deep frying pan. Add onion, capsicum, zucchini, fennel, garlic and herbes de provence and cook over medium heat, stirring occasionally, 10 minutes, or until softened and lightly browned.

2 Meanwhile, brush lamb steaks with remaining oil and season lightly with salt and pepper. Cook, turning once, in a hot chargrill pan or heavy-based frying pan, or under a preheated grill (broiler), 5–8 minutes, depending on the steaks' thickness. They should still be slightly pink in the centre. Remove from heat and keep warm.

3 Add tomatoes and tapenade to the vegetables, then simmer a further 3–4 minutes, or until softened. Add lamb steaks to the pan and heat through, then serve on four individual plates.

NUTRIENTS PER SERVING

1437 kJ, 343 kcal, 31 g protein, 20 g fat (6 g saturated fat), 11 g carbohydrate

VARIATION

To give the dish a warm, aniseed flavour, replace herbes de provence (a combination of thyme, summer savory, lavender and rosemary) with 2–3 teaspoons fennel seeds.

COOK'S TIP

The vegetables can be cooked in advance, then cooled and stored, covered, in the refrigerator. You'll find the flavours actually improve with a few hours' keeping. Eat within 2 days, served cold or reheated gently until boiling.

ROSEMARY-GLAZED LAMB CHOPS

TIME **25 MINUTES** SERVES **4**

INGREDIENTS

2 tablespoons redcurrant jelly

2 teaspoons dijon mustard

4 teaspoons chopped fresh rosemary

4 lean lamb loin chops
  (about 175 g/6 oz each)

3–4 tablespoons olive oil

salt and freshly ground black pepper

1 eggplant (aubergine), thickly sliced

8 slices ciabatta or sourdough

fresh redcurrants, to garnish (optional)

METHOD

1 Preheat grill (broiler) to high. In a small saucepan, combine redcurrant jelly, mustard and rosemary.

2 Put lamb chops on the grill rack, brush lightly with oil, then season with salt and pepper. Arrange eggplant slices on the rack and brush with oil. Grill 6–8 minutes, turning lamb once and eggplant slices occasionally, until golden.

3 Gently heat rosemary glaze in the small saucepan, then brush a little over the lamb and grill a further 2 minutes. Turn the lamb and glaze the other side, then cook a further 1–2 minutes.

4 While the lamb finishes cooking, brush ciabatta or sourdough slices with a little oil and add to the grill rack. (Move eggplant slices to make room, or remove from the rack and keep warm if already golden.) Grill until golden on both sides.

5 Heat remaining glaze until almost boiling. Put lamb and eggplant on individual serving plates, then spoon the hot glaze over the lamb. Serve garnished with redcurrants, if you like, and accompanied by the toasted ciabatta or sourdough slices.

NUTRIENTS PER SERVING

2277 kJ, 544 kcal, 42 g protein, 28 g fat (9 g saturated fat), 31 g carbohydrate

COOK'S TIP

You could brush the eggplant, lamb chops and ciabatta or sourdough slices with a little oil and cook on a hot chargrill pan or plate.

Left Rosemary-glazed lamb chops

LAMB ROGAN JOSH

TIME **30 MINUTES** SERVES **4**

INGREDIENTS

2 tablespoons peanut (groundnut)
  or vegetable oil

1 onion, roughly chopped

1 orange capsicum (bell pepper),
  seeds removed, diced

1 orange sweet potato (kumara), diced

1 clove garlic, crushed

1 tablespoon medium curry powder

500 g (1 lb) lamb fillet, cut into
  bite-sized chunks

200 ml (7 fl oz) lamb or beef stock

2 tablespoons tomato paste
  (concentrated purée)

salt and freshly ground black pepper

4 tablespoons natural (plain) yogurt

2 tablespoons chopped fresh coriander
  (cilantro) leaves

2 tablespoons flaked almonds

METHOD

1 Heat oil in a large frying pan. Add onion, capsicum, sweet potato and garlic and fry 4–5 minutes, stirring occasionally, until starting to soften but not browned.

2 Stir in curry powder and cook a further 1 minute, then add lamb, stirring to coat evenly with the spicy mixture.

3 Add stock and tomato paste, then bring to a boil. Reduce heat, cover and simmer 15 minutes, or until lamb and vegetables are tender. Adjust seasoning if necessary. Stir in yogurt and coriander, sprinkle with flaked almonds and serve.

NUTRIENTS PER SERVING

1601 kJ, 382 kcal, 32 g protein, 22 g fat (6 g saturated fat), 13 g carbohydrate

COOK'S TIP

Serve with garlic and coriander or plain naan; warm it gently in the oven while the curry cooks.

SPICED LAMB SKEWERS WITH PITAS

TIME **30 MINUTES** SERVES **4**

INGREDIENTS

2 tablespoons olive oil

2 cloves garlic, crushed

2 teaspoons ground cumin

1/2 teaspoon cayenne pepper

750 g (1 1/2 lb) lamb fillet or lean lamb leg
    steak, cut into bite-sized pieces

1 baby cos (little gem) or mignonette
    lettuce, shredded

1/2 cucumber, diced

4 tomatoes, chopped

1 red onion, chopped

4 tablespoons chopped fresh mint,
    plus extra leaves, to garnish

3/4 cup (185 g) natural (plain) yogurt

salt and freshly ground black pepper

4 large or 8 small pitas

METHOD

1 Put oil, garlic, cumin and cayenne
   pepper in a bowl and mix well.

2 Toss meat in the seasoned oil,
   then thread onto metal skewers
   and set aside.

3 Preheat grill (broiler) to high.
   Put lettuce, cucumber, tomatoes,
   onion and chopped mint in a
   salad bowl and toss. Put yogurt
   in a serving bowl and season with
   salt and pepper.

4 Grill lamb skewers 6 minutes,
   turning once.

5 Meanwhile cut each large pita
   into four pieces, or slit open small
   pitas if using. Place pitas with the
   salad on individual serving plates.
   Top with the lamb skewers and
   garnish with mint leaves. Serve
   with the yogurt.

NUTRIENTS PER SERVING

3846 kJ, 919 kcal, 53 g protein, 39 g fat
(15 g saturated fat), 95 g carbohydrate

LAMB KOFTAS WITH TOMATO SALSA

TIME **30 MINUTES** SERVES **4**

INGREDIENTS

3 teaspoons butter

1 onion, 1/4 finely sliced, 3/4 chopped

2 cups (400 g) long-grain or
    basmati rice

salt and freshly ground black pepper

1/3 cup (20 g) chopped fresh
    coriander (cilantro) leaves, plus
    extra leaves, to garnish

5 mm (1/4 inch) piece fresh ginger,
    peeled and chopped

1 clove garlic, chopped

500 g (1 lb) minced (ground) lamb

3 teaspoons amchur (mango powder)
    or lemon juice

1 teaspoon garam masala

1 teaspoon ground cumin

1 teaspoon chilli powder

1 tablespoon besan (chickpea flour)

2 tablespoons natural (plain) yogurt

1–2 tablespoons vegetable oil

TOMATO SALSA

1 tablespoon olive oil

1 teaspoon white wine vinegar

1 large ripe tomato, seeds removed,
    diced

1 clove garlic, crushed

1 small green or red chilli,
    finely chopped

METHOD

1 Melt butter in a saucepan. Add finely sliced onion and fry gently
   3 minutes. Stir in rice and fry 1 minute.

2 Pour 3 cups (750 ml) boiling water over rice, add salt, cover and return
   to a boil. Reduce heat and simmer 15 minutes.

3 Meanwhile, put one-third of chopped coriander, along with chopped
   onion, ginger, garlic, lamb, amchur or lemon juice, garam masala,
   ground cumin, chilli powder, besan, yogurt and some salt and pepper
   in a food processor or blender. Process to a paste.

4 Preheat grill (broiler) to high. Divide lamb mixture into eight portions
   and mould each into a sausage shape around a lightly greased metal
   skewer. Brush all over with oil and grill 6–8 minutes, turning once.

5 Meanwhile, to make the salsa, whisk oil and vinegar together in a bowl.
   Add tomato, garlic, chilli and the remaining chopped coriander to the
   bowl. Season with salt and pepper and stir well.

6 Spoon cooked rice onto serving plates, top with the koftas and spoon
   the salsa alongside. Garnish with coriander leaves and serve.

NUTRIENTS PER SERVING

2651 kJ, 633 kcal, 36 g protein, 23 g fat (4 g saturated fat), 69 g carbohydrate

COOK'S TIP

Both besan (made from ground chickpeas) and amchur are available from
larger supermarkets and Indian grocers.

Right Lamb koftas with tomato salsa (top); Spiced lamb skewers with pitas (bottom)

SAUSAGES WITH MUSTARD MASHED POTATO AND RED ONION GRAVY

TIME **30 MINUTES** SERVES **4**

INGREDIENTS

1 tablespoon olive oil

1 red onion, thinly sliced

2 teaspoons soft brown sugar

1 kg (2 lb) boiling (waxy) potatoes, peeled and diced

8 good-quality sausages

1 tablespoon plain (all-purpose) flour

1¼ cups (310 ml) hot beef stock

100 ml (3½ fl oz) red wine

1 tablespoon worcestershire sauce

100 ml (3½ fl oz) milk, warmed

50 g (1¾ oz) butter

2–3 teaspoons wholegrain mustard

METHOD

1 Preheat grill (broiler) to high. Heat oil in a large frying pan. Add onion and sprinkle with sugar, then cook gently, stirring from time to time, 12–15 minutes, or until onion is lightly caramelised.

2 While onion is cooking, boil potatoes in a large saucepan of lightly salted water 15 minutes, or until tender. Grill sausages, turning regularly, about 15 minutes, or until evenly browned.

3 Sprinkle flour over caramelised onion, stir and cook 1 minute, then gradually stir in stock, wine and worcestershire sauce. Bring to a boil, then reduce heat and simmer gravy gently.

4 Drain potatoes and return to the saucepan. Mash with warmed milk, butter and mustard to taste.

5 Spoon a mound of mashed potato onto each plate, lay two sausages on top and spoon over the gravy.

NUTRIENTS PER SERVING

3261 kJ, 779 kcal, 30 g protein, 55 g fat (26 g saturated fat), 41 g carbohydrate

COOK'S TIP

To keep mashed potato hot for a few minutes, cover the pan with a clean tea towel (dish towel) instead of a lid — the potatoes will stay light and fluffy.

SPICY CHIPOLATAS IN BATTER
TIME **30 MINUTES** SERVES **4**

METHOD

1 Preheat oven to 220°C (425°F/Gas 7). Brush a 12-hole standard muffin tin with oil and heat in oven until hot. Add sausages, placing two halves in each hole, and bake 5 minutes. Turn sausages, then divide tomato halves among the holes and bake a further 2 minutes.

2 Meanwhile, put flour, eggs, milk, hot chilli sauce and a little salt in a bowl and beat until smooth and bubbly.

3 Remove muffin tin from oven and quickly pour a little batter into each hole. Return to the oven and bake 20 minutes, or until well risen and golden brown. Serve immediately.

NUTRIENTS PER SERVING

2969 kJ, 709 kcal, 31 g protein, 51 g fat (17 g saturated fat), 33 g carbohydrate

VARIATION

Try some of the unusual chipolatas available, such as a pack of mixed types. Or use cocktail sausages instead of chipolatas.

COOK'S TIP

For an extra-light batter, use half milk and half water instead of all milk.

INGREDIENTS

2 tablespoons vegetable oil

12 good-quality pork chipolatas or other spicy small sausages, halved crosswise

200 g (7 oz) red cherry tomatoes, halved

¾ cup (110 g) plain (all-purpose) flour

2 eggs

1¼ cups (310 ml) low-fat milk

1½ teaspoons hot chilli sauce

salt

SAUSAGES WITH SPICED WINE AND APPLES

TIME **25 MINUTES** SERVES **2**

INGREDIENTS

1¼ cups (310 ml) dry white wine

250 g (8 oz) good-quality pork or
chicken sausages

3 tablespoons butter, softened

1 French shallot (eschalot) or ½ small
onion, grated

2 crisp red apples, peeled, quartered,
cored and sliced

200 ml (7 fl oz) chicken or vegetable stock

2 tablespoons soft brown sugar

½ teaspoon ground cinnamon

METHOD

1 Bring wine to a boil in a large
frying pan and poach sausages
gently 10 minutes. Remove the
sausages from the pan, reserving
the wine. Discard any loose skins.

2 Gently melt 1 tablespoon butter
in a second frying pan over low
heat. Add sausages and fry slowly
until browned all over.

3 Meanwhile, add French shallot
or onion to the white wine in the
first pan, along with apples, stock,
sugar, cinnamon and remaining
butter. Bring to a boil, lower heat
and simmer until the apples are
tender and the liquid is reduced to
a thin syrup. Serve the sausages
with the spiced wine and apples.

NUTRIENTS PER SERVING

3888 kJ, 929 kcal, 15 g protein, 69 g fat
(34 g saturated fat), 42 g carbohydrate

COOK'S TIP

Good-quality sausages are essential,
but choose a mild variety or the
flavour may clash with the apple
sauce.

ITALIAN SPIRALS WITH BURST TOMATOES

TIME **30 MINUTES** SERVES **4**

INGREDIENTS

2 tablespoons olive oil

2 cloves garlic, crushed

1 teaspoon dried oregano

½ teaspoon dried red chilli flakes

750 g (1½ lb) ripe red cherry
tomatoes

500 g (1 lb) length of thin Italian
peppered or spiced sausage
(salsiccia)

salt and freshly ground black pepper

fresh basil leaves, to garnish

METHOD

1 Heat oil in a large frying pan. Add garlic, oregano and chilli flakes and
fry gently over low heat about 30 seconds, without allowing the garlic
to change colour.

2 Spread tomatoes in a single layer on top of garlic and chilli. Cover and
cook over low heat about 10–12 minutes, or until most of the tomatoes
have burst and are half-submerged in their juices.

3 Meanwhile, preheat grill (broiler) to high. Cut sausage into four shorter
lengths and wind each into a coil. Pass a thin metal skewer horizontally
through each coil to hold it in place, then arrange all four skewers on
the grill rack.

4 Grill sausage coils 5–6 minutes on each side, turning them so that they
become evenly crusty and brown on all sides.

5 Uncover tomatoes, increase heat to medium and cook a further
5 minutes, or until the juices have reduced and thickened. Press lightly
occasionally with the back of a spoon so that all the tomatoes burst.

6 Season the tomato sauce to taste with salt and pepper, then pour onto
four warmed serving plates and put a sausage coil in the centre of each.
Scatter basil leaves over the top and serve.

NUTRIENTS PER SERVING

2059 kJ, 492 kcal, 30 g protein, 38 g fat (15 g saturated fat), 7 g carbohydrate

VARIATION

Other thin spicy sausages can be used instead of salsiccia. If long lengths
are unavailable in the sausage of your choice, untwist the links and
smooth the sausage meat into a solid column with your fingers before
winding it into coils.

COOK'S TIP

Mashed potatoes, or polenta or cornmeal cooked with cheese, would
provide a creamy contrast to the tomato and chilli sauce.

Right Sausages with spiced wine and apples (top); Italian spirals with burst tomatoes (bottom)

ROQUEFORT PORK CHOPS

TIME **25 MINUTES** SERVES **4**

INGREDIENTS

4 thick rindless pork loin chops
   (about 250 g/8 oz each)
50 g (1¾ oz) roquefort cheese,
   crumbled
grated zest of ½ lemon, plus
   lemon wedges, to serve

1 tablespoon vegetable oil
salt and freshly ground black pepper
2 tablespoon chopped fresh rosemary
250 g (8 oz) baby spinach leaves
1 teaspoon freshly grated nutmeg

METHOD

1 With a sharp knife, make a horizontal slit in the fat side of each pork chop without cutting all the way through. Gently open out into a pocket through the meat.

2 Mix cheese with lemon zest, then tuck this mixture into the pocket of each chop, pressing the meat back over firmly to enclose.

3 Brush pork chops lightly with oil on both sides and season with salt and pepper. Heat a frying pan until hot, then reduce heat and fry chops over medium heat 6–7 minutes on each side, or until golden brown and evenly cooked. Sprinkle rosemary over chops and turn once or twice to coat. Transfer chops to a plate and keep warm.

4 Add spinach to the pan and stir until just wilted. Divide spinach among four serving plates. Add a pork chop to each, then sprinkle lightly with nutmeg. Serve with lemon wedges to squeeze over the chops.

NUTRIENTS PER SERVING

2044 kJ, 488 kcal, 68 g protein, 23 g fat (8 g saturated fat), 4 g carbohydrate

VARIATION

Instead of roquefort and lemon, try brie or camembert with 1 tablespoon sweet chilli sauce.

COOK'S TIP

Take care not to overcook the chops, or they may become dry.

Left Roquefort pork chops

MAPLE HAM STEAKS WITH MANGO–GINGER SALSA

TIME **25 MINUTES** SERVES **4**

INGREDIENTS

1 ripe mango
2 tomatoes, finely chopped
1 spring onion (scallion), finely chopped
1 tablespoon grated fresh ginger
juice of 1 lime
2 tablespoons maple syrup
4 ham steaks (about 200 g/7 oz each),
   trimmed of fat
1 bunch (250 g/8 oz) watercress,
   trimmed, to serve

METHOD

1 Using a sharp knife, cut the flesh off each cheek of the mango along either side of the stone. Holding a cheek in one hand, slice through the flesh (but not through the skin) in a criss-cross pattern. Push against the skin, turning it inside out; the flesh will pop up in small cubes. Slice these off. Repeat with the other cheek. Cut the skin off the section containing the mango stone, and slice away the flesh. Chop all mango flesh finely.

2 Mix mango with tomatoes and spring onion in a bowl. Add ginger and half the lime juice and stir to mix well.

3 Preheat grill (broiler) to medium. Mix the remaining lime juice with maple syrup and brush over ham steaks.

4 Place ham steaks on the grill rack and cook 3–4 minutes each side, or until golden brown. Serve on a bed of watercress with a spoonful of salsa alongside.

NUTRIENTS PER SERVING

1721 kJ, 411 kcal, 41 g protein, 16 g fat (6 g saturated fat), 26 g carbohydrate

PORK SAUSAGES WITH CELERIAC AND PEAR PURÉE

TIME **30 MINUTES** SERVES **4**

INGREDIENTS

1 tablespoon olive oil

1 tablespoon butter

1 head celeriac (celery root) (about 650 g/
    1 lb 7 oz), peeled and chopped

1 large onion, chopped

2 large juicy pears, peeled and
    roughly chopped

juice of 1/2 lemon

4 cups (1 litre) chicken stock

8 thin pork sausages (about 350 g/
    12 oz in total)

salt and freshly ground black pepper

2 tablespoons chopped fresh flat-leaf
    (Italian) parsley

1/2 teaspoon mild paprika

METHOD

1 Heat oil and butter in a large saucepan. Stir in celeriac, onion and pears. Add lemon juice. Cover and cook over low heat 10 minutes, stirring occasionally. Add 1 cup (250 ml) stock and cook a further 5 minutes, or until vegetables have softened. If you have time, allow to cool a little before puréeing.

2 While vegetables and fruit are cooking, preheat grill (broiler) to hot. Grill sausages, turning occasionally, about 10 minutes, or until golden brown. Drain on paper towel and keep warm.

3 Tip vegetables and fruit into a food processor or blender, add remaining stock and process until it is a smooth, soup-like purée. Season with salt and pepper, return to the pan and heat through gently.

4 Slice the sausages thickly and add to the purée. Stir in parsley, then ladle into bowls and sprinkle over paprika.

NUTRIENTS PER SERVING

1940 kJ, 463 kcal, 17 g protein, 28 g fat (11 g saturated fat), 37 g carbohydrate

VARIATION

You could replace the celeriac with swedes (rutabaga) or turnips, plus 2 chopped celery stalks.

GINGERED PORK ON WATERCRESS

TIME **30 MINUTES** SERVES **2**

INGREDIENTS

250 g (8 oz) pork fillet, trimmed of fat,
   sliced 1 cm ($\frac{1}{2}$ inch) thick

1$\frac{1}{2}$ teaspoons grated fresh ginger

250 g (8 oz) new waxy (boiling) potatoes,
   cut into 1 cm ($\frac{1}{2}$ inch) slices

salt and freshly ground black pepper

2 teaspoons sesame seeds

1 large egg

2 teaspoons sesame oil

2 tablespoons vegetable oil

$\frac{1}{2}$ teaspoon cornflour (cornstarch)

2 tablespoons dry sherry

3 teaspoons soy sauce

1 bunch (250 g/8 oz) watercress,
   trimmed

METHOD

1 Put pork slices in a bowl. Stir in
   ginger and set aside.

2 Put potatoes in a saucepan of
   salted boiling water and cook
   10–12 minutes, until tender.

3 Meanwhile, dry-fry sesame seeds
   in a frying pan over medium heat,
   shaking, until lightly toasted, then
   leave to cool.

4 Lightly beat egg, salt and pepper
   in a small bowl, then stir in the
   sesame seeds. Heat sesame oil and
   1 teaspoon vegetable oil in the
   frying pan. Add beaten egg and
   swirl over the base of the pan to
   make a thin omelette. When it is
   cooked, turn out onto a plate, roll
   up and slice thinly. Set aside.

5 Blend cornflour and 2 tablespoons
   cold water in a small bowl, then
   stir in sherry and soy sauce.

6 Heat remaining vegetable oil in
   the frying pan over high heat. Add
   pork and fry 1–2 minutes on each
   side until golden brown. Transfer
   to a plate and keep warm.

7 Pour cornflour mixture into the pan and stir over medium heat until
   it boils and thickens. Return pork to the pan with any juices and heat
   through gently.

8 Drain the potatoes and arrange on two plates. Place watercress and pork
   slices on top and pour over the sauce. Garnish with the omelette ribbons
   and serve immediately.

NUTRIENTS PER SERVING

2209 kJ, 528 kcal, 34 g protein, 33 g fat (6 g saturated fat), 19 g carbohydrate

THAI PORK PATTIES WITH BOK CHOY
TIME **30 MINUTES** SERVES **4**

...HOD

...ix spring onions, pork, curry paste, lemongrass and eggwhite in a bowl
...ntil all ingredients are thoroughly bound together, pressing the mixture
...rmly with the back of the mixing spoon (or use your hands to mix).
...ivide mixture into 12 portions, then shape each into a round patty.
...eat 1 tablespoon oil in a heavy-based frying pan and fry patties, turning
...nce, 8–10 minutes, or until golden brown and thoroughly cooked.
...eanwhile, heat remaining oil in a wide frying pan or wok and add bok
...noy and mushrooms. Stir-fry over high heat 2–3 minutes to soften.
...tir coconut milk and fish sauce into vegetables, bring to a boil, then
...mmer 1 minute. Serve patties with the bok choy mixture, sprinkled
...ith sesame seeds.

...TRIENTS PER SERVING

...3 kJ, 404 kcal, 30 g protein, 30 g fat (14 g saturated fat), 4 g carbohydrate

...RIATION

...) THAI BEEF PATTIES WITH VEGETABLES Prepare 500 g
...) minced (ground) lean beef as for step 1 using 3 finely chopped spring
...ons, 1½ teaspoons red curry paste, 1 crushed clove garlic and 1 eggwhite.
...pe into 12 patties and fry as for step 3. Stir-fry 350 g (12 oz) mixed
...etables, such as broccoli florets, snow peas (mangetout) and baby corn,
... tablespoons oil until just tender, then add a 125 g (4 oz) can bamboo
...ots, drained, and ¾ cup (180 ml) coconut milk. Bring to a boil, stir in
...blespoons chopped fresh coriander (cilantro) leaves and serve.

...OK'S TIP

...seful alternative to fresh lemongrass is a jar or tube of crushed lemongrass
...e, which can be stored in the fridge. Dried lemongrass sticks are also
...venient to use and store. They can be crumbled straight into Thai-style
...es. You will need 1 teaspoon dried lemongrass for this recipe.

INGREDIENTS

4 spring onions (scallions), finely chopped

500 g (1 lb) minced (ground) lean pork

1½ teaspoons green curry paste

2 teaspoons crushed lemongrass,
     from a jar

1 eggwhite

2 tablespoons peanut (groundnut)
     or vegetable oil

200 g (7 oz) bok choy, sliced lengthwise

175 g (6 oz) oyster mushrooms, sliced

¾ cup (180 ml) coconut milk

1 teaspoon fish sauce

1 tablespoon sesame seeds, to garnish

CHINESE FIVE-SPICE PORK
AND NOODLE STIR-FRY
TIME **20 MINUTES** SERVES **4**

INGREDIENTS

2/3 cup (100 g) cashew nuts

1 tablespoons peanut (groundnut) oil

500 g (1 lb) minced lean pork

1 clove garlic, crushed

2–3 teaspoons Chinese five-spice

6 spring onions (scallions), chopped

100 g (3 1/2 oz) baby corn

100 g (3 1/2 oz) snow peas (mangetout),
   topped and tailed

juice of 1 lime

500 g (1 lb) wok-ready hokkien (egg)
   or Singapore noodles

METHOD

1 Toast cashew nuts in a dry wok or large frying pan over medium–high heat, tossing regularly, 3 minutes, or until golden brown. Set aside.

2 Heat oil in the wok. Add pork and stir-fry 3 minutes, or until light golden brown. Stir in garlic, Chinese five-spice to taste and spring onions and stir-fry 1 minute.

3 Add baby corn and snow peas and stir-fry 6 minutes, or until just tender.

4 Add lime juice and noodles. Cook, stirring occasionally, 2 minutes, or until thoroughly heated through. Stir in the toasted cashew nuts and serve.

NUTRIENTS PER SERVING

2341 kJ, 559 kcal, 36 g protein, 27 g fat (7 g saturated fat), 43 g carbohydrate

PORK FILLET WITH MUSTARD SAUCE

TIME **30 MINUTES** SERVES **4**

INGREDIENTS

1½ tablespoons butter

600 g (1 lb 5 oz) pork fillet, trimmed of fat,
    sliced 1 cm (½ inch) thick

4 spring onions (scallions), chopped

1 tablespoon plain (all-purpose) flour

¾ cup (180 ml) chicken stock

1 teaspoon fresh thyme

2 small sweet red apples, quartered,
    cored and sliced

3 tablespoons wholegrain mustard

salt and freshly ground black pepper

4 tablespoons thick (heavy/double) cream

2 tablespoons calvados or brandy

METHOD

1 Melt half the butter in a large
frying pan. Add pork slices and
fry over high heat 1 minute on
each side, or until pork is very
lightly browned. Remove from the
pan and keep warm.

2 Heat the remaining butter in the
pan, add spring onions and cook
1–2 minutes, until softened. Stir
in flour, add stock and bring to a
boil, stirring.

3 Add thyme, apples, mustard and
salt and pepper to taste to the pan.
Cook over medium heat a further
4 minutes.

4 Stir in cream and simmer gently
2 minutes. Pour in calvados or
brandy, increase heat slightly and
cook gently a further 2 minutes.
Transfer to four warmed plates
and serve immediately.

NUTRIENTS PER SERVING

2260 kJ, 540 kcal, 36 g protein, 37 g fat
(16 g saturated fat), 11 g carbohydrate

COOK'S TIP

Tender baby peas cooked with shredded lettuce make a good accompaniment
to this dish.

PORK FILLET WITH PEARS AND TARRAGON

TIME **25 MINUTES** SERVES **4**

INGREDIENTS

15 g (¹/₂ oz) butter

1 tablespoon olive oil

2 ripe pears, quartered, cored and
   sliced lengthwise

2 French shallots (eschalots),
   finely chopped

2 pork fillets (about 500 g/1 lb in total),
   thinly sliced

²/₃ cup (150 ml) dry white wine

2 tablespoons chopped fresh tarragon

4 tablespoons light sour cream

salt and freshly ground black pepper

METHOD

1 Melt half the butter with ¹/₂ tablespoon oil in a frying pan and fry pears
   quickly over a high heat, turning once, 3 minutes each side, or until golden
   all over. Remove from pan to a warmed plate and cover.

2 Add remaining butter and oil to the pan, stir in French shallots and cook
   over medium heat, stirring occasionally, 3–4 minutes, or until softened
   and golden.

3 Push shallots to one side of the pan, add pork slices and fry 5–6 minutes,
   or until lightly browned, turning once.

4 Pour wine into the pan, bring to a boil and boil 1–2 minutes to reduce
   slightly. Stir in tarragon and sour cream and boil a further 1 minute. Add
   salt and pepper to taste. Serve pork slices topped with the pears, then
   spoon the sauce over.

NUTRIENTS PER SERVING

1311 kJ, 313 kcal, 28 g protein, 15 g fat (6 g saturated fat), 11 g carbohydrate

VARIATION

Replace the pears and white wine with apple rings and dry alcoholic (hard)
cider. Instead of the pork fillet, use lamb leg steaks or lamb fillet, sliced into
medallions, and simmer in step 3 for 15–20 minutes, or until tender.

QUICK CASSOULET
TIME **30 MINUTES** SERVES **4**

METHOD

1 Heat oil in a large flameproof casserole dish or large heavy-based saucepan and add sausages and bacon. Fry over medium–high heat 8 minutes, until sausages are golden on all sides and bacon is cooked.

2 Remove sausages and bacon from the dish, drain on paper towel and set aside. Pour off all but 2 tablespoons fat from the dish. Add onion and garlic and cook over medium heat 5 minutes, until softened.

3 Stir in tomatoes, then add mixed dried herbs, mustard and tomato paste. Fill the tomato can one-third with water, stir well and add to the mixture. Bring to a boil, stirring, then add butterbeans and cannellini beans.

4 Return sausages and bacon to the dish and season to taste. Reduce heat, cover and cook gently 10 minutes, or until sausages are cooked through. Serve immediately.

NUTRIENTS PER SERVING
2971 kJ, 710 kcal, 29 g protein, 48 g fat (17 g saturated fat), 41 g carbohydrate

VARIATION
Replace one of the cans of beans with 250 g (8 oz) frozen corn kernels, peas or broad (fava) beans.

COOK'S TIP
Serve with a green salad and mashed potatoes, or some warm crusty bread.

INGREDIENTS

1 tablespoon vegetable oil

8 large pork sausages, cut into bite-sized pieces

125 g (4 oz) rindless bacon (bacon strips), diced

1 large onion, halved and sliced

2 cloves garlic, crushed

410 g (15 oz) can chopped tomatoes

1–2 teaspoons mixed dried herbs

1 tablespoon wholegrain mustard

2 tablespoons tomato paste (concentrated purée)

1½ x 200 g (7 oz) cans butterbeans (lima beans), rinsed and drained

400 g (14 oz) can cannellini beans, rinsed and drained

salt and freshly ground black pepper

PLUM-GLAZED PORK WITH SPICY CABBAGE

TIME **30 MINUTES** SERVES **4**

INGREDIENTS

2 tablespoons good plum jam

1 tablespoon soy sauce

$1/2$ teaspoon ground allspice

$1/2$ teaspoon cayenne pepper

4 pork loin chops or steaks
(about 200 g/7 oz each)

2 tablespoons cider vinegar

salt and freshly ground black pepper

2 tablespoons olive oil

1 red chilli, halved, seeds removed, finely
chopped

2 cloves garlic, chopped

750 g ($1 1/2$ lb) crisp green cabbage,
such as savoy, coarsely chopped

METHOD

1 Gently warm plum jam and soy
sauce in a small pan. Season with
allspice and cayenne pepper, then
sieve, if necessary.

2 Preheat grill (broiler) to high.
Trim fat off pork chops or steaks
and discard the bones. Arrange
pork on the grill rack and cook
5–7 minutes each side, basting
with the plum glaze halfway
through.

3 Meanwhile, mix cider vinegar
with 2 tablespoons water and
some salt and pepper.

4 Heat oil in a large saucepan. Fry
chilli and garlic 30–40 seconds.
Add cabbage and toss in the oil.
Stir in diluted vinegar, then cover
and cook 4 minutes.

5 Uncover the pan, raise the heat
and cook the cabbage until all the
liquid has evaporated.

6 Serve the cabbage on individual
plates with the plum-glazed pork.

NUTRIENTS PER SERVING

2377 kJ, 568 kcal, 32 g protein, 41 g fat
(13 g saturated fat), 19 g carbohydrate

SPICY PORK BURGERS WITH GUACAMOLE
TIME 30 MINUTES SERVES 4

METHOD

1 Heat 2 teaspoons oil in a small frying pan. Add onion and half the garlic and fry until the onion is soft. Stir in half the chillies, the ground coriander and cumin and fry gently 3 minutes, or until soft but not browned.

2 Transfer the fried onion mixture to a large bowl. Add pork, 1 tablespoon chopped fresh coriander, the egg, lemon or lime zest, and salt and pepper to taste. Stir the mixture to combine; it should be slightly soft. Divide into four portions and shape each portion into a fairly flat burger.

3 Heat the remaining oil in a large frying pan. Fry the burgers over medium heat 5–6 minutes on each side, until cooked through.

4 Meanwhile, make the guacamole. Put the remaining chopped coriander, remaining garlic, remaining chillies and the lemon or lime juice in a bowl. Add avocado flesh, season, then mash together well.

5 Drain the cooked burgers on paper towel. Serve on individual plates with the guacamole and corn chips or soft tortillas divided among them.

NUTRIENTS PER SERVING
2838 kJ, 678 kcal, 32 g protein, 48 g fat (11 g saturated fat), 33 g carbohydrate

COOK'S TIP
Use a food processor or blender to save time making the guacamole. First process all the coriander, set aside 1 tablespoon for the burgers, then add the other guacamole ingredients to the processor and blend.

INGREDIENTS

2 tablespoons vegetable oil

1 small onion, finely chopped

2 cloves garlic, crushed

2 red or green chillies, finely chopped

1 teaspoon ground coriander

1 teaspoon ground cumin

500 g (1 lb) minced (ground) pork

2 tablespoons chopped fresh coriander (cilantro) leaves

1 small egg

finely grated zest of 1 lemon or lime, plus juice of $1/2$ lemon or lime

salt and freshly ground black pepper

1 large avocado

corn chips or soft tortillas, to serve

HAM AND LEEK PIE

TIME **30 MINUTES** SERVES **4**

INGREDIENTS

1 kg (2 lb) boiling (waxy) potatoes, diced
salt and freshly ground black pepper
3 tablespoons butter
500 g (1 lb) leeks, sliced
500 g (1 lb) lean ham pieces, diced
2 tablespoons plain (all-purpose) flour
1 teaspoon mixed dried herbs
1¼ cups (310 ml) milk, plus extra
   1–2 tablespoons
¾ cup (90 g) mature cheddar, grated
125 g (4 oz) red cherry tomatoes, halved
fresh flat-leaf (Italian) parsley leaves,
   to garnish

METHOD

1 Put potatoes in a saucepan of salted boiling water and cook, covered, 8–10 minutes until tender.
2 Meanwhile, melt 1 tablespoon butter in a frying pan over medium heat. Fry leeks 6–8 minutes, stirring frequently, until softened but not browned. Remove from heat and keep warm.
3 Melt 1 tablespoon butter in a flameproof casserole dish about 25 cm (10 inches) wide and 5 cm (2 inches) deep, or in a frying pan with a flameproof handle. Add ham and fry over medium heat 5 minutes, stirring frequently.
4 Stir in flour and mixed dried herbs and cook 1 minute. Add 1¼ cups milk and stir until it comes to a boil. Add cheese, stir until it melts, then add leeks, season to taste and reduce heat to low.
5 Preheat grill (broiler) to high. Drain potatoes, then mash with pepper, the remaining butter and 1–2 tablespoons milk. Place large spoonfuls of mashed potato in a circle around the top of the ham and leek mixture and place cherry tomatoes in the centre.
6 Grill the pie 2–3 minutes, or until the top of the mash is golden. Scatter over parsley and serve immediately.

NUTRIENTS PER SERVING
2411 kJ, 576 kcal, 37 g protein, 30 g fat (18 g saturated fat), 42 g carbohydrate

COOK'S TIP
Serve with a plain green vegetable, such as brussels sprouts.

CHAPTER 9

Vegetables

ROAST PUMPKIN AND ZUCCHINI WITH BUTTERBEANS

TIME **30 MINUTES** SERVES **4**

INGREDIENTS

1 butternut pumpkin (squash) (about
  750 g/1^1/$_2$ lb), cut into small chunks

2 red onions, each cut into 8 wedges

2 tablespoons olive oil

salt and freshly ground black pepper

2 zucchini (courgettes), thickly sliced

4 small sprigs fresh thyme

1 teaspoon ground cardamom

^{1}/$_2$ teaspoon soft brown sugar

4 tablespoons orange juice

2 teaspoons balsamic vinegar

400 g (14 oz) can butterbeans
  (lima beans), rinsed and drained

^{1}/$_3$ cup (90 g) light sour cream

METHOD

1 Preheat oven to 230°C (450°F/Gas 8) and put a roasting pan (baking dish) or large non-stick baking tray (sheet) in the oven to heat. Put pumpkin and onions in a bowl and drizzle over 1^1/$_2$ tablespoons oil. Add a little salt and pepper and toss vegetables with your hands or a large spoon to coat.

2 Remove the pan from the oven and tip the vegetables into it, spreading them out in a single layer. Roast 10 minutes. Meanwhile, put zucchini in the bowl, add thyme and drizzle with remaining oil. Toss to coat, then set aside.

3 Mix cardamom, sugar, orange juice and vinegar in a small bowl.

4 Turn the vegetables in the pan, then add thyme-coated zucchini and butterbeans. Drizzle everything with the cardamom glaze. Roast a further 10 minutes, or until the vegetables are tender and lightly charred.

5 Remove the vegetables from the oven and spoon into a warmed serving dish or onto individual plates. Top with small spoonfuls of sour cream, then serve.

NUTRIENTS PER SERVING

1354 kJ, 323 kcal, 9 g protein, 15 g fat (5 g saturated fat), 39 g carbohydrate

VARIATION

You could use any other type of pumpkin (winter squash) and replace the zucchini with green capsicums (bell peppers).

ROAST NEW POTATOES WITH ROSEMARY

TIME **30 MINUTES** SERVES **4**

INGREDIENTS

750 g (1¹/₂ lb) even-sized small
   new potatoes
2 tablespoons olive oil
grated zest of 1 lemon
2–3 large sprigs fresh rosemary
salt and freshly ground black pepper

METHOD

1 Preheat oven to 230°C (450°F/Gas 8). Gently cook potatoes in a large saucepan of boiling water 5 minutes.
2 Meanwhile, pour oil into a large shallow roasting pan (baking dish) and put in the oven to heat.
3 Drain potatoes. Put into the hot oil in the pan and stir well to coat evenly. Sprinkle lemon zest, rosemary leaves and some salt and pepper over. Make sure the oil is really hot before you begin roasting — the potatoes should start to sizzle as soon as you put them into the pan.
4 Roast potatoes on the top shelf of the oven 20 minutes, until golden.

NUTRIENTS PER SERVING

745 kJ, 178 kcal, 3 g protein, 8 g fat (1 g saturated fat), 25 g carbohydrate

COOK'S TIP

Choose tiny new potatoes, about the size of a marble, for this elegant dish. If larger, cut into halves or quarters.

SWEET POTATO RÖSTI
TIME **30 MINUTES** SERVES **4**

METHOD

1 Line a baking tray (sheet) with a double thickness of paper towel and set aside.

2 Put sweet potatoes in a mixing bowl. Season with salt and pepper and mix well. Divide the mixture into eight, then shape each portion into a round patty about 1 cm ($\frac{1}{2}$ inch) thick and press firmly.

3 Heat half the oil in a large non-stick frying pan, then add half the butter. As soon as it begins to sizzle, carefully place 4 patties in the pan.

4 Cook the rösti over medium heat 5 minutes, or until crisp and golden brown underneath, then turn carefully with a fish slice and cook a further 5 minutes (do not worry if the patties break up as you turn them — simply pat back into shape).

5 When the first batch is cooked, transfer to the lined tray to drain off excess cooking oil and keep warm.

6 Add the remaining oil and butter to the pan, heat until sizzling and fry the remaining rösti as in step 4.

INGREDIENTS

750 g (1 $\frac{1}{2}$ lb) orange sweet potatoes (kumara), peeled and coarsely grated

salt and freshly ground black pepper

2 tablespoons vegetable oil

1 tablespoon butter

NUTRIENTS PER SERVING

975 kJ, 233 kcal, 2 g protein, 14 g fat (5 g saturated fat), 28 g carbohydrate

COOK'S TIP

The rösti can also be cooked in one large cake and divided into eight portions at the table. You can add finely chopped bacon or ham for extra flavour.

MIXED MUSHROOMS WITH BRANDY

TIME **30 MINUTES** SERVES **4**

INGREDIENTS

30 g (1 oz) dried morels or
   cep mushrooms
1 tablespoon butter
1 tablespoon olive oil
1 onion, finely chopped
2 cloves garlic, crushed
200 g (7 oz) Swiss brown or porcini
   mushrooms, halved
200 g (7 oz) open cap mushrooms, sliced
150 g (5 oz) oyster mushrooms,
   tough stalks discarded, sliced
1–2 tablespoons brandy
salt and freshly ground black pepper
3 tablespoons chopped fresh parsley

METHOD

1 Put dried morels or cep mushrooms into a bowl, cover with ¾ cup (180 ml) boiling water and leave to soak.
2 Meanwhile, heat butter and oil in a large frying pan over medium heat. Add onion and fry 5 minutes, to soften.
3 Increase heat and add garlic and Swiss brown or porcini, open cap and oyster mushrooms. Stir-fry 5 minutes, until mushrooms are just softened.
4 Meanwhile, line a sieve with paper towel and place it over a bowl. Pour the soaked mushrooms into it, so the paper towel catches any grit and the soaking water drains into the bowl. Reserve this liquid. Rinse and chop the drained mushrooms.
5 With a slotted spoon, remove the onions and mushrooms from the pan and put in a bowl, leaving the juices in the pan.
6 Add drained mushrooms and their soaking liquid to the pan. Boil rapidly until the liquid has a syrupy consistency.
7 Stir in brandy. Return onion and mushroom mixture to the pan, season to taste with salt and pepper, stir in the parsley and reheat. Transfer to a warmed dish to serve.

NUTRIENTS PER SERVING
527 kJ, 126 kcal, 5 g protein, 11 g fat (4 g saturated fat), 4 g carbohydrate

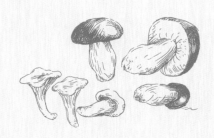

ITALIAN PAN-FRIED MUSHROOMS
TIME 25 MINUTES SERVES 4

METHOD

1 Put pine nuts in a large dry non-stick frying pan and toast 2–3 minutes over medium heat, stirring frequently, until light golden brown. Remove from pan and set aside.

2 Add oil and French shallot to pan; cook 2 minutes, or until starting to soften. Stir in garlic.

3 Increase heat a little, add butter and Swiss brown or porcini mushrooms and cook 2 minutes. Add mixed mushrooms and continue cooking 2–3 minutes, stirring occasionally, until liquid evaporates and mushrooms are tender. Sprinkle over vinegar, thyme and salt and pepper to taste. Heat a further few seconds, then stir in the reserved pine nuts and serve.

INGREDIENTS

$^1/_3$ cup (50 g) pine nuts

1 tablespoon olive oil

1 French shallot, finely chopped

1 clove garlic, crushed

15 g ($^1/_2$ oz) butter

350 g (12 oz) Swiss brown or porcini mushrooms, thickly sliced

100 g (3$^1/_2$ oz) mixed exotic mushrooms, thickly sliced

2 teaspoons balsamic vinegar

1 teaspoon chopped fresh thyme

salt and freshly ground black pepper

NUTRIENTS PER SERVING

762 kJ, 182 kcal, 6 g protein, 17 g fat (3 g saturated fat), 3 g carbohydrate

VARIATION

Replace the pine nuts with 250 g (8 oz) smoked tofu. Dice and fry in 2 teaspoons olive oil 2–3 minutes. Tip into a bowl and sprinkle with 1 teaspoon dark soy sauce. Stir into the cooked mushrooms.

COOK'S TIP

To serve the mushrooms, toss freshly cooked pasta with 2 tablespoons crème fraîche or sour cream, 250 g (8 oz) English spinach (cooked in the microwave on High 2 minutes) and freshly grated nutmeg. Top with mushrooms and scatter with grated parmesan. Or cut a slightly stale ciabatta or baguette into diagonal slices. Brush with olive oil on both sides. Cook on a chargrill pan or under a hot grill 1 minute on each side, or until lightly browned. Serve the mushrooms on top of the toasts.

ORANGE AND SESAME CARROTS

TIME **25 MINUTES** SERVES **4**

INGREDIENTS

500 g (1 lb) small carrots
grated zest and juice of 1 orange
3 teaspoons butter or vegetable oil
salt and freshly ground black pepper
1 tablespoon sesame seeds

METHOD

1 If carrots are very small, leave whole; otherwise, cut them in half lengthwise.
2 Put orange zest and juice in a large saucepan, then add butter or oil and bring to a boil over medium heat.
3 Add carrots to the saucepan, then season to taste with salt and pepper. Bring back to a boil, reduce heat, cover and simmer 10–12 minutes, shaking the pan occasionally, until the carrots are tender but not soft.
4 Meanwhile, put sesame seeds in a small frying pan and dry-fry over medium–high heat about 2 minutes, shaking the pan, until golden.
5 Stir sesame seeds into the carrots and serve.

NUTRIENTS PER SERVING

364 kJ, 87 kcal, 2 g protein, 6 g fat (2 g saturated fat), 8 g carbohydrate

LEEK AND CARROT STIR-FRY

TIME **20 MINUTES** SERVES **4**

INGREDIENTS

750 g (1¹/₂ lb) leeks
2 tablespoons olive oil
250 g (8 oz) carrots, grated
salt and freshly ground black pepper
1 large sprig fresh tarragon, chopped

METHOD

1 Discard tough outer leaves and two-thirds of the green tops of the leeks. Slice thinly. Put in a colander and rinse under cold running water to clean well, then drain well.
2 Heat oil in a wok or large frying pan over medium heat. Add leeks and fry about 2 minutes, or until just beginning to wilt.
3 Stir in carrots and add salt, pepper and tarragon. Continue to cook a further 2 minutes, then serve.

NUTRIENTS PER SERVING

373 kJ, 89 kcal, 2 g protein, 8 g fat (1 g saturated fat), 7 g carbohydrate

CURRIED PARSNIP PURÉE

TIME **20 MINUTES** SERVES **4**

INGREDIENTS

500 g (1 lb) parsnips, cut into
    small chunks
salt and freshly ground black pepper
1 tablespoon butter
1 tablespoon medium or hot curry powder
4 tablespoons sour cream
2 tablespoons chopped fresh parsley,
    to garnish

METHOD

1 Add parsnips to a saucepan of salted boiling water. Bring back to a boil, then reduce heat and simmer 8–10 minutes, or until tender. Drain thoroughly, then return to the saucepan and mash.
2 Add butter, curry powder and sour cream, season well with pepper, and beat until the parsnips are puréed. Transfer the purée to a heated serving dish. Sprinkle parsley over the top and serve.

NUTRIENTS PER SERVING

678 kJ, 162 kcal, 3 g protein, 10 g fat (6 g saturated fat), 16 g carbohydrate

Right Orange and sesame carrots (top left); Leek and carrot stir-fry (top right);
Curried parsnip purée (bottom)

CHUNKY VEGETABLE FRICASSEE
TIME **30 MINUTES** SERVES **4**

METHOD

1 Preheat oven to 220°C (425°F/Gas 7). Add vegetables to a saucepan of boiling water, bring back to a boil and cook 3 minutes, or until just tender (or use a steamer if you prefer). Drain.

2 Reserve 2 tablespoons of cheddar for topping and stir remainder into crème fraîche or sour cream in a large bowl. Mix in the eggs. Season to taste with plenty of pepper. Mix in the cooked vegetables, then transfer to a warm, greased, shallow ovenproof dish.

3 Mix grissini with the remaining cheddar and hazelnuts, then scatter over the vegetables.

4 Bake on the top shelf of the oven 12–15 minutes, or until golden and slightly puffed. Serve immediately.

NUTRIENTS PER SERVING

1959 kJ, 468 kcal, 19 g protein, 37 g fat (23 g saturated fat), 14 g carbohydrate

VARIATION

Instead of the ready-sliced mixed vegetables, use cooked small new potatoes plus your favourite vegetables, such as baby leeks, zucchini (courgettes) and carrots, as well as green beans or broad (fava) beans.

COOK'S TIP

Baked potatoes would go well with the fricassee. Serve with 8 slices of cooked bacon, for non-vegetarians, if you like.

INGREDIENTS

750 g (1½ lb) fresh or frozen
  ready-sliced mixed vegetables

1 cup (125 g) grated mature cheddar

¾ cup (185 g) crème fraîche or
  sour cream

2 eggs, beaten

freshly ground black pepper

4 grissini (thin breadsticks), crushed

2 tablespoons chopped hazelnuts

SPICY BROCCOLI AND CAULIFLOWER
TIME 25 MINUTES SERVES 4

INGREDIENTS

1½ tablespoons olive oil

5 cloves garlic, thinly sliced

1 green chilli, seeds removed, chopped

500 g (1 lb) broccoli florets

500 g (1 lb) cauliflower florets

salt and freshly ground black pepper

50 g (1¾ oz) grated gruyère

50 g (1¾ oz) grated parmesan

3 tablespoons dry packaged breadcrumbs

2 tablespoons capers, rinsed and
   squeezed dry

1–2 tablespoons green peppercorns
   in brine

METHOD

1 Heat oil in a large frying pan or wok with a lid. Add garlic and chilli, stir in broccoli and cauliflower florets, sprinkle with salt and pepper and add ²/₃ cup (150 ml) boiling water. Cover and cook vegetables over high heat 4–5 minutes, or until tender. Stir halfway through the cooking time.

2 Meanwhile, mix gruyère, parmesan and breadcrumbs together. Preheat grill (broiler) to high.

3 Stir capers and peppercorns into the vegetables. Transfer to a shallow flameproof dish, sprinkle with the cheese and breadcrumb mixture, and cook under the grill until the cheese melts and the topping turns golden. Serve hot.

NUTRIENTS PER SERVING

1197 kJ, 286 kcal, 20 g protein, 16 g fat (6 g saturated fat), 16 g carbohydrate

COOK'S TIP

For a complete vegetarian meal, serve these vegetables with some rice or potatoes.

PUNJABI POTATO PATTIES
TIME **30 MINUTES** SERVES **4**

METHOD

1 Put potatoes in a saucepan and cover with cold salted water. Cover, bring to a boil and cook gently 10 minutes, until tender but not disintegrating.

2 Put grated onion on a double thickness of paper towel. Squeeze out any juice, then put onion in a bowl. Add chilli powder, garam masala, lemon juice and chopped coriander and a pinch of salt.

3 Drain potatoes, add to the onion mixture and mash roughly, mixing together. Shape into eight patties, each about 5 cm (2 inches) wide.

4 Heat oil and butter in a large frying pan until sizzling, then fry patties 2–3 minutes on each side, until crisp and golden.

5 Drain the patties on paper towel and serve immediately, garnished with coriander sprigs.

NUTRIENTS PER SERVING
812 kJ, 194 kcal, 3 g protein, 12 g fat (3 g saturated fat), 21 g carbohydrate

COOK'S TIP
The patties can be made from leftover potatoes. They can also be mixed and shaped in advance, then kept in the refrigerator until needed.

INGREDIENTS

500 g (1 lb) potatoes, diced

salt

1 onion, coarsely grated

¼ teaspoon chilli powder

1 teaspoon garam masala

2 teaspoons lemon juice

3 tablespoons chopped fresh coriander (cilantro) leaves, plus extra sprigs, to garnish

2 tablespoons vegetable oil

3 teaspoons butter

BABY VEGETABLES WITH SOUR CREAM

TIME **20 MINUTES** SERVES **4**

INGREDIENTS

175 g (6 oz) baby carrots, halved
   lengthwise if large
250 g (8 oz) baby zucchini (courgettes),
   halved lengthwise
1 baby cauliflower, quartered
250 g (8 oz) young asparagus spears,
   trimmed
3/4 cup (185 g) sour cream
2 teaspoons wholegrain or dijon mustard
2–3 teaspoons butter, softened
freshly ground black pepper

METHOD

1 Prepare a steamer by half-filling the bottom pan with water and putting it on to boil.
2 Put carrots in the steamer basket, cover and steam 5 minutes. Layer zucchini over the carrots, then cauliflower over the zucchini, and asparagus over the cauliflower. Cover and steam a further 5 minutes.
3 Meanwhile, put sour cream in a saucepan and stir in mustard. Heat mixture very gently until just warmed through.
4 Put the vegetables in a warmed serving bowl and stir in butter and some pepper. Pour over the sour cream mixture, or put in a separate bowl, and serve at once.

NUTRIENTS PER SERVING
712 kJ, 170 kcal, 5 g protein, 14 g fat (8 g saturated fat), 7 g carbohydrate

VARIATION
Replace the asparagus with small green beans. You can also use small florets of cauliflower or broccoli.

COOK'S TIP
You can use a conventional steamer or a Chinese bamboo steamer set over a large wok of boiling water for the vegetables. If you do not have either, you can successfully compromise with a metal sieve and a saucepan. Ensure the sieve sits above the level of the water so that the steam circulates all round.

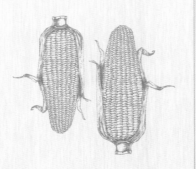

BACON AND BEAN STEW

TIME **30 MINUTES** SERVES **4**

INGREDIENTS

2 tablespoons olive oil

1 red onion, roughly chopped

1 clove garlic, crushed

1 kg (2 lb) butternut pumpkin (squash),
   cut into bite-sized chunks

410 g (15 oz) can chopped tomatoes

1¼ cups (310 ml) vegetable, chicken
   or ham stock

6–8 semi-dried (sun-blushed) tomatoes,
   roughly chopped

4 slices lean rindless bacon (bacon strips)

250 g (8 oz) frozen corn

250 g (8 oz) frozen green beans

salt and freshly ground black pepper

2 tablespoons chopped fresh parsley,
   to garnish

METHOD

1 Heat oil in a large flameproof casserole dish or heavy-based saucepan. Add onion, garlic and pumpkin, and cook gently 5 minutes, or until softened.

2 Stir in canned tomatoes, stock and semi-dried tomatoes. Bring to a boil, then reduce heat. Cover and cook gently 10 minutes.

3 Meanwhile, preheat grill (broiler) to medium–high, then grill bacon until crisp.

4 When tomatoes and pumpkin have been cooking 10 minutes, stir in corn and green beans. Return to a boil, cover and cook gently a further 5 minutes, or until all vegetables are cooked. Add salt and pepper to taste.

5 Lay bacon over the top of the stew in the dish, sprinkle with parsley and serve immediately.

NUTRIENTS PER SERVING

2013 kJ, 481 kcal, 15 g protein, 26 g fat (7 g saturated fat), 50 g carbohydrate

VARIATION

If you have some stew left over, turn it into a delicious soup for another meal by adding extra stock. Purée in a food processor or blender to form a smooth consistency, or process it only partially if you prefer a slightly chunky texture. Serve sprinkled with grated mature cheddar. This soup can be frozen for 1 month. To use, thaw, reheat and simmer 3 minutes.

COOK'S TIP

If you use a jar of semi-dried tomatoes in oil, you could replace the olive oil with the oil from the jar.

POTATO AND CAMEMBERT BAKE

TIME **30 MINUTES** SERVES **4**

INGREDIENTS

750 g (1$^1/_2$ lb) small new potatoes, unpeeled

4 slices lean rindless bacon (bacon strips)

4 spring onions (scallions), sliced

$^1/_2$ round of camembert, reblochon de Savoie or raclette cheese (about 250 g/8 oz)

freshly ground black pepper

100 ml (3$^1/_2$ fl oz) cream

METHOD

1 Preheat oven to 230°C (450°F/ Gas 8). Cook the potatoes in a large saucepan of boiling water 12–15 minutes, or until tender. Drain thoroughly and tip into a greased shallow ovenproof dish.

2 Meanwhile, cut bacon into thin strips using kitchen scissors. Put in a cold non-stick frying pan and cook over high heat 1 minute, or until crisp. Remove from pan and mix with spring onions.

3 Cut the semicircle of cheese in half horizontally to make two semicircles (if using raclette, first remove the hard rind). Score rind in a criss-cross pattern to help the cheese melt.

4 Scatter bacon and spring onions over potatoes. Season with plenty of pepper, then pour over cream. Set cheese on top, rind side up, and bake 7–10 minutes, or until cheese is melting and bubbling. Serve piping hot.

NUTRIENTS PER SERVING

1982 kJ, 473 kcal, 26 g protein, 30 g fat (18 g saturated fat), 26 g carbohydrate

VARIATION

Replace the potatoes with 750 g (1$^1/_2$ lb) cooked beetroot (without vinegar), peeled and thickly sliced. Arrange in a greased roasting pan (baking dish), scatter with diced ham or bacon, add the cream and top with 250 g (8 oz) blue brie, cut into slices. Bake as for the basic recipe.

CABBAGE WITH CREAM AND BLUE CHEESE

TIME **20 MINUTES** SERVES **4**

INGREDIENTS

1 tablespoon olive oil

1 large onion, finely chopped

1 small savoy cabbage (about 500 g/1 lb),
    outer leaves discarded, finely shredded

3/4 cup (180 ml) cream

125 g (4 oz) stilton or other blue
    cheese, cubed

freshly ground black pepper

METHOD

1 Heat oil in a large saucepan. Add
   onion and cook gently, 5 minutes,
   or until softened.

2 Stir in cabbage, then cover and
   cook over medium heat, shaking
   frequently, 6–8 minutes. (You do
   not need to add salt as the cheese
   will make it salty enough.)

3 Remove pan from heat. Stir in
   cream, stilton or other blue cheese
   and a generous grinding of black
   pepper, then return to the heat.
   Stir until cheese has melted, but
   do not allow to boil. (The melted
   cheese will thicken the cream.)
   Serve immediately.

NUTRIENTS PER SERVING

1189 kJ, 294 kcal, 10 g protein, 25 g fat
(13 g saturated fat), 10 g carbohydrate

STIR-FRIED CABBAGE AND CASHEW NUTS

TIME **20 MINUTES** SERVES **4**

INGREDIENTS

2 tablespoons sesame oil

1/3 cup unsalted cashew nuts

2 cloves garlic, chopped

2 cm (3/4 inch) piece fresh ginger,
    grated

2 celery stalks, sliced

4 spring onions (scallions), sliced

350 g (12 oz) white cabbage,
    shredded

350 g (12 oz) green cabbage,
    shredded

light soy sauce, to serve

METHOD

1 Heat sesame oil in a large frying pan and fry cashew nuts 30 seconds,
   until just beginning to turn brown.

2 Add garlic, ginger, celery and spring onions and cook 30 seconds, being
   careful not to burn the garlic.

3 Add shredded white and green cabbage and stir-fry 3–5 minutes, until
   just softened but not wilted.

4 Serve sprinkled with soy sauce.

NUTRIENTS PER SERVING

762 kJ, 182 kcal, 7 g protein, 13 g fat (2 g saturated fat), 10 g carbohydrate

COOK'S TIP

This vegetable dish can accompany plainly grilled pork chops or steaks;
it also teams well as part of an Asian meal.

Right Cabbage with cream and blue cheese (top); Stir-fried cabbage and cashew nuts (bottom)

LEMON ZUCCHINI
TIME **15 MINUTES** SERVES **4**

INGREDIENTS
1 tablespoon olive oil

500 g (1 lb) small zucchini (courgettes),
   thinly sliced on the diagonal

finely grated zest of 1 lemon

sea salt and freshly ground black pepper

METHOD
1 Heat oil in a large frying pan. Add zucchini and fry, stirring frequently, 5 minutes, or until tender.
2 Sprinkle over lemon zest and season well with sea salt and pepper. Serve immediately.

NUTRIENTS PER SERVING
234 kJ, 56 kcal, 2 g protein, 4 g fat (1 g saturated fat), 2 g carbohydrate

COOK'S TIP
This lightly flavoured vegetable is a delicious accompaniment to many main course dishes, especially chicken. Try it also with plainly grilled fish.

EGGPLANT WITH TAHINI DRESSING
TIME **25 MINUTES** SERVES **4**

METHOD

1 Prepare a steamer by half-filling the bottom pan with water and putting it on to boil.

2 Halve eggplant lengthwise if large, then cut crosswise into slices about 5 mm (¼ inch) thick. Put in the steamer basket, then cover and cook 6–8 minutes, or until softened.

3 Meanwhile, make the tahini dressing. Put garlic, lemon juice, tahini and oil in a small bowl. Season to taste with salt and pepper, then mix.

4 Transfer cooked eggplant to a colander and press down firmly with a spoon to remove as much liquid as possible — do not worry if the slices break up. Then transfer eggplant to a serving bowl and stir in spring onions and sun-dried tomatoes.

5 Pour over the tahini dressing and toss well. Scatter over dill, then leave to cool 5 minutes to let the flavour develop before serving.

INGREDIENTS

400 g (14 oz) eggplant (aubergine)

4 spring onions (scallions), thinly sliced

¼ cup (35 g) sun-dried tomatoes in oil, drained and chopped

1 tablespoon chopped fresh dill, to garnish

TAHINI DRESSING

1 clove garlic, crushed

2 tablespoons lemon juice

3 teaspoons tahini

2 tablespoons olive oil

salt and freshly ground black pepper

NUTRIENTS PER SERVING

1005 kJ, 240 kcal, 2 g protein, 13 g fat (2 g saturated fat), 4 g carbohydrate

COOK'S TIP

This dish goes particularly well with simple grilled lamb or chicken. It can also be served as a starter, accompanied by some hot crusty bread.

ZUCCHINI, APPLES AND PERSILLADE
TIME **25 MINUTES** SERVES **4**

METHOD

1 Heat 2 tablespoons oil in a frying pan. Add onion and cook over low heat 7–8 minutes, until softened.

2 Stir in apple and tomato and cook over low heat 5 minutes, stirring occasionally.

3 Meanwhile, sprinkle zucchini with salt and toss well. Heat remaining oil in a separate frying pan and fry zucchini over medium heat until it releases its moisture. Increase heat and continue cooking until the liquid has evaporated, shaking the pan to make sure the zucchini does not burn.

4 Reduce heat, then stir in apple, tomato and onion mixture and simmer 5–6 minutes.

5 Meanwhile, mix parsley and garlic together in a small bowl to make the persillade.

6 Stir the persillade into the vegetables. Simmer 3–4 minutes until the garlic is cooked, then season with pepper and more salt if necessary. Serve the vegetables immediately.

INGREDIENTS

3 tablespoons olive oil

1 red or white onion, thinly sliced

1 apple, quartered, cored and diced

1 tomato, diced

500 g (1 lb) small zucchini (courgettes), cut into thin strips

salt and freshly ground black pepper

4 tablespoons chopped fresh parsley

1 clove garlic, crushed

NUTRIENTS PER SERVING
628 kJ, 150 kcal, 3 g protein, 12 g fat (2 g saturated fat), 9 g carbohydrate

VARIATION
This vegetable dish can be turned into a light main course by stirring $1^2/_3$ cups (250 g) chopped cooked ham into the mixture and heating gently until just warmed through, before adding the persillade.

COOK'S TIP
Persillade is a combination of chopped parsley and garlic. It gives a wonderful flavour to this dish, which goes well with pan-fried or grilled (broiled) pork chops or steaks.

POTATO AND GREEN BEAN CURRY
TIME **30 MINUTES** SERVES **4**

INGREDIENTS
3 teaspoons butter

2 tablespoons vegetable oil

2 small green chillies

1/2 teaspoon cumin seeds

1/2 teaspoon ground turmeric

1/4 teaspoon garam masala

1 clove garlic, crushed

500 g (1 lb) small new potatoes,
   thickly sliced

salt

250 g (8 oz) small green beans,
   topped and tailed, cut into 2.5 cm
   (1 inch) pieces

METHOD
1 Heat butter and oil in a wide shallow saucepan or frying pan over high heat. When it begins to sizzle, stir in whole green chillies, cumin seeds, turmeric, garam masala and garlic. Fry, stirring, 30 seconds.
2 Add potatoes and season with salt. Stir until coated with the spice mixture.
3 Stir in beans, then reduce heat to medium. Cover and cook 15 minutes, stirring occasionally. The curry is ready to serve as soon as the potatoes are cooked through.

NUTRIENTS PER SERVING
825 kJ, 197 kcal, 3 g protein, 12 g fat (3 g saturated fat), 20 g carbohydrate

COOK'S TIP
These lightly spiced vegetables go beautifully with a chicken curry and dal. Serve some steamed or boiled basmati rice on the side.

DAL
TIME 25 MINUTES SERVES 4

METHOD

1 Pick over lentils and remove any small pieces of grit, then put in a sieve and rinse under cold running water.
2 Put lentils in a saucepan and cover with 5 cups (1.25 litres) boiling water. Add turmeric, chilli powder, ginger and garlic. Cover and bring to a boil. Reduce heat and simmer gently 10 minutes, or until lentils are soft and almost all the liquid has been absorbed.
3 Stir in garam masala, then add some salt to taste and cook the dal a further 5 minutes, leaving the pan uncovered if the mixture is still soupy.
4 Meanwhile, heat butter and cumin in a small frying pan. Add onion and fry gently until soft.
5 Transfer the dal to a warmed serving dish, stir in the fried onion and serve hot.

INGREDIENTS

1 1/3 cups (340 g) red lentils
1 teaspoon ground turmeric
1/2 teaspoon chilli powder
1 cm (1/2 inch) piece fresh ginger, peeled and thinly sliced
2 cloves garlic, crushed
1/2 teaspoon garam masala
salt
1 tablespoon butter
1 pinch ground cumin
1 small onion, chopped

NUTRIENTS PER SERVING
1394 kJ, 333 kcal, 21 g protein, 6 g fat (4 g saturated fat), 51 g carbohydrate

COOK'S TIP
Many pulses require soaking in cold water followed by a long period of boiling, but red lentils are ideal for meals in a hurry. They do not need soaking and cook very quickly.

GRILLED WITLOF AND BEETROOT
TIME 25 MINUTES SERVES 4

INGREDIENTS

4 large witlof (Belgian endive)
   (about 150–175 g/5–6 oz each),
   trimmed and halved lengthwise

3 tablespoons olive oil

250 g (8 oz) cooked baby beetroot (beets)

fresh chives (optional), to garnish

DRESSING

1 tablespoon orange juice

2 tablespoons mayonnaise

2 teaspoons wholegrain mustard

METHOD

1 Preheat grill (broiler) to medium–high. Put witlof halves on the grill rack, cut side down, brush with half the oil and grill 5 minutes, about 10 cm (4 inches) from the heat. Turn witlof, brush with the remaining oil, and grill a further 3 minutes, or until the edges begin to char.

2 Meanwhile, make the dressing. Stir orange juice into mayonnaise in a small bowl, then stir in mustard.

3 Remove witlof from the grill. Arrange, cut side up, in a serving bowl with beetroot alongside. Drizzle dressing over the top and garnish with chives, if using.

NUTRIENTS PER SERVING

933 kJ, 223 kcal, 2 g protein, 21 g fat (3 g saturated fat), 10 g carbohydrate

COOK'S TIP

You could brush the witlof with oil and cook on a medium–hot chargrill pan, turning once, until cooked and starting to brown.

ITALIAN BAKED WITLOF
TIME **30 MINUTES** SERVES **4**

METHOD

1 Preheat oven to 200°C (400°F/Gas 6). If using the slice of bread, process in a food processor or blender to make breadcrumbs. Mix breadcrumbs and parmesan together in a small bowl, then set aside.

2 Put lemon juice in a large shallow ovenproof dish. Stir in 1 tablespoon oil. Arrange witlof quarters, cut side up, in the dish. Drizzle over remaining oil, then season with pepper.

3 Scatter sun-dried tomatoes over the witlof, followed by olives, then sprinkle parmesan and breadcrumb mixture over the top. Bake 15 minutes, until the topping is golden brown.

NUTRIENTS PER SERVING
791 kJ, 189 kcal, 5 g protein, 16 g fat (4 g saturated fat), 7 g carbohydrate

INGREDIENTS

1 slice day-old bread, crusts removed, or
  ¼ cup (20 g) fresh white breadcrumbs

⅓ cup (40 g) grated parmesan

1 tablespoon lemon juice

2 tablespoons olive oil

4 large witlof (Belgian endive)
  (about 150–175 g/5–6 oz each),
  trimmed and quartered lengthwise

freshly ground black pepper

6 sun-dried tomatoes in oil,
  drained and chopped

16 pitted black olives

PARSNIP AND APPLE CREAM

TIME **20 MINUTES** SERVES **4**

INGREDIENTS

2 tablespoons olive oil

500 g (1 lb) parsnips, coarsely grated

1 tart green apple, such as granny smith, peeled and coarsely grated

salt and freshly ground black pepper

1 teaspoon lemon juice

3 sprigs fresh thyme, leaves stripped

1/3 cup (80 ml) thick (heavy/double) cream

METHOD

1 Heat oil in a large shallow saucepan. Add parsnips and cook over medium heat, stirring occasionally, 5 minutes.

2 Stir in apple and season with salt and pepper. Add lemon juice and thyme and cook a further 3–5 minutes, or until parsnips are tender.

3 Pour cream into the pan and stir until heated through. Spoon into a warmed serving dish and serve.

NUTRIENTS PER SERVING

887 kJ, 212 kcal, 2 g protein, 18 g fat (7 g saturated fat), 17 g carbohydrate

COOK'S TIP

If the parsnips are old, cut them into quarters and discard the woody cores before grating.

CAULIFLOWER AND BROCCOLI WITH GORGONZOLA

TIME **30 MINUTES** SERVES **4**

METHOD

1 Drop the cauliflower and broccoli into a saucepan of boiling water and cook 3–4 minutes, or until just tender. Drain, reserving cooking water, and set aside.

2 Melt butter in the same saucepan. Stir in onion and cook gently 5 minutes without browning. Stir in flour with a wooden spoon, then gradually add milk and ⅔ cup (150 ml) reserved cooking water. Bring to a boil, stirring constantly, then simmer 2 minutes to make a smooth light sauce. Remove from heat.

3 Preheat grill (broiler) to high. Stir two-thirds of the cheese into the sauce. Season with salt and pepper, then gently fold in cooked cauliflower and broccoli. Spoon into a warmed shallow ovenproof dish.

4 Arrange tomato slices on top, then scatter with remaining cheese. Grill 4–5 minutes, or until browned and bubbling.

INGREDIENTS

300 g (10 oz) cauliflower,
    divided into florets
250 g (8 oz) broccoli, divided into florets
40 g (1½ oz) butter
1 small onion, finely chopped
2½ tablespoons plain (all-purpose) flour
1¼ cups (310 ml) low-fat milk
150 g (5 oz) gorgonzola cheese,
    roughly chopped or crumbled
salt and freshly ground black pepper
2 tomatoes, sliced

NUTRIENTS PER SERVING

1298 kJ, 310 kcal, 17 g protein, 20 g fat (13 g saturated fat), 14 g carbohydrate

VARIATION

TRADITIONAL CAULIFLOWER CHEESE Use 600 g (1 lb 5 oz) cauliflower florets (or the florets from 1 very large cauliflower) and omit the broccoli. Increase the cooking water added in step 2 to 200 ml (7 fl oz). Instead of the gorgonzola cheese, use grated extra-mature cheddar. Add 1 teaspoon dijon mustard or 1 good pinch English mustard powder with the salt and pepper in step 3.

BAKED POTATO WITH SPRING ONION AND CHEESE TOPPING

TIME **20 MINUTES** SERVES **4**

INGREDIENTS

8 potatoes (about 175 g/6 oz each), scrubbed
30 g (1 oz) butter
5 spring onions (scallions), sliced diagonally
1 clove garlic, halved
salt and freshly ground black pepper
150 g (5 oz) smoked cheese, diced

METHOD

1 Prick potatoes in several places with a sharp knife to stop them from exploding. Microwave four potatoes on High 5 minutes. Turn and cook a further 2–3 minutes, or until tender. Repeat with the remaining potatoes. Leave cooked potatoes to rest about 2–3 minutes before handling.

2 Meanwhile, heat butter in a small frying pan and gently cook spring onions and garlic 3–4 minutes, or until tender. Discard garlic, then season spring onions with salt and pepper.

3 Cut a deep cross in the top of each baked potato and squeeze it open, holding with a clean tea towel (dish towel). Spoon half the spring onions and all the garlicky butter from the pan between them, then scatter cheese and remaining spring onions on top.

NUTRIENTS PER SERVING

1723 kJ, 412 kcal, 17 g protein, 16 g fat (10 g saturated fat), 49 g carbohydrate

BAKED POTATO WITH BLACK OLIVE, BEAN AND JALAPEÑO CHILLI TOPPING

TIME **20 MINUTES** SERVES **4**

INGREDIENTS

8 potatoes (about 175 g/6 oz each), scrubbed
400 g (14 oz) can red kidney beans, rinsed and drained
2 tablespoons extra virgin olive oil
1/2 teaspoon ground cumin
salt and freshly ground black pepper
1/3 cup (50 g) pitted black olives in oil, drained and roughly chopped
1 jalapeño chilli in brine, rinsed and drained, finely chopped
2/3 cup (160 g) sour cream or crème fraîche (optional)

METHOD

1 Prick potatoes in several places with a sharp knife to stop them from exploding. Microwave four potatoes on High 5 minutes. Turn and cook a further 2–3 minutes, or until tender. Repeat with remaining potatoes. Leave cooked potatoes to rest about 2–3 minutes before handling.

2 Meanwhile, tip half the kidney beans into a bowl, add oil, cumin and salt and black pepper to taste. Roughly crush with a fork. Stir in the remaining beans, olives and jalapeño chilli.

3 Cut a deep cross in the top of each baked potato and squeeze it open, holding with a clean tea towel (dish towel). Divide bean mixture among them, then spoon sour cream or crème fraîche over the top, if you like.

NUTRIENTS PER SERVING

2099 kJ, 501 kcal, 14 g protein, 22 g fat (8 g saturated fat), 60 g carbohydrate

COOK'S TIP

If you have time, you can bake the potatoes in the oven. Preheat the oven to 220°C (425°F/Gas 7). Scrub potatoes with a brush and prick all over with a fork. Push a metal skewer through each potato (this conducts heat to the middle of the potato so that it cooks faster). Bake 50–60 minutes; the skewers will come out easily when the potatoes are cooked. Cut a deep cross in the top of each potato and squeeze it open, holding it with a clean tea towel.

BAKED POTATO WITH GOAT'S CHEESE AND PESTO TOPPING

TIME **20 MINUTES** SERVES 4

INGREDIENTS

8 potatoes (about 175 g/6 oz each),
    scrubbed
30 g (1 oz) pine nuts
150 g (5 oz) soft goat's cheese
4 tablespoons pesto

METHOD

1 Prick potatoes in several places
   with a sharp knife to stop them
   from exploding. Microwave four
   potatoes on High 5 minutes. Turn
   and cook a further 2–3 minutes,
   or until tender. Repeat with the
   remaining potatoes. Leave cooked
   potatoes to rest about 2–3 minutes
   before handling.

2 Meanwhile, toast pine nuts in a
   small non-stick frying pan over
   medium–high heat 2–3 minutes,
   stirring constantly, until golden.
   Tip onto a plate and set aside.

3 Cut a deep cross in the top of
   each baked potato and squeeze it
   open, holding it with a clean tea
   towel (dish towel). Divide goat's
   cheese among them. Drizzle each
   potato with $1/2$ tablespoon pesto,
   then scatter over pine nuts.

NUTRIENTS PER SERVING
1629 kJ, 387 kcal, 17 g protein, 14 g fat
(6 g saturated fat), 48 g carbohydrate

COOK'S TIP

For a single 175 g (6 oz) potato,
microwave on High $3^{1}/_{2}$ minutes.
Turn and cook a further 1–2 minutes,
or until tender.

CHINESE-STYLE VEGETABLE STIR-FRY
TIME **30 MINUTES** SERVES **4**

INGREDIENTS

2 tablespoons hoisin sauce

2 tablespoons soy sauce

1 tablespoon sherry vinegar

1 tablespoon honey

2 tablespoons peanut (groundnut) oil

300 g (10 oz) firm tofu, drained and diced

3 tablespoons vegetable stock or water

2.5 cm (1 inch) piece fresh ginger,
  grated

1 red capsicum (bell pepper), seeds
  removed, halved and sliced

100 g (3½ oz) small button mushrooms,
  halved

400 g (14 oz) Chinese greens,
  such as bok choy, shredded

cooked rice or noodles, to serve

1 tablespoon toasted sesame seeds,
  to garnish

METHOD

1 Preheat oven to 220°C (425°F/Gas 7). Combine hoisin sauce, soy sauce, vinegar, honey and 2 teaspoons oil in a small jug. Put tofu in a small shallow non-stick roasting pan (baking dish), pour over two-thirds of the marinade and toss to coat tofu well. Bake 8 minutes, then turn tofu over and cook a further 6–8 minutes.

2 Meanwhile, blend remaining marinade with stock or water and set aside. Heat a wok or large heavy-based non-stick frying pan over high heat. Heat remaining oil in the wok. Add ginger and cook 20 seconds, stirring. Add capsicum and mushrooms and stir-fry 2 minutes. Add Chinese greens and the reserved stock mixture. Stir-fry a further 2–3 minutes, or until the greens are wilted.

3 Stir in tofu and cook to heat through, then pile high onto bowls of rice or noodles. Sprinkle with toasted sesame seeds and serve.

NUTRIENTS PER SERVING

1083 kJ, 259 kcal, 13 g protein, 17 g fat (3 g saturated fat), 15 g carbohydrate

VARIATION

Replace half the Chinese greens with 125 g (4 oz) green beans, cut into bite-sized pieces. Add with the capsicum and mushrooms in step 2.

COOK'S TIP

Tofu is a great source of protein and calcium and is also low in fat, but it has little flavour of its own, so it is best when marinated or brushed with a basting sauce during cooking.

SAUTÉED BRUSSELS SPROUTS
TIME **25 MINUTES** SERVES **4**

METHOD

1 Heat vegetable oil in a frying pan. Add bacon and fry 2–3 minutes, until golden brown.

2 Add orange zest, butter, mustard and brussels sprouts to the pan. Cook over medium–high heat 5 minutes, stirring, until the sprouts are crisp.

3 Stir in water chestnuts and cook 3–4 minutes, until the sprouts are golden and the chestnuts are heated through. Add salt and pepper to taste and serve immediately.

NUTRIENTS PER SERVING
938 kJ, 224 kcal, 8 g protein, 20 g fat (9 g saturated fat), 7 g carbohydrate

INGREDIENTS

3 teaspoons vegetable oil

100 g (3¹/₂ oz) thick rindless bacon (bacon strips), diced

grated zest of 1 orange

3 tablespoons butter

2 teaspoons wholegrain mustard

500 g (1 lb) small brussels sprouts, trimmed and halved

125 g (4 oz) drained canned water chestnuts, chopped

salt and freshly ground black pepper

STUFFED TOMATOES
TIME **30 MINUTES** SERVES **4**

INGREDIENTS

4 large tomatoes (about 200 g/7 oz each)

salt and freshly ground black pepper

2 tablespoons butter

1 onion, finely chopped

1 cup (125 g) rolled (porridge) oats

2 tablespoons chopped fresh parsley,
   to garnish

METHOD

1 Preheat oven to 200°C (400°F/
Gas 6). Halve the tomatoes
horizontally and make deep criss-
cross slashes over the cut sides.
Place, cut side up, on a baking
tray (sheet). Season with salt and
pepper and bake 20 minutes.

2 Meanwhile, melt butter in a frying
pan, then add onion and cook
over low heat, stirring frequently,
15 minutes.

3 When onion is soft and begins
to brown, stir in oats and add salt
and pepper. Increase the heat to
medium and cook 5–10 minutes,
stirring, until the oats are toasted.

4 Pile the onion and oat mixture
into the tomatoes and sprinkle
with parsley.

NUTRIENTS PER SERVING

1155 kJ, 276 kcal, 6 g protein, 14 g fat
(6 g saturated fat), 33 g carbohydrate

Left Celery and apple (top right); Glazed onions
(middle); Stuffed tomatoes (bottom)

GLAZED ONIONS

TIME **30 MINUTES** SERVES 4

INGREDIENTS

500 g (1 lb) pickling onions
1/2–1 teaspoon dried rosemary
1 tablespoon butter
2 teaspoons dijon mustard

2 teaspoons treacle or 3 teaspoons
  honey
3 teaspoons soy sauce
1 sprig fresh rosemary, to garnish

METHOD

1 Cook onions in a large saucepan of boiling water over medium heat
  5 minutes. Drain into a colander and put under cold running water.
  When they are cool enough to handle, drain well and peel.
2 Crush dried rosemary as finely as possible, using a pestle and mortar or
  the end of a rolling pin.
3 Melt butter gently in a large frying pan over medium heat. Add crushed
  dried rosemary, mustard, treacle or honey and soy sauce and mix well
  to form an emulsion.
4 Stir in onions and cook gently, stirring and basting with the glaze,
  10–15 minutes, until the glaze has thickened and the onions are tender.
  Watch continuously to make sure the glaze does not burn.
5 Tip the onions into a warmed serving bowl and garnish with fresh
  rosemary.

NUTRIENTS PER SERVING
462 kJ, 110 kcal, 2 g protein, 6 g fat (3 g saturated fat), 14 g carbohydrate

COOK'S TIP

These onions make a sweet and spicy accompaniment to roasted or grilled
(broiled) red meats.

CELERY AND APPLE

TIME **30 MINUTES** SERVES 4

INGREDIENTS

1 bunch young celery
2 tablespoons olive oil
12 fresh sage leaves, snipped
1 large clove garlic, crushed
3 sweet red apples, quartered, cored
  and finely sliced
1 bay leaf
1/2–3/4 cup (125–180 ml) dry white wine
1 tablespoon capers, rinsed and
  squeezed dry (optional)
salt and freshly ground black pepper

METHOD

1 Trim off the leaves and the root
  end of celery. Thinly slice stalks
  on the diagonal, cutting across the
  entire head, then set aside.
2 Generously cover the bottom of a
  large frying pan with oil, and heat
  until it shows a haze. Add sage
  and garlic and allow to sizzle a
  few seconds, then quickly add
  celery, apples and bay leaf and
  cook over high heat 1 minute,
  stirring well.
3 Pour in enough white wine to
  cover the mixture. Cook over
  high heat, stirring occasionally,
  2–3 minutes, until the celery is
  cooked but still crunchy. If the
  mixture dries out before the celery
  is cooked, add a little more wine.
4 When the celery is done to your
  liking, stir in capers, if using, and
  heat through quickly. Season with
  salt and pepper to taste, discard
  the bay leaf and serve.

NUTRIENTS PER SERVING
590 kJ, 141 kcal, 1 g protein, 7 g fat
(1 g saturated fat), 13 g carbohydrate

SPICY POTATOES WITH SPINACH AND LENTILS
TIME **30 MINUTES** SERVES **4**

INGREDIENTS

750 g (1¹/₂ lb) boiling (waxy) potatoes,
   peeled and diced

salt

250 g (8 oz) baby spinach leaves

3¹/₂ tablespoons peanut (groundnut) oil

1 onion, finely sliced

5 cm (2 inch) piece fresh ginger,
   peeled and finely chopped

1 small green chilli, halved, seeds
   removed, finely sliced

1 teaspoon ground coriander

¹/₄ teaspoon ground turmeric

2 x 400 g (14 oz) cans green lentils,
   rinsed and drained

2 cloves garlic, cut into fine shreds

¹/₂ teaspoon cumin seeds

2 tablespoons chopped fresh coriander
   (cilantro) leaves

METHOD

1 Cook potatoes in a large saucepan of salted boiling water 8–10 minutes, or until just tender. Drain.

2 While potatoes are boiling, cook spinach in a steamer basket over the potatoes 3–4 minutes, or put in a covered microwave-safe container and microwave on Medium 2–3 minutes, or until wilted. Tip into a colander and drain, squeezing out the excess liquid by pressing with the back of a spoon.

3 Heat 3 tablespoons oil in a large frying pan or wok. Add onion and cook over medium heat 2 minutes, then stir in ginger, chilli, ground coriander and turmeric. Cook a few seconds, stirring, then add potato and stir-fry 3–4 minutes. Separate spinach leaves with two forks, then stir into potato mixture with lentils. Add salt to taste. Heat gently until very hot.

4 Meanwhile, heat remaining oil in a small frying pan over low–medium heat. Add garlic and cumin seeds and cook 1–2 minutes, or until lightly browned. Stir in 1 tablespoon fresh coriander. Tip the potato, spinach and lentil mixture into a warmed serving dish and sprinkle with the garlic and cumin mixture and the remaining fresh coriander.

NUTRIENTS PER SERVING
1490 kJ, 356 kcal, 13 g protein, 17 g fat (3 g saturated fat), 38 g carbohydrate

EGGPLANT PARMIGIANA
TIME **25 MINUTES** SERVES **4**

METHOD

1 Heat 1 tablespoon oil in a large frying pan, or two smaller pans, and fry eggplant in batches over medium–high heat, turning once, until golden brown. Add more oil to the pan as necessary.

2 Preheat grill (broiler) to high. When the eggplant is ready, arrange in layers in a wide shallow flameproof dish. Alternate with layers of mozzarella, tomato passata, basil or oregano, salt and pepper.

3 Scatter parmesan over the top layer, then grill 4–5 minutes, or until golden brown and bubbling.

NUTRIENTS PER SERVING

1352 kJ, 323 kcal, 12 g protein, 28 g fat (8 g saturated fat), 5 g carbohydrate

COOK'S TIP

Serve with grilled meats, such as lamb cutlets or steak, or with simply cooked white fish or alongside a vegetarian risotto.

INGREDIENTS

4–8 tablespoons olive oil

500 g (1 lb) eggplant (aubergine), thinly sliced crosswise

125 g (4 oz) mozzarella, thinly sliced

200 g (7 oz) tomato passata (puréed tomatoes)

2 tablespoons chopped fresh basil or oregano

salt and freshly ground black pepper

1/3 cup (35 g) grated parmesan

THAI VEGETABLES WITH COCONUT AND CASHEW NUTS

TIME **30 MINUTES** SERVES **4**

INGREDIENTS

$^1/_2$ cup (80 g) unsalted cashew nuts

2 tablespoons vegetable oil

1 onion, finely chopped

100 g (3$^1/_2$ oz) button mushrooms, sliced

125 g (4 oz) snow peas (mangetout),
   topped and tailed

125 g (4 oz) baby corn, halved lengthwise

1 green capsicum (bell pepper),
   seeds removed, sliced

3 teaspoons green curry paste,
   or to taste

400 ml (14 fl oz) can light coconut milk

100 g (3$^1/_2$ oz) bean sprouts, trimmed

METHOD

1 Heat a large frying pan over medium heat 1 minute. Add cashew nuts and toast, stirring frequently, 2–3 minutes, or until the nuts are golden brown. Tip onto a plate and set aside.

2 Add oil to the pan and cook onion 2 minutes, or until beginning to soften. Increase heat a little and add mushrooms. Continue cooking 2–3 minutes, stirring constantly, then add snow peas, baby corn and capsicum. Cook a further 2 minutes, stirring.

3 Stir in curry paste and 3 tablespoons coconut milk and cook, stirring, 1 minute. Stir in remaining coconut milk and bean sprouts. Simmer, stirring occasionally, 2 minutes, or until all vegetables are tender and the coconut milk has reduced a little. Stir in half the cashew nuts, then pile the mixture onto warmed plates, scatter over the remaining cashew nuts and serve.

NUTRIENTS PER SERVING

1568 kJ, 375 kcal, 9 g protein, 31 g fat (14 g saturated fat), 15 g carbohydrate

VARIATION

Instead of the green curry paste, use 1 tablespoon red curry paste, which is much spicier and richer and goes well with more robust vegetables. Dice 350 g (12 oz) orange sweet potatoes (kumara) or parsnips and stir-fry with the mushrooms in step 2. Replace the snow peas, corn and capsicum with 150 g (5 oz) broccoli florets and cook 2 minutes in step 2. After adding the coconut milk in step 3, simmer 4 minutes before adding the bean sprouts.

CHAPTER 10

Desserts

PASSIONFRUIT AND HONEY ZABAGLIONE

TIME 15 MINUTES SERVES 4

INGREDIENTS

4 ripe passionfruit
3 tablespoons honey
4 large egg yolks
2 teaspoons lemon juice

METHOD

1 Cut each passionfruit in half and scoop out all the pulp and seeds into a sieve set over a large heatproof bowl. Sieve the fruit thoroughly, then trickle 1 tablespoon boiling water over the seed mixture in the sieve and scrape again with a spoon. Scrape any small amount of pulp from underneath the sieve into the bowl too. Discard the seeds.

2 Half-fill a saucepan with boiling water and heat to simmering point. Put honey, egg yolks and lemon juice in the bowl with the passionfruit juice and whisk well with an electric mixer. Set the bowl over the pan of hot water and continue to whisk until the mixture is pale and thick and holds a trail when the beaters are lifted out. This takes about 10 minutes and the mixture will look like a slightly soft, whisked sponge mixture when ready. Keep the water barely simmering — do not let it bubble too fiercely or the eggs will cook and separate.

3 Remove the bowl from the pan and continue to whisk 1 minute. Spoon, ladle or pour the mixture into four small glasses. Serve immediately.

NUTRIENTS PER SERVING

544 kJ, 130 kcal, 3 g protein, 5 g fat (1 g saturated fat), 19 g carbohydrate

VARIATION

Instead of the passionfruit, honey and lemon juice, use $^2/_3$ cup (150 ml) pure fruit juice such as mango, or fruit purée such as raspberry, and 3 tablespoons caster (superfine) sugar.

POACHED FRUIT WITH CHOCOLATE SAUCE
TIME **20 MINUTES** SERVES **4**

INGREDIENTS

90 g (3 oz) white chocolate melts
    (buttons) or solid white chocolate,
    broken into pieces

1 cup (250 ml) apple juice

1 teaspoon caster (superfine) sugar

1 tablespoon brandy

4 large figs, quartered, or 8 small figs,
    halved

2 large peaches or nectarines, stoned
    and each cut into 8 slices

2/3 cup (160 g) crème fraîche or
    light sour cream

grated zest of 1/2 orange and
    2 tablespoons orange juice

METHOD

1 Put some hot water into a small saucepan. Set a heatproof bowl over it, making sure the base is clear of the water. Put chocolate in the bowl; bring the water to simmering point. Stir chocolate a little as it melts, but do not allow the water to boil as the chocolate will overheat. When it has melted, set the bowl aside, leaving the pan of hot water for later.

2 Pour apple juice into a shallow saucepan or a frying pan with a lid. Add caster sugar and brandy, bring to a boil, then reduce heat.

3 Add figs and peaches or nectarines to the pan, cover and poach gently 4 minutes. If the skins come off the peaches or nectarines, remove them.

4 While the fruit is poaching, stir crème fraîche into the melted chocolate gradually with a balloon whisk, then beat until smooth. Put the bowl back on the pan of hot water while you finish off the fruit.

5 Transfer the poached fruit to a serving dish with a slotted spoon. Boil the juice 5 minutes, or until reduced to a slightly heavy syrup, then pour over the fruit.

6 Stir orange zest into the chocolate mixture, then add juice. Stir the sauce and serve with the fruit.

NUTRIENTS PER SERVING
1544 kJ, 369 kcal, 5 g protein, 22 g fat (14 g saturated fat), 36 g carbohydrate

COOK'S TIP
Melt the white chocolate quickly in a microwave oven. Put the chocolate pieces into a bowl, heat on Low 30 seconds, then stir. If lumps remain, cook in 10 second bursts then stir, until smooth.

HOT BANANA AND WALNUT SUNDAE
TIME 15 MINUTES SERVES 4

METHOD

1 Melt butter in a large frying pan, preferably non-stick. Add walnuts and fry over medium heat 1 minute. Add brown sugar and cook, stirring, 2 minutes.

2 Push walnuts to one side of the pan to make room for bananas, then add them and cook 30 seconds. Turn bananas and cook a further 30 seconds, shaking the pan gently.

3 Carefully tip orange zest and juice into the pan (the mixture will bubble up and create a lot of steam, so take care). Shake the pan and stir walnuts and sugar, then bring to a boil. Allow to boil vigorously 1 minute, moving the bananas a little with a spoon and fork so that the syrup boils evenly. The syrup should be reduced and just beginning to sizzle in places. It should form a sticky coating on and around the walnuts. Remove pan from heat.

4 Cut bananas in half crosswise and put two halves on each plate. Spoon over the walnut and toffee glaze. Top each with two scoops of ice cream and serve immediately.

INGREDIENTS
40 g (1½ oz) butter
¾ cup (90 g) walnut pieces
3 tablespoons dark brown sugar
4 bananas
grated zest and juice of 1 orange
8 small scoops vanilla ice cream

NUTRIENTS PER SERVING
1953 kJ, 466 kcal, 7 g protein, 31 g fat (10 g saturated fat), 42 g carbohydrate

COOK'S TIP
Any sugar will work well in this recipe. Dark brown or dark muscovado sugars make a dark rich glaze, whereas light brown or light muscovado sugars are not quite as rich. White (granulated) sugar will produce a light fruity glaze.

TROPICAL FRUIT TRIFLE

TIME **10 MINUTES** SERVES **6**

INGREDIENTS

250 g (8 oz) amaretti or other small soft
  almond-flavoured biscuits (cookies)

¾ cup (180 ml) sweet sherry

410 g (15 oz) can fruit salad in syrup

2 cups (500 g) low-fat custard

¾ cup (180 ml) thick (heavy/double)
  cream

METHOD

1 Divide amaretti among six 200 ml (7 fl oz) dessert glasses or trifle dishes. Sprinkle about 1½ tablespoons sherry over the biscuits in each glass.

2 Drain fruit, reserving syrup. Spoon 2 tablespoons syrup into each glass. Reserve four or five pieces of fruit for decoration, then divide remainder among the glasses.

3 Spoon custard over the fruit, then top each serving with a large spoonful of cream. Chop reserved fruit into small pieces and scatter over cream. Chill in the fridge until ready to serve.

NUTRIENTS PER SERVING

1871 kJ, 447 kcal, 8 g protein, 20 g fat (10 g saturated fat), 57 g carbohydrate

VARIATION

MANDARIN AND LEMON MERINGUE TRIFLES Cut 4 slices madeira (pound) cake or other plain cake, then spread with lemon curd and lay in four dishes. Drain a 310 g (10 oz) can mandarin segments and divide among the dishes. Stir 4 tablespoons lemon curd into 2 cups (500 g) low-fat natural (plain) yogurt and spread over the fruit. Top with small meringues.

STRAWBERRY CLOUDS

TIME **20 MINUTES** SERVES **4**

INGREDIENTS

1²/₃ cups (250 g) strawberries, hulled
¼ cup (55 g) caster (superfine)
   sugar, plus 1 tablespoon extra
2 large eggwhites

1 cup (250 g) natural (plain) yogurt,
   chilled
½ teaspoon vanilla extract
almond biscotti or bread, to serve

METHOD

1 Halve two large strawberries and set aside for decoration. Put the remaining strawberries in a bowl. Sprinkle with 1 tablespoon caster sugar and crush with a fork.
2 In a large mixing bowl, whisk eggwhites until they form soft peaks, then gradually add the remaining caster sugar, whisking well after each addition, to make a stiff meringue.
3 Add yogurt and vanilla extract and gently fold into the meringue with a metal spoon.
4 Fold mashed strawberries and their juice into the mixture. Be careful not to mix too vigorously, or the light airy texture will be lost.
5 Spoon the meringue into four 200 ml (7 fl oz) dessert glasses and decorate with the reserved strawberry halves. Serve immediately with almond biscotti or bread, or chill 2–3 hours before serving.

NUTRIENTS PER SERVING

691 kJ, 165 kcal, 6 g protein, 6 g fat (3 g saturated fat), 23 g carbohydrate

MANGO BRÛLÉE

TIME **20 MINUTES** SERVES **4**

INGREDIENTS

2 large mangoes (about 400 g/
   14 oz each)
2 tablespoons rum
½ teaspoon ground cinnamon
1¹/₃ cups (350 g) natural (plain) yogurt
½ cup (95 g) soft brown sugar

METHOD

1 Preheat grill (broiler) to high.
2 Peel mangoes, cut off the two fat cheeks and dice, then cut off and dice the remaining flesh. Half-fill four deep flameproof ramekin or dariole moulds with the fruit.
3 Drizzle rum over the fruit and sprinkle with cinnamon. Spoon in yogurt and smooth it level, then sprinkle evenly with brown sugar.
4 Put ramekins under the grill, about 10 cm (4 inches) from the heat, and cook 4–5 minutes, until the sugar melts and turns golden brown. Serve hot or cold.

NUTRIENTS PER SERVING

1318 kJ, 315 kcal, 7 g protein, 8 g fat (5 g saturated fat), 52 g carbohydrate

RASPBERRY CRUNCH

TIME **10 MINUTES** SERVES **4**

INGREDIENTS

2³/₄ cups (350 g) raspberries,
   plus extra, to garnish
2 tablespoons caster (superfine) sugar
2 cups (500 g) natural (plain) yogurt
1½ cups (200 g) muesli (granola),
   plus extra, to garnish
1 tablespoon honey, plus extra, to garnish

METHOD

1 Put raspberries and caster sugar in a bowl. Mix and put aside.
2 In another bowl, mix yogurt with muesli. Add honey, stirring lightly so that the mixture is streaky.
3 Divide two-thirds of the mixture among four wide 250 ml (8 fl oz) dessert glasses. Top with the sweetened raspberries, then add remaining mixture. Drizzle a little extra honey over the top, sprinkle with extra muesli and decorate with extra raspberries.
4 If it is served immediately, this dessert has a crunchy texture; if you prefer a softer creamier texture, chill 3–4 hours before serving.

NUTRIENTS PER SERVING

1331 kJ, 318 kcal, 14 g protein, 7 g fat (3 g saturated fat), 52 g carbohydrate

Left Raspberry crunch (top left); Strawberry clouds (middle); Mango brûlée (bottom)

SESAME FRUIT FRITTERS

TIME **10 MINUTES** SERVES **4**

INGREDIENTS

225 g (8 oz) can pineapple slices
   in light syrup (4 slices)
2 tablespoons caster (superfine)
   sugar

2 tablespoons toasted sesame seeds
75 g (2¹/₂ oz) self-raising flour
vegetable oil, for shallow-frying

METHOD

1 Drain pineapple in a sieve over a measuring jug, reserving syrup. Put a double thickness of paper towel on a plate and lay pineapple slices on it. Cover with more paper towel to dry the fruit.
2 Mix caster sugar and sesame seeds. Spread on a plate ready for coating the cooked fritters.
3 Make up the syrup from the pineapple to 100 ml (3¹/₂ fl oz) with a little cold water, if necessary. Put flour in a bowl and make a well in the centre, then pour in about half the syrup. Gradually mix the flour and syrup to make a smooth, very thick batter. Add a little more syrup, if necessary, beating to remove any lumps. Then mix in the remaining liquid to make a smooth thick batter.
4 Pour oil into a frying pan to a depth of about 1 cm (¹/₂ inch). Heat oil, checking the temperature by dropping a teaspoonful of batter into the oil; the batter should immediately sizzle, rise and set, then brown in about 30 seconds. Using a draining spoon, remove and discard the piece of batter, or it will burn.
5 Put a pineapple slice in the batter and use a spoon and fork to turn it so that it is well coated all over. Carefully drop pineapple into the hot oil. Cook 30–60 seconds, turning the fritter when the bottom edge is bubbly and crisp. If the batter is well browned on the second side but the first side is a little pale, turn the fritter a second time. Cook the fritters in pairs (or four at once if your pan is large enough).
6 Remove fritters using a slotted spoon, allow to drain a little, then put onto the sesame sugar. Turn quickly to coat both sides. Serve at once.

NUTRIENTS PER SERVING

1016 kJ, 243 kcal, 4 g protein, 13 g fat (1 g saturated fat), 29 g carbohydrate

VARIATION

Use fresh fruit and apple or orange juice for the batter. To prepare fresh fruit: halve 4 bananas crosswise; peel, quarter and core 3 apples; halve and stone 2 nectarines (add them to the pan rounded side down first).

FRESH FIG PUFFS

TIME **20 MINUTES** SERVES **6**

INGREDIENTS

¹/₂ x 375 g (13 oz) ready-rolled puff
   pastry, thawed if frozen
2 tablespoons rosewater
¹/₃ cup (35 g) chopped pistachios, plus
   extra pistachios, to decorate (optional)
2 tablespoons sugar
6 ripe figs
¹/₂ cup (125 g) Greek-style yogurt
3 tablespoons honey

METHOD

1 Preheat oven to 240°C (460°F/ Gas 8). If time allows, leave pastry, still wrapped, at room temperature 20 minutes. Unroll pastry and cut in half. Keep one half for another recipe. Cut the other half into six equal-sized pieces and put on a baking tray (sheet).
2 Sprinkle pastry with rosewater and top with pistachios and sugar. Bake 10–12 minutes, or until well puffed and browned.
3 Meanwhile, trim stalks off figs and cut each fig lengthwise into six wedges. Put a cooked pastry piece onto each plate and top with three fig wedges. Add a dollop of yogurt at the side and arrange another three fig wedges around, and partly in, the yogurt. Drizzle honey over all fig wedges, sprinkle with extra pistachios, if you like, and serve at once.

NUTRIENTS PER SERVING

1179 kJ, 282 kcal, 5 g protein, 13 g fat (6 g saturated fat), 39 g carbohydrate

Right Fresh fig puffs

MAGIC TIRAMISU
TIME 20 MINUTES SERVES 8

INGREDIENTS

4 teaspoons instant coffee granules

100 ml (3½ fl oz) boiling water

4 tablespoons grappa, Tia Maria, Kahlúa, Marsala or sherry

200 g (7 oz) sponge finger biscuits (savoiardi)

2 tablespoons caster (superfine) sugar

⅔ cup (160 g) natural (plain) yogurt

500 g (1 lb) mascarpone

60–75 g (2–2½ oz) plain chocolate, grated, or crumbled flaked chocolate bars

METHOD

1 Dissolve coffee in boiling water. Add 100 ml (3½ fl oz) cold water and grappa, Tia Maria, Kahlúa, Marsala or sherry.

2 Arrange half the sponge fingers in a 20 cm (8 inch) square shallow dish or cake tin. Spoon half the coffee mixture evenly over biscuits.

3 Beat caster sugar and yogurt into mascarpone, then spread half of this mixture over the biscuits. Cover mascarpone with remaining biscuits, then sprinkle with remaining coffee mixture. Spread remaining mascarpone over the second layer of biscuits. Spoon grated chocolate evenly over the top, then press down. Chill 10 minutes in the freezer, if possible.

NUTRIENTS PER SERVING

2049 kJ, 489 kcal, 5 g protein, 40 g fat (26 g saturated fat), 27 g carbohydrate

VARIATION

Instead of mascarpone, use low-fat cream cheese.

COOK'S TIP

This dessert freezes well. Cover the dish with plastic wrap and freeze until hard, then place in a freezer bag. Eat within 3 months. You can also open-freeze individual portions, then pack in plastic wrap and a freezer bag.

HOT CHOCOLATE SOUFFLÉS WITH RUM

TIME **30 MINUTES** SERVES **4**

INGREDIENTS

3 teaspoons unsalted butter, softened

⅓ cup (80 g) caster (superfine) sugar

1 cup (250 ml) milk

100 g (3½ oz) dark (semi-sweet) chocolate, broken into pieces

2 tablespoons cornflour (cornstarch)

2 tablespoons thick (heavy/double) cream

2 tablespoons rum

5 eggs, separated

1 tablespoon icing (confectioner's) sugar, for dusting

METHOD

1 Carefully butter the insides and rims of four 200 ml (7 fl oz) soufflé dishes, then coat evenly with 1 tablespoon caster sugar.

2 Pour milk into a small saucepan and put over medium heat. Stir in chocolate. As soon as the milk reaches scalding point, remove from heat, cover and leave to stand 2–3 minutes, or until the chocolate has melted.

3 Put 2 tablespoons caster sugar and the cornflour in a large saucepan. Over low heat, gradually whisk in the chocolate milk to form a smooth paste. Increase the heat, beating continuously, until the sauce boils and becomes stiff.

4 Remove from heat and beat in cream, rum and 3 egg yolks. (The other 2 yolks are not needed and can be kept for another purpose.) Scrape the mixture from the side of the pan with a spatula and cover with the lid to prevent a skin forming, then set aside.

5 Preheat oven to 230°C (450°F/ Gas 8). Put a baking tray (sheet) with a raised edge in the oven to heat.

6 Put eggwhites in a large clean bowl and whisk with an electric mixer until they form soft peaks. Add remaining caster sugar and whisk again until the whites are stiff and shiny.

7 Fold a large spoonful of eggwhites into the chocolate sauce, then gently fold in all the remaining eggwhites. Spoon the mixture into the soufflé dishes and put on the baking tray.

8 Bake 8–10 minutes, or until well risen and lightly set, with soft centres. Remove from oven, dust with icing sugar and serve immediately.

NUTRIENTS PER SERVING

1988 kJ, 475 kcal, 9 g protein, 24 g fat (13 g saturated fat), 53 g carbohydrate

WARM PEAR AND MANGO COMPOTE

TIME 15 MINUTES SERVES 4

INGREDIENTS

410 g (15 oz) can mango slices
   in syrup
410 g (15 oz) pear halves in syrup
coarsely grated or finely pared zest
   and juice of 1 lime

9 green cardamom pods,
   lightly crushed
2 tablespoons chopped pistachios

METHOD

1 Drain mango slices and pear halves in a sieve over a saucepan. Shake sieve well, then set it aside over a bowl. If the mango slices are large, cut into thinner slices. Cut the pear halves in half.
2 Add lime zest and juice and cardamom pods to the saucepan with the drained syrup. Bring to a boil and boil vigorously 5–6 minutes, or until reduced by about half and aromatic with cardamom.
3 Meanwhile, arrange mango slices and pear quarters in four shallow dessert dishes. Spoon over the reduced syrup (strain to remove the cardamom pods, if you like), sprinkle with pistachios and serve.

NUTRIENTS PER SERVING

753 kJ, 180 kcal, 3 g protein, 4 g fat (0 g saturated fat), 34 g carbohydrate

VARIATION

Replace the lime and cardamom with the grated zest of 1 orange (without the juice) and 1 cinnamon stick.

COOK'S TIP

This compote is a terrific make-ahead dessert. Arrange the fruit in a large bowl, pour over syrup (with the cardamom pods) and chill for several hours or overnight.

Left Warm pear and mango compote

SPICED FRUIT AND NUT FREEZER CAKE

TIME 30 MINUTES SERVES 6

INGREDIENTS

100 g (3½ oz) dark (semi-sweet)
   chocolate, broken into pieces
100 g (3½ oz) toasted flaked almonds
   or chopped hazelnuts
200 g (7 oz) dried fruit medley (fruit mix)
100 g (3½ oz) dried figs, chopped
1 cup (100 g) almond meal
   (ground almonds)
2 teaspoons ground coriander
2 teaspoons ground cinnamon
2 tablespoons honey
icing (confectioner's) sugar, for dusting

METHOD

1 Set a heatproof bowl over a saucepan of simmering water. Add chocolate and melt, stirring occasionally. Put a 23 cm (9 inch) round cake tin in the freezer.
2 Put almonds or hazelnuts, dried fruit medley, figs, almond meal, coriander and cinnamon in a large bowl and mix. Pour chocolate over, add honey and mix well until thoroughly combined.
3 Lay a large piece of plastic wrap in cake tin and press in to line the tin, leaving excess overhanging the rim. Spoon mixture into tin and press it down a little with the back of a spoon, then cover with overhanging plastic wrap. Press out evenly with the heel of your hand until fairly smooth on top.
4 Chill in the freezer 10 minutes, or until mixture has firmed a little. Uncover the cake and turn out on a platter. Remove plastic wrap, dust generously with icing sugar and cut into 12 wedges to serve.

NUTRIENTS PER SERVING

1836 kJ, 439 kcal, 10 g protein, 23 g fat (4 g saturated fat), 52 g carbohydrate

RHUBARB AND STRAWBERRY COMPOTE
TIME **20 MINUTES** SERVES **4**

INGREDIENTS
650 g (1 lb 7 oz) rhubarb, trimmed
    and cut into bite-sized pieces
1/4 cup (55 g) caster (superfine) sugar
100 ml (3 1/2 fl oz) orange juice
1 2/3 cups (250 g) strawberries, hulled,
    halved or quartered if large
3/4 cup (180 ml) thick (heavy/double)
    cream

METHOD
1 Put rhubarb in a large saucepan with caster sugar and orange juice.
   Cover, bring to a boil, then reduce heat and simmer gently, uncovered,
   5–6 minutes, stirring occasionally.
2 Add strawberries and simmer gently 4–5 minutes, or until slightly softened.
   They should maintain their shape and still have some bite.
3 Taste and add a little more sugar if necessary. Transfer the compote to a
   serving dish and serve while still warm with cream.

NUTRIENTS PER SERVING
1327 kJ, 317 kcal, 3 g protein, 24 g fat (15 g saturated fat), 24 g carbohydrate

VARIATION
If you prefer, you can refrigerate the compote and serve it chilled,
accompanied by ice cream or a little pouring custard.

COOK'S TIP
When buying rhubarb, choose a fresh-looking bunch with firm red stalks; any
stalks with green tinges will be too sour. When cooking rhubarb, always use a
stainless steel or enamel saucepan.

FLAMBÉED PINEAPPLE AND BANANAS
TIME **30 MINUTES** SERVES **4**

METHOD

1 Peel pineapple, cut in half lengthwise and remove and discard the centre core. Cut each half crosswise into eight slices, reserving any juice.

2 Melt butter and brown sugar in a large stainless steel or enamel frying pan over medium heat.

3 Add pineapple and cook over medium–high heat 1–2 minutes. Add bananas and cook a further 2–3 minutes, until heated through.

4 Pour rum into the pan, heat a few seconds, then stand well back and set alight with a match. Allow the rum to burn, shaking the pan very gently, until the flames die down. Pour any reserved pineapple juice into the pan and continue to heat a further 1 minute.

5 Transfer the flambéed fruit to individual dishes and serve with whipped cream or ice cream.

INGREDIENTS

1 pineapple (about 800 g/1¾ lb)

1 tablespoon unsalted butter

⅓ cup (60 g) soft brown sugar

3 large firm ripe bananas, halved crosswise then lengthwise

3 tablespoons rum

whipped cream or vanilla ice cream, to serve

NUTRIENTS PER SERVING

1170 kJ, 280 kcal, 3 g protein, 4 g fat (3 g saturated fat), 50 g carbohydrate

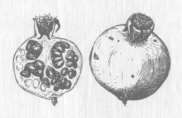

SPICED ORANGE WITH POMEGRANATE

TIME **10 MINUTES** SERVES **4**

INGREDIENTS

6 oranges, preferably seedless
freshly grated nutmeg
1 pomegranate
4 tablespoons grenadine cordial
4 fresh mint leaves, finely chopped (optional)

METHOD

1　Slice tops and bottoms off oranges. Using a sharp knife, cut off the peel and pith in one go, in wide strips down the side of the oranges. Slice oranges and arrange on four plates. Sprinkle with a little nutmeg.
2　Cut pomegranate into quarters. Remove seeds with your fingers over a bowl, discarding the membranes, peel and pith. Sprinkle seeds over the oranges. Drizzle 1 tablespoon grenadine cordial over the top of each serving. Sprinkle over mint, if you like, and serve.

NUTRIENTS PER SERVING
483 kJ, 115 kcal, 3 g protein, 0 g fat, 26 g carbohydrate

PEPPERED STRAWBERRIES AND BLUEBERRIES

TIME **5 MINUTES** SERVES **4**

INGREDIENTS

2²/₃ cups (400 g) strawberries, hulled
1²/₃ cups (250 g) blueberries
freshly ground black pepper
4 lemon wedges
caster (superfine) sugar, to serve

METHOD

1　Halve any large strawberries and arrange on four plates. Divide blueberries among the plates.
2　Grind some pepper over the fruit. Put a lemon wedge on each plate and serve with caster sugar and extra pepper.

NUTRIENTS PER SERVING
202 kJ, 48 kcal, 2 g protein, 0 g fat, 9 g carbohydrate

GUAVAS AND PLUMS WITH VANILLA SYRUP AND PISTACHIOS

TIME **10 MINUTES** SERVES **4**

INGREDIENTS

¹/₂ x 825 g (28 oz) can plums,
　drained and syrup reserved,
　fruit stoned if necessary
410 g (15 oz) can guava halves, drained
　and syrup reserved
1 teaspoon vanilla extract
50 g (1³/₄ oz) chopped pistachios

METHOD

1　Pour syrup from canned plums and guavas into a saucepan. Boil vigorously 4–5 minutes, or until reduced by about half.
2　Meanwhile, divide plums and guavas among four bowls.
3　Stir vanilla extract into the syrup, then spoon over the fruit. Sprinkle with pistachios and serve.

NUTRIENTS PER SERVING
897 kJ, 212 kcal, 3 g protein, 7 g fat (1 g saturated fat), 35 g carbohydrate

Right Peppered strawberries and blueberries

BAKED APPLE WITH BRIOCHE

TIME **30 MINUTES** SERVES **4**

METHOD

1 Preheat oven to 220°C (425°F/Gas 7) and heat an ovenproof dish.
2 Core apples, then cut in half lengthwise. Score the skins deeply several times with a sharp knife. Place apples, cut side down, in the heated dish, and dot the tops with butter.
3 Put orange zest and juice in a bowl. Stir in cinnamon and 1 tablespoon brown sugar. Pour the mixture over the apples.
4 Cover the dish with a lid or foil and bake 10–15 minutes, or until the apples are tender.
5 Meanwhile, cut brioche rolls in half crosswise, then cut off the top and bottom crusts.
6 Toast brioche slices about 1 minute each side, or until just lightly browned. Put two slices on each warmed individual serving plate and carefully place an apple half on top of each slice.
7 Spoon the cooking juices over the apples, sprinkle with the remaining brown sugar, and serve immediately with yogurt or whipped cream.

INGREDIENTS

4 sweet apples (about 150 g/5 oz each)
3 teaspoons butter
finely grated zest and juice
of 1 large orange
$1/2$ teaspoon ground cinnamon
2 tablespoons soft brown sugar
4 brioche rolls or other sweet yeast bread
$2/3$ cup (160 g) natural (plain) yogurt or
$2/3$ cup (150 ml) thick (heavy/double) cream, whipped

NUTRIENTS PER SERVING

1800 kJ, 430 kcal, 6 g protein, 23 g fat (11 g saturated fat), 52 g carbohydrate

MAPLE CREAMS

TIME **20 MINUTES** SERVES **4**

INGREDIENTS

6 tablespoons maple syrup   grated zest of 1 lemon

¼ cup (30 g) cornflour (cornstarch)   ⅔ cup (150 ml) thick

2 eggs, separated   (double/heavy) cream

METHOD

1 Preheat oven to 230°C (450°F/Gas 8). Set four 150 ml (5 fl oz) ramekin moulds on a baking tray (sheet) and put 1 tablespoon maple syrup in each mould. (There is no need to grease the moulds.)
2 Put cornflour in a bowl and add egg yolks, remaining maple syrup and lemon zest. Stir yolks and syrup into the cornflour until smooth, then gradually and gently fold in cream until thoroughly combined.
3 Put eggwhites in a separate bowl that is thoroughly clean and dry. Whisk with an electric mixer until stiff but not dry. Using a large metal spoon, fold eggwhites into cream mixture until well combined. Take care not to stir out the air.
4 Divide mixture among the ramekin moulds and bake about 10 minutes, or until mixture is puffed up, browned and just set. Set the hot moulds on small plates or saucers and serve immediately.

NUTRIENTS PER SERVING

1228 kJ, 293 kcal, 4 g protein, 16 g fat (10 g saturated fat), 34 g carbohydrate

VARIATION

Instead of maple syrup, put a generous 1 tablespoon fruit jam, such as black cherry or plum, into each ramekin mould. Add 1 tablespoon caster (superfine) sugar and 1 teaspoon pure vanilla extract to the cream mixture.

COOK'S TIP

Use the thickest type of cream, which may be called double thick cream or thick double cream and has a fat content of about 50 per cent. It holds its shape when spooned or dolloped. It can't be whipped, or even stirred vigorously, or it will become grainy and stiff.

CHEESECAKE PAIRS

TIME **20 MINUTES** SERVES **4**

INGREDIENTS

8 good-quality round butter shortbread biscuits (cookies)

grated zest and juice of 1 small lemon

3 tablespoons lemon curd

1 cup (250 g) low-fat cream cheese, chilled

4 teaspoons icing (confectioner's) sugar

8 strawberries, hulled and sliced

METHOD

1 Put shortbread biscuits on a board. Brush tops generously with some of the lemon juice. Spread with half the lemon curd, keeping it in the centre of the biscuits.
2 Stir the remaining lemon juice, the lemon zest and icing sugar into the cream cheese. Divide the cheese mixture among biscuits, piling it on with a teaspoon.
3 Spread the remaining lemon curd over the tops — there should be just enough to cover the centres thinly. Top each cheesecake with a sliced strawberry and serve.

NUTRIENTS PER SERVING

1272 kJ, 304 kcal, 10 g protein, 12 g fat (7 g saturated fat), 39 g carbohydrate

VARIATION

Replace the cream cheese with mascarpone, and try different biscuit bases, such as chocolate chip or crunchy oat biscuits.

Right Cheesecake pairs

APRICOT AND SOUR CREAM CLAFOUTIS
TIME **30 MINUTES** SERVES 4

INGREDIENTS
butter, for greasing

825 g (28 oz) can apricot halves
  in natural juice

crème fraîche or thick (double/heavy)
  cream, to serve

BATTER
²/₃ cup (160 g) sour cream

1 cup (150 g) plain (all-purpose) flour

2 large eggs

¹/₂ cup (95 g) soft brown sugar

3–4 drops vanilla extract

TOPPING
3 teaspoons butter

2 tablespoons soft brown sugar

METHOD

1 Preheat oven to 200°C (400°F/Gas 6) and grease a shallow ovenproof dish, 25–30 cm (10–12 inches) in diameter, with butter.

2 Drain canned apricots, reserving 100 ml (3¹/₂ fl oz) juice, and arrange them, cut side down, in the bottom of the dish.

3 To make the batter, stir sour cream into the reserved apricot juice. Place flour in a separate bowl and make a well in the centre. Add eggs, brown sugar and vanilla extract and whisk into the flour to make a smooth paste. Gradually whisk in the apricot juice and sour cream mixture.

4 Pour the batter over the apricots in the dish and bake 15 minutes.

5 Meanwhile, make the topping by mixing the butter and brown sugar together with a fork in a small bowl.

6 Remove the clafoutis from the oven and dot evenly with the topping. Bake a further 5 minutes, or until the batter is golden and puffed up.

7 Serve hot with crème fraîche or thick cream.

NUTRIENTS PER SERVING
2151 kJ, 513 kcal, 11 g protein, 18 g fat (11 g saturated fat), 78 g carbohydrate

VARIATION
Canned peaches, plums or cherries can be used instead of the apricots.

CINNAMON APPLE FRITTERS
TIME **15 MINUTES** SERVES **2**

METHOD

1 Half-fill a large wok or deep-fryer with oil and put on to heat.

2 Break egg into a bowl, add salt and whisk until frothy. Quickly whisk in mineral water, then flour — you are not aiming for a smooth batter.

3 Mix caster sugar and cinnamon together on a saucer and set aside. Peel, core and slice apples crosswise into rings about 5 mm ($^{1}/_{4}$ inch) thick.

4 When the oil has reached a temperature of 190°C (375°F), and a few drops of the batter sizzle as soon as they are dropped in, use a fork to dip each apple slice into the batter, then drop it into the oil. Deep-fry the coated apple slices in two or three batches, 1–2 minutes each batch, or until puffed and golden, turning carefully with a slotted spoon halfway through the cooking time.

5 Drain on paper towel, sprinkle with the cinnamon sugar and serve.

INGREDIENTS

vegetable oil, for deep-frying

1 egg

1 pinch salt

4 tablespoons sparkling mineral water

3 tablespoons plain (all-purpose) flour

2 tablespoons caster (superfine) sugar

1 teaspoon ground cinnamon

2 crisp sweet apples

NUTRIENTS PER SERVING

1729 kJ, 413 kcal, 5 g protein, 25 g fat (4 g saturated fat), 45 g carbohydrate

CINNAMON RICE WITH HOT PLUMS

TIME **10 MINUTES** SERVES **4**

INGREDIENTS

2 x 425 g (15 oz) cans creamed rice
425 g (15 oz) can plums in syrup
1/4 teaspoon ground cinnamon,
    plus extra, to serve (optional)

METHOD

1 Heat creamed rice in a saucepan.
2 Put plums and their syrup in a
   separate saucepan, add cinnamon
   and heat.
3 Divide rice among four bowls
   and top with the plums. Sprinkle
   with extra cinnamon, if you like.
   Serve immediately.

NUTRIENTS PER SERVING

1232 kJ, 294 kcal, 6 g protein, 8 g fat
(5 g saturated fat), 50 g carbohydrate

QUICK RICE PUDDING

TIME **30 MINUTES** SERVES **4**

INGREDIENTS

1/2 cup (95 g) short-grain rice
3 1/4 cups (800 ml) low-fat milk
4–5 teaspoons sugar

METHOD

1 Put rice in a heavy-based saucepan, preferably non-stick, and add
   2 cups (500 ml) milk. Bring to a boil, stirring occasionally. Reduce heat
   to the lowest setting and stir until milk sinks back, then cover and cook
   gently 15 minutes, giving the pan a shake occasionally.
2 Stir in remaining milk and return to a boil, stirring all the time. Boil,
   stirring constantly, 7 minutes.
3 Remove from heat and stir 1 minute, then stir in sugar and serve.

NUTRIENTS PER SERVING

845 kJ, 202 kcal, 11 g protein, 1 g fat (0 g saturated fat), 38 g carbohydrate

COOK'S TIP

This is a creamy dessert, with soft grains of rice, like a traditional baked
rice pudding. Rice pudding is best cooked slowly, so the rice will absorb
all the milk and soften. Traditional rice pudding is normally baked at a
low temperature in the oven; when making it on the stovetop, as above,
keep the heat very low and stir the mixture frequently.

INDIAN-STYLE RICE PUDDING

TIME **5 MINUTES** SERVES **4**

INGREDIENTS

2 x 425 g (15 oz) cans creamed rice
1/4 teaspoon ground cardamom
4 tablespoons chopped pistachios or
   toasted flaked almonds
1–3 teaspoons rosewater, to taste,
3 tablespoons sultanas (golden raisins)
   or chopped dried apricots

METHOD

1 Empty creamed rice into a serving bowl.
2 Sprinkle with cardamom, then scatter over pistachios or almonds,
   rosewater to taste and sultanas or dried apricots. Serve cold.

NUTRIENTS PER SERVING

1427 kJ, 341 kcal, 8 g protein, 15 g fat (6 g saturated fat), 44 g carbohydrate

Left Cinnamon rice with hot plums

PEACH AND RASPBERRY CROUSTADES

TIME **30 MINUTES** SERVES **4**

INGREDIENTS

2 tablespoons good-quality raspberry jam

3 tablespoons unsalted butter

150 g (5 oz) filo pastry

4 firm ripe peaches, halved,
    stoned and sliced

1 cup (125 g) raspberries

2 tablespoons icing (confectioner's) sugar,
    for dusting

cream or crème fraîche, to serve

METHOD

1 Preheat oven to 200°C (400°F/Gas 6).

2 Melt jam in a saucepan over low heat, then sieve into a small heatproof container. Put some hot water in a small bowl and stand the container of jam in the water to keep warm; set aside.

3 Gently melt butter in a small saucepan. Cut filo pastry into 12 rectangles, each about 25 x 12 cm (10 x 4 inches).

4 Lightly brush a baking tray (sheet) with some of the melted butter. Put 1 filo strip on the tray and brush with butter. Place another filo strip on top and brush with butter, then repeat with a third strip to make the base of one croustade. Repeat this to make three more bases.

5 Place your hands at the short end of each rectangle of pastry and gently push the ends together, pleating and scrunching, until you have made a corrugated croustade about 15 x 12 cm (6 x 4 inches).

6 Carefully arrange peach slices inside the folds on top of the pastry. Scatter raspberries over the top. Brush with the jam and bake 15–20 minutes, or until the pastry is crisp and golden.

7 Transfer the croustades to individual dishes and dust with icing sugar. Serve hot or warm, accompanied by cream or crème fraîche.

NUTRIENTS PER SERVING

1365 kJ, 326 kcal, 6 g protein, 13 g fat (8 g saturated fat), 46 g carbohydrate

FRESH BERRIES WITH SABAYON SAUCE

TIME **20 MINUTES** SERVES **4**

INGREDIENTS

1²/₃ cups (250 g) strawberries, hulled,
    or 1 cup (150 g) blueberries

1 cup (125 g) raspberries

3 egg yolks

¹/₃ cup (80 g) caster (superfine) sugar

¹/₂ cup (125 ml) brandy, rum
    or orange-flavoured liqueur

METHOD

1 Divide strawberries or blueberries and raspberries among four dessert glasses.

2 Beat egg yolks and caster sugar in the top half of a double boiler, over gently simmering water, 2–3 minutes, until creamy.

3 Beating the egg yolk mixture continuously, add brandy, rum or liqueur in a thin steady stream. Continue to beat over gently simmering water 10–12 minutes, until the sauce is thick. Remove from heat.

4 Spoon the sauce over the berries and serve immediately.

NUTRIENTS PER SERVING

1043 kJ, 249 kcal, 3 g protein, 4 g fat (1 g saturated fat), 36 g carbohydrate

COOK'S TIP

If you do not have a double boiler, the sabayon can be made in a heatproof bowl placed over a saucepan of gently simmering water. Make sure no water splashes into the bowl.

OAT-TOPPED NECTARINES
TIME **20 MINUTES** SERVES **4**

METHOD

1 Mix oats and brown or muscovado sugar in a bowl. Melt butter in a large frying pan over medium heat. Reduce heat slightly, add the oat mixture and stir well, then spread out evenly in the pan and cook gently 3 minutes.

2 Meanwhile, put nectarines, white sugar and 1 tablespoon water in a large saucepan. Cook over medium–high heat, stirring continuously, 2–3 minutes, or until the fruit is juicy, sticky and slightly softened around the edges. It should be sizzling in the pan. Remove pan from heat, cover and set aside.

3 Increase heat under the oats to medium and cook, stirring continuously, 5–6 minutes, or until lightly browned. Reduce heat if the oats begin to brown quickly, or increase it if they are still pale and floury.

4 Turn the nectarines into a serving dish, spreading them out evenly. Top with the oats, spreading them out and pressing them down gently with the back of a spoon. Serve at once, or leave to stand for a while, if you prefer.

INGREDIENTS

100 g (3½ oz) rolled (porridge) oats

2 tablespoons soft brown sugar or light muscovado sugar

50 g (1¾ oz) unsalted butter

4 firm ripe nectarines, halved, stoned and sliced

2 tablespoons white (granulated) sugar

NUTRIENTS PER SERVING
1248 kJ, 298 kcal, 4 g protein, 13 g fat (8 g saturated fat), 41 g carbohydrate

VARIATION
Instead of nectarines, use 500 g (1 lb) apples, peeled, cored and thinly sliced, cooked with 4 tablespoons sugar and 1 tablespoon water 5 minutes, or until tender.

FRUITY YOGURT WITH CHOCOLATE CHIP AND NUT CRUNCH

TIME **5 MINUTES** SERVES **4**

METHOD

1 Put biscuits in a plastic bag and crush coarsely using a rolling pin. Tip into a bowl and mix with toasted hazelnuts and honey.
2 Mix bananas and apricots into yogurt and divide among four bowls. Top with biscuit, nut and honey mixture and serve.

NUTRIENTS PER SERVING

1306 kJ, 312 kcal, 13 g protein, 11 g fat (2 g saturated fat), 40 g carbohydrate

VARIATION

PRALINE Try this topping with the natural yogurt. Brush a baking tray (sheet) or a piece of foil with oil. Put 4 tablespoons caster (superfine) sugar and $1/2$ cup (45 g) flaked almonds in a frying pan, then heat until the sugar melts. Continue to heat over high heat $1^1/2$–2 minutes, watching carefully, as the sugar caramelises quickly once it melts. Have a spatula ready and scrape all the almonds and caramel out onto the tray or foil as soon as they are brown — they will quickly burn if left in the pan. Leave to set, then break up and sprinkle over the yogurt (or over ice cream, rice pudding or semolina).

INGREDIENTS

4 chocolate chip biscuits (cookies)
$1/3$ cup (45 g) toasted hazelnuts, chopped
2 tablespoons honey
2 small ripe bananas, sliced
4 dried apricots, chopped
$2^1/2$ cups (625 g) low-fat natural (plain) yogurt

FRUITY SEMOLINA
TIME **15 MINUTES** SERVES **4**

INGREDIENTS
50 g (1¾ oz) semolina
2 cups (500 ml) milk
2 tablespoons sugar
grated zest of 1 orange
1 cup (150 g) blueberries

METHOD
1 Put semolina in a large saucepan and gradually stir in milk. Bring to a boil over medium heat, stirring continuously, about 5 minutes. Reduce heat and simmer, stirring, a further 5 minutes, or until semolina is thick, creamy and smooth.
2 Remove pan from heat and stir in sugar and orange zest. Add blueberries and fold through gently, then divide semolina among four bowls and serve immediately.

NUTRIENTS PER SERVING
733 kJ, 175 kcal, 6 g protein, 5 g fat (3 g saturated fat), 27 g carbohydrate

VARIATION
To make chocolate semolina, replace blueberries with 100 g (3½ oz) chopped dark (semi-sweet) or milk chocolate or chocolate melts (buttons) and 1 teaspoon vanilla extract. It's good hot or chilled (with cream).

COOK'S TIP
For the best result, take time to bring the semolina and milk to a boil slowly. It should take about 5 minutes. Stir continuously during this process to avoid any lumps forming.

HOT RASPBERRY SOUFFLÉS
TIME **25 MINUTES** SERVES **4**

METHOD

1 Preheat oven to 190°C (375°F/Gas 5). Grease the insides of four 200 ml (7 fl oz) soufflé dishes or ramekin moulds with butter, then coat evenly with 1 tablespoon caster sugar, tipping out any surplus. Place the dishes on a baking tray (sheet).

2 Purée raspberries by pressing the fruit through a nylon or stainless steel sieve with the back of a spoon. Stir kirsch, if using, into the purée.

3 Put eggwhites in a bowl that is thoroughly clean and dry, and whisk with an electric mixer until stiff but not dry. Gradually whisk in the remaining caster sugar and beat until the mixture is shiny.

4 Carefully fold the raspberry purée into the eggwhites, then spoon the mixture into the dishes, making a swirl on top of each. Cook in the centre of the oven 12–14 minutes, or until well risen and lightly set.

5 Remove the soufflés from the oven, dust evenly with icing sugar and serve with cream.

INGREDIENTS

2 teaspoons unsalted butter, softened

$^{1}/_{2}$ cup (115 g) caster (superfine) sugar

2 cups (250 g) raspberries

1 tablespoon kirsch (optional)

4 large eggwhites

1 tablespoon icing (confectioner's) sugar, for dusting

thick (heavy/double) cream, to serve

NUTRIENTS PER SERVING

743 kJ, 177 kcal, 4 g protein, 2 g fat (1 g saturated fat), 36 g carbohydrate

SPICED PEACHES WITH MASCARPONE

TIME **25 MINUTES** SERVES **4**

INGREDIENTS

¹/₂ cup (115 g) caster (superfine) sugar,
   plus 1 tablespoon extra

2 star anise

1 cm (¹/₂ inch) piece cinnamon stick

1 red chilli

2 thin slices fresh ginger

juice and 3 strips zest of 1 lemon

1 kg (2 lb) firm ripe peaches,
   halved and stoned

200 g (7 oz) mascarpone

METHOD

1 Put ²/₃ cup (150 ml) water in a large saucepan and add ¹/₂ cup (115 g) caster sugar, star anise, cinnamon stick, chilli and ginger. Stir over medium heat until the sugar has dissolved, then bring to a boil. Add lemon zest, then reduce heat and simmer while preparing the peaches.

2 Put peaches in a bowl, cover with boiling water and leave 1–2 minutes, then drain and peel. Cut each half into 4–6 slices.

3 Add peaches to the syrup and bring to a boil. Reduce heat and simmer 4–5 minutes, or until just softened.

4 Stir the remaining caster sugar into the mascarpone in a small bowl.

5 Remove the peaches from the heat and add lemon juice. Transfer the peaches to four individual dishes, pour over a little syrup and divide the mascarpone among the dishes. Serve warm or cold.

NUTRIENTS PER SERVING

1687 kJ, 403 kcal, 4 g protein, 21 g fat (13 g saturated fat), 54 g carbohydrate

COOK'S TIP

When served warm, this dessert makes an excellent accompaniment to pancakes, waffles or ice cream.

BAKED ALMOND PEARS
TIME **30 MINUTES** SERVES **4**

METHOD

1 Preheat oven to 200°C (400°F/Gas 6). Grease a shallow round ovenproof dish with half the butter and sprinkle caster sugar evenly over to coat.

2 Peel, halve and core pears, then cut lengthwise into slices about 1 cm (½ inch) thick. Arrange in a single overlapping layer in the dish.

3 Mix wine or orange juice with apricot jam or honey and pour the mixture over the pears.

4 Sprinkle crushed amaretti or finely chopped almonds over the pears. Dot the remaining butter evenly over the top. Bake 15–20 minutes, until the pears have softened and the topping is lightly browned. Serve with cream or yogurt.

INGREDIENTS

2½ tablespoons butter, softened

1 tablespoon caster (superfine) sugar

4 large firm ripe pears

3 tablespoons white wine or orange juice

¼ cup (80 g) apricot jam or
    2 tablespoons honey

6 amaretti, coarsely crushed, or
    ½ cup (60 g) blanched almonds,
    finely chopped

cream or natural (plain) yogurt, to serve

NUTRIENTS PER SERVING

1407 kJ, 336 kcal, 2 g protein, 13 g fat (7 g saturated fat), 55 g carbohydrate

VARIATION

For a faster dessert, substitute 8 canned pear halves, sliced or left whole, for the fresh pears, and mix 2 tablespoons juice from the can with 2 tablespoons orange juice to replace the white wine. Bake in the oven about 10 minutes to heat through and lightly brown the top.

FRUITY BREAD AND BUTTER PUDDING

TIME **30 MINUTES** SERVES **4**

INGREDIENTS

300 g (10 oz) fresh or frozen mixed
    summer fruit, such as berries and
    stone fruits

2 tablespoons butter, softened

8 slices wholemeal (whole-wheat) bread,
    crusts removed

2 tablespoons soft brown sugar

2 large eggs

1½ cups (375 ml) milk, warmed

½ teaspoon vanilla extract

freshly grated nutmeg

1 teaspoon icing (confectioner's) sugar,
    for dusting

thick (double/heavy) cream or natural
    (plain) yogurt, to serve

METHOD

1 Preheat oven to 220°C (425°F/Gas 7). If you are using frozen fruit, spread out on a plate to thaw a little.

2 Grease four 300 ml (10 fl oz) ovenproof dishes with a little butter. Spread the remaining butter over the bread, then cut each slice into four triangles.

3 Arrange a few pieces of bread in the bottom of each dish. Add a spoonful of mixed fruit and a sprinkling of sugar, then repeat the layers until all the fruit and sugar has been used, then end with a layer of bread.

4 Put eggs in a bowl and whisk lightly, then stir in warmed milk and vanilla. Whisk, then carefully pour the mixture evenly over each dish.

5 Grate a little nutmeg over, then transfer the dishes to a baking tray (sheet) and bake 15 minutes, or until just set and golden brown on top.

6 Dust with icing sugar and serve warm with cream or yogurt.

NUTRIENTS PER SERVING

1470 kJ, 351 kcal, 12 g protein, 16 g fat (9 g saturated fat), 38 g carbohydrate

COOK'S TIP

You can prepare the puddings up to the end of step 4 a few hours ahead of serving and keep in the fridge. Return to room temperature 30 minutes before you are ready to bake them.

OATY PLUM CRUMBLE
TIME **30 MINUTES** SERVES **4**

METHOD

1 Preheat oven to 230°C (450°F/Gas 8).
2 Put plums in a flameproof casserole dish, about 20 cm (8 inches) in diameter and 5 cm (2 inches) deep. Add caster sugar and 2–3 tablespoons water. Cover and poach over medium heat 8–10 minutes, stirring occasionally, until the plums begin to soften.
3 Meanwhile, melt butter in a frying pan. Add mixed spice, rolled oats, brown sugar and nuts and stir to combine.
4 Spoon the oat mixture evenly over the plums. Bake 12–15 minutes, checking regularly, until the oats are golden brown.
5 Serve the crumble straight from the dish, hot or warm, with whipped cream or ice cream.

INGREDIENTS

1 kg (2 lb) firm ripe plums, halved and stoned, quartered if large
1/2 cup (115 g) caster (superfine) sugar
3 tablespoons unsalted butter
1 teaspoon mixed (pumpkin pie) spice
3/4 cup (90 g) rolled (porridge) oats
1/3 cup (60 g) light brown sugar
1/2 cup (60 g) mixed nuts, chopped
whipped cream or ice cream, to serve

NUTRIENTS PER SERVING

2244 kJ, 536 kcal, 7 g protein, 23 g fat (10 g saturated fat), 76 g carbohydrate

COOK'S TIP

If you do not have a flameproof casserole dish, poach the plums in a large saucepan, then transfer to an ovenproof dish, spoon over the oat mixture and bake.

DARK CHOCOLATE POTS WITH WHITE CHOCOLATE CREAM

TIME 30 MINUTES SERVES 6

INGREDIENTS

200 g (7 oz) dark (semi-sweet) chocolate, broken into pieces

1³/₄ cups (435 g) low-fat custard, at room temperature

1 tablespoon brandy

¹/₂ cup (125 ml) cream

30 g (1 oz) white chocolate, finely grated

METHOD

1 Put six small glass dishes, ramekin moulds or shallow tumblers in the freezer to chill. Put dark chocolate in a heatproof bowl set over a saucepan of simmering water. Stir until chocolate has melted — this will take about 3 minutes. Remove the bowl from the pan as soon as the chocolate has melted and stir until smooth.

2 Pour in a third of the custard and stir lightly. The chocolate will begin to thicken and become glossy, so do not overmix. Pour in the remaining custard and stir to combine. It will thicken as the chocolate cools. Stir in brandy.

3 Spoon mixture into the chilled dishes. Put in the freezer to chill 20 minutes, or until set.

4 Meanwhile, put cream in a bowl and whip until it just begins to thicken and hold its shape. Stir in white chocolate and chill in the fridge until you need it. Spoon the cream onto the chocolate pots and serve at once.

NUTRIENTS PER SERVING

1395 kJ, 333 kcal, 5 g protein, 19 g fat (12 g saturated fat), 35 g carbohydrate

Left Dark chocolate pots with white chocolate cream

TRIPLE CHOCOLATE ROULADE

TIME 30 MINUTES SERVES 6

INGREDIENTS

3 eggs

²/₃ cup (145 g) caster (superfine) sugar

¹/₂ cup (75 g) plain (all-purpose) flour

45 g (1¹/₂ oz) unsweetened cocoa powder

1 tablespoon brandy

¹/₂ teaspoon vanilla extract

20 g (²/₃ oz) butter

1 tablespoon icing (confectioner's) sugar

90 g (3 oz) chocolate or chocolate–hazelnut spread

METHOD

1 Preheat oven to 220°C (425°F/Gas 7). Cover a large baking tray with baking paper (or a large baking sheet with parchment paper).

2 Whisk eggs and half the caster sugar with an electric mixer on high speed until pale and very thick; the mixture should hold its shape.

3 Sift flour and 2 tablespoons cocoa powder evenly over the mixture, then use a large metal spoon to fold it in, turning the mixture over in big scoops rather than stirring it.

4 Pour mixture onto baking paper and spread out lightly into a rectangle about 23 x 33 cm (9 x 13 inches). (Do not press heavily — it does not matter if the edges are not quite square.) Bake 8–10 minutes, or until sponge is risen, set and springy in the middle when lightly pressed.

5 Meanwhile, put remaining caster sugar, 2 tablespoons cocoa powder and ²/₃ cup (150 ml) water in a saucepan. Bring to a boil, stirring, then boil 2 minutes. Remove from heat and stir in brandy, vanilla extract and butter. Set aside over a low heat to keep warm.

6 Dampen a clean tea towel (dish towel) with hot water, then lay it on a clean surface. Lay a sheet of baking paper on top and sift remaining cocoa powder and icing sugar over the paper, covering an area about the size of the sponge. Remove the sponge from the oven and invert it onto the cocoa and sugar mixture on the paper.

7 Peel off lining paper and trim off crisp edges. Make a shallow cut about 1 cm (¹/₂ inch) in from a long edge, but don't cut right through. Dollop the chocolate spread over the sponge and spread it out thickly. Roll up the sponge and filling from the long edge with the cut, using the cut to start the roll tightly. Hold the paper and damp towel to guide the roll, then hold the roll firmly for a minute, so that it sets in place.

8 Remove the towel and paper, sprinkling the cocoa mixture over the roll. Don't worry if the roll is slightly cracked. Cut six slices of roll, using a serrated knife, and arrange them on serving plates, then spoon the warm syrup over the top.

NUTRIENTS PER SERVING

1370 kJ, 327 kcal, 7 g protein, 12 g fat (5 g saturated fat), 46 g carbohydrate

CINNAMON STRAWBERRY PANCAKE

TIME **20 MINUTES** SERVES **4**

INGREDIENTS

$^2/_3$ cup (100 g) self-raising flour

1 teaspoon baking powder

1 teaspoon caster (superfine) sugar

1 egg

1 teaspoon vanilla extract (optional)

100 ml (3$^1/_2$ fl oz) low-fat milk

20 g ($^2/_3$ oz) butter

2$^2/_3$ cups (400 g) strawberries,
    hulled and halved

$^1/_2$ teaspoon ground cinnamon

3 tablespoons white (granulated) sugar

fresh mint sprigs, to garnish (optional)

METHOD

1 Mix flour, baking powder and caster sugar in a bowl. Make a well in the centre and add egg and vanilla extract, if using. Pour in a little milk, then beat egg lightly until mixed with the milk and vanilla. Gradually stir in the flour mixture and pour in remaining milk a little at a time. Before all the milk is added and while the mixture is quite thick, beat well with an electric mixer to remove all the lumps, then gradually beat in remaining milk to make a smooth batter.

2 Preheat grill (broiler) to high. On the stovetop, melt butter in a 20–23 cm (8–9 inch) frying pan that can be used under the grill (wrap a wooden handle with foil). Swirl the butter around the pan, then pour in the batter and cook over medium heat until the pancake is golden underneath. The batter should have risen and almost set on top. The surface of the pancake will break into little bubbles.

3 Slide frying pan under the grill and cook 1 minute. Scatter strawberries evenly over the pancake. Sprinkle with cinnamon and white sugar, then grill a further 3 minutes, or until sugar has melted. Cut into four wedges, garnish with mint, if you like, and serve at once.

NUTRIENTS PER SERVING

952 kJ, 227 kcal, 7 g protein, 6 g fat (3 g saturated fat), 36 g carbohydrate

VARIATION

Instead of making the pancake, use bought pancakes. Heat 4 large pancakes, one at a time, in a little melted unsalted butter in a frying pan for about 30 seconds each, or following packet instructions. Fold each pancake into four. Put all pancakes back in the pan, add the strawberries, cinnamon and sugar as for the basic recipe and grill about 1 minute.

INDEX

NOTE TO READERS

WEIGHTS AND MEASURES Australian metric cup and spoon measurements have been used throughout this book: 1 cup = 250 ml; 1 tablespoon = 20 ml and 1 teaspoon = 5 ml. If using the smaller imperial cup and spoon measures (where 1 cup = 235 ml and 1 tablespoon = 15 ml), some adjustments may need to be made. A small variation in the weight or volume of most ingredients is unlikely to adversely affect a recipe. The exceptions are yeast, baking powder and bicarbonate of soda (baking soda). For these ingredients, adjust the recipe accordingly. All cup and spoon measures are level, unless stated otherwise. Ingredients are generally listed by their weight or volume with cup measurements given for convenience, unless the conversion is imperfect, whereby the ingredients are listed by weight or volume only.

Sometimes conversions within a recipe are not exact but are the closest conversion that is a suitable measurement for each system. Use either the metric or the imperial measurements; do not mix the two systems.

CAN SIZES Can sizes vary between countries and manufacturers; if the stated size is unavailable, use the nearest equivalent.

Here are the metric and imperial measurements for can sizes used in this book: 225 g = 8 oz; 300 g = 10 oz; 350 g = 12 oz; 400/410 g = 14 oz = 398 ml/410 ml; 425 g = 15 oz = 540 ml; 800 g = 28 oz = 796 ml.

NUTRITIONAL ANALYSIS Serving suggestions, garnishes and optional ingredients are not included in the nutritional analysis. For the recipe analysis we used FoodWorks ®.

INGREDIENTS Please note the following:
* All fruits and vegetables are medium sized unless the recipe says otherwise.
* Peel any fruits and vegetables (such as apples, bananas, oranges, carrots, garlic, onions, potatoes, pumpkin and sweet potatoes) that would normally be peeled before cooking. If they aren't meant to be peeled, the recipe will say so.
* Pasta is dried unless it says otherwise.
* Nuts are raw and unsalted unless it says otherwise.
* Dairy foods (such as milk, cream, sour cream and yogurt) are full fat unless it says otherwise. Using a low-fat dairy product in a recipe written for a full-fat product may give a different result.

OVEN TEMPERATURES These recipes have been written for a regular oven. If you have a fan-forced (convection) oven, reduce the temperature by 20°C. If you have a broiler (grill) where the temperature cannot be adjusted by a temperature dial or knob, lower the rack down from the element: MEDIUM – about half or two-thirds of the way down. MEDIUM-HOT – about a third of the way down.

ALTERNATIVE TERMS AND SUBSTITUTES

BABY COS LETTUCE little gem, romaine
BENCHTOP countertop
BLACK-EYED PEAS cowpeas
BURGHUL bulgur
BUTTERBEANS lima beans
CAPSICUM bell pepper, sweet pepper
CHINESE FIVE SPICE five-spice powder
CORIANDER cilantro
COS LETTUCE romaine lettuce
CREAM where a recipe doesn't specify a type of cream, use pure, light, single or pouring cream
EGGPLANT aubergine, brinjal
ENGLISH SPINACH baby spinach; not the heavily veined, thick-leafed vegetable sold as spinach or silverbeet
FILO phyllo
FISH SUBSTITUTES for blue-eye, bream, ling, snapper, flathead, use any firm white-fleshed fish, such as cod, coley, hake or kabeljou
FRESH SHIITAKE MUSHROOMS rehydrated dried shiitake mushrooms
HOKKIEN NOODLES 2-minute noodles or other fast-cooking noodles

LEBANESE CUCUMBER Mediterranean cucumber, short cucumber
LOW-FAT MILK 1% milk
OREGANO oreganum
PAPAYA pawpaw
PASSIONFRUIT granadilla
PEPITAS (PUMPKIN SEEDS) use sunflower seeds
POT STICKERS Chinese dumplings
RICE NOODLES rice vermicelli
ROCKMELON spanspek, cantaloupe
SELF-RAISING FLOUR self-rising flour
SILVERBEET Swiss chard, often sold as spinach in South Africa
SOLID VEGETABLE SHORTENING solid (white) fat
SWISS BROWN MUSHROOMS brown mushrooms
VANILLA EXTRACT vanilla essence
VEGETABLE OIL canola oil
WHOLEMEAL whole-wheat
WHOLEGRAIN MUSTARD seeded mustard
WITLOF witloof, Belgian endive
ZUCCHINI baby marrow, courgette

QUICK & EASY COOKING

EDITOR Bronwyn Sweeney
DESIGNER Sarah Odgers
PROOFREADER Susan McCreery
INDEXER Diane Harriman
SENIOR PRODUCTION CONTROLLER Monique Tesoriero
EDITORIAL PROJECT MANAGER GENERAL BOOKS Deborah Nixon

READER'S DIGEST GENERAL BOOKS
EDITORIAL DIRECTOR Lynn Lewis
MANAGING EDITOR Rosemary McDonald
ART DIRECTOR Carole Orbell

Quick & Easy Cooking is published by
Reader's Digest (Australia) Pty Limited,
80 Bay Street, Ultimo, NSW 2007
www.readersdigest.com.au, www.readersdigest.co.nz,
www.readersdigest.co.za, www.rd.com, www.readersdigest.ca

First published 2012. Reprinted 2013.
Copyright © Reader's Digest (Australia) Pty Limited 2012
Copyright © Reader's Digest Association Far East Limited
    2012 Philippines
Copyright © Reader's Digest Association Far East Limited
    2012

Quick & Easy Cooking contains some material first
published in the following Reader's Digest books:
30 Minute Cookbook and *Midweek Meals Made Easy*.

All images except the following are the copyright of
Reader's Digest.
4 Shutterstock, 10 t, c, b iStockphoto; 11 c iStockphoto,
b Shutterstock; 14 Shutterstock; 60 Shutterstock;
110 Shutterstock; 156 Shutterstock; 206 Shutterstock;
254 Shutterstock; 312 Shutterstock; 362 Shutterstock;
416 Shutterstock; 456 Shutterstock.

National Library of Australia Cataloguing-in-Publication entry

Title: Quick & easy cooking
ISBN: 978-1-921744-03-7 (hbk)
ISBN: 978-1-921744-33-4 (pbk)
ISBN: 978-1-55475-101-3 (North America)
Notes: Includes index.
Subjects: Quick and easy cooking.
Cooking.
Dewey Number: 641.555

Prepress by Sinnott Bros, Sydney
Printed and bound by Leo Paper Products, China

We are interested in receiving your comments on the contents
of this book. Write to: The Editor, General Books Editorial,
Reader's Digest (Australia) Pty Limited, GPO Box 4353,
Sydney, NSW 2001, or email us at bookeditors.au@
readersdigest.com

To order additional copies of this book, please contact us
as follows:
www.readersdigest.com.au, 1300 300 030 (Australia);
www.readersdigest.co.nz, 0800 400 060 (New Zealand);
www.readersdigest.co.za, 0800 980 572 (South Africa)
www.rd.com, 1 800 846 2100 (United States);
www.readersdigest.ca, 1 800 465 0780 (Canada);
or email us at customerservice@readersdigest.com.au

CONCEPT CODE: AU 0906/IC
PRODUCT CODES: 041 4488 (HBK)
              041 4546 (PBK)